W9-DAS-830

LOVELESS

G. WILLOW WILSON
WRITER

JESÚS MERINO
TOM DERENICK
XERMANICO
LEE GARBETT
SCOT EATON
VICENTE CIFUENTES
TREVOR SCOTT
NORM RAPMUND
WAYNE FAUCHER
JOSÉ MARZÁN JR.
SCOTT HANNA
ARTISTS

ROMULO FAJARDO JR.
COLORIST

PAT BROSSEAU
LETTERER

JESÚS MERINO AND ROMULO FAJARDO JR.
COLLECTION COVER ARTISTS

WONDER WOMAN CREATED BY WILLIAM MOULTON MARSTON

BRIAN CUNNINGHAM
Editor – Original Series

BRITTANY HOLZHERR
Associate Editor – Original Series

JEB WOODARD
Group Editor – Collected Editions

ROBIN WILDMAN
Editor – Collected Edition

STEVE COOK
Design Director – Books

MEGEN BELLERSEN
Publication Design

DANIELLE DIGRADO
Publication Production

BOB HARRAS
Senior VP – Editor-in-Chief, DC Comics

JIM LEE
Publisher & Chief Creative Officer

BOBBIE CHASE
VP – Global Publishing Initiatives & Digital Strategy

DON FALLETTI
VP – Manufacturing Operations & Workflow Management

LAWRENCE GANEM
VP – Talent Services

ALISON GILL
Senior VP – Manufacturing & Operations

HANK KANALZ
Senior VP – Publishing Strategy & Support Services

DAN MIRON
VP – Publishing Operations

NICK J. NAPOLITANO
VP – Manufacturing Administration & Design

NANCY SPEARS
VP – Sales

JONAH WEILAND
VP – Marketing & Creative Services

MICHELE R. WELLS
VP & Executive Editor, Young Reader

WONDER WOMAN VOL. 3: LOVELESS

Published by DC Comics. Compilation and all new material Copyright © 2020 DC Comics.
All Rights Reserved. Originally published in single magazine form in *Wonder Woman* 74-81.
Copyright © 2019, 2020 DC Comics. All Rights Reserved. All characters, their distinctive
likenesses, and related elements featured in this publication are trademarks of DC Comics. The
stories, characters, and incidents featured in this publication are entirely fictional. DC Comics
does not read or accept unsolicited submissions of ideas, stories, or artwork.
DC – a WarnerMedia Company.

DC Comics, 2900 West Alameda Ave., Burbank, CA 91505
Printed by LSC Communications, Owensville, MO, USA. 11/20/20. First Printing.
ISBN: 978-1-77950-253-7

Library of Congress Cataloging-in-Publication Data is available.

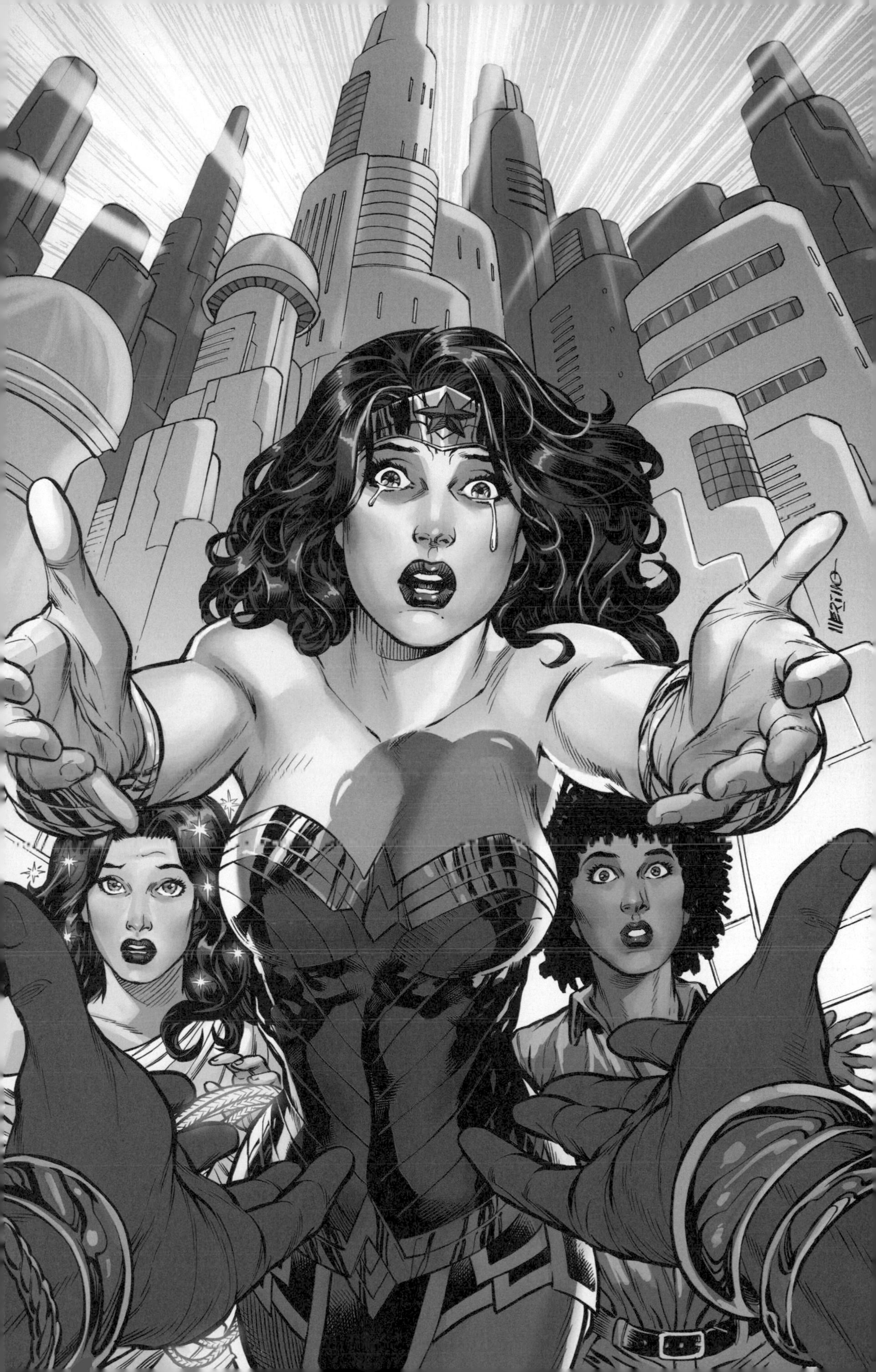

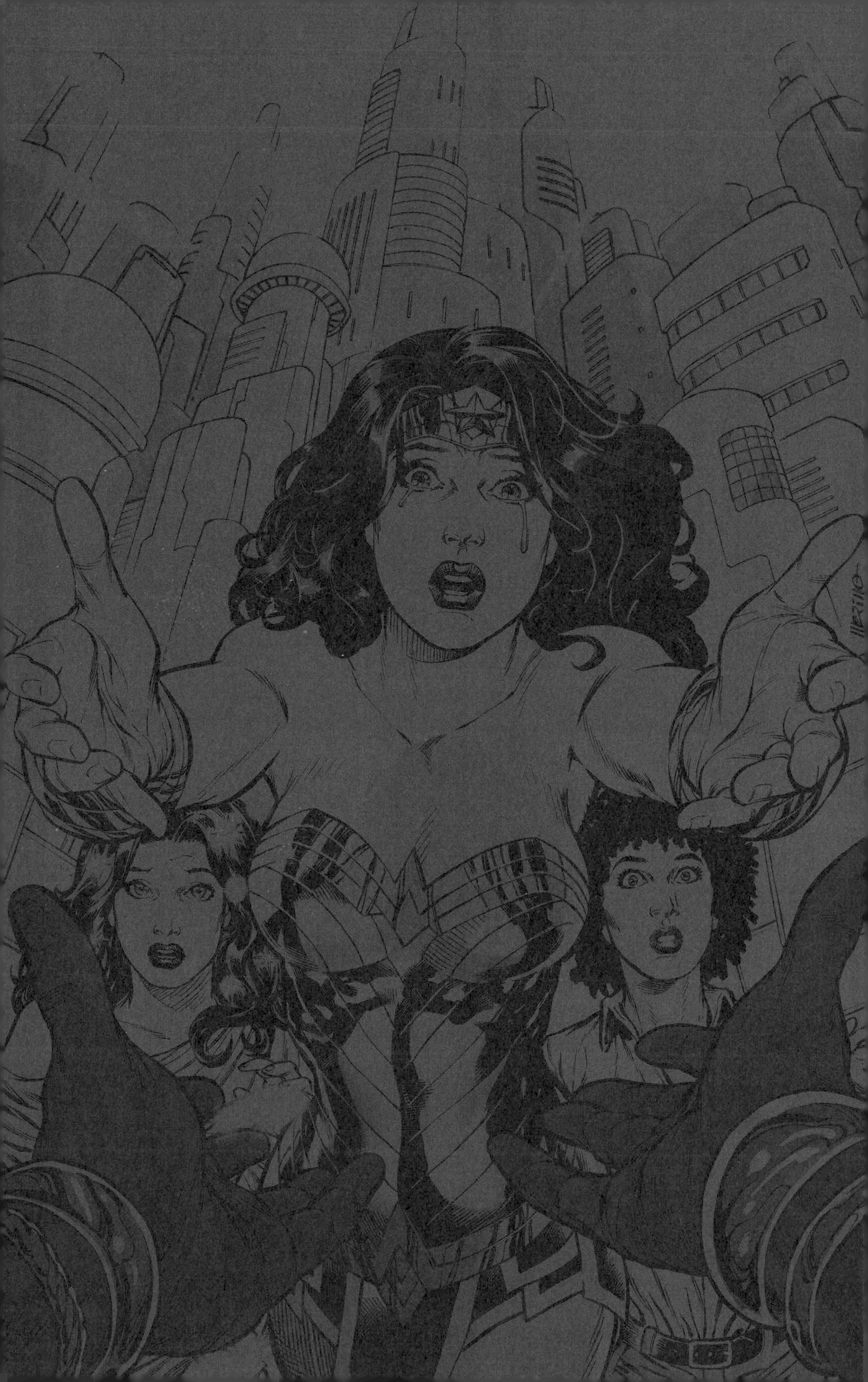

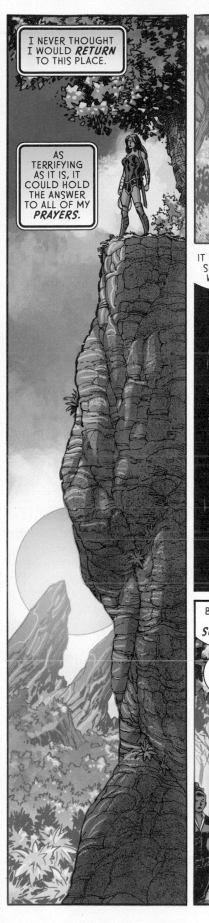

I NEVER THOUGHT I WOULD *RETURN* TO THIS PLACE.

AS TERRIFYING AS IT IS, IT COULD HOLD THE ANSWER TO ALL OF MY *PRAYERS*.

CAN IT BE, DIANA? CAN THE AMAZONS REALLY BE *ALIVE* IN THIS PLACE-- THIS--

DIMENSION CHI. IT ONLY EXISTS AT MY MOTHER'S *WHIM.*

IT WAS HER WAY OF SEEING A FUTURE WITHOUT YOU?

YES, A FUTURE IN WHICH SHE WAS NOT HAMPERED BY A *CHILD*...

BUT IF THIS PLACE *SURVIVES*...

...CAN, TOO, MY MOTHER AND THE REST OF THE AMAZONS?

PERHAPS, DAUGHTER OF HIPPOLYTA.

IF *YOUR* WORLD COLLAPSED AND YOU WERE TRYING TO *SAVE* WHAT WAS LEFT...WHERE *ELSE* WOULD YOU FLEE BUT TO A REALM OF YOUR OWN MAKING?

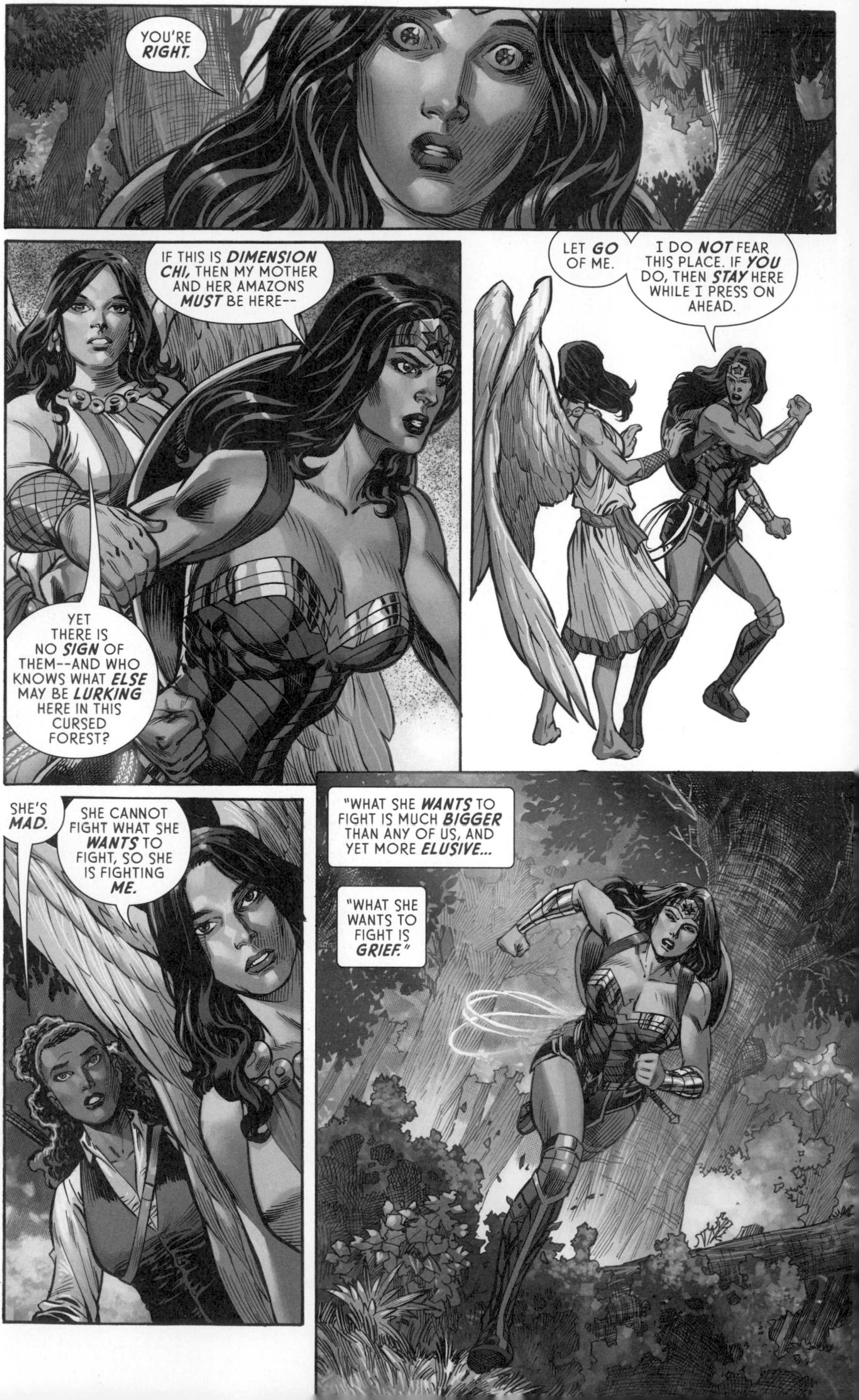
YOU'RE RIGHT.
IF THIS IS DIMENSION CHI, THEN MY MOTHER AND HER AMAZONS MUST BE HERE--
YET THERE IS NO SIGN OF THEM--AND WHO KNOWS WHAT ELSE MAY BE LURKING HERE IN THIS CURSED FOREST?
LET GO OF ME.
I DO NOT FEAR THIS PLACE. IF YOU DO, THEN STAY HERE WHILE I PRESS ON AHEAD.
SHE'S MAD.
SHE CANNOT FIGHT WHAT SHE WANTS TO FIGHT, SO SHE IS FIGHTING ME.
"WHAT SHE WANTS TO FIGHT IS MUCH BIGGER THAN ANY OF US, AND YET MORE ELUSIVE...
"WHAT SHE WANTS TO FIGHT IS GRIEF."

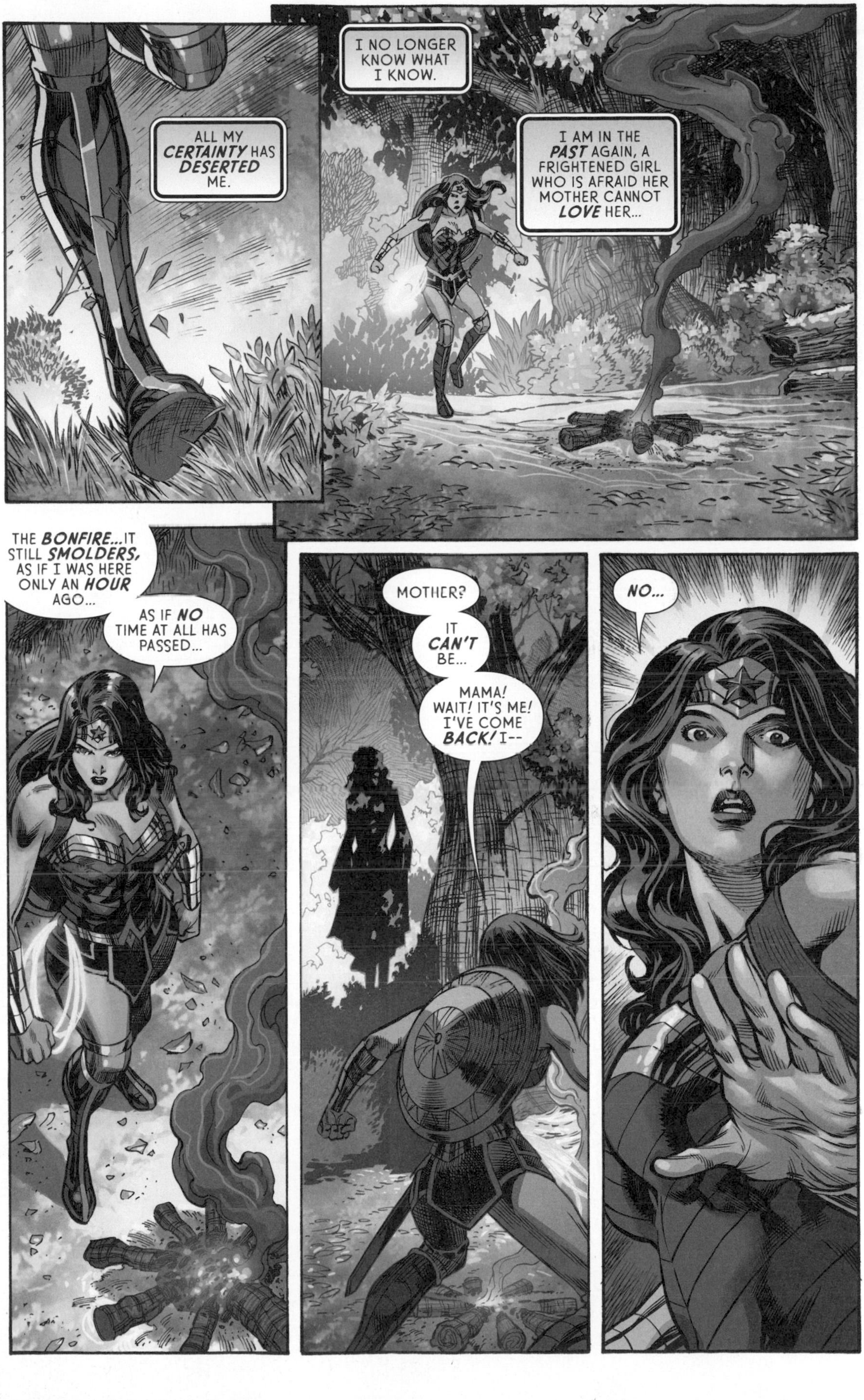
ALL MY CERTAINTY HAS DESERTED ME.
I NO LONGER KNOW WHAT I KNOW.
I AM IN THE PAST AGAIN, A FRIGHTENED GIRL WHO IS AFRAID HER MOTHER CANNOT LOVE HER...
THE BONFIRE...IT STILL SMOLDERS, AS IF I WAS HERE ONLY AN HOUR AGO...
AS IF NO TIME AT ALL HAS PASSED...
MOTHER?
IT CAN'T BE...
MAMA! WAIT! IT'S ME! I'VE COME BACK! I--
NO...

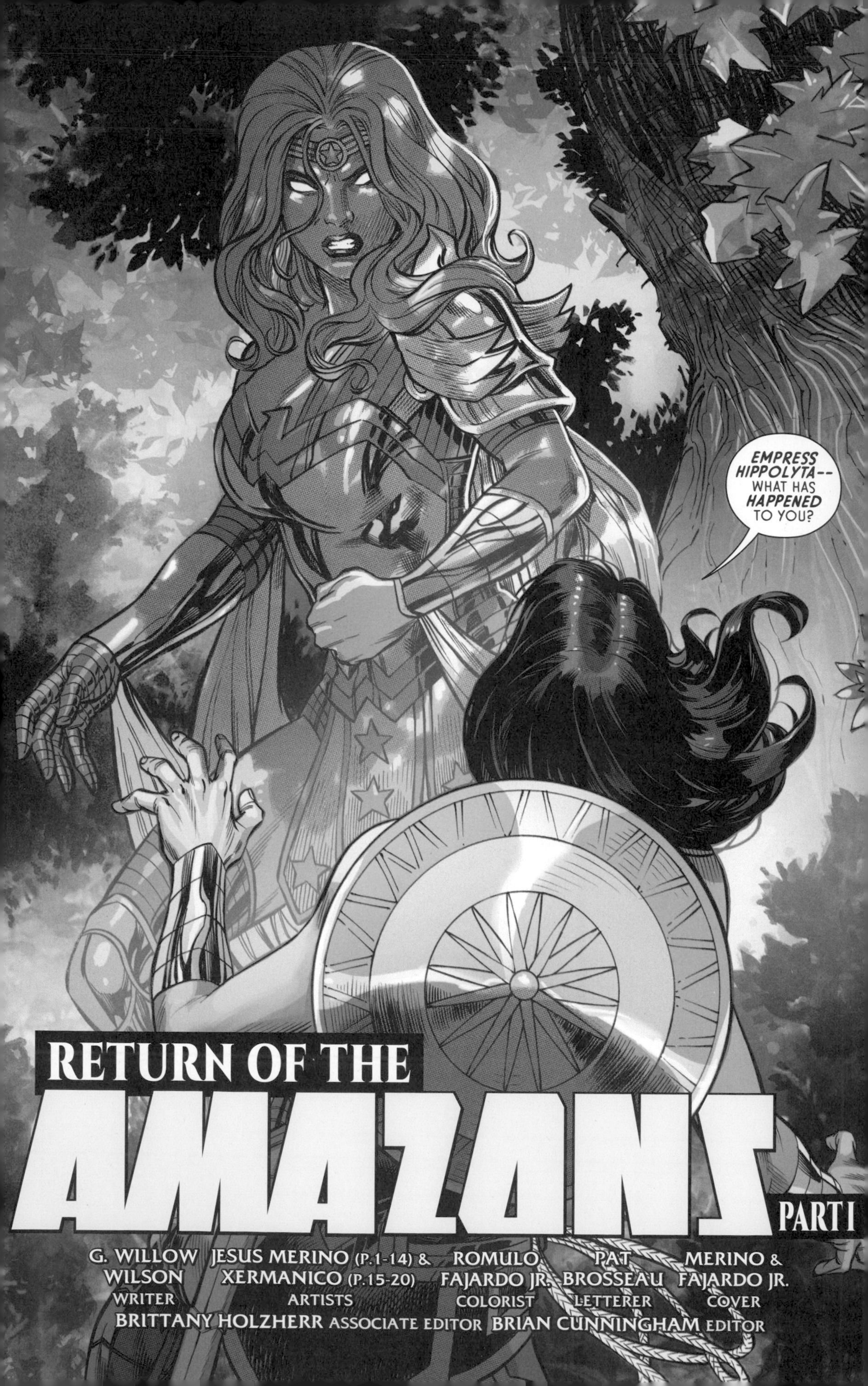
EMPRESS HIPPOLYTA-- WHAT HAS HAPPENED TO YOU?
RETURN OF THE AMAZONS PART I
G. WILLOW WILSON WRITER
JESUS MERINO (P.1-14) & XERMANICO (P.15-20) ARTISTS
ROMULO FAJARDO JR. COLORIST
PAT BROSSEAU LETTERER
MERINO & FAJARDO JR. COVER
BRITTANY HOLZHERR ASSOCIATE EDITOR BRIAN CUNNINGHAM EDITOR

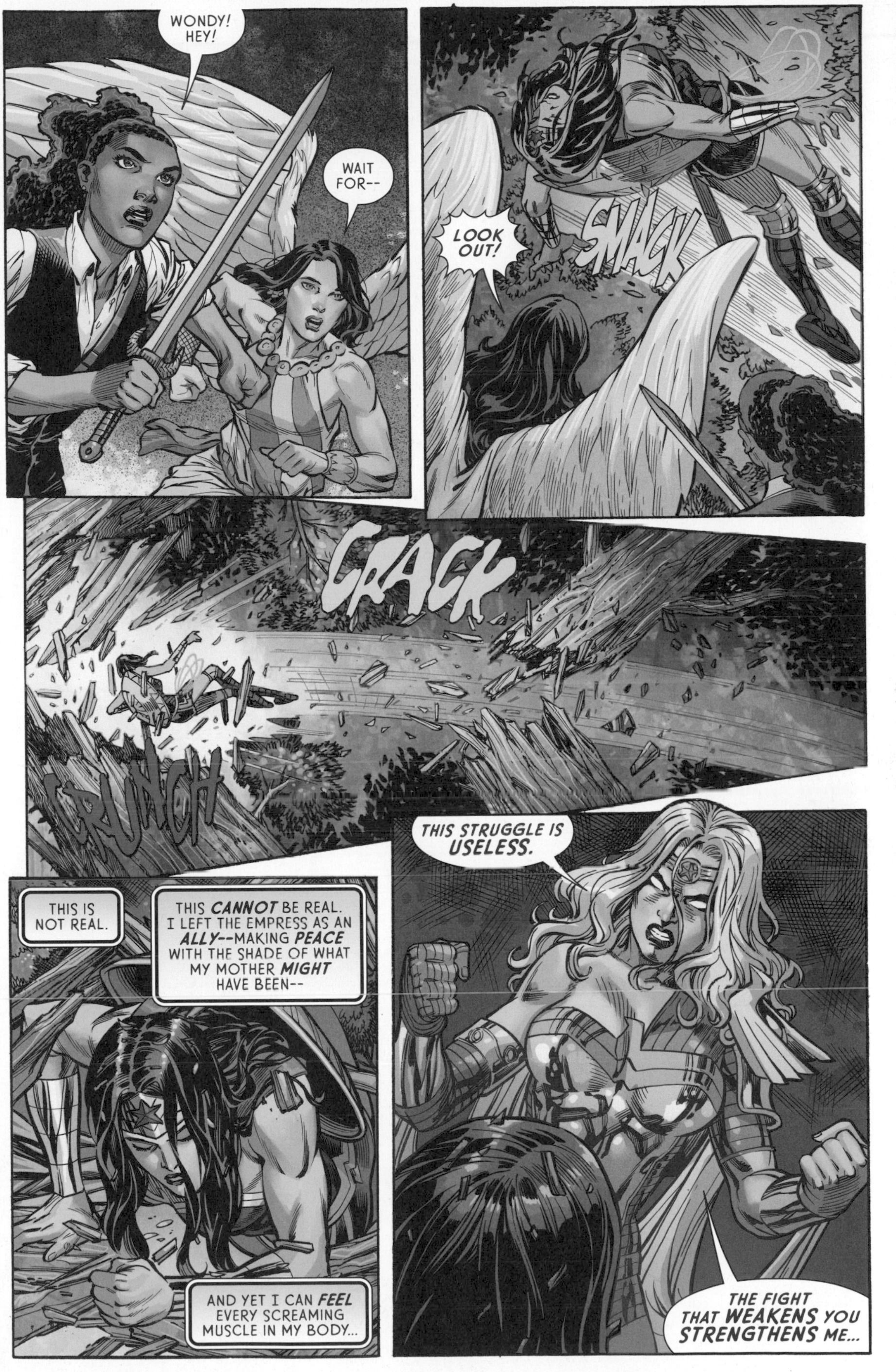
WONDY! HEY!
WAIT FOR--
LOOK OUT!
SMACK
CRACK
CRUNCH
THIS IS NOT REAL.
THIS CANNOT BE REAL. I LEFT THE EMPRESS AS AN ALLY--MAKING PEACE WITH THE SHADE OF WHAT MY MOTHER MIGHT HAVE BEEN--
AND YET I CAN FEEL EVERY SCREAMING MUSCLE IN MY BODY...
THIS STRUGGLE IS USELESS.
THE FIGHT THAT WEAKENS YOU STRENGTHENS ME...

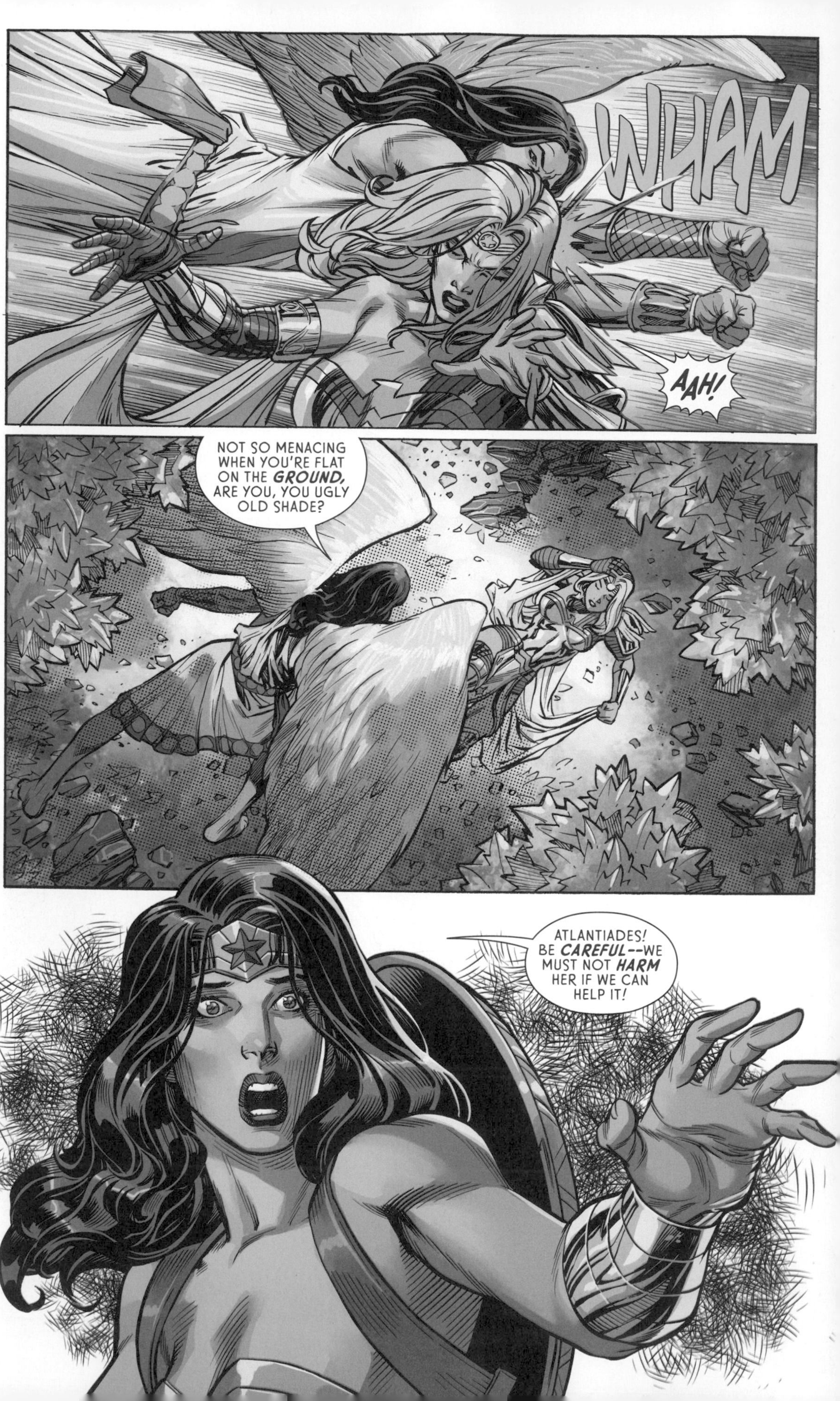
WHAM
AAH!
NOT SO MENACING WHEN YOU'RE FLAT ON THE GROUND, ARE YOU, YOU UGLY OLD SHADE?
ATLANTIADES! BE CAREFUL--WE MUST NOT HARM HER IF WE CAN HELP IT!

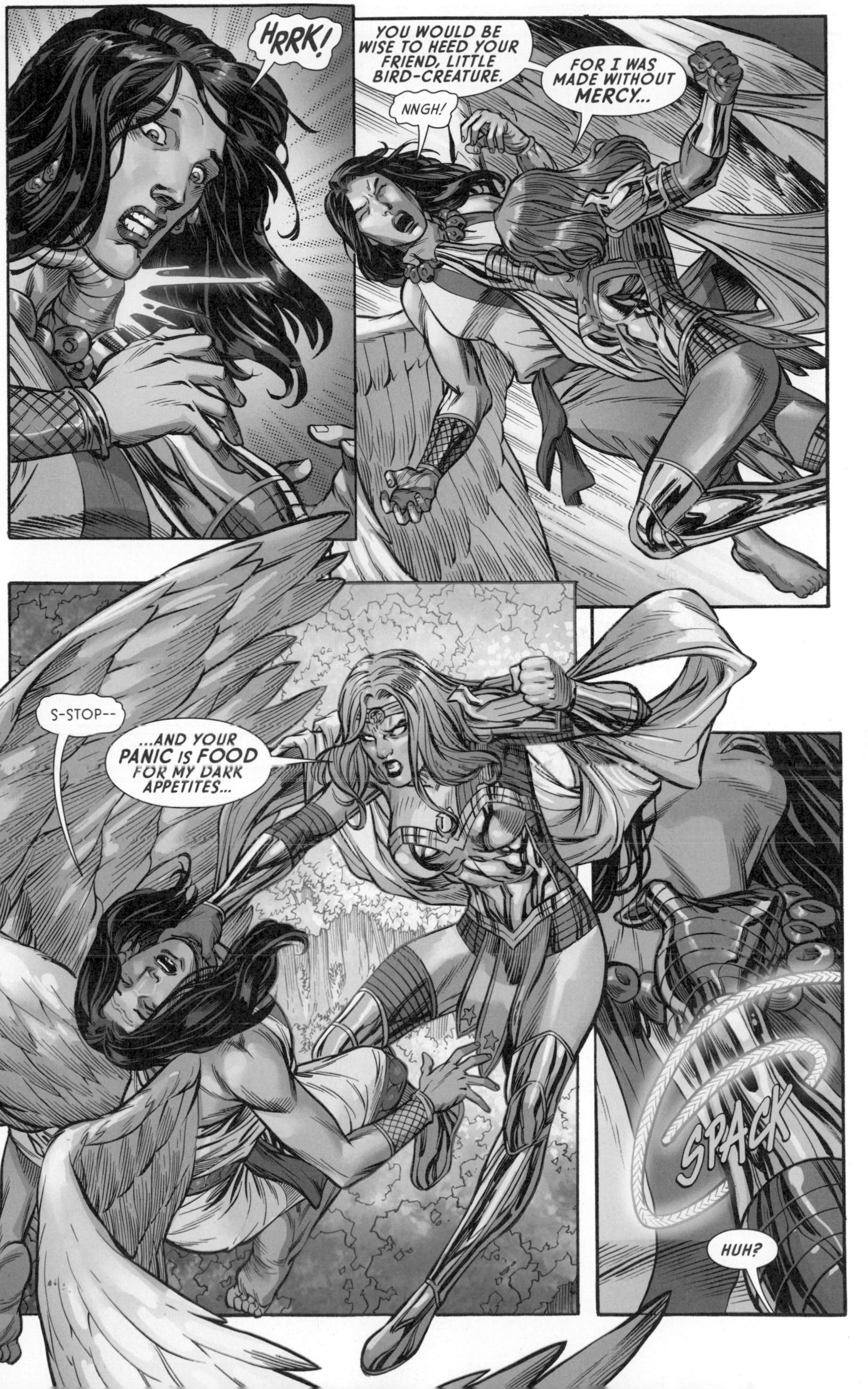
HRRK!
YOU WOULD BE WISE TO HEED YOUR FRIEND, LITTLE BIRD-CREATURE.
NNGH!
FOR I WAS MADE WITHOUT MERCY...
S-STOP--
...AND YOUR PANIC IS FOOD FOR MY DARK APPETITES...
SPACK
HUH?

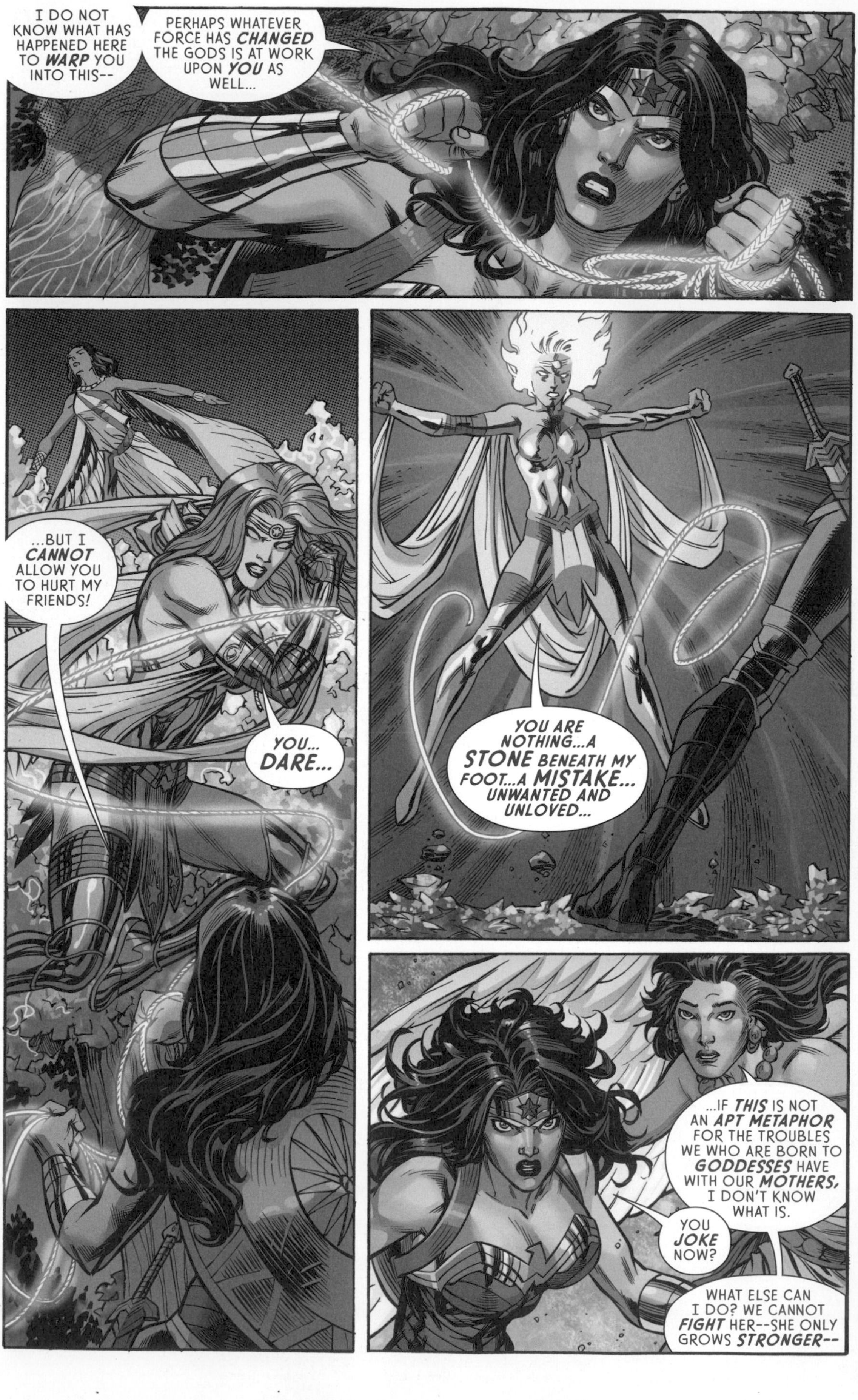
I DO NOT KNOW WHAT HAS HAPPENED HERE TO WARP YOU INTO THIS--
PERHAPS WHATEVER FORCE HAS CHANGED THE GODS IS AT WORK UPON YOU AS WELL...
...BUT I CANNOT ALLOW YOU TO HURT MY FRIENDS!
YOU... DARE...
YOU ARE NOTHING...A STONE BENEATH MY FOOT...A MISTAKE... UNWANTED AND UNLOVED...
...IF THIS IS NOT AN APT METAPHOR FOR THE TROUBLES WE WHO ARE BORN TO GODDESSES HAVE WITH OUR MOTHERS, I DON'T KNOW WHAT IS.
YOU JOKE NOW?
WHAT ELSE CAN I DO? WE CANNOT FIGHT HER--SHE ONLY GROWS STRONGER--

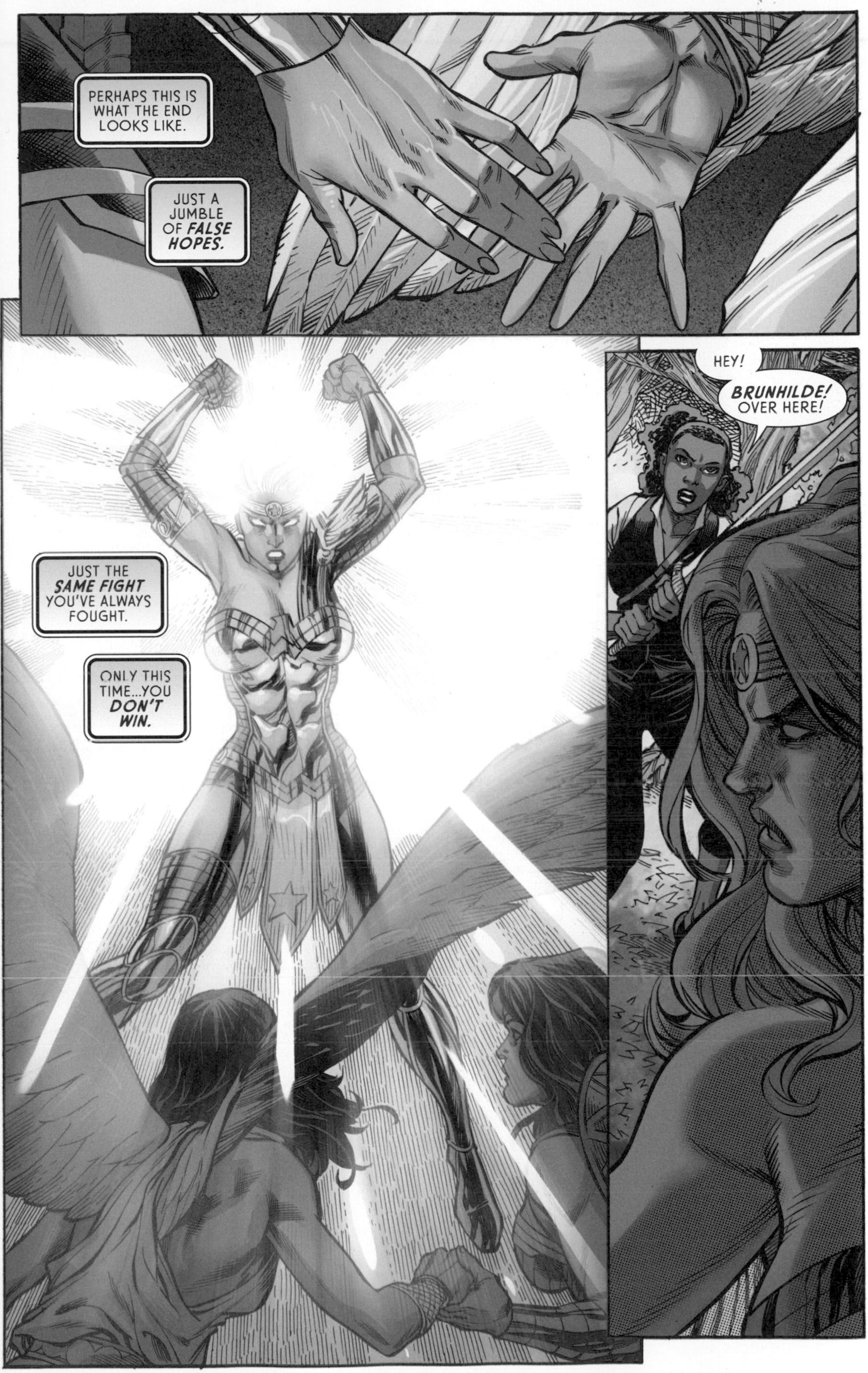
PERHAPS THIS IS WHAT THE END LOOKS LIKE.
JUST A JUMBLE OF FALSE HOPES.
JUST THE SAME FIGHT YOU'VE ALWAYS FOUGHT.
ONLY THIS TIME...YOU DON'T WIN.
HEY!
BRUNHILDE! OVER HERE!

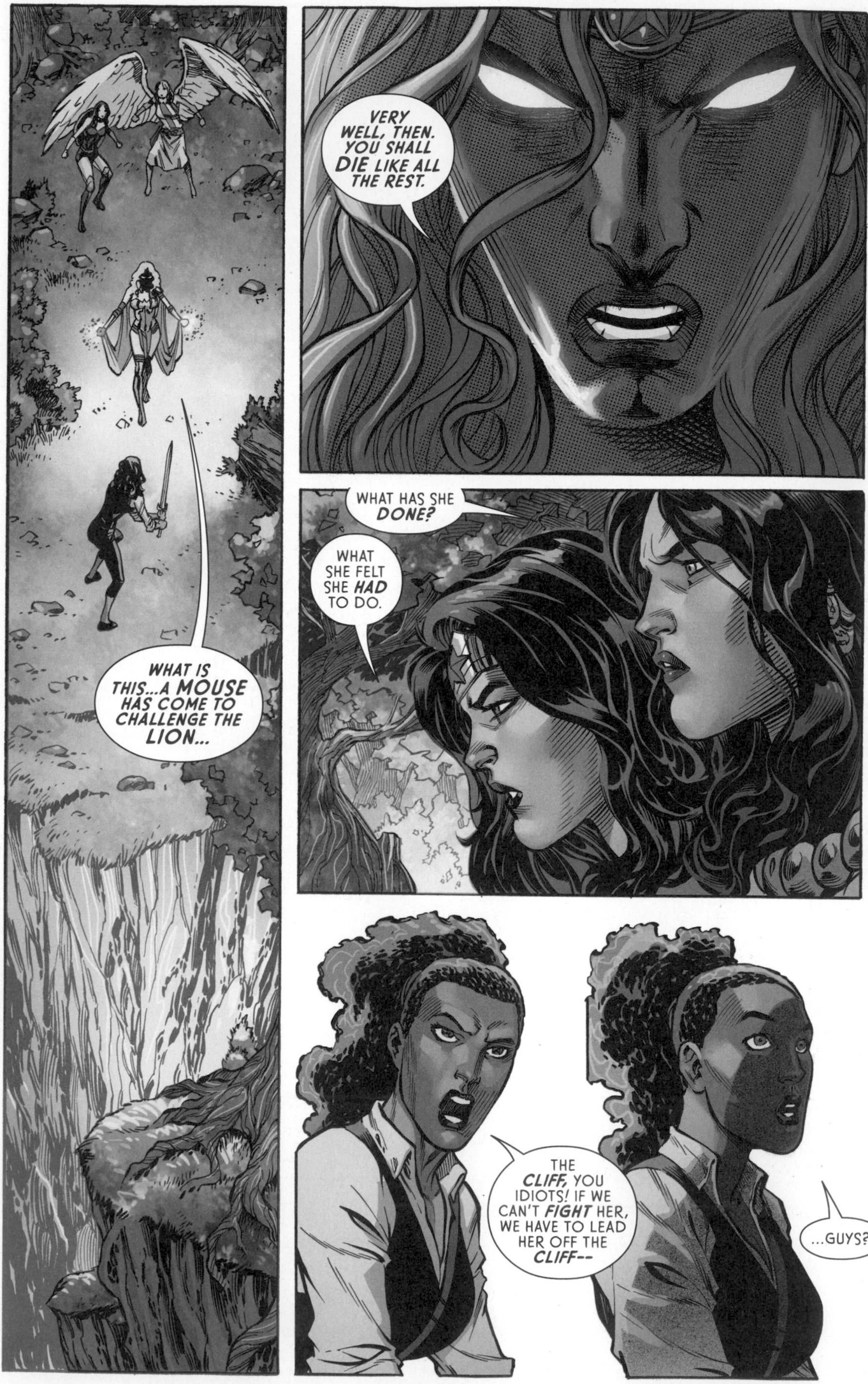
WHAT IS THIS...A MOUSE HAS COME TO CHALLENGE THE LION...
VERY WELL, THEN. YOU SHALL DIE LIKE ALL THE REST.
WHAT HAS SHE DONE?
WHAT SHE FELT SHE HAD TO DO.
THE CLIFF, YOU IDIOTS! IF WE CAN'T FIGHT HER, WE HAVE TO LEAD HER OFF THE CLIFF--
...GUYS?

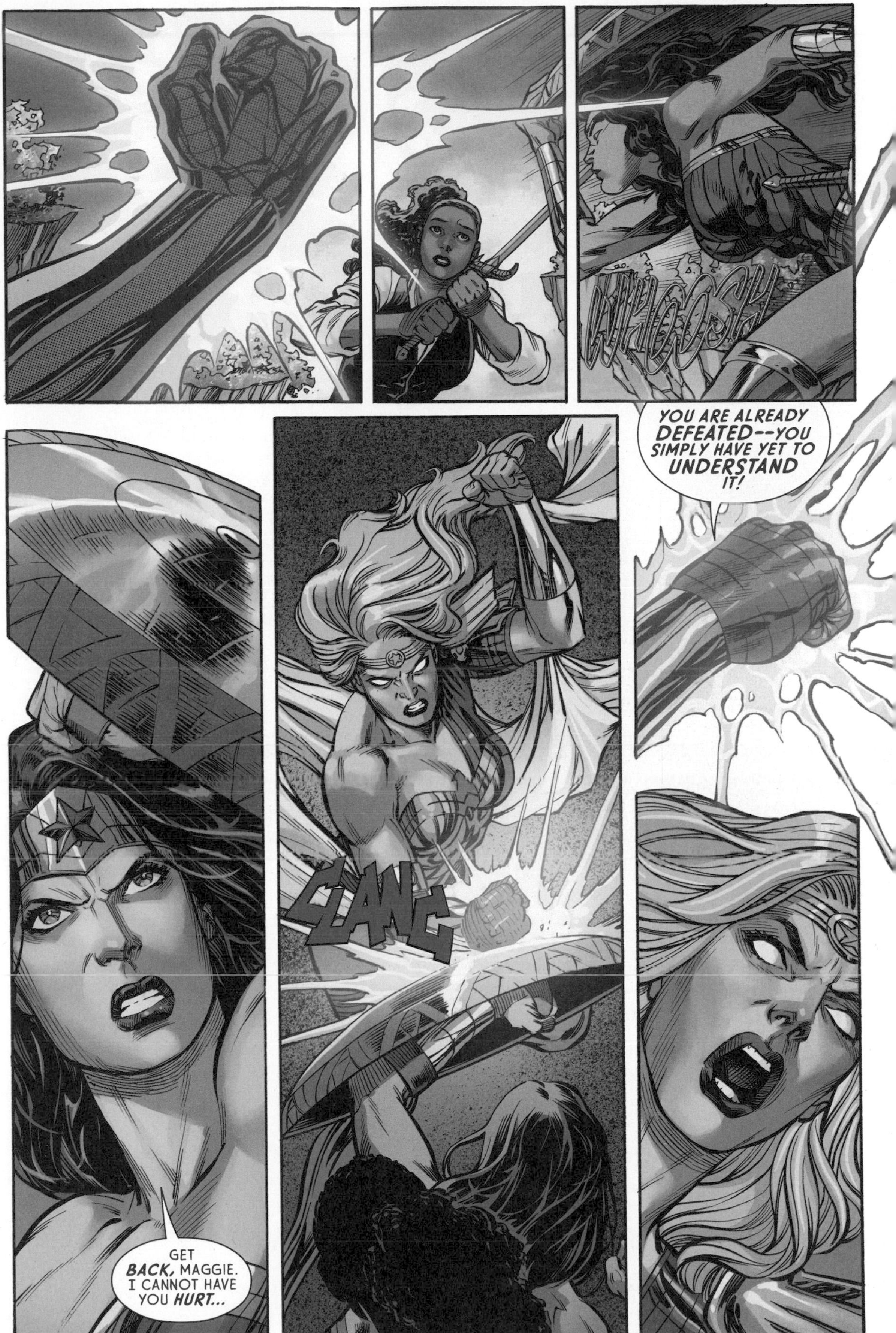
WHOOOSH
YOU ARE ALREADY DEFEATED--YOU SIMPLY HAVE YET TO UNDERSTAND IT!
GET BACK, MAGGIE. I CANNOT HAVE YOU HURT...
CLANG

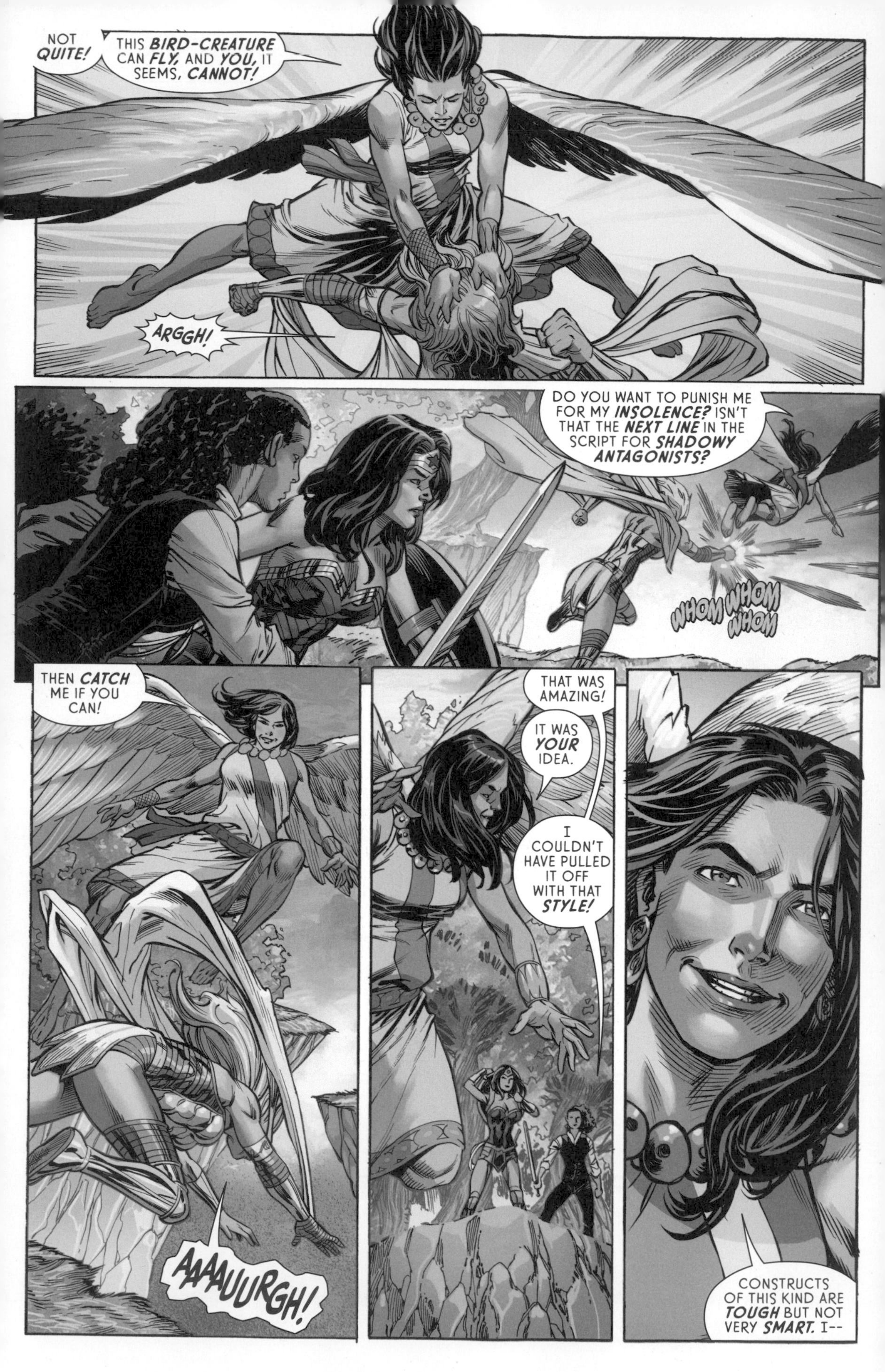

NOT QUITE!
THIS BIRD-CREATURE CAN FLY, AND YOU, IT SEEMS, CANNOT!
ARGGH!
DO YOU WANT TO PUNISH ME FOR MY INSOLENCE? ISN'T THAT THE NEXT LINE IN THE SCRIPT FOR SHADOWY ANTAGONISTS?
WHOM WHOM WHOM
THEN CATCH ME IF YOU CAN!
AAAAUURGH!
THAT WAS AMAZING!
IT WAS YOUR IDEA.
I COULDN'T HAVE PULLED IT OFF WITH THAT STYLE!
CONSTRUCTS OF THIS KIND ARE TOUGH BUT NOT VERY SMART. I--

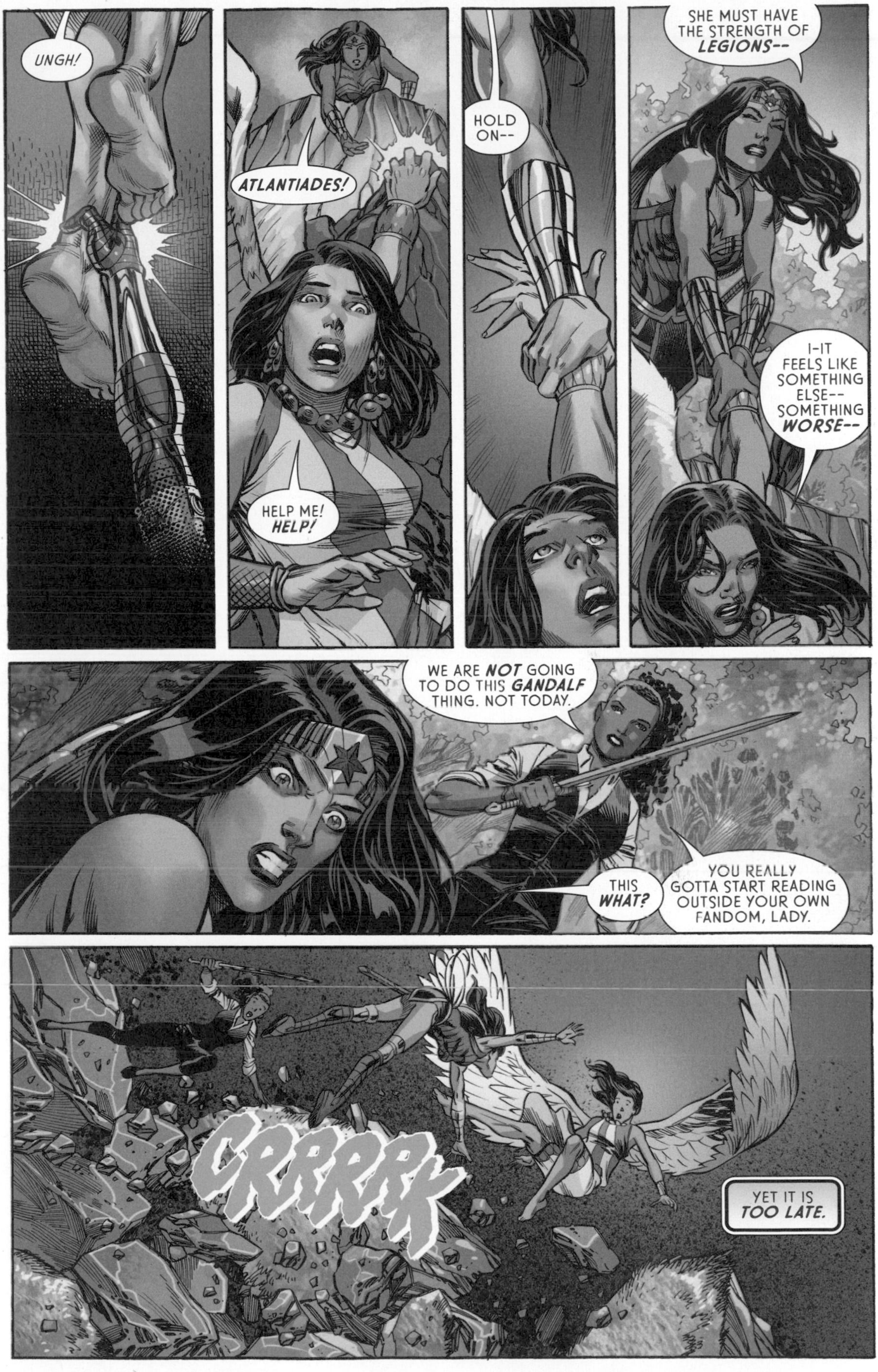
UNGH!
ATLANTIADES!
HELP ME! HELP!
HOLD ON--
SHE MUST HAVE THE STRENGTH OF LEGIONS--
I-IT FEELS LIKE SOMETHING ELSE-- SOMETHING WORSE--
WE ARE NOT GOING TO DO THIS GANDALF THING. NOT TODAY.
THIS WHAT?
YOU REALLY GOTTA START READING OUTSIDE YOUR OWN FANDOM, LADY.
CRRRRK
YET IT IS TOO LATE.

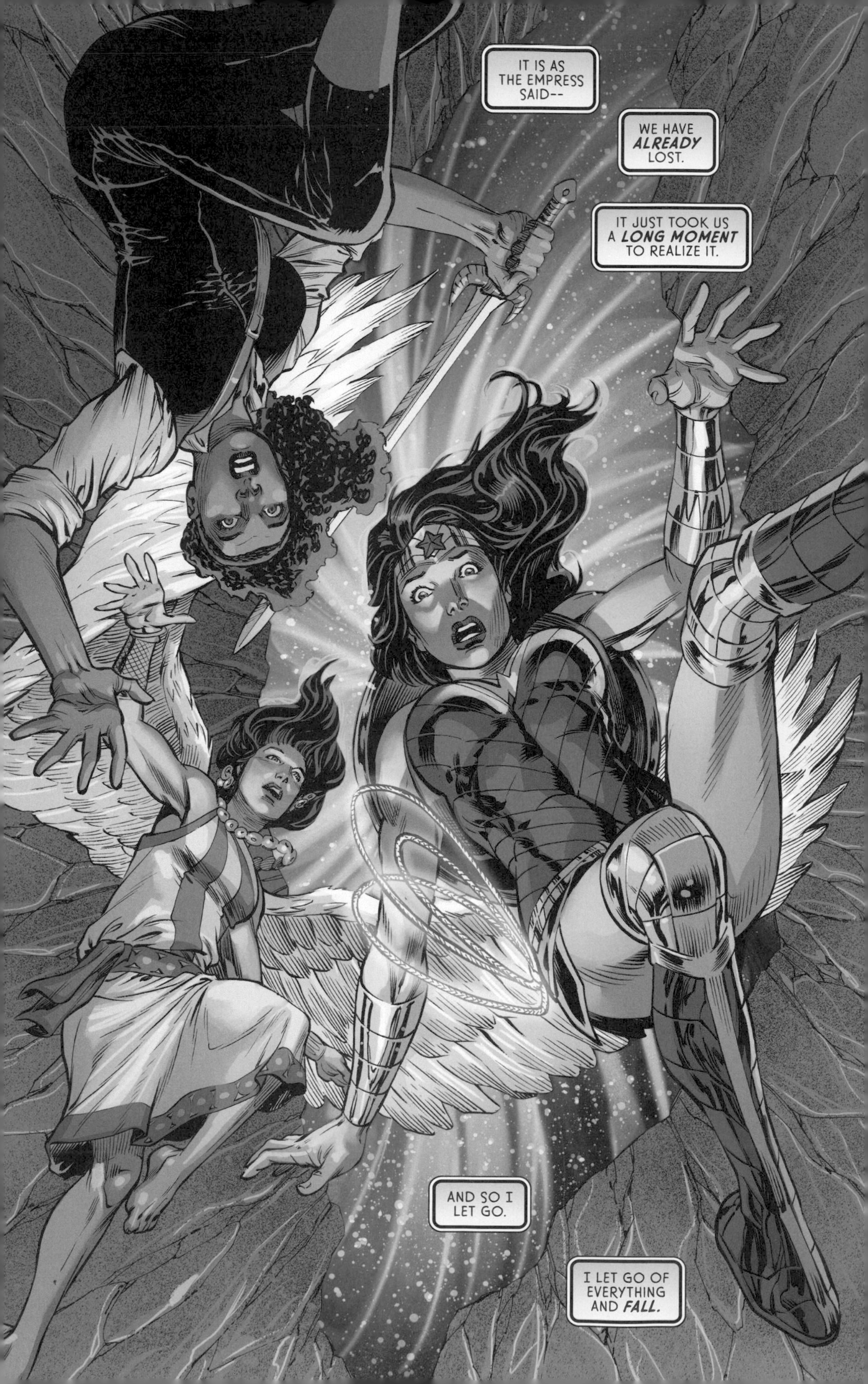
IT IS AS THE EMPRESS SAID--
WE HAVE **ALREADY** LOST.
IT JUST TOOK US A **LONG MOMENT** TO REALIZE IT.
AND SO I LET GO.
I LET GO OF EVERYTHING AND **FALL.**

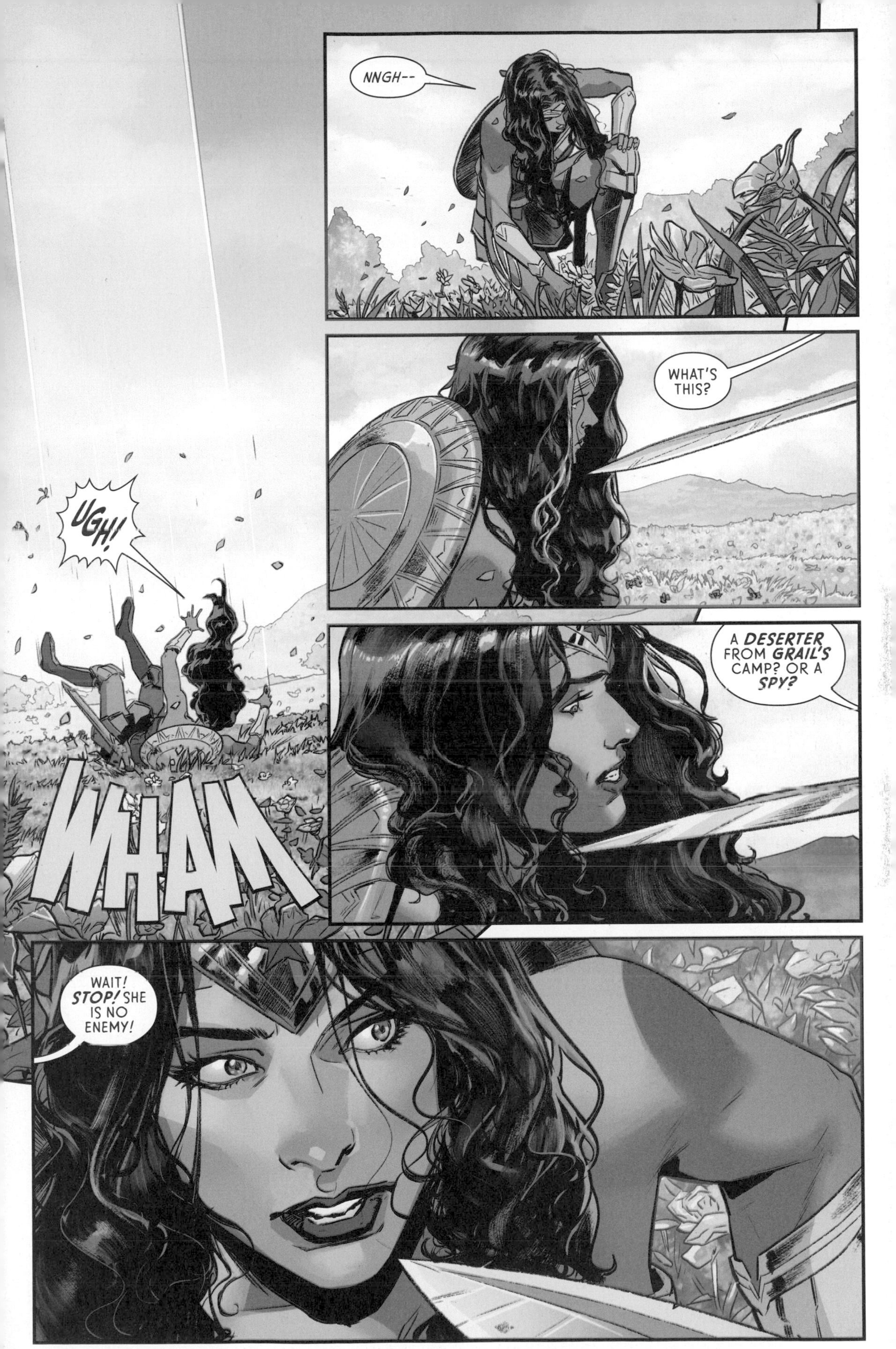
NNGH--
WHAT'S THIS?
UGH!
WHAM
A DESERTER FROM GRAIL'S CAMP? OR A SPY?
WAIT! STOP! SHE IS NO ENEMY!

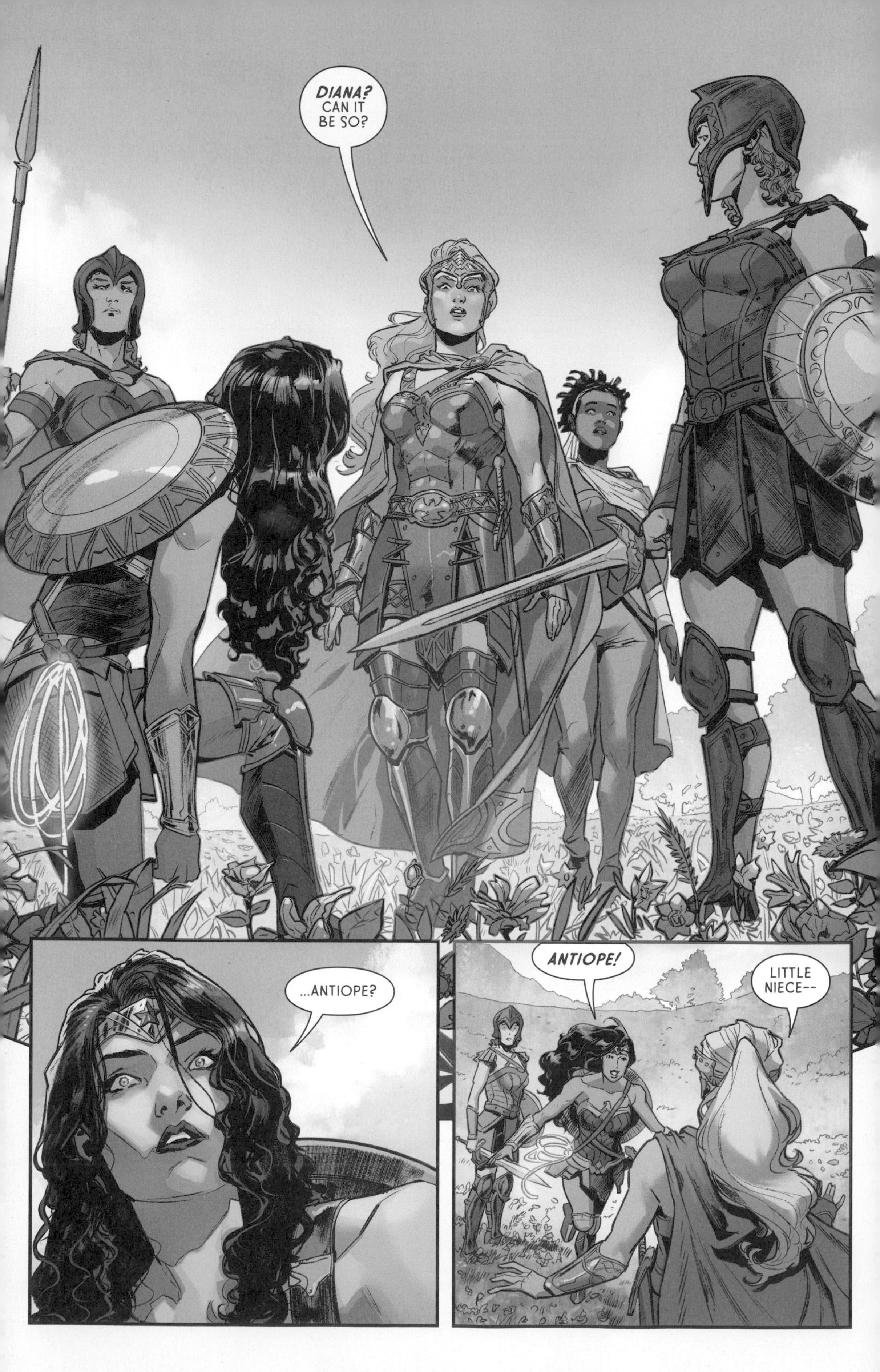
DIANA? CAN IT BE SO?
...ANTIOPE?
ANTIOPE!
LITTLE NIECE--

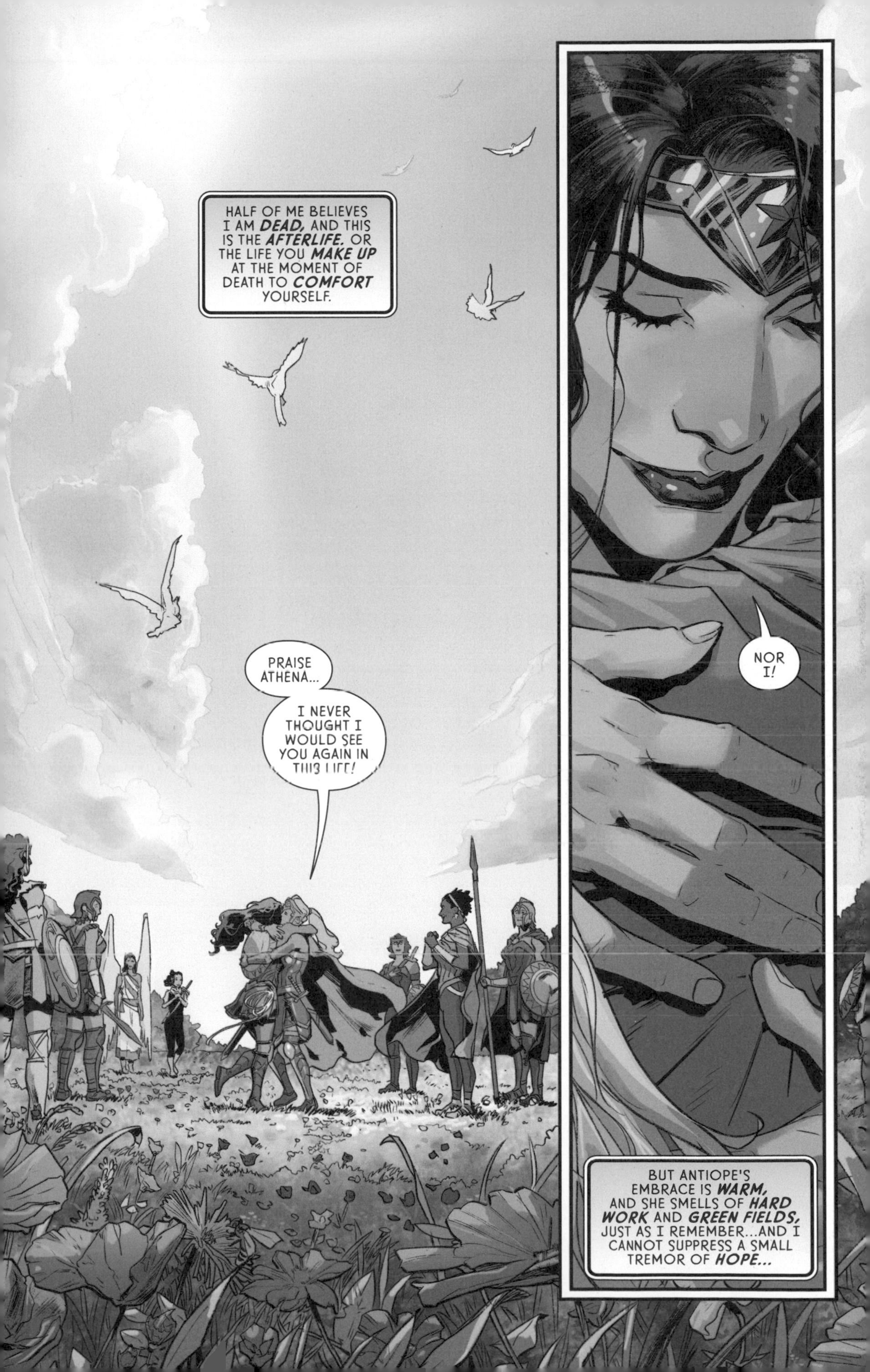
HALF OF ME BELIEVES I AM DEAD, AND THIS IS THE AFTERLIFE. OR THE LIFE YOU MAKE UP AT THE MOMENT OF DEATH TO COMFORT YOURSELF.
PRAISE ATHENA...
I NEVER THOUGHT I WOULD SEE YOU AGAIN IN THIS LIFE!
NOR I!
BUT ANTIOPE'S EMBRACE IS WARM, AND SHE SMELLS OF HARD WORK AND GREEN FIELDS, JUST AS I REMEMBER...AND I CANNOT SUPPRESS A SMALL TREMOR OF HOPE...

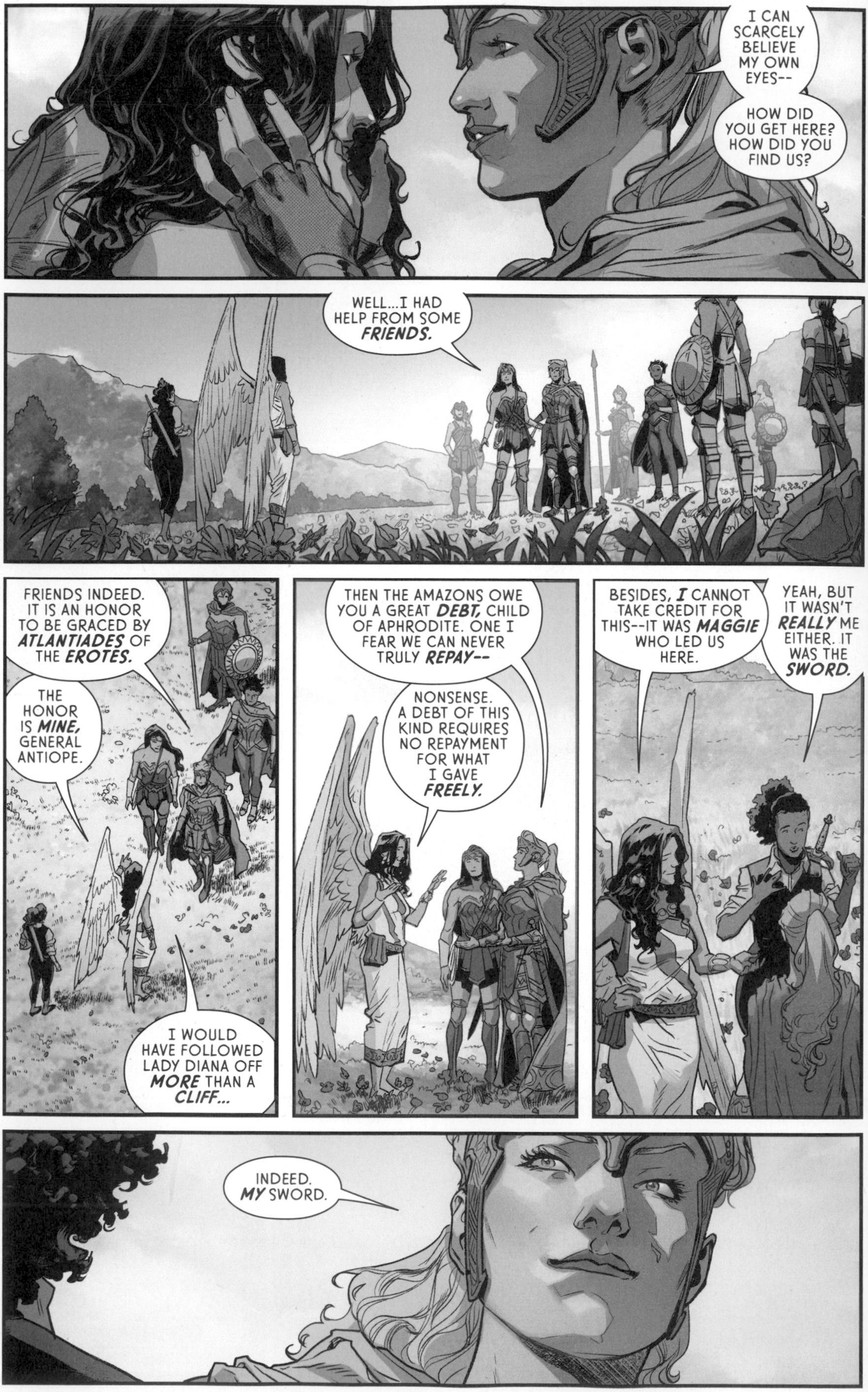

I CAN SCARCELY BELIEVE MY OWN EYES--
HOW DID YOU GET HERE? HOW DID YOU FIND US?
WELL...I HAD HELP FROM SOME **FRIENDS.**
FRIENDS INDEED. IT IS AN HONOR TO BE GRACED BY **ATLANTIADES** OF THE **EROTES.**
THE HONOR IS **MINE,** GENERAL ANTIOPE.
I WOULD HAVE FOLLOWED LADY DIANA OFF **MORE** THAN A **CLIFF...**
THEN THE AMAZONS OWE YOU A GREAT **DEBT,** CHILD OF APHRODITE. ONE I FEAR WE CAN NEVER TRULY **REPAY--**
NONSENSE. A DEBT OF THIS KIND REQUIRES NO REPAYMENT FOR WHAT I GAVE **FREELY.**
BESIDES, **I** CANNOT TAKE CREDIT FOR THIS--IT WAS **MAGGIE** WHO LED US HERE.
YEAH, BUT IT WASN'T **REALLY** ME EITHER. IT WAS THE **SWORD.**
INDEED. **MY** SWORD.

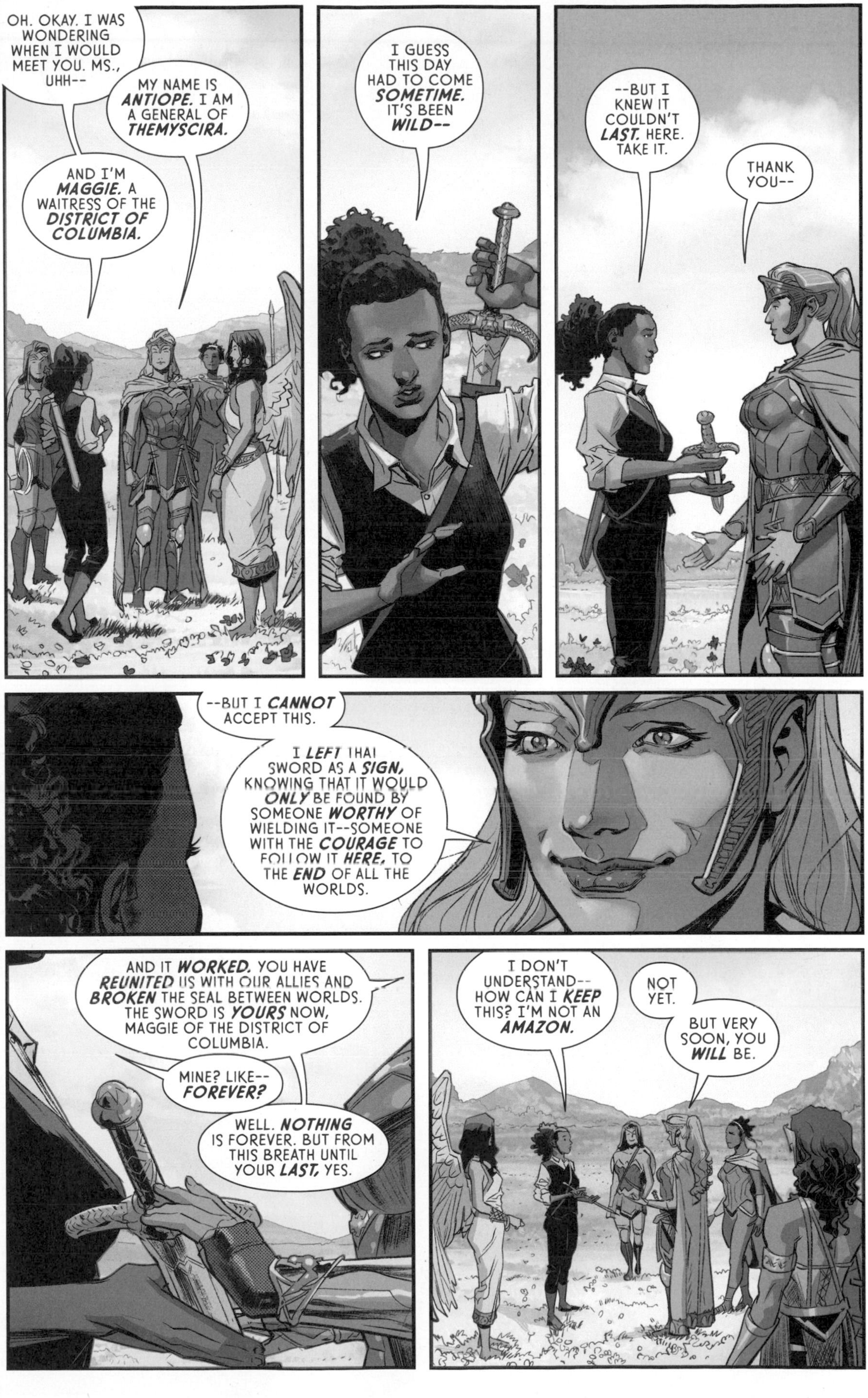

OH. OKAY. I WAS WONDERING WHEN I WOULD MEET YOU. MS., UHH--
MY NAME IS ANTIOPE. I AM A GENERAL OF THEMYSCIRA.
AND I'M MAGGIE. A WAITRESS OF THE DISTRICT OF COLUMBIA.
I GUESS THIS DAY HAD TO COME SOMETIME. IT'S BEEN WILD--
--BUT I KNEW IT COULDN'T LAST. HERE. TAKE IT.
THANK YOU--
--BUT I CANNOT ACCEPT THIS.
I LEFT THAT SWORD AS A SIGN, KNOWING THAT IT WOULD ONLY BE FOUND BY SOMEONE WORTHY OF WIELDING IT--SOMEONE WITH THE COURAGE TO FOLLOW IT HERE, TO THE END OF ALL THE WORLDS.
AND IT WORKED. YOU HAVE REUNITED US WITH OUR ALLIES AND BROKEN THE SEAL BETWEEN WORLDS. THE SWORD IS YOURS NOW, MAGGIE OF THE DISTRICT OF COLUMBIA.
MINE? LIKE-- FOREVER?
WELL. NOTHING IS FOREVER. BUT FROM THIS BREATH UNTIL YOUR LAST, YES.
I DON'T UNDERSTAND-- HOW CAN I KEEP THIS? I'M NOT AN AMAZON.
NOT YET.
BUT VERY SOON, YOU WILL BE.

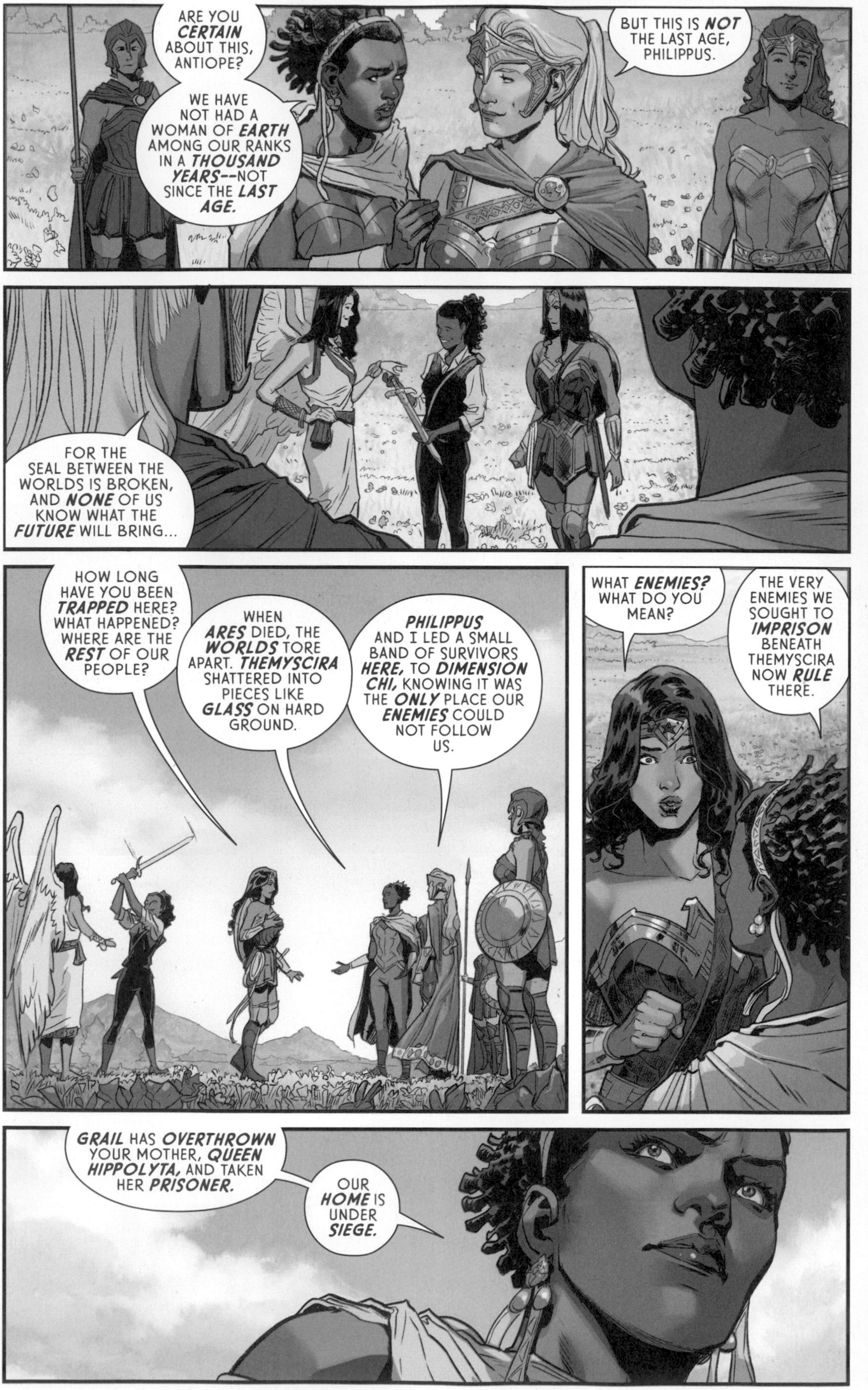
ARE YOU CERTAIN ABOUT THIS, ANTIOPE?
WE HAVE NOT HAD A WOMAN OF EARTH AMONG OUR RANKS IN A THOUSAND YEARS--NOT SINCE THE LAST AGE.
BUT THIS IS NOT THE LAST AGE, PHILIPPUS.
FOR THE SEAL BETWEEN THE WORLDS IS BROKEN, AND NONE OF US KNOW WHAT THE FUTURE WILL BRING...
HOW LONG HAVE YOU BEEN TRAPPED HERE? WHAT HAPPENED? WHERE ARE THE REST OF OUR PEOPLE?
WHEN ARES DIED, THE WORLDS TORE APART. THEMYSCIRA SHATTERED INTO PIECES LIKE GLASS ON HARD GROUND.
PHILIPPUS AND I LED A SMALL BAND OF SURVIVORS HERE, TO DIMENSION CHI, KNOWING IT WAS THE ONLY PLACE OUR ENEMIES COULD NOT FOLLOW US.
WHAT ENEMIES? WHAT DO YOU MEAN?
THE VERY ENEMIES WE SOUGHT TO IMPRISON BENEATH THEMYSCIRA NOW RULE THERE.
GRAIL HAS OVERTHROWN YOUR MOTHER, QUEEN HIPPOLYTA, AND TAKEN HER PRISONER.
OUR HOME IS UNDER SIEGE.

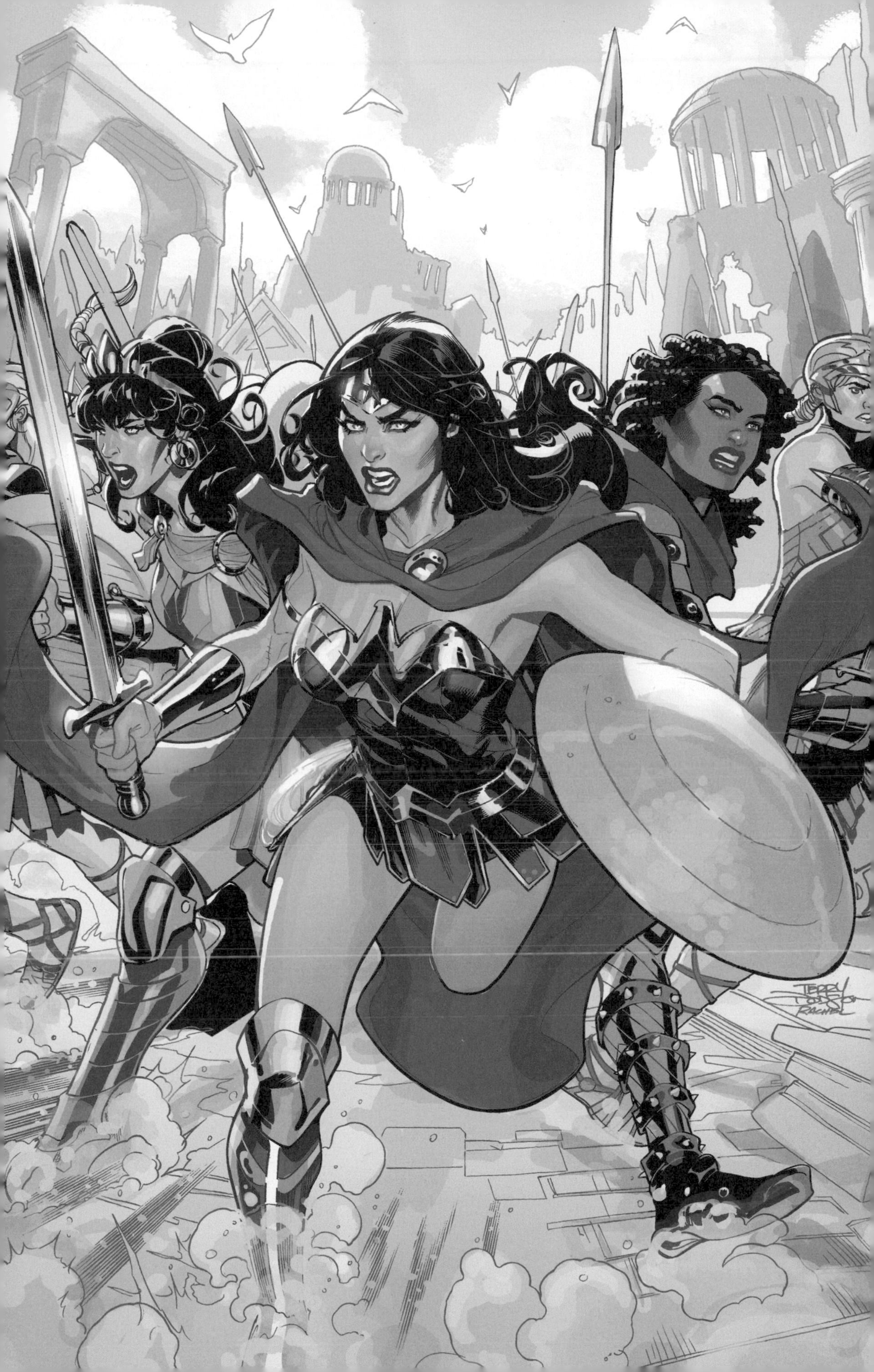

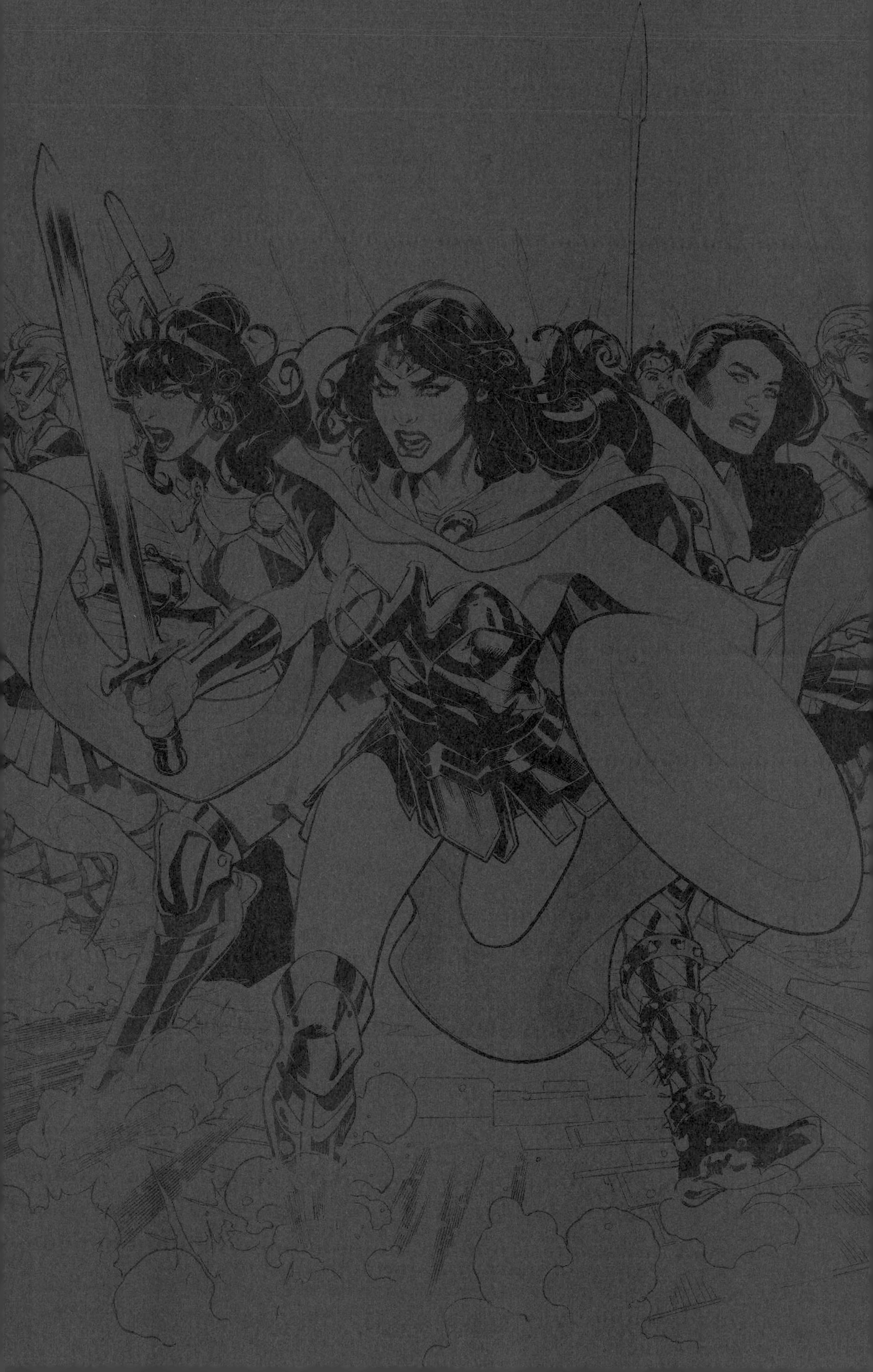

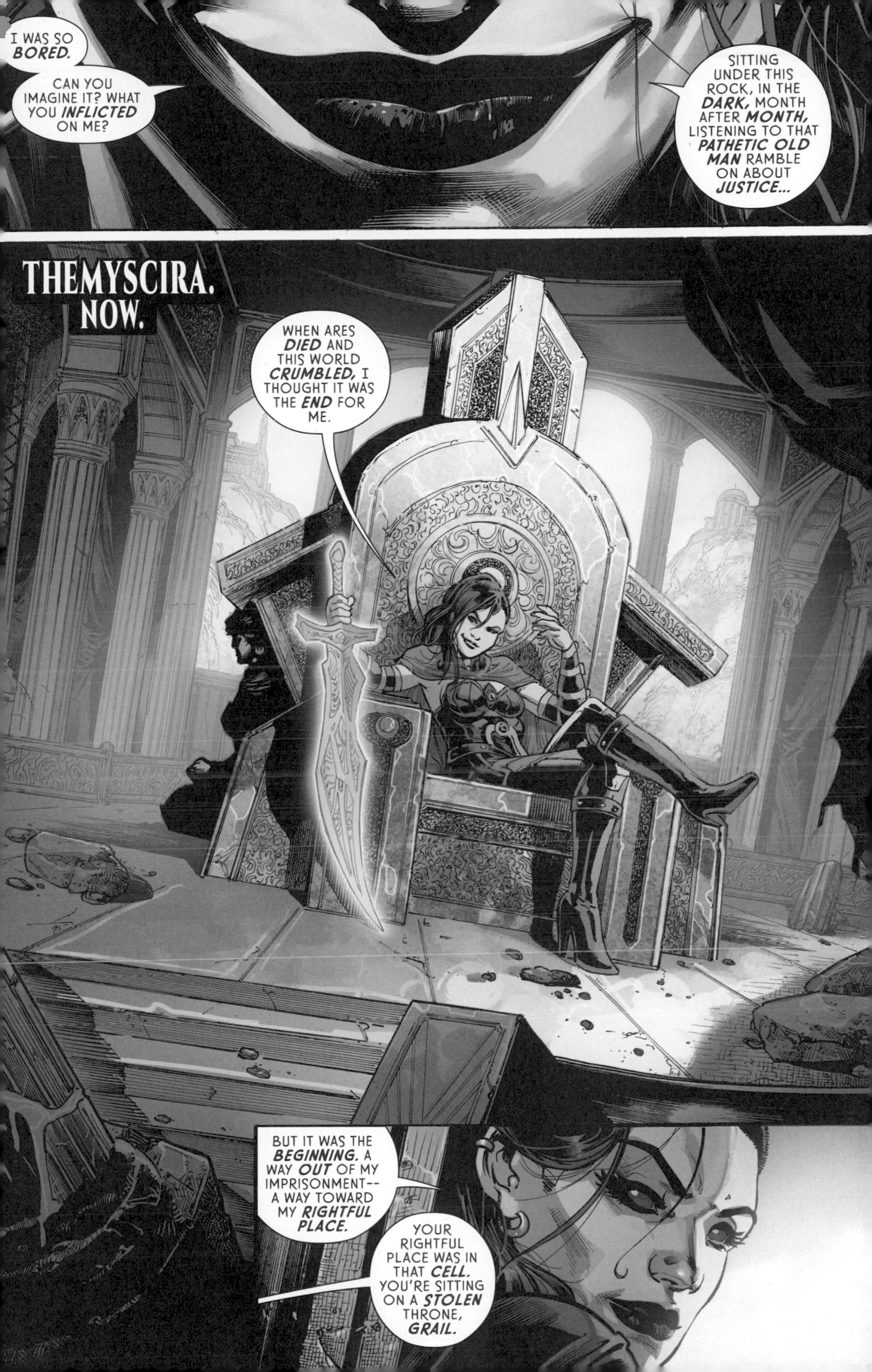
I WAS SO BORED.
CAN YOU IMAGINE IT? WHAT YOU INFLICTED ON ME?
SITTING UNDER THIS ROCK, IN THE DARK, MONTH AFTER MONTH, LISTENING TO THAT PATHETIC OLD MAN RAMBLE ON ABOUT JUSTICE...
THEMYSCIRA. NOW.
WHEN ARES DIED AND THIS WORLD CRUMBLED, I THOUGHT IT WAS THE END FOR ME.
BUT IT WAS THE BEGINNING. A WAY OUT OF MY IMPRISONMENT-- A WAY TOWARD MY RIGHTFUL PLACE.
YOUR RIGHTFUL PLACE WAS IN THAT CELL. YOU'RE SITTING ON A STOLEN THRONE, GRAIL.

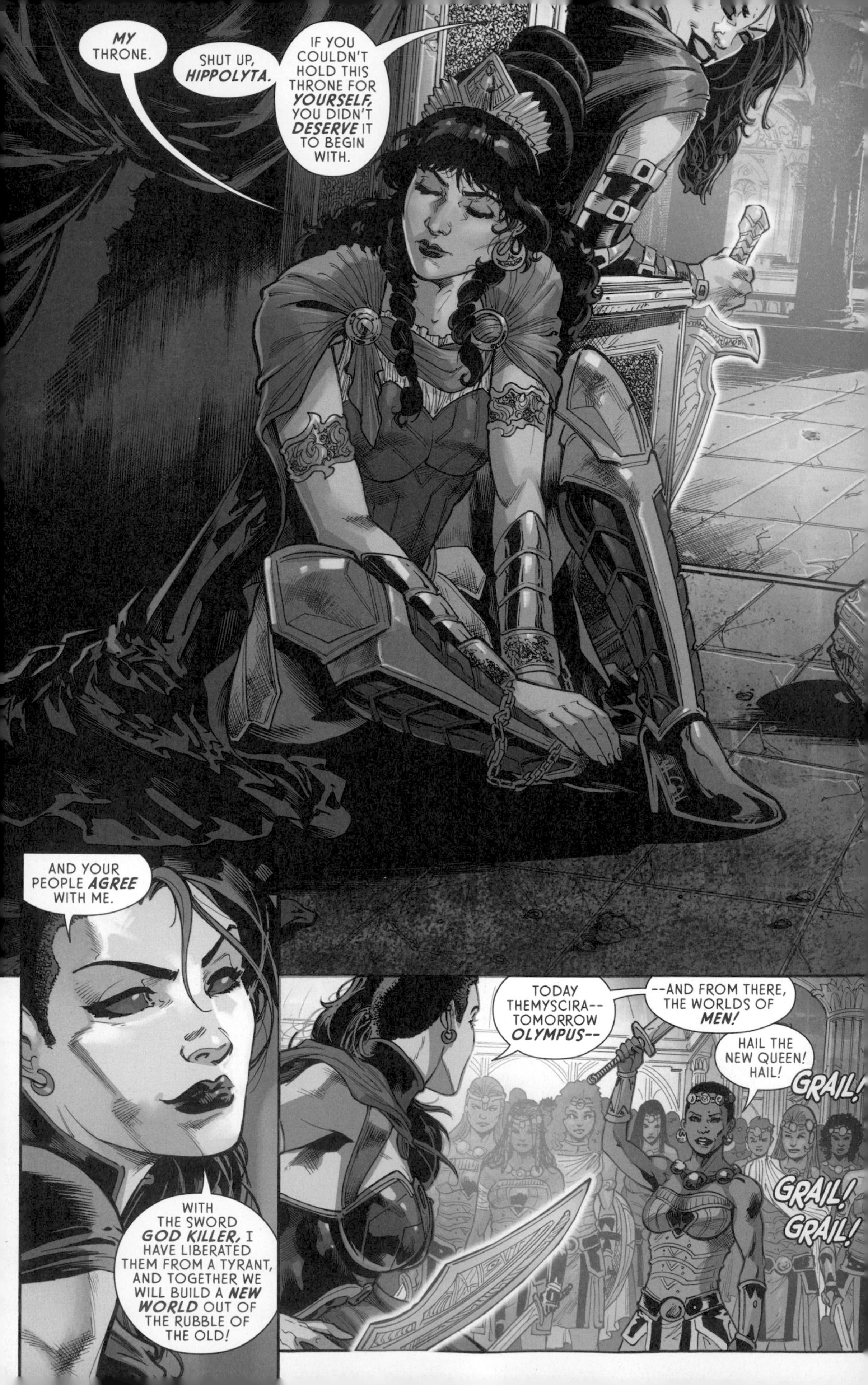
MY THRONE.
SHUT UP, HIPPOLYTA.
IF YOU COULDN'T HOLD THIS THRONE FOR YOURSELF, YOU DIDN'T DESERVE IT TO BEGIN WITH.
AND YOUR PEOPLE AGREE WITH ME.
WITH THE SWORD GOD KILLER, I HAVE LIBERATED THEM FROM A TYRANT, AND TOGETHER WE WILL BUILD A NEW WORLD OUT OF THE RUBBLE OF THE OLD!
TODAY THEMYSCIRA-- TOMORROW OLYMPUS--
--AND FROM THERE, THE WORLDS OF MEN!
HAIL THE NEW QUEEN! HAIL!
GRAIL!
GRAIL!
GRAIL!

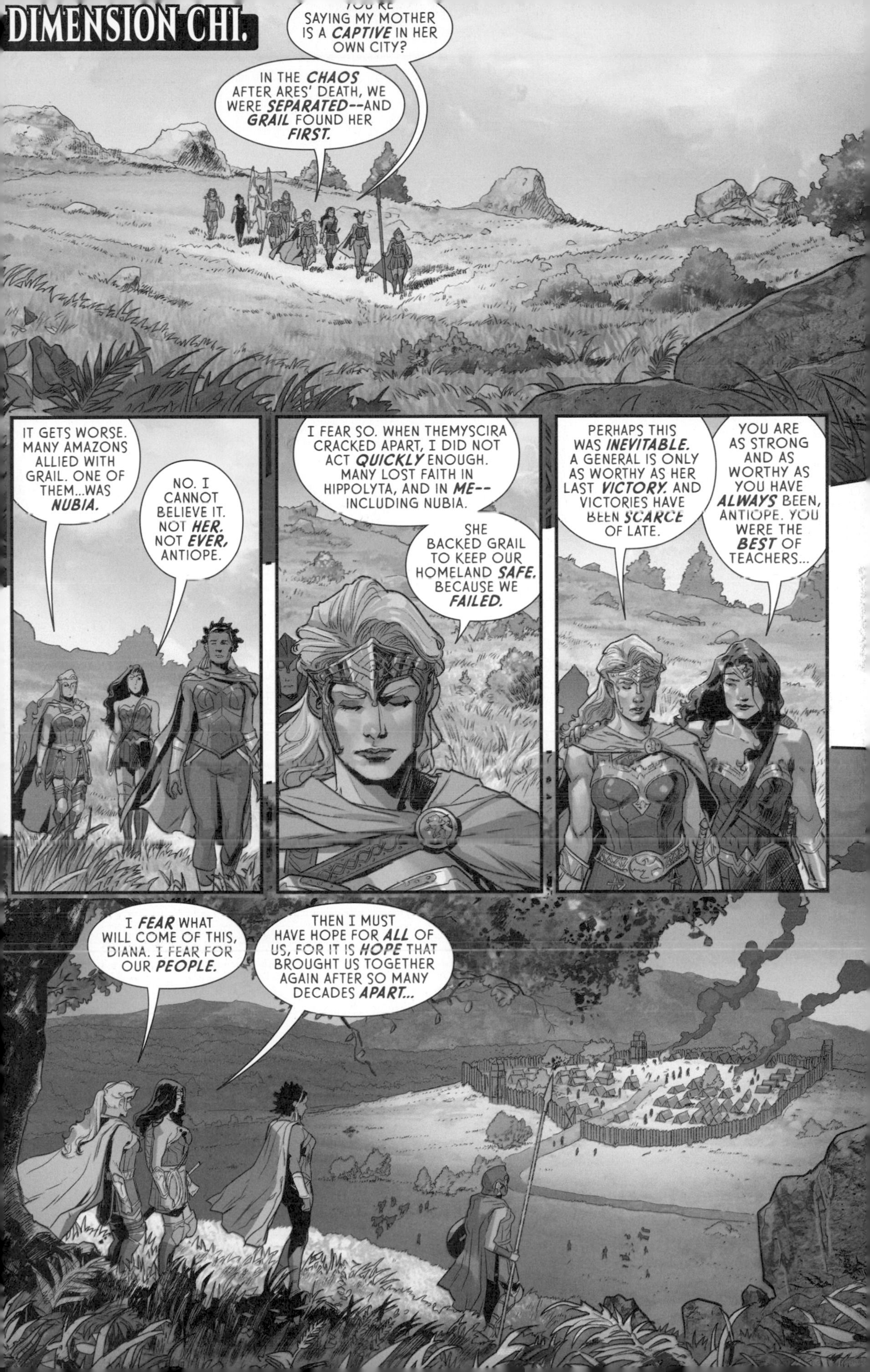
DIMENSION CHI.
YOU'RE SAYING MY MOTHER IS A CAPTIVE IN HER OWN CITY?
IN THE CHAOS AFTER ARES' DEATH, WE WERE SEPARATED--AND GRAIL FOUND HER FIRST.
IT GETS WORSE. MANY AMAZONS ALLIED WITH GRAIL. ONE OF THEM...WAS NUBIA.
NO. I CANNOT BELIEVE IT. NOT HER. NOT EVER, ANTIOPE.
I FEAR SO. WHEN THEMYSCIRA CRACKED APART, I DID NOT ACT QUICKLY ENOUGH. MANY LOST FAITH IN HIPPOLYTA, AND IN ME--INCLUDING NUBIA.
SHE BACKED GRAIL TO KEEP OUR HOMELAND SAFE. BECAUSE WE FAILED.
PERHAPS THIS WAS INEVITABLE. A GENERAL IS ONLY AS WORTHY AS HER LAST VICTORY. AND VICTORIES HAVE BEEN SCARCE OF LATE.
YOU ARE AS STRONG AND AS WORTHY AS YOU HAVE ALWAYS BEEN, ANTIOPE. YOU WERE THE BEST OF TEACHERS...
I FEAR WHAT WILL COME OF THIS, DIANA. I FEAR FOR OUR PEOPLE.
THEN I MUST HAVE HOPE FOR ALL OF US, FOR IT IS HOPE THAT BROUGHT US TOGETHER AGAIN AFTER SO MANY DECADES APART...

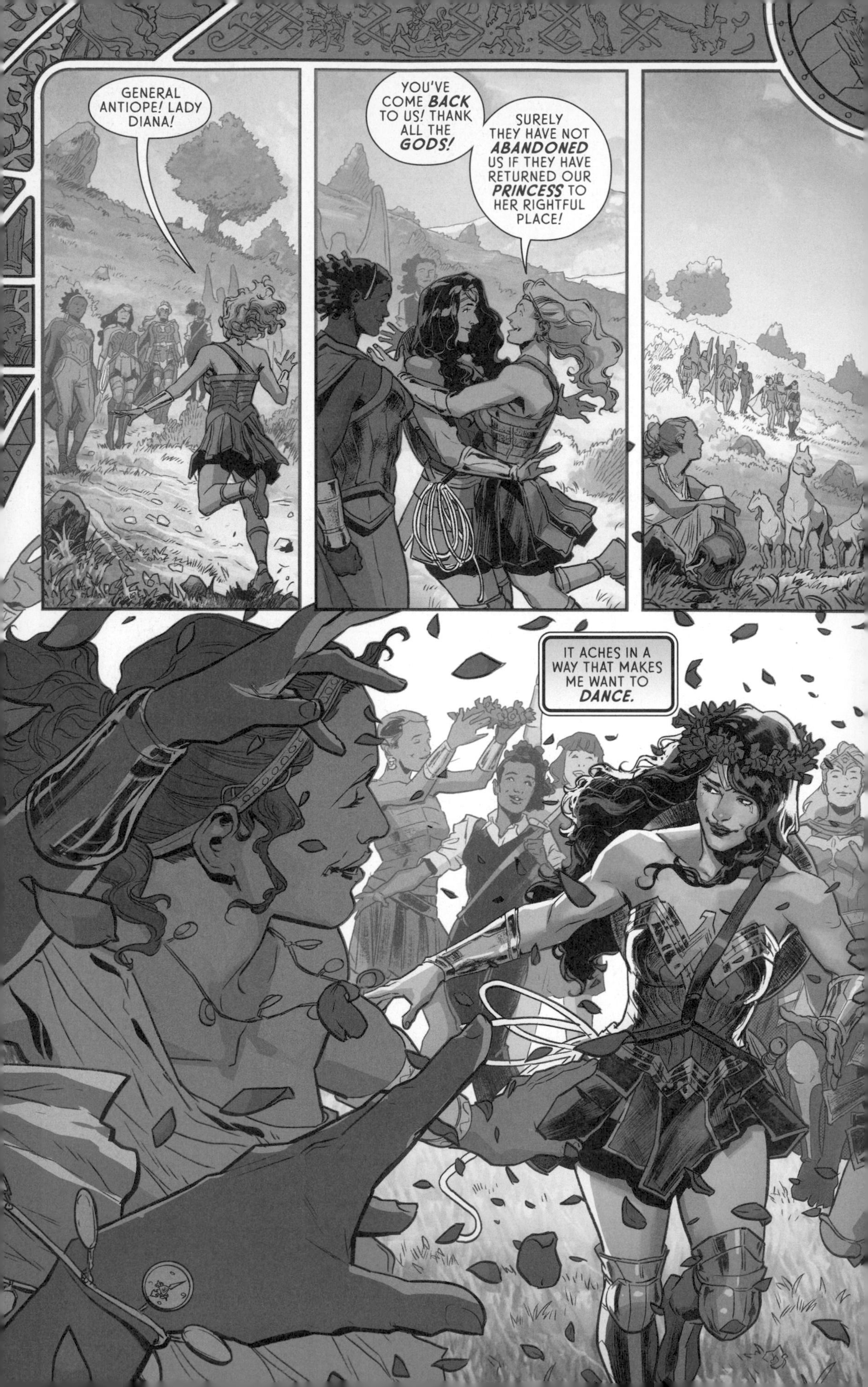
GENERAL ANTIOPE! LADY DIANA!
YOU'VE COME BACK TO US! THANK ALL THE GODS!
SURELY THEY HAVE NOT ABANDONED US IF THEY HAVE RETURNED OUR PRINCESS TO HER RIGHTFUL PLACE!
IT ACHES IN A WAY THAT MAKES ME WANT TO DANCE.

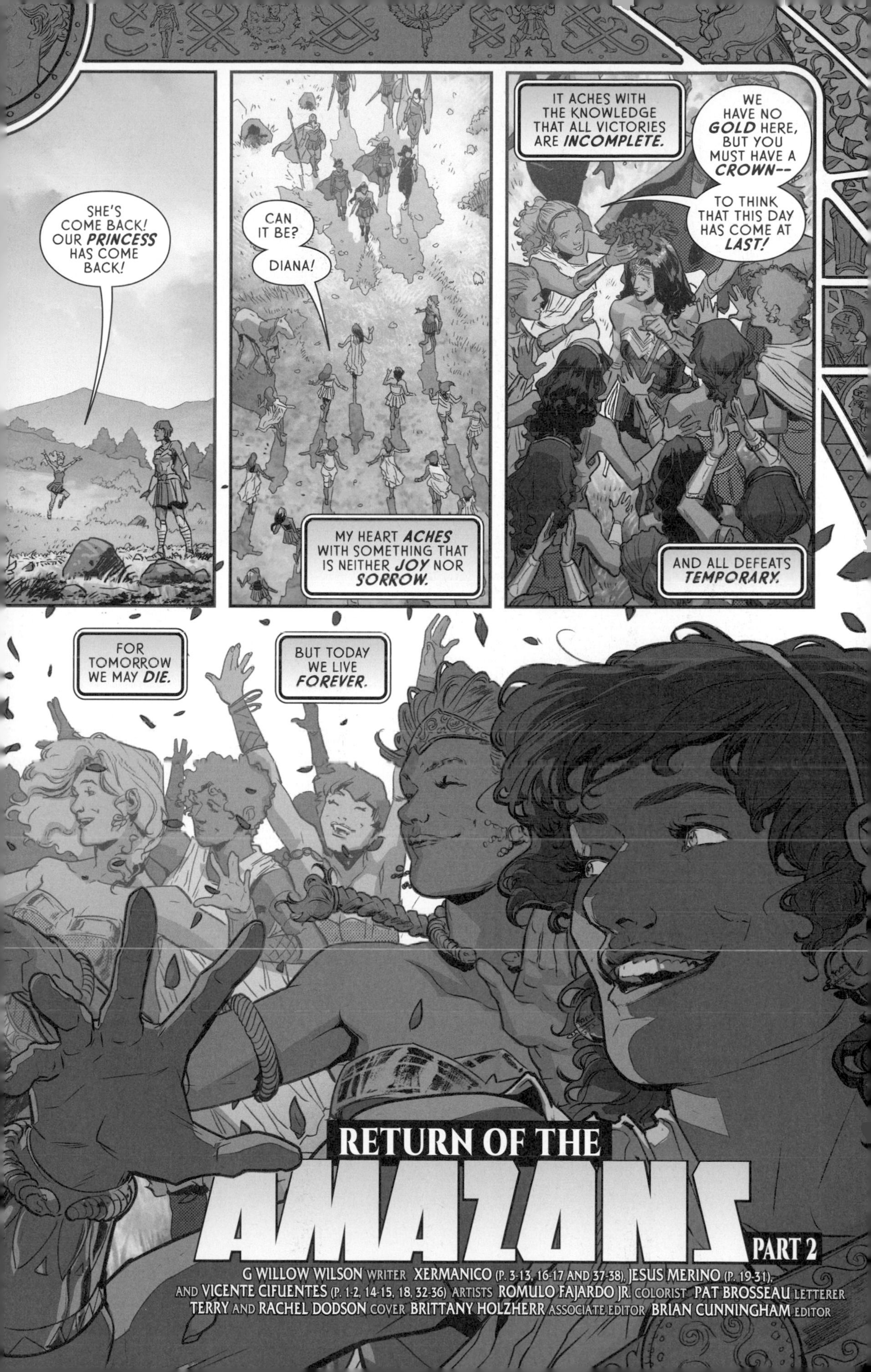
SHE'S COME BACK! OUR PRINCESS HAS COME BACK!
CAN IT BE?
DIANA!
MY HEART ACHES WITH SOMETHING THAT IS NEITHER JOY NOR SORROW.
IT ACHES WITH THE KNOWLEDGE THAT ALL VICTORIES ARE INCOMPLETE.
WE HAVE NO GOLD HERE, BUT YOU MUST HAVE A CROWN--
TO THINK THAT THIS DAY HAS COME AT LAST!
AND ALL DEFEATS TEMPORARY.
FOR TOMORROW WE MAY DIE.
BUT TODAY WE LIVE FOREVER.
RETURN OF THE AMAZONS PART 2
G WILLOW WILSON WRITER XERMANICO (P. 3-13, 16-17 AND 37-38), JESUS MERINO (P. 19-31), AND VICENTE CIFUENTES (P. 1-2, 14-15, 18, 32-36) ARTISTS ROMULO FAJARDO JR. COLORIST PAT BROSSEAU LETTERER
TERRY AND RACHEL DODSON COVER BRITTANY HOLZHERR ASSOCIATE EDITOR BRIAN CUNNINGHAM EDITOR

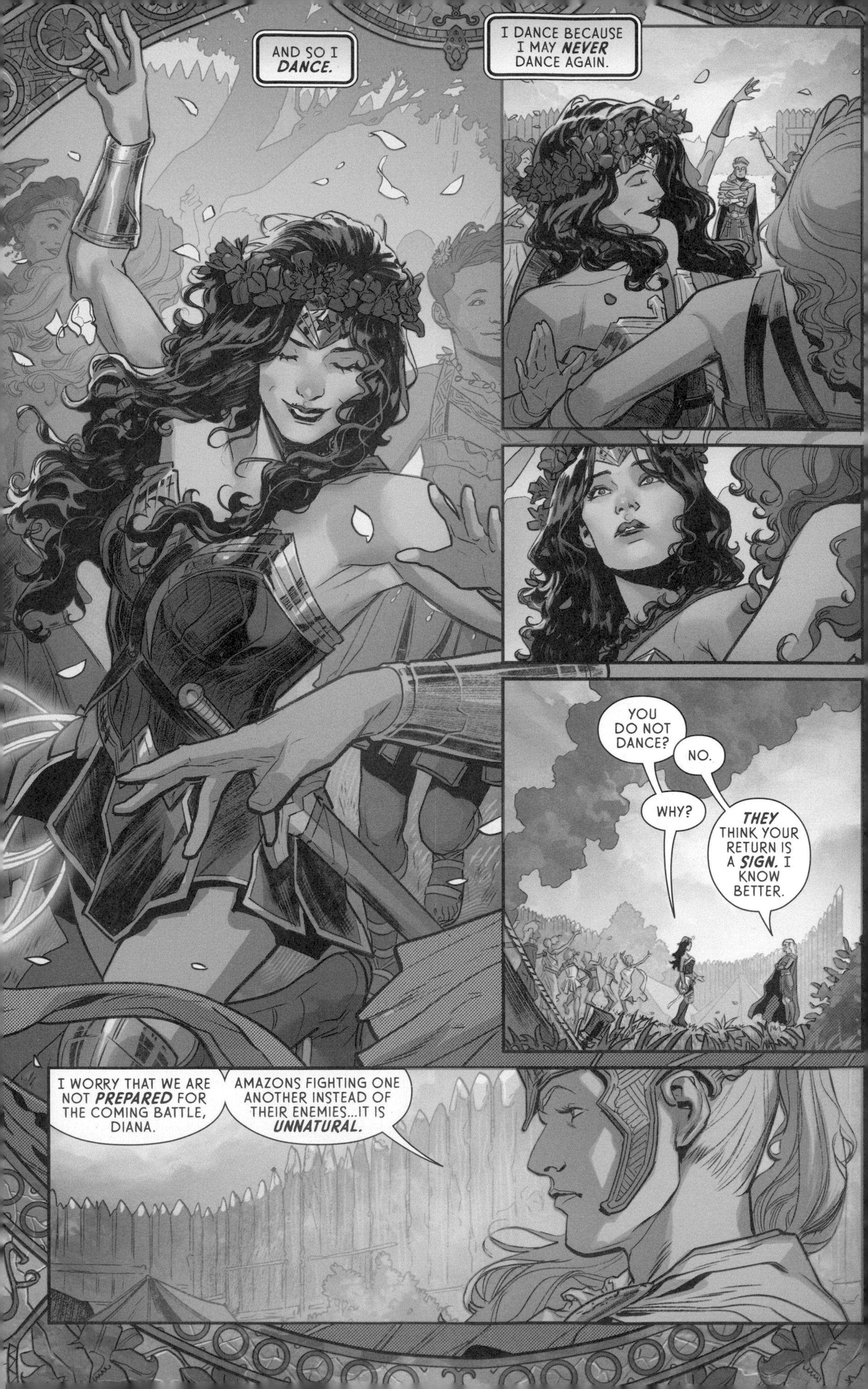
AND SO I DANCE.
I DANCE BECAUSE I MAY NEVER DANCE AGAIN.
YOU DO NOT DANCE?
NO.
WHY?
THEY THINK YOUR RETURN IS A SIGN. I KNOW BETTER.
I WORRY THAT WE ARE NOT PREPARED FOR THE COMING BATTLE, DIANA.
AMAZONS FIGHTING ONE ANOTHER INSTEAD OF THEIR ENEMIES...IT IS UNNATURAL.

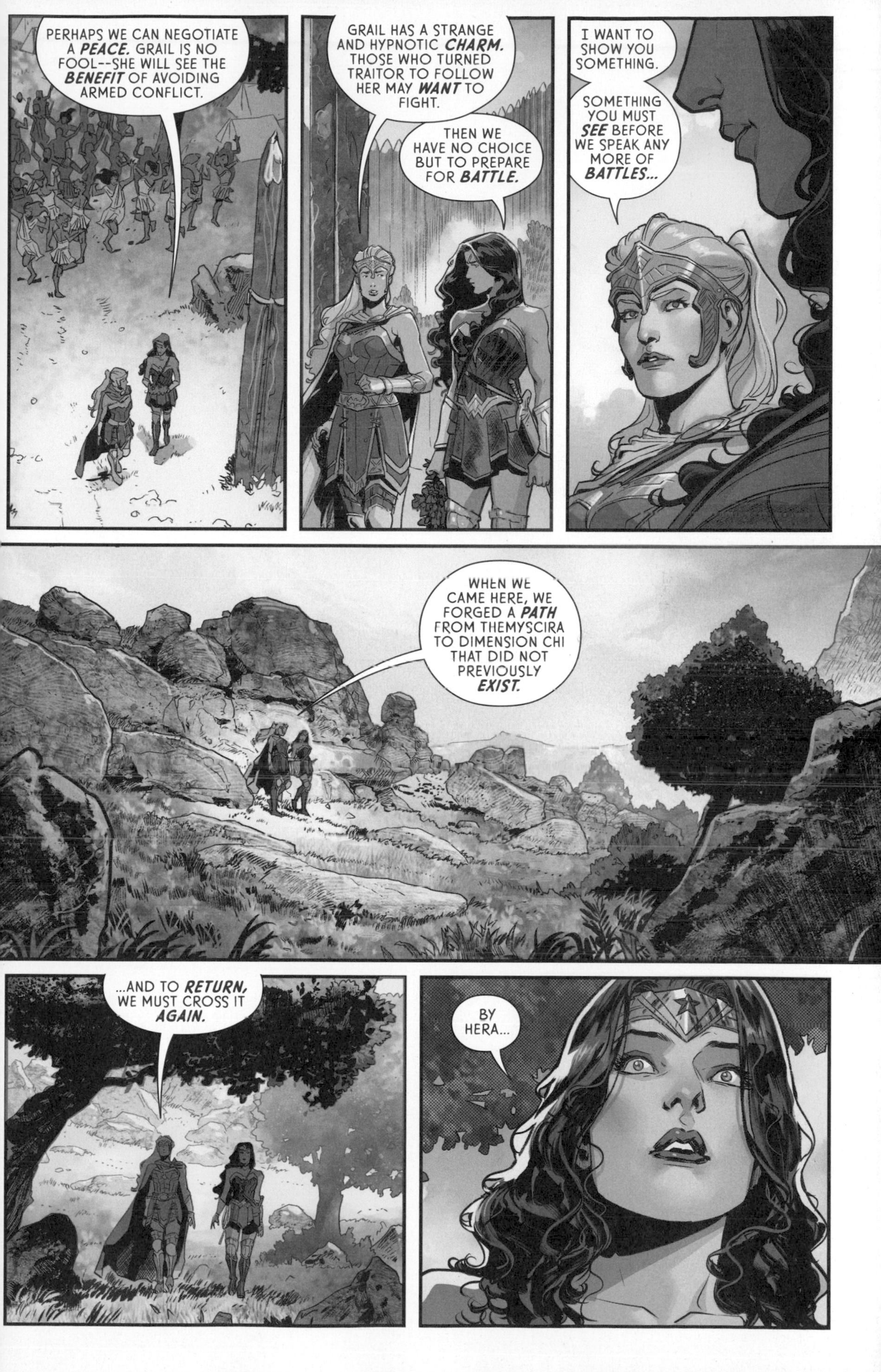
PERHAPS WE CAN NEGOTIATE A PEACE. GRAIL IS NO FOOL--SHE WILL SEE THE BENEFIT OF AVOIDING ARMED CONFLICT.
GRAIL HAS A STRANGE AND HYPNOTIC CHARM. THOSE WHO TURNED TRAITOR TO FOLLOW HER MAY WANT TO FIGHT.
THEN WE HAVE NO CHOICE BUT TO PREPARE FOR BATTLE.
I WANT TO SHOW YOU SOMETHING.
SOMETHING YOU MUST SEE BEFORE WE SPEAK ANY MORE OF BATTLES...
WHEN WE CAME HERE, WE FORGED A PATH FROM THEMYSCIRA TO DIMENSION CHI THAT DID NOT PREVIOUSLY EXIST.
...AND TO RETURN, WE MUST CROSS IT AGAIN.
BY HERA...

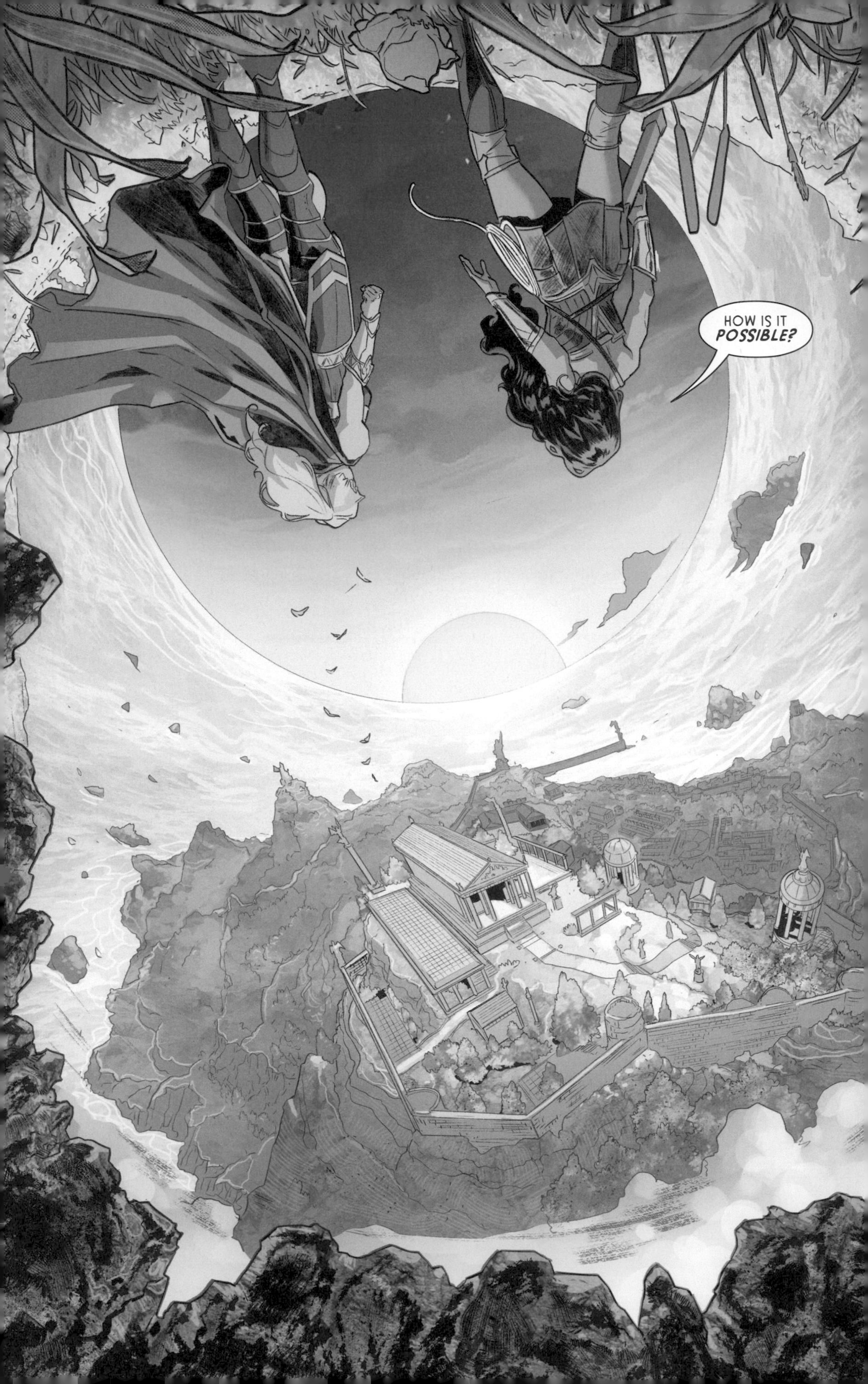
HOW IS IT POSSIBLE?

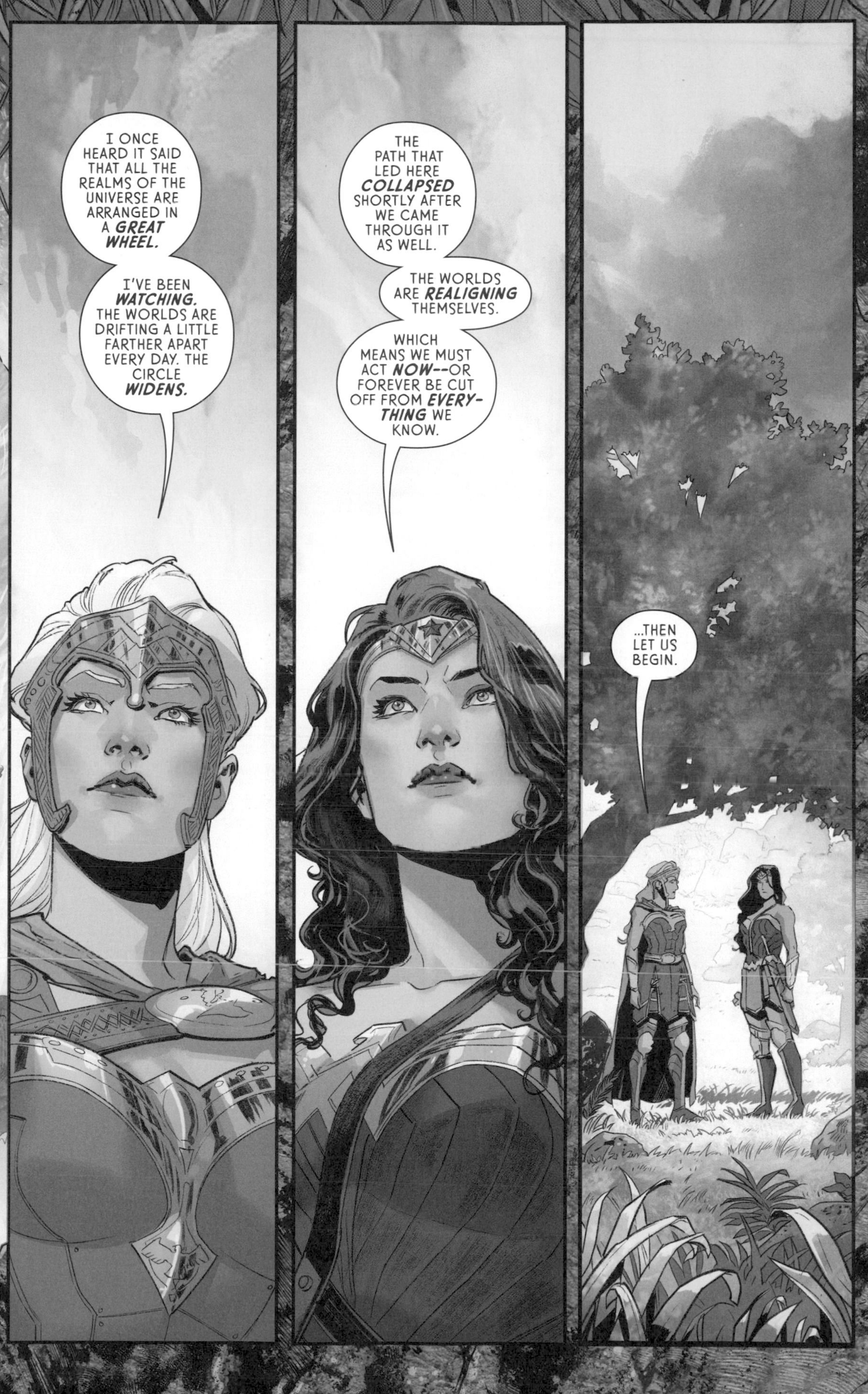
I ONCE HEARD IT SAID THAT ALL THE REALMS OF THE UNIVERSE ARE ARRANGED IN A **GREAT WHEEL.**
I'VE BEEN **WATCHING.** THE WORLDS ARE DRIFTING A LITTLE FARTHER APART EVERY DAY. THE CIRCLE **WIDENS.**
THE PATH THAT LED HERE **COLLAPSED** SHORTLY AFTER WE CAME THROUGH IT AS WELL.
THE WORLDS ARE **REALIGNING** THEMSELVES.
WHICH MEANS WE MUST ACT **NOW**--OR FOREVER BE CUT OFF FROM **EVERY-THING** WE KNOW.
...THEN LET US BEGIN.

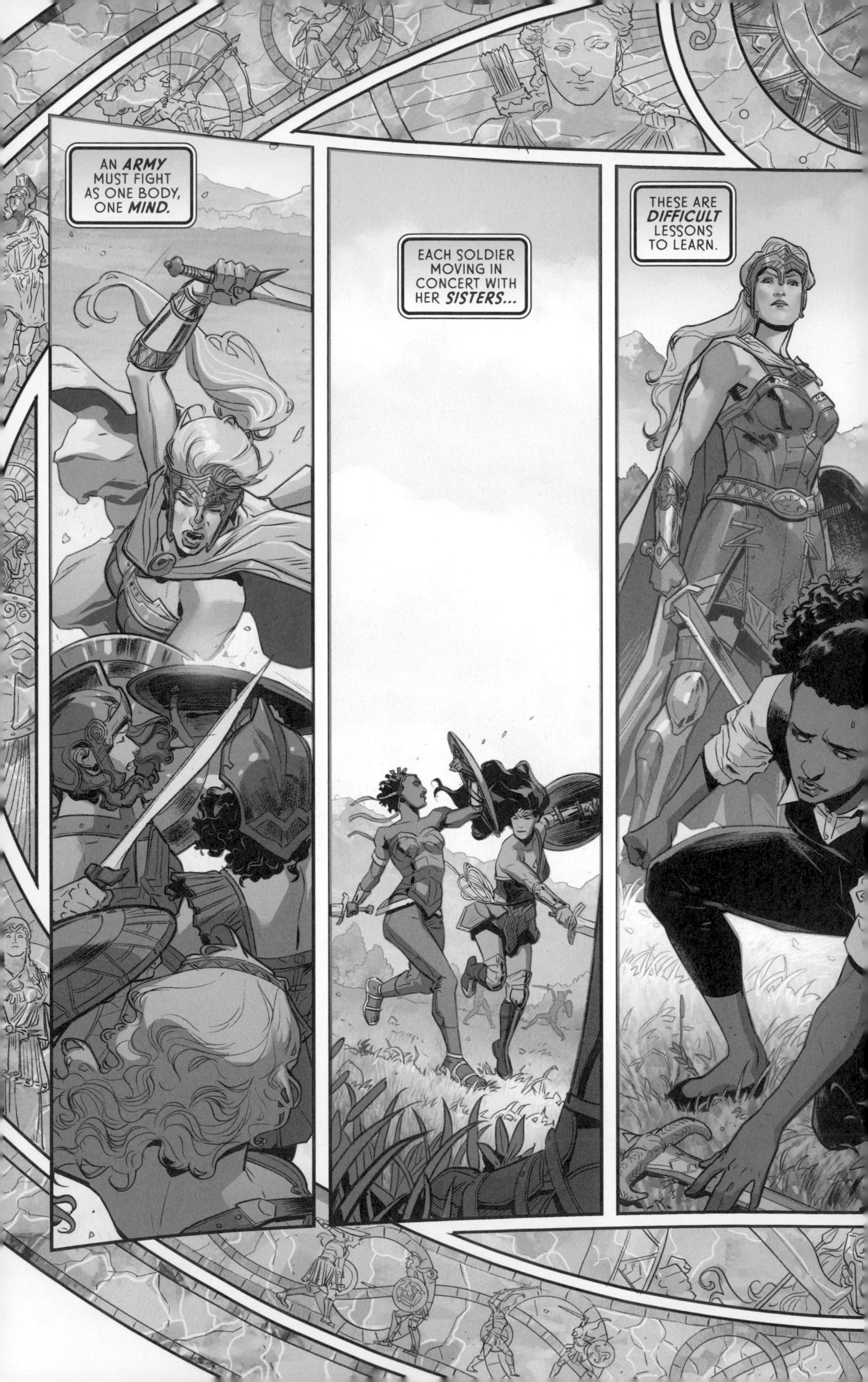
AN *ARMY* MUST FIGHT AS ONE BODY, ONE *MIND.*
EACH SOLDIER MOVING IN CONCERT WITH HER *SISTERS...*
THESE ARE *DIFFICULT* LESSONS TO LEARN.

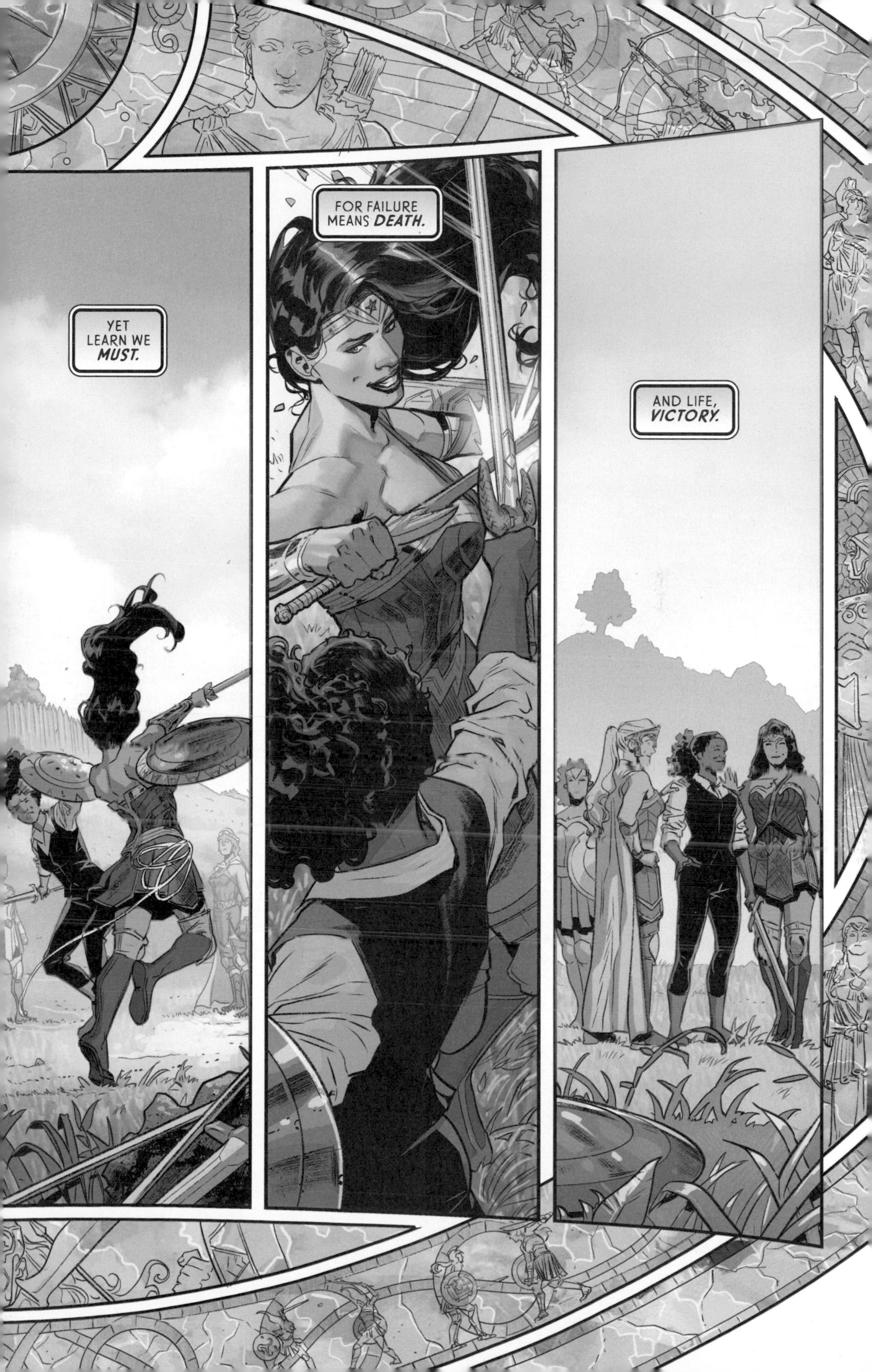
YET LEARN WE *MUST.*
FOR FAILURE MEANS *DEATH.*
AND LIFE, *VICTORY.*

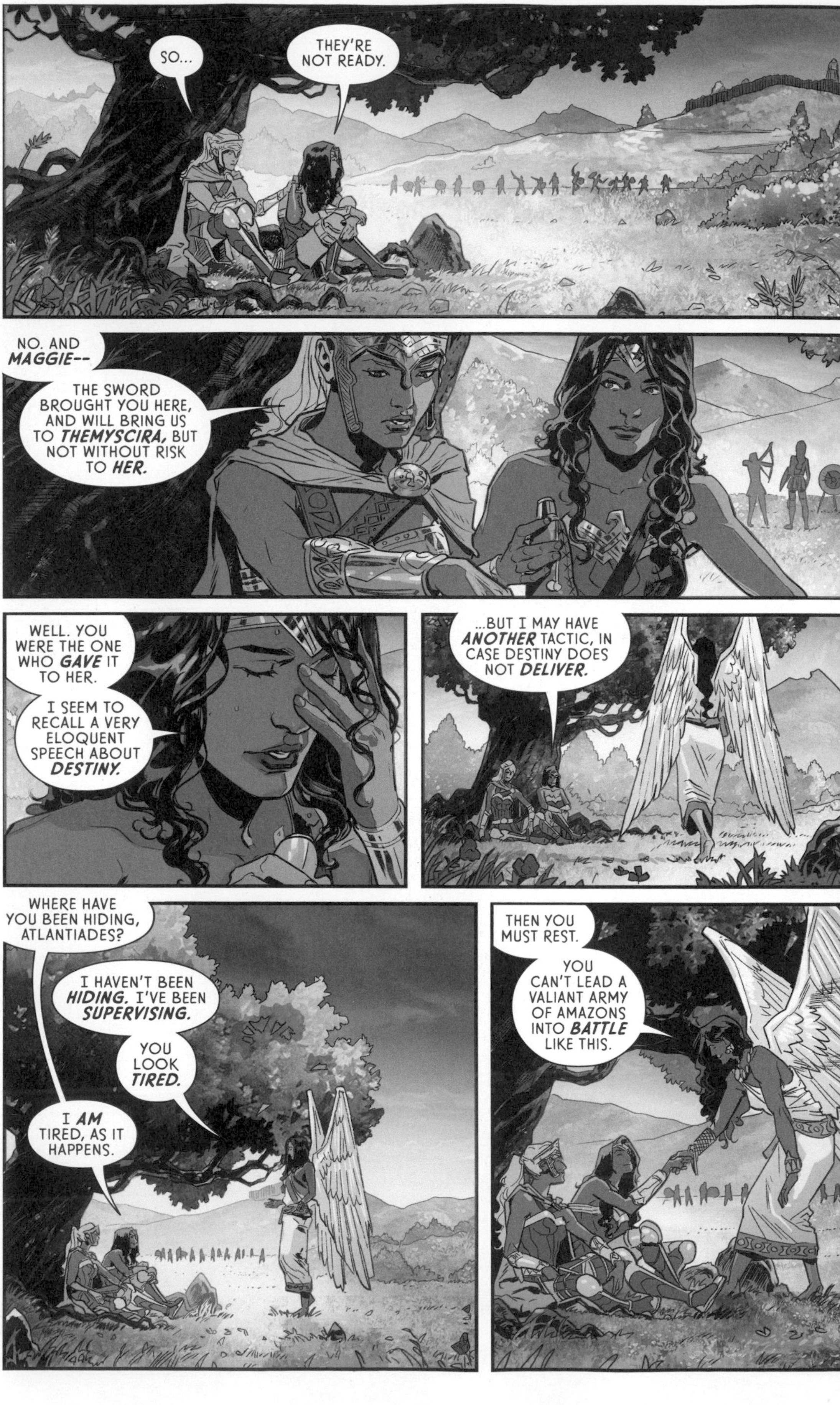
SO...
THEY'RE NOT READY.
NO. AND MAGGIE--
THE SWORD BROUGHT YOU HERE, AND WILL BRING US TO THEMYSCIRA, BUT NOT WITHOUT RISK TO HER.
WELL. YOU WERE THE ONE WHO GAVE IT TO HER.
I SEEM TO RECALL A VERY ELOQUENT SPEECH ABOUT DESTINY.
...BUT I MAY HAVE ANOTHER TACTIC, IN CASE DESTINY DOES NOT DELIVER.
WHERE HAVE YOU BEEN HIDING, ATLANTIADES?
I HAVEN'T BEEN HIDING. I'VE BEEN SUPERVISING.
YOU LOOK TIRED.
I AM TIRED, AS IT HAPPENS.
THEN YOU MUST REST.
YOU CAN'T LEAD A VALIANT ARMY OF AMAZONS INTO BATTLE LIKE THIS.

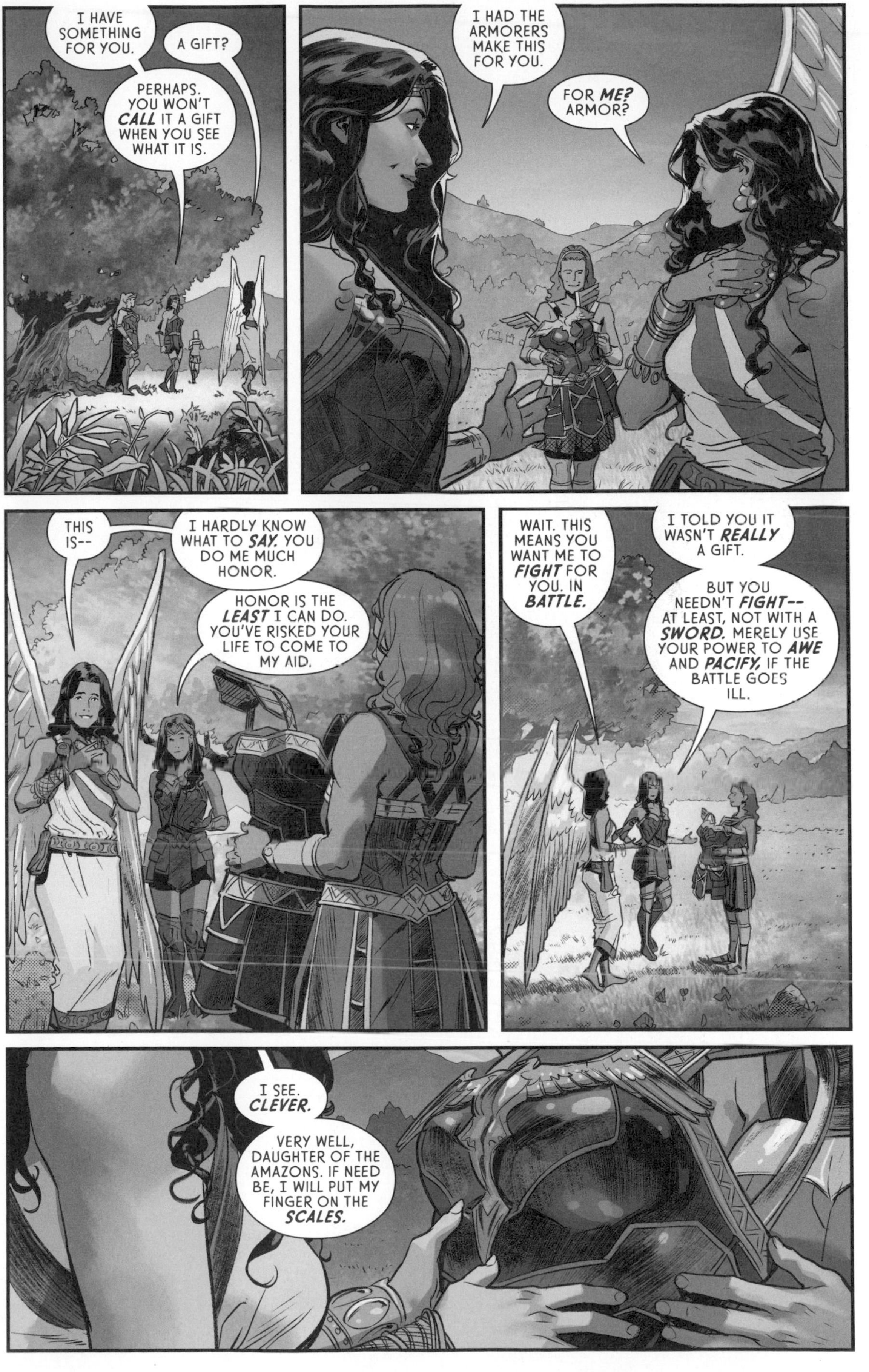
I HAVE SOMETHING FOR YOU.
A GIFT?
PERHAPS. YOU WON'T **CALL** IT A GIFT WHEN YOU SEE WHAT IT IS.
I HAD THE ARMORERS MAKE THIS FOR YOU.
FOR **ME?** ARMOR?
THIS IS--
I HARDLY KNOW WHAT TO **SAY.** YOU DO ME MUCH HONOR.
HONOR IS THE **LEAST** I CAN DO. YOU'VE RISKED YOUR LIFE TO COME TO MY AID.
WAIT. THIS MEANS YOU WANT ME TO **FIGHT** FOR YOU. IN **BATTLE.**
I TOLD YOU IT WASN'T **REALLY** A GIFT.
BUT YOU NEEDN'T **FIGHT--** AT LEAST, NOT WITH A **SWORD.** MERELY USE YOUR POWER TO **AWE** AND **PACIFY,** IF THE BATTLE GOES ILL.
I SEE. **CLEVER.**
VERY WELL, DAUGHTER OF THE AMAZONS. IF NEED BE, I WILL PUT MY FINGER ON THE **SCALES.**

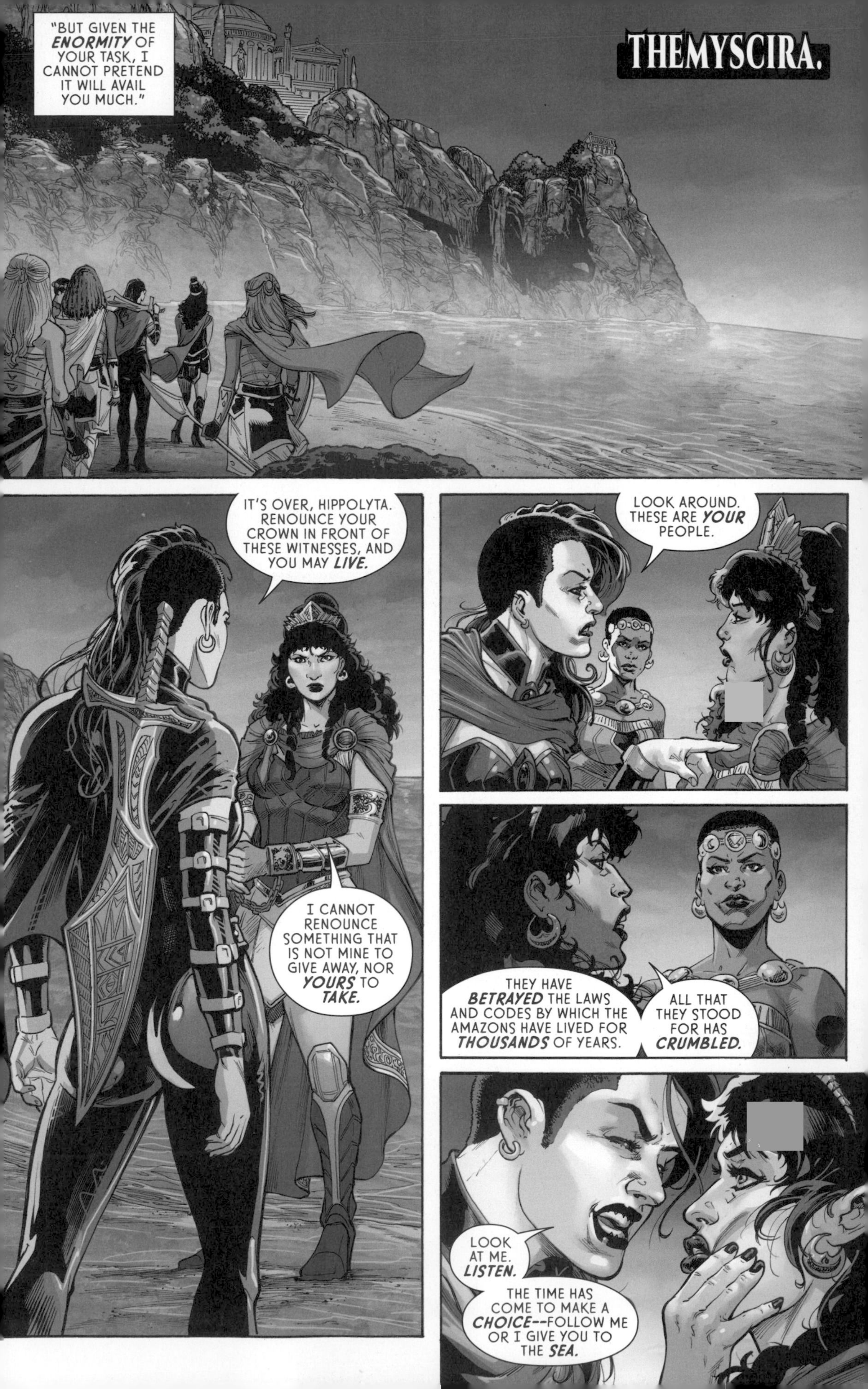
"BUT GIVEN THE ENORMITY OF YOUR TASK, I CANNOT PRETEND IT WILL AVAIL YOU MUCH."
THEMYSCIRA.
IT'S OVER, HIPPOLYTA. RENOUNCE YOUR CROWN IN FRONT OF THESE WITNESSES, AND YOU MAY LIVE.
I CANNOT RENOUNCE SOMETHING THAT IS NOT MINE TO GIVE AWAY, NOR YOURS TO TAKE.
LOOK AROUND. THESE ARE YOUR PEOPLE.
THEY HAVE BETRAYED THE LAWS AND CODES BY WHICH THE AMAZONS HAVE LIVED FOR THOUSANDS OF YEARS.
ALL THAT THEY STOOD FOR HAS CRUMBLED.
LOOK AT ME. LISTEN.
THE TIME HAS COME TO MAKE A CHOICE--FOLLOW ME OR I GIVE YOU TO THE SEA.

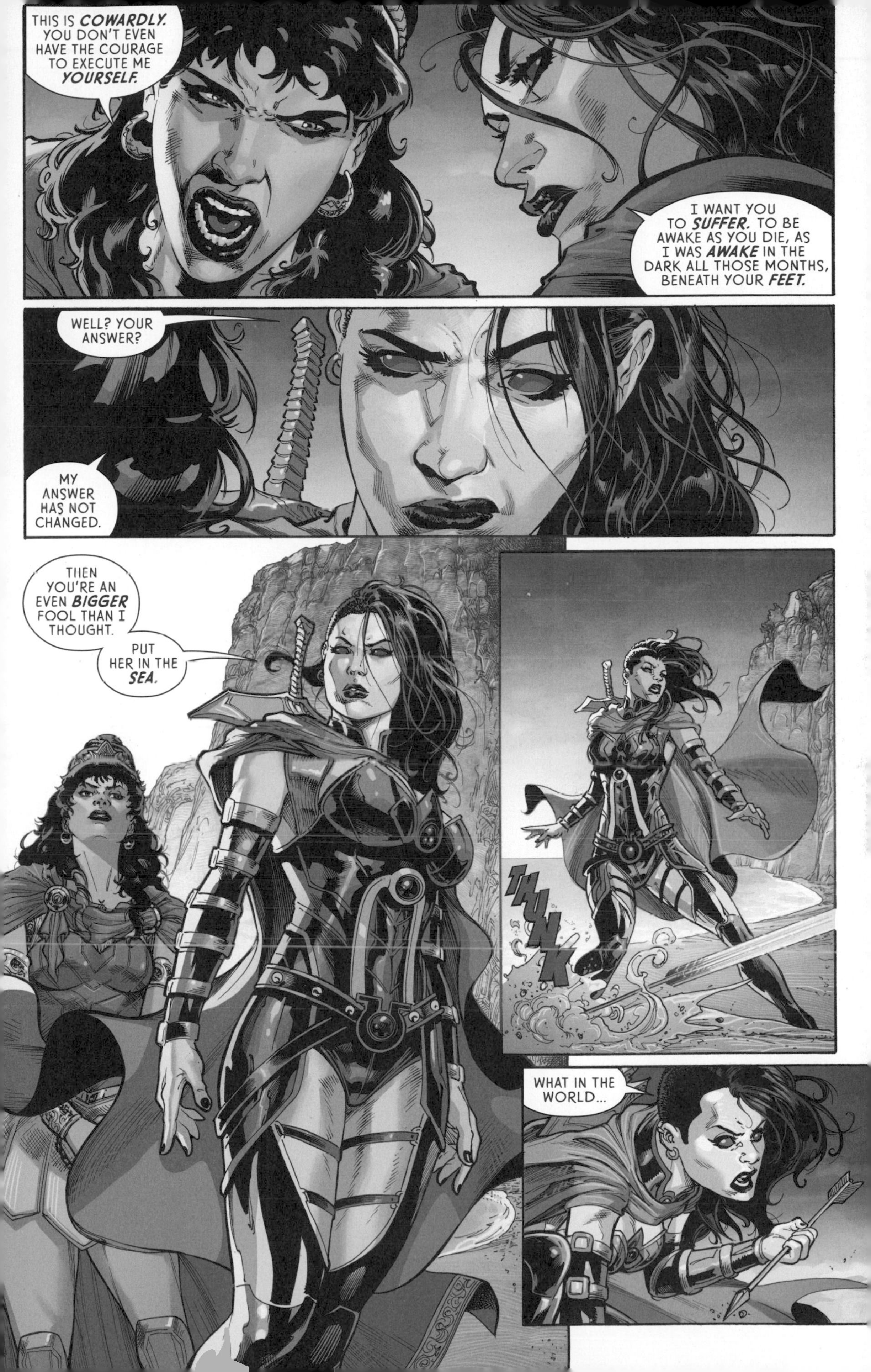
THIS IS COWARDLY. YOU DON'T EVEN HAVE THE COURAGE TO EXECUTE ME YOURSELF.
I WANT YOU TO SUFFER. TO BE AWAKE AS YOU DIE, AS I WAS AWAKE IN THE DARK ALL THOSE MONTHS, BENEATH YOUR FEET.
WELL? YOUR ANSWER?
MY ANSWER HAS NOT CHANGED.
THEN YOU'RE AN EVEN BIGGER FOOL THAN I THOUGHT.
PUT HER IN THE SEA.
THUNK
WHAT IN THE WORLD...

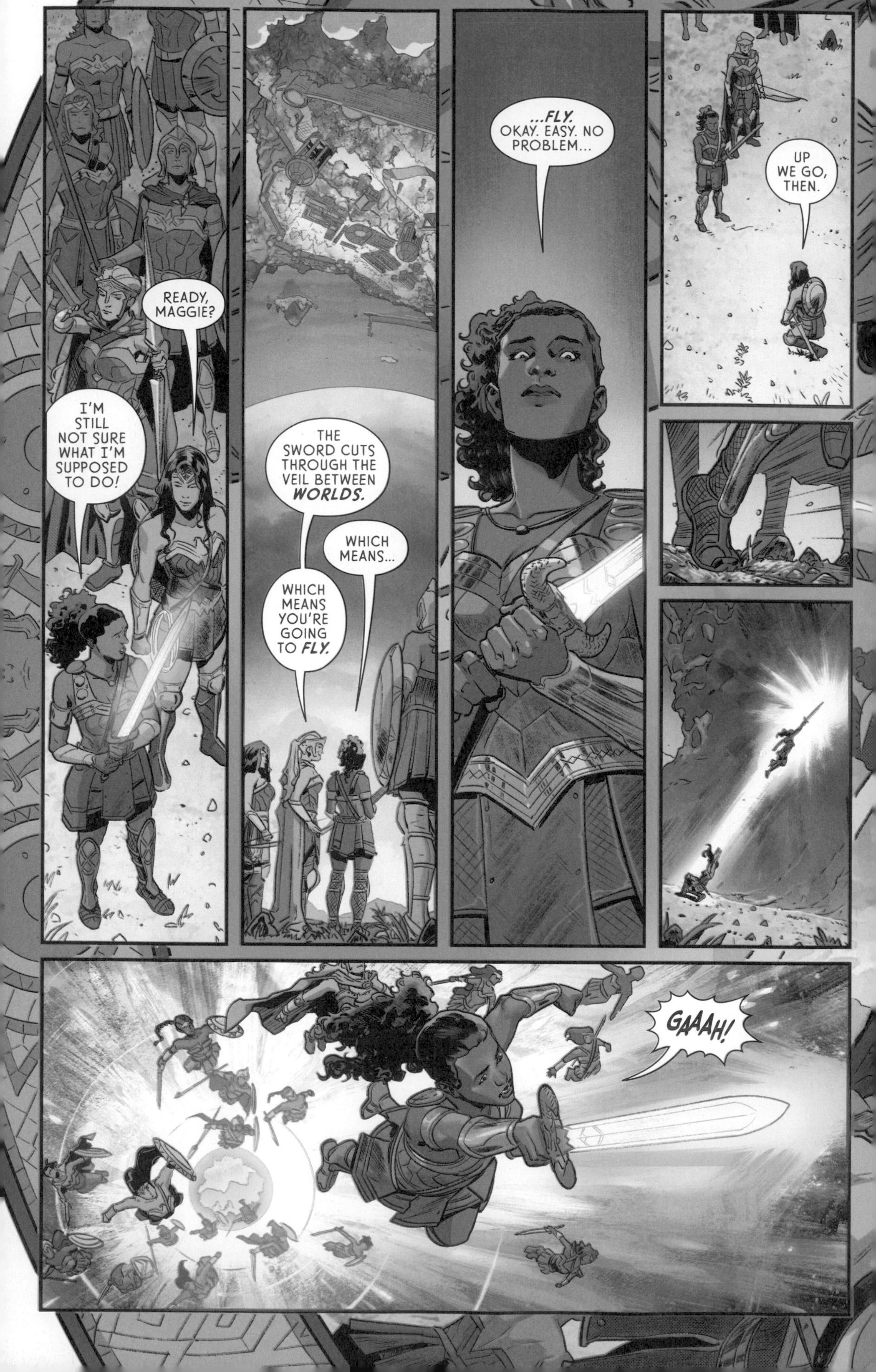
READY, MAGGIE?
I'M STILL NOT SURE WHAT I'M SUPPOSED TO DO!
THE SWORD CUTS THROUGH THE VEIL BETWEEN WORLDS.
WHICH MEANS...
WHICH MEANS YOU'RE GOING TO FLY.
...FLY. OKAY. EASY. NO PROBLEM...
UP WE GO, THEN.
GAAAH!

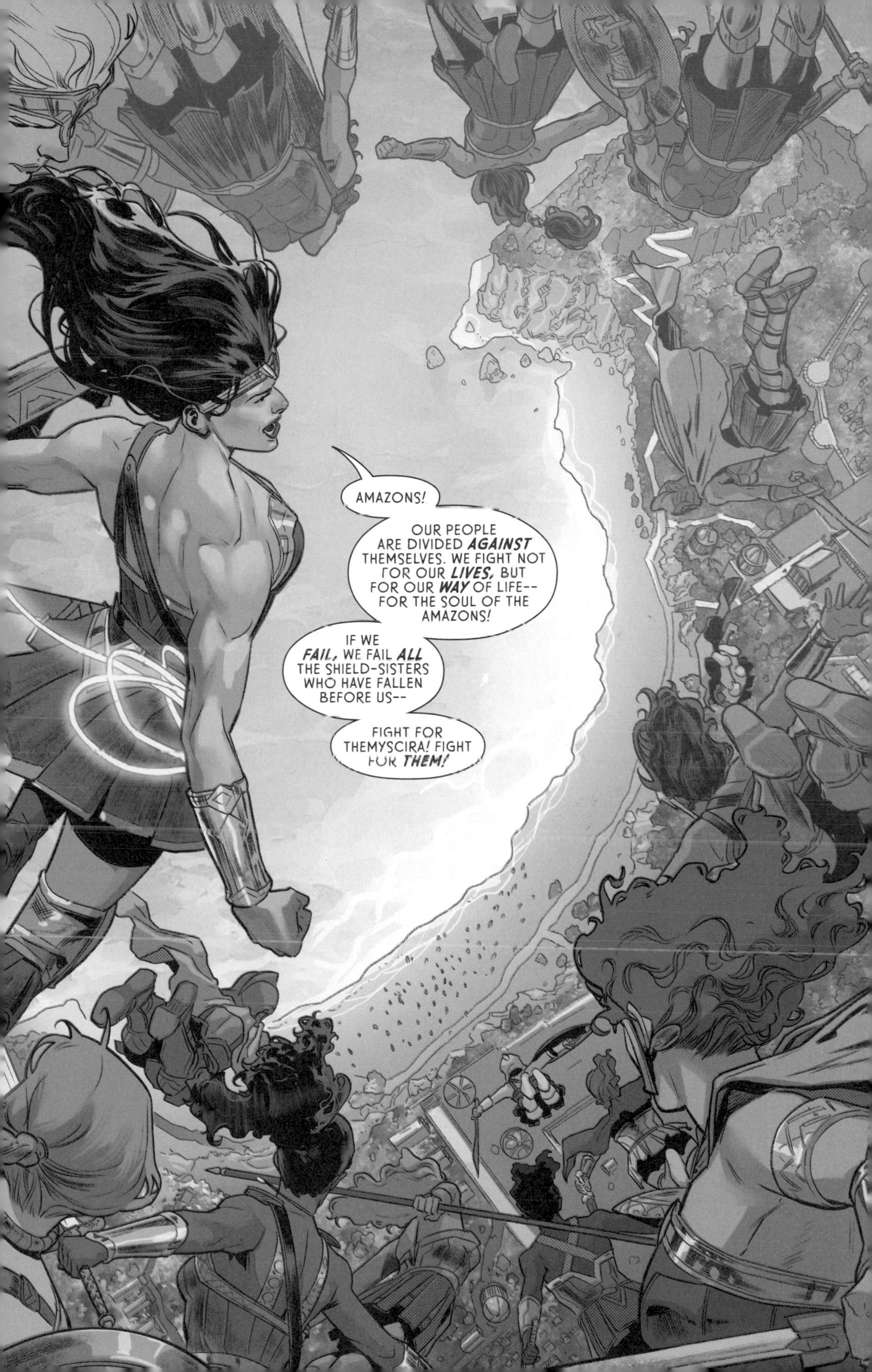
AMAZONS!
OUR PEOPLE ARE DIVIDED AGAINST THEMSELVES. WE FIGHT NOT FOR OUR LIVES, BUT FOR OUR WAY OF LIFE-- FOR THE SOUL OF THE AMAZONS!
IF WE FAIL, WE FAIL ALL THE SHIELD-SISTERS WHO HAVE FALLEN BEFORE US--
FIGHT FOR THEMYSCIRA! FIGHT FOR THEM!

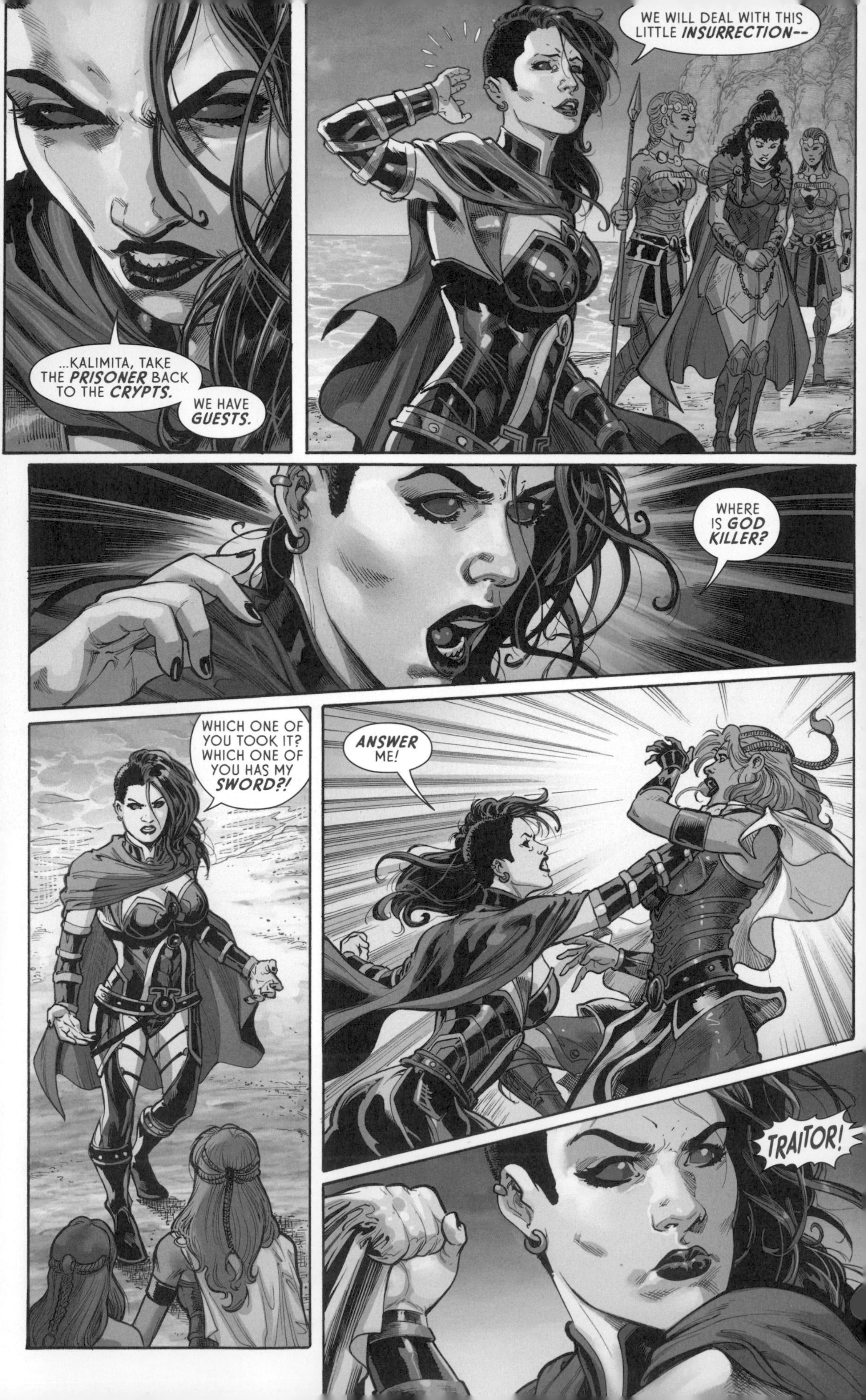
...KALIMITA, TAKE THE PRISONER BACK TO THE CRYPTS.
WE HAVE GUESTS.
WE WILL DEAL WITH THIS LITTLE INSURRECTION--
WHERE IS GOD KILLER?
WHICH ONE OF YOU TOOK IT? WHICH ONE OF YOU HAS MY SWORD?!
ANSWER ME!
TRAITOR!

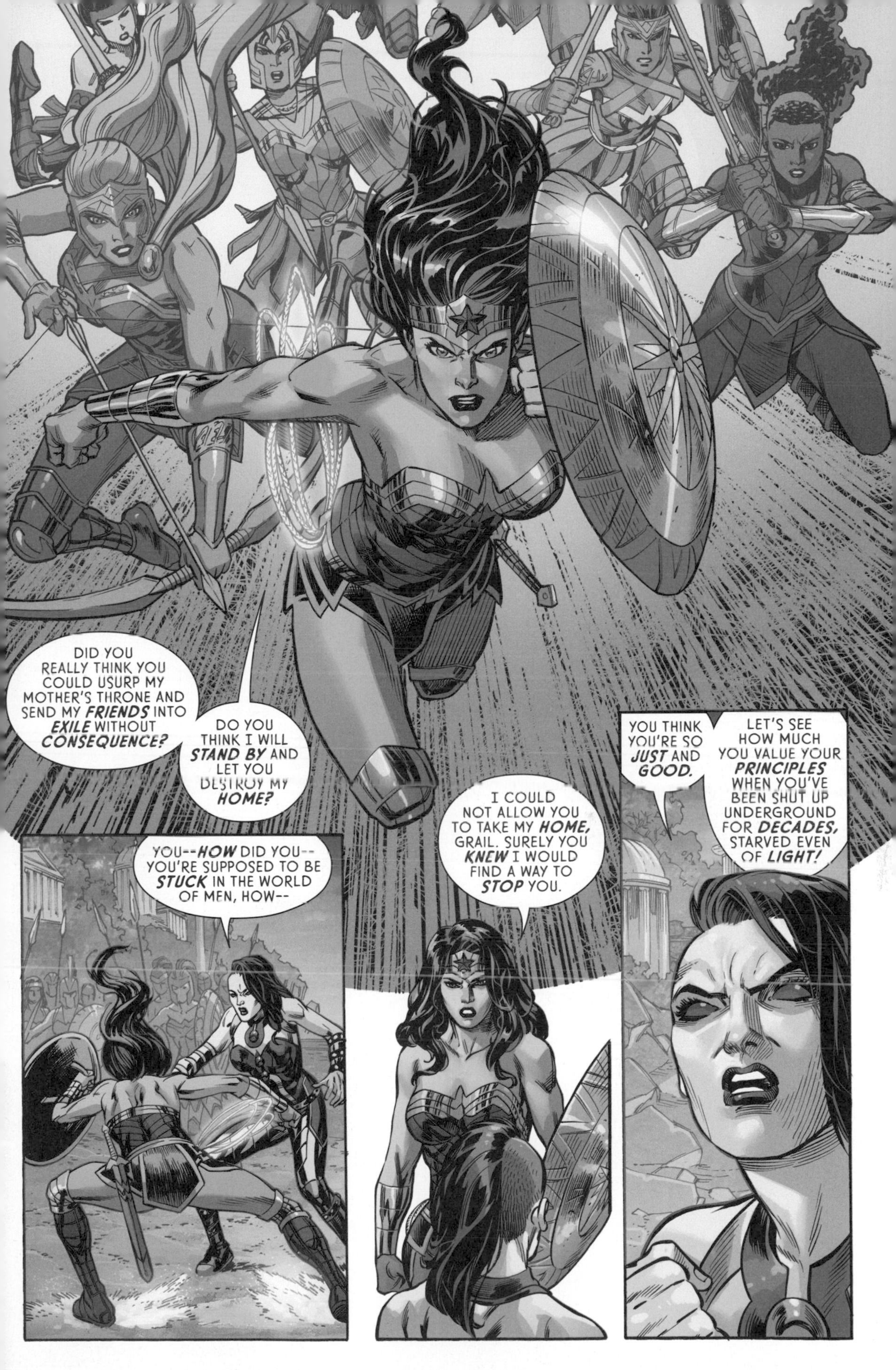
DID YOU REALLY THINK YOU COULD USURP MY MOTHER'S THRONE AND SEND MY FRIENDS INTO EXILE WITHOUT CONSEQUENCE?
DO YOU THINK I WILL STAND BY AND LET YOU DESTROY MY HOME?
YOU--HOW DID YOU--YOU'RE SUPPOSED TO BE STUCK IN THE WORLD OF MEN, HOW--
I COULD NOT ALLOW YOU TO TAKE MY HOME, GRAIL. SURELY YOU KNEW I WOULD FIND A WAY TO STOP YOU.
YOU THINK YOU'RE SO JUST AND GOOD.
LET'S SEE HOW MUCH YOU VALUE YOUR PRINCIPLES WHEN YOU'VE BEEN SHUT UP UNDERGROUND FOR DECADES, STARVED EVEN OF LIGHT!

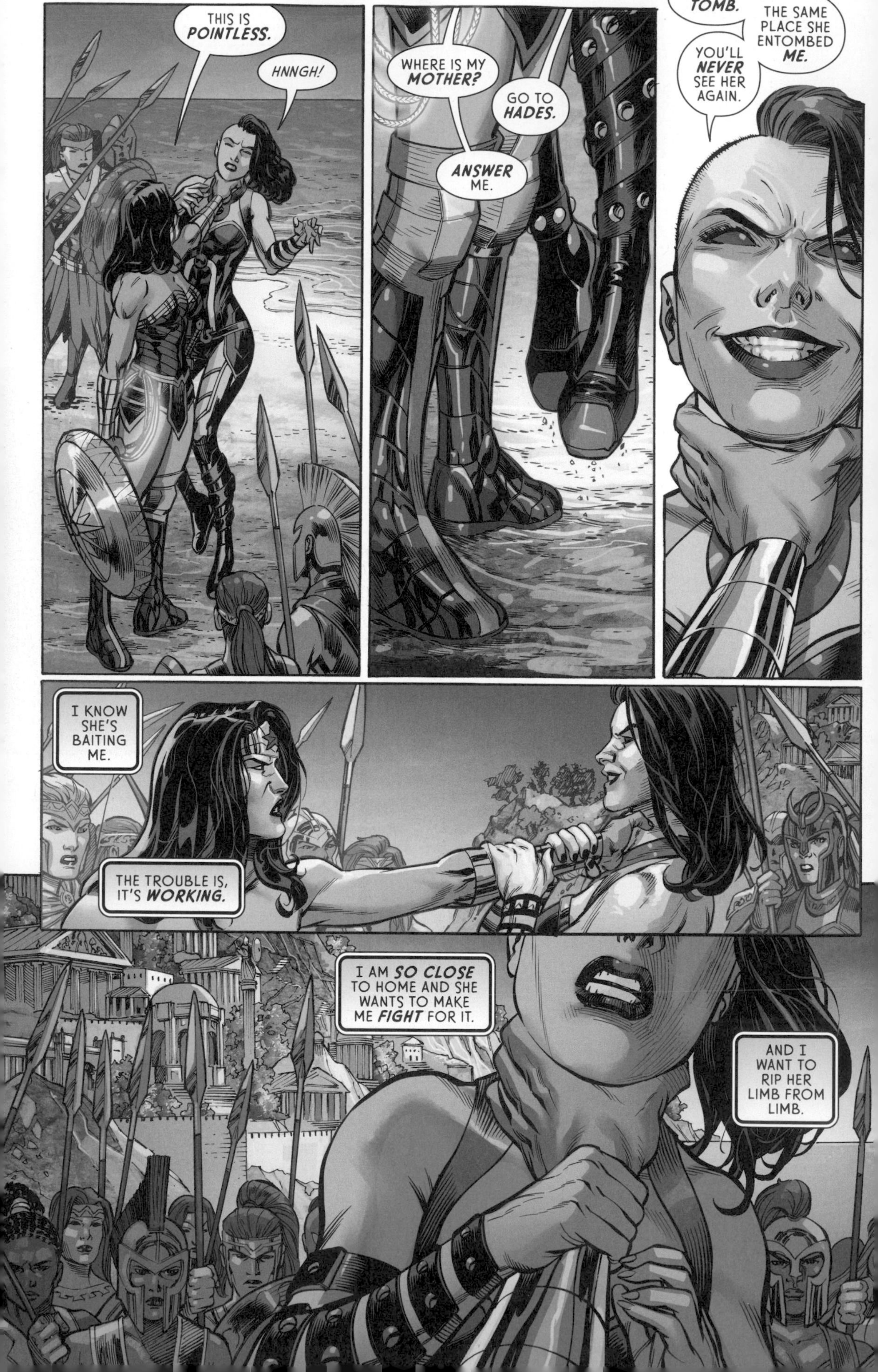
THIS IS POINTLESS.
HNNGH!
WHERE IS MY MOTHER?
GO TO HADES.
ANSWER ME.
SHE'S IN A TOMB.
THE SAME PLACE SHE ENTOMBED ME.
YOU'LL NEVER SEE HER AGAIN.
I KNOW SHE'S BAITING ME.
THE TROUBLE IS, IT'S WORKING.
I AM SO CLOSE TO HOME AND SHE WANTS TO MAKE ME FIGHT FOR IT.
AND I WANT TO RIP HER LIMB FROM LIMB.

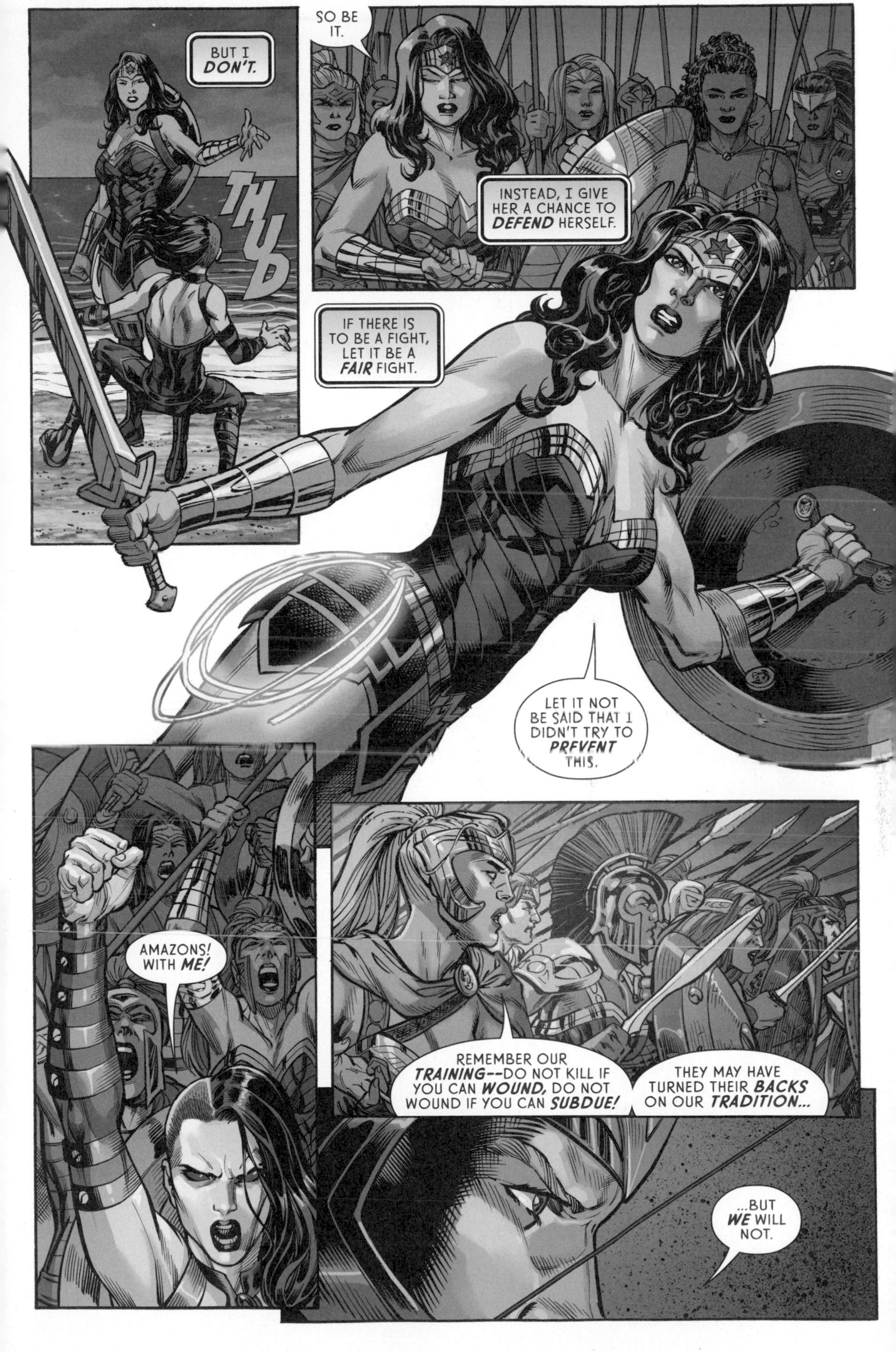

BUT I DON'T.
THUD
SO BE IT.
INSTEAD, I GIVE HER A CHANCE TO DEFEND HERSELF.
IF THERE IS TO BE A FIGHT, LET IT BE A FAIR FIGHT.
LET IT NOT BE SAID THAT I DIDN'T TRY TO PREVENT THIS.
AMAZONS! WITH ME!
REMEMBER OUR TRAINING--DO NOT KILL IF YOU CAN WOUND, DO NOT WOUND IF YOU CAN SUBDUE!
THEY MAY HAVE TURNED THEIR BACKS ON OUR TRADITION...
...BUT WE WILL NOT.

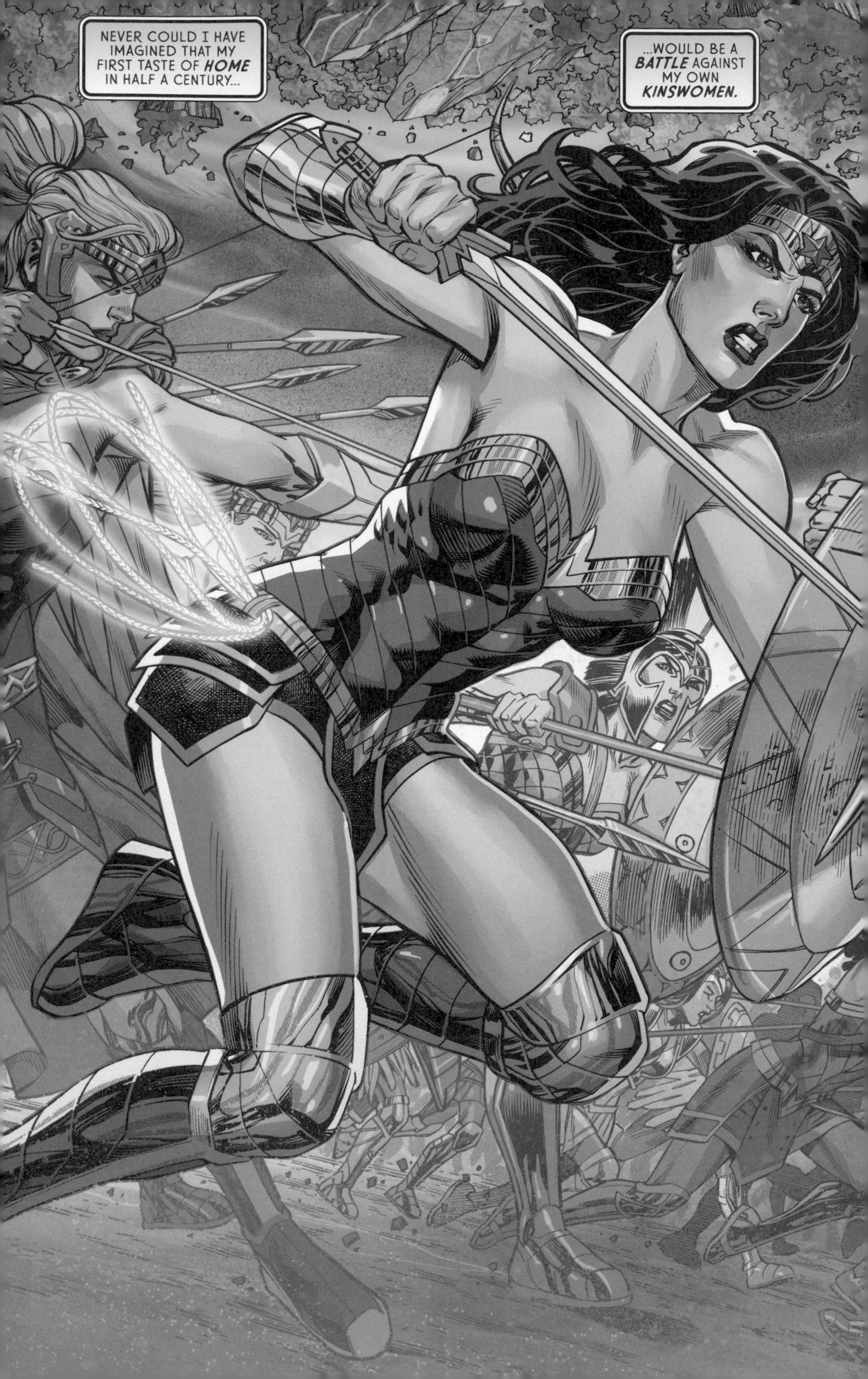
NEVER COULD I HAVE IMAGINED THAT MY FIRST TASTE OF HOME IN HALF A CENTURY...
...WOULD BE A BATTLE AGAINST MY OWN KINSWOMEN.

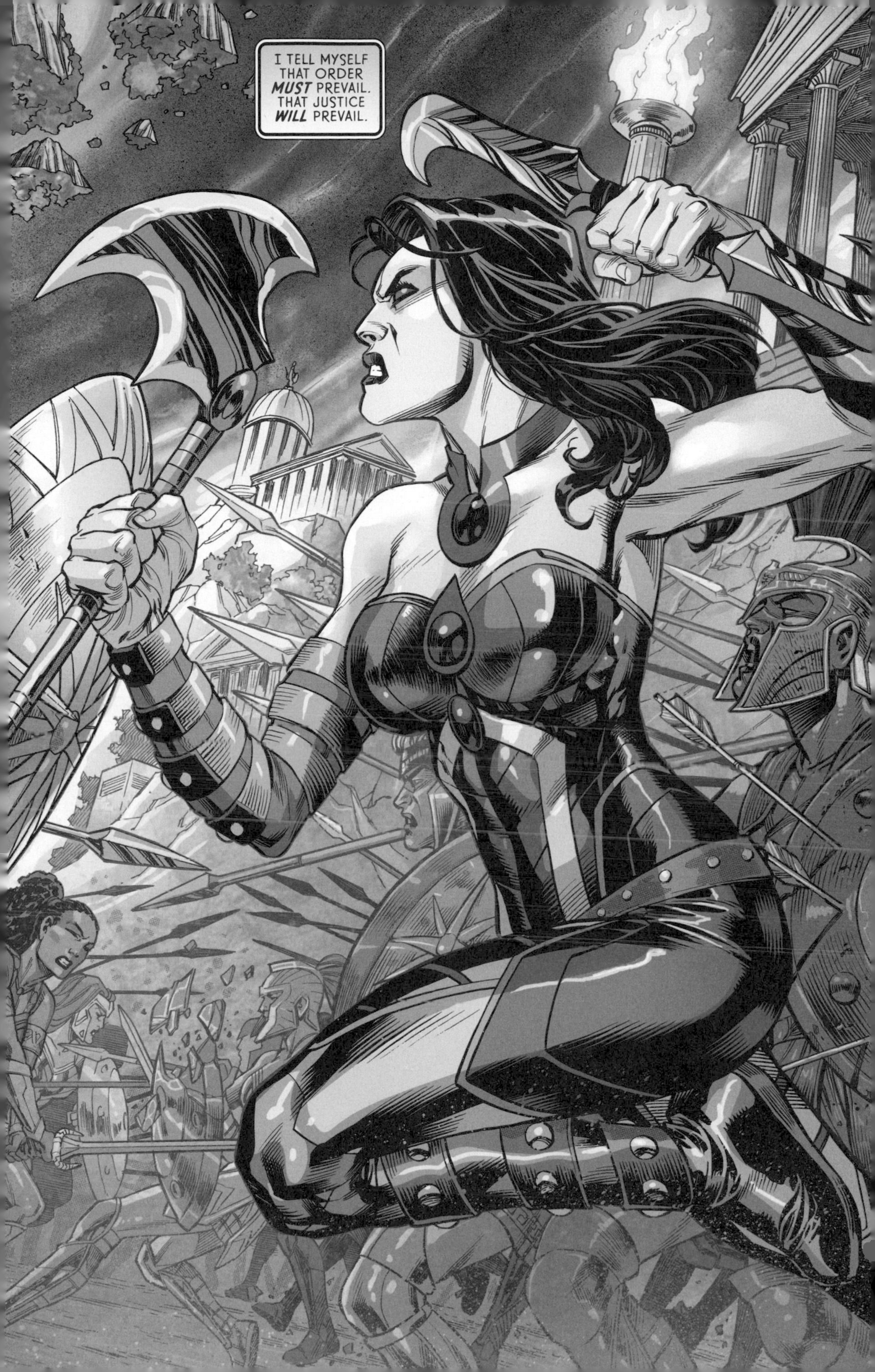
I TELL MYSELF THAT ORDER MUST PREVAIL. THAT JUSTICE WILL PREVAIL.

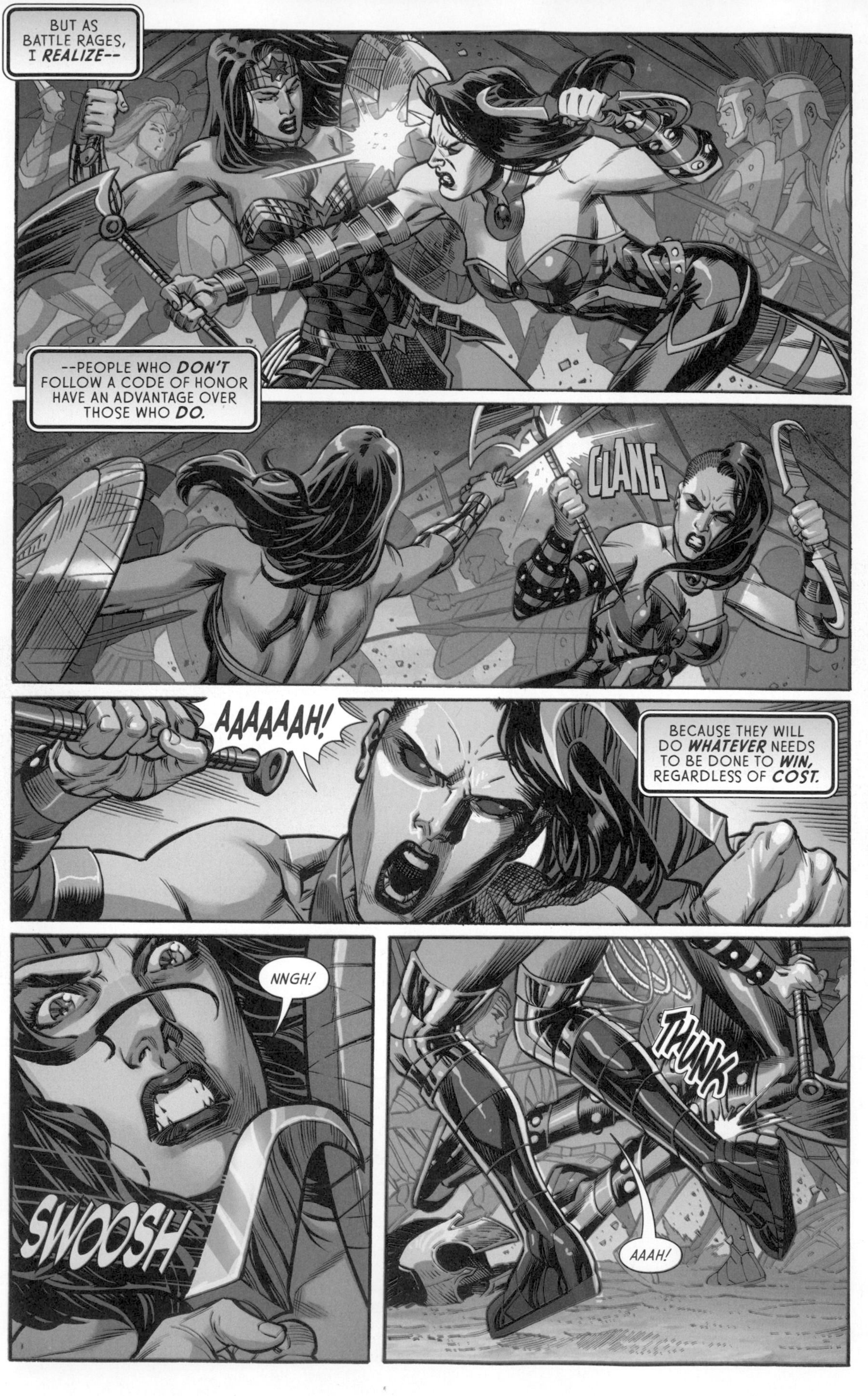
BUT AS BATTLE RAGES, I REALIZE--
--PEOPLE WHO DON'T FOLLOW A CODE OF HONOR HAVE AN ADVANTAGE OVER THOSE WHO DO.
CLANG
AAAAAAH!
BECAUSE THEY WILL DO WHATEVER NEEDS TO BE DONE TO WIN, REGARDLESS OF COST.
NNGH!
SWOOSH
THUNK
AAAH!

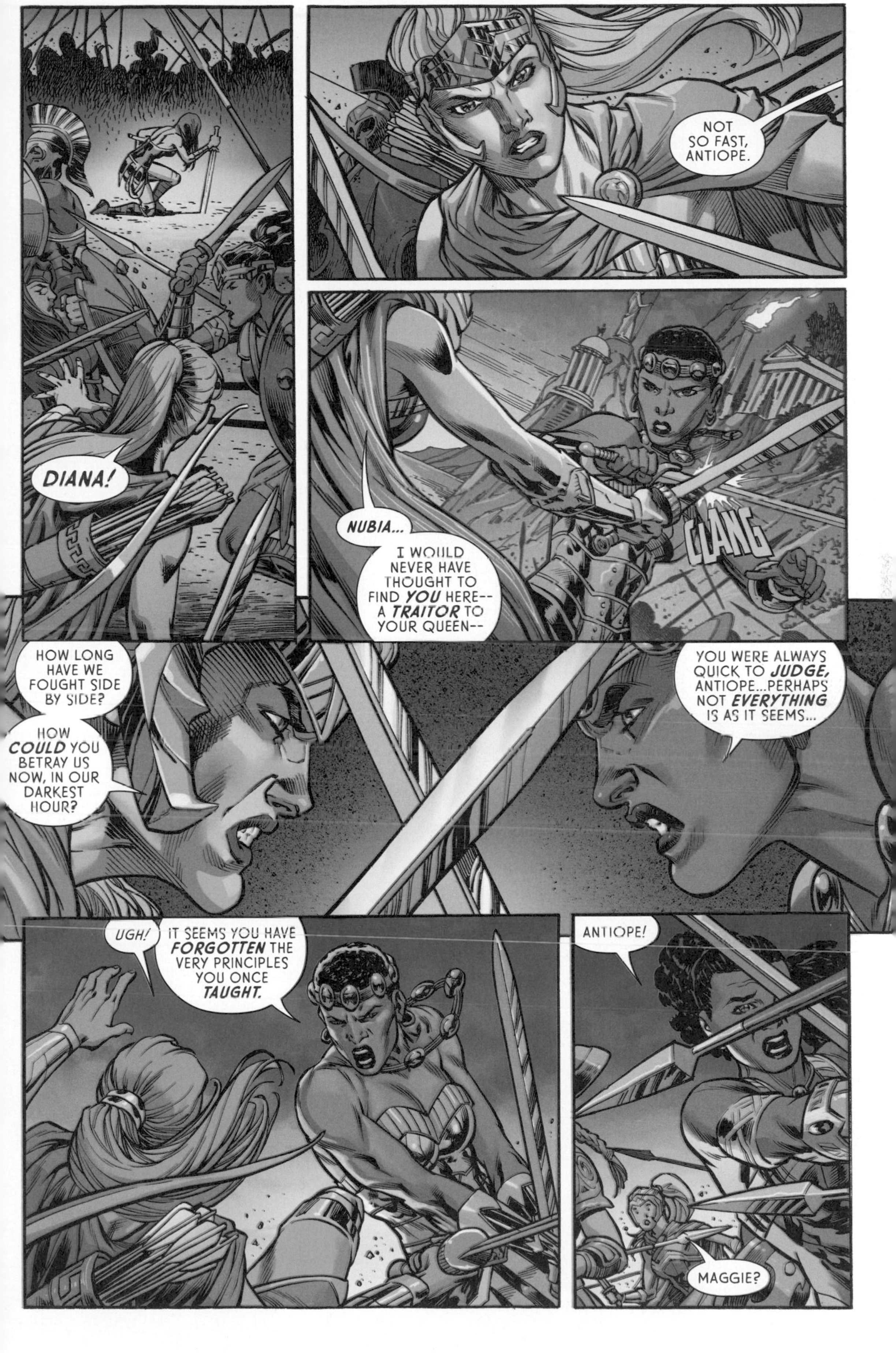
DIANA!
NOT SO FAST, ANTIOPE.
NUBIA...
I WOULD NEVER HAVE THOUGHT TO FIND YOU HERE-- A TRAITOR TO YOUR QUEEN--
CLANG
HOW LONG HAVE WE FOUGHT SIDE BY SIDE?
HOW COULD YOU BETRAY US NOW, IN OUR DARKEST HOUR?
YOU WERE ALWAYS QUICK TO JUDGE, ANTIOPE...PERHAPS NOT EVERYTHING IS AS IT SEEMS...
UGH!
IT SEEMS YOU HAVE FORGOTTEN THE VERY PRINCIPLES YOU ONCE TAUGHT.
ANTIOPE!
MAGGIE?

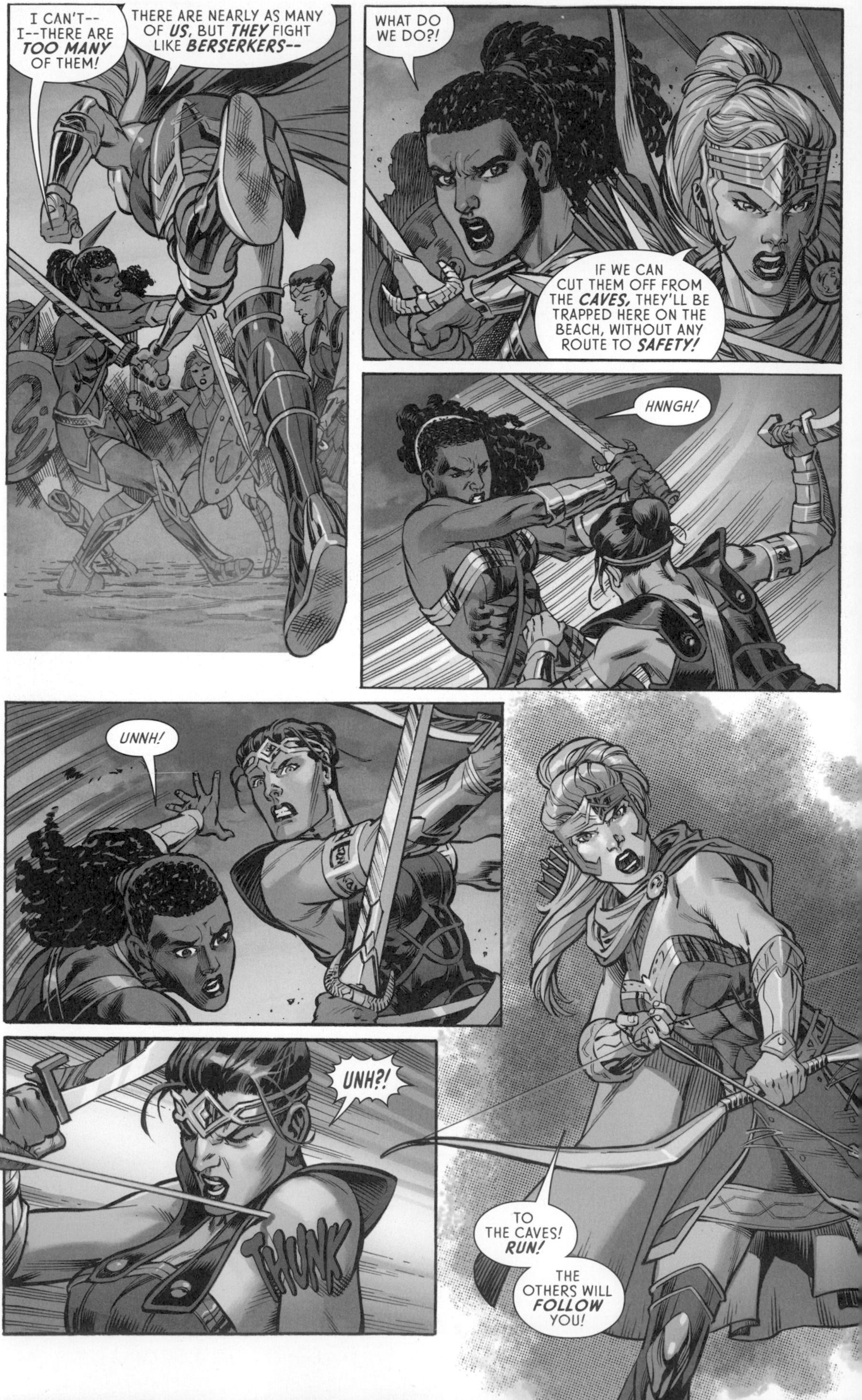
I CAN'T-- I--THERE ARE TOO MANY OF THEM!
THERE ARE NEARLY AS MANY OF US, BUT THEY FIGHT LIKE BERSERKERS--
WHAT DO WE DO?!
IF WE CAN CUT THEM OFF FROM THE CAVES, THEY'LL BE TRAPPED HERE ON THE BEACH, WITHOUT ANY ROUTE TO SAFETY!
HNNGH!
UNNH!
UNH?!
THUNK
TO THE CAVES! RUN!
THE OTHERS WILL FOLLOW YOU!

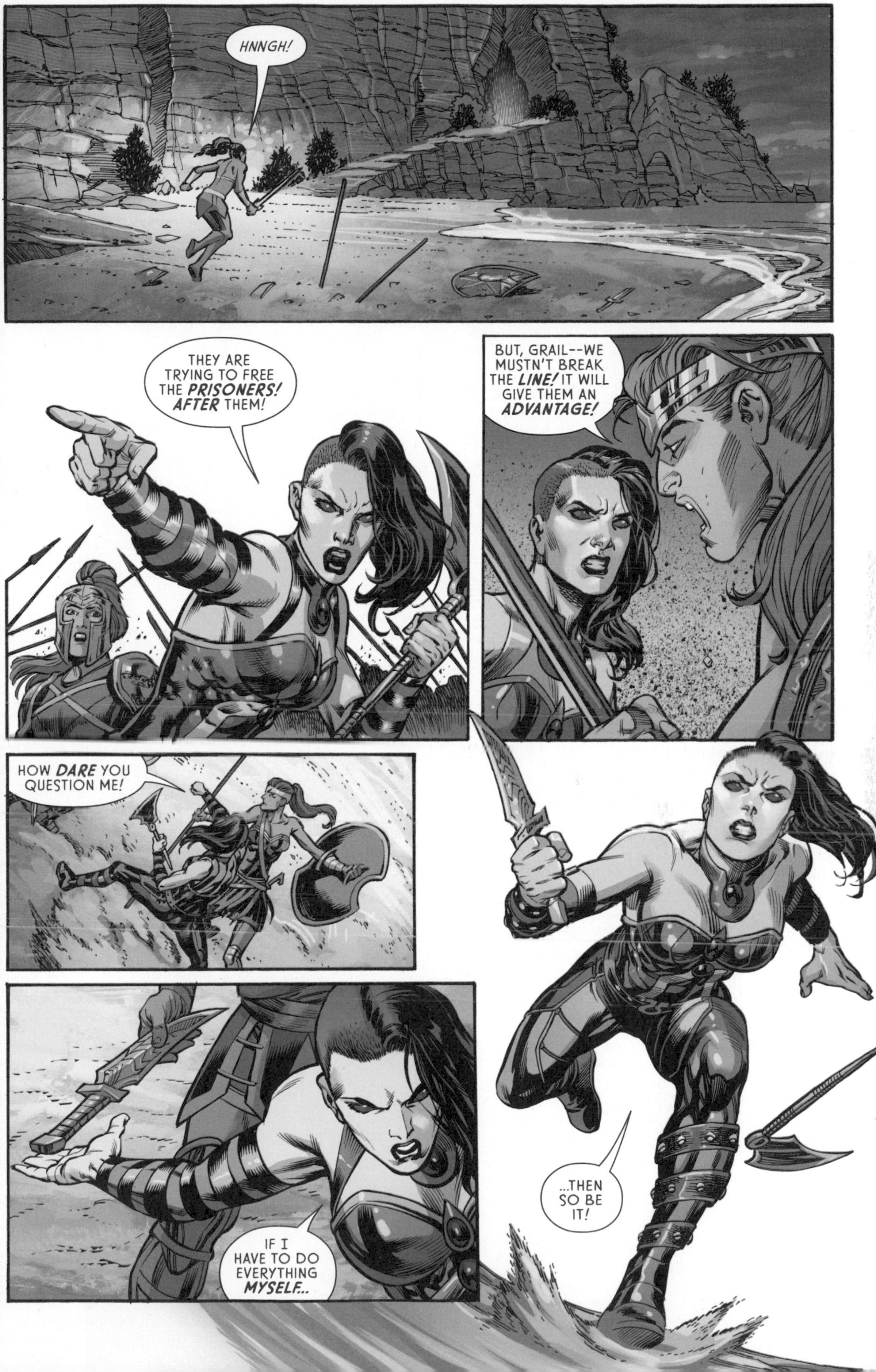
HNNGH!
THEY ARE TRYING TO FREE THE PRISONERS! AFTER THEM!
BUT, GRAIL--WE MUSTN'T BREAK THE LINE! IT WILL GIVE THEM AN ADVANTAGE!
HOW DARE YOU QUESTION ME!
IF I HAVE TO DO EVERYTHING MYSELF...
...THEN SO BE IT!

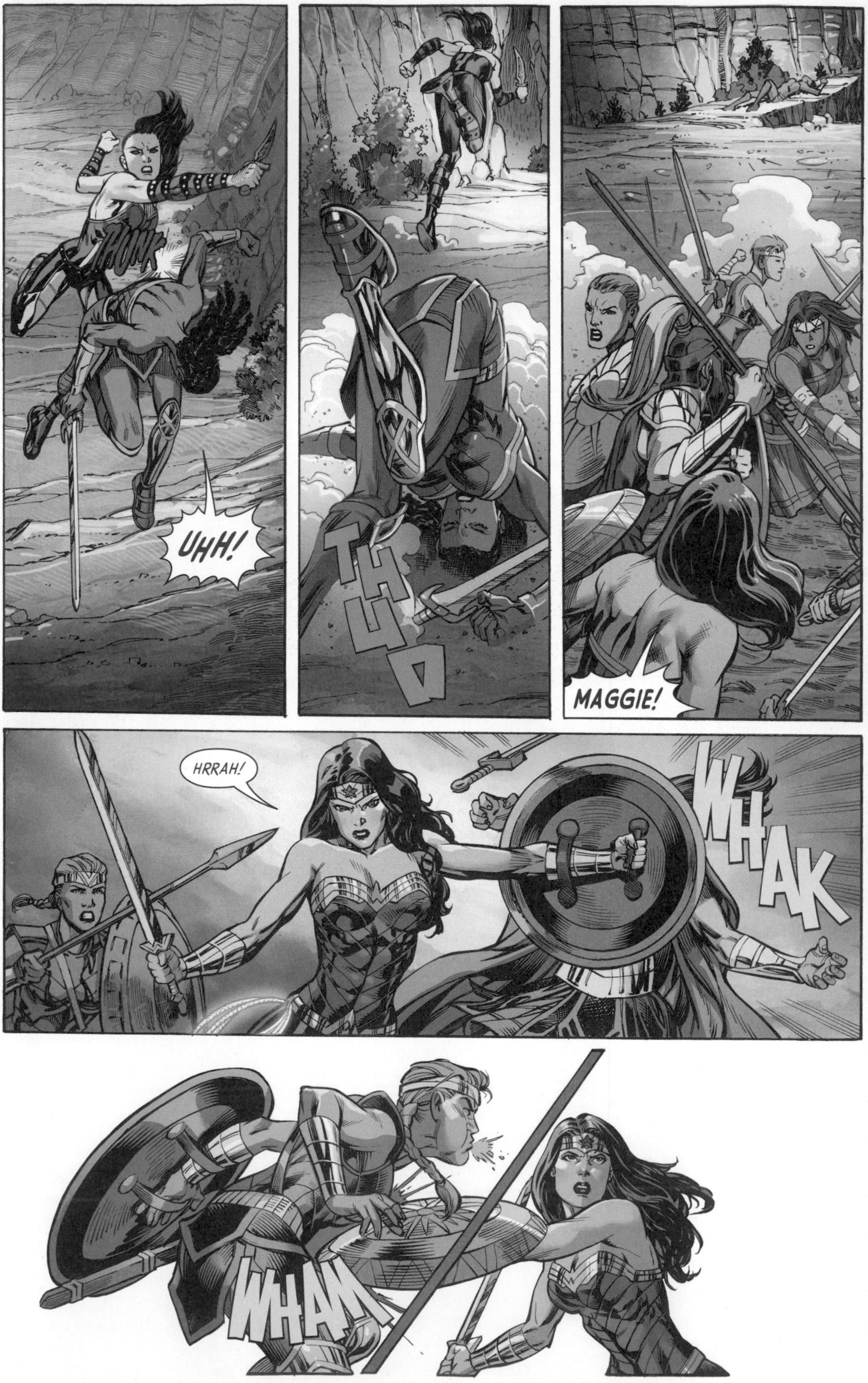
THONK
UHH!
THUD
MAGGIE!
HRRAH!
WHAK
WHAM

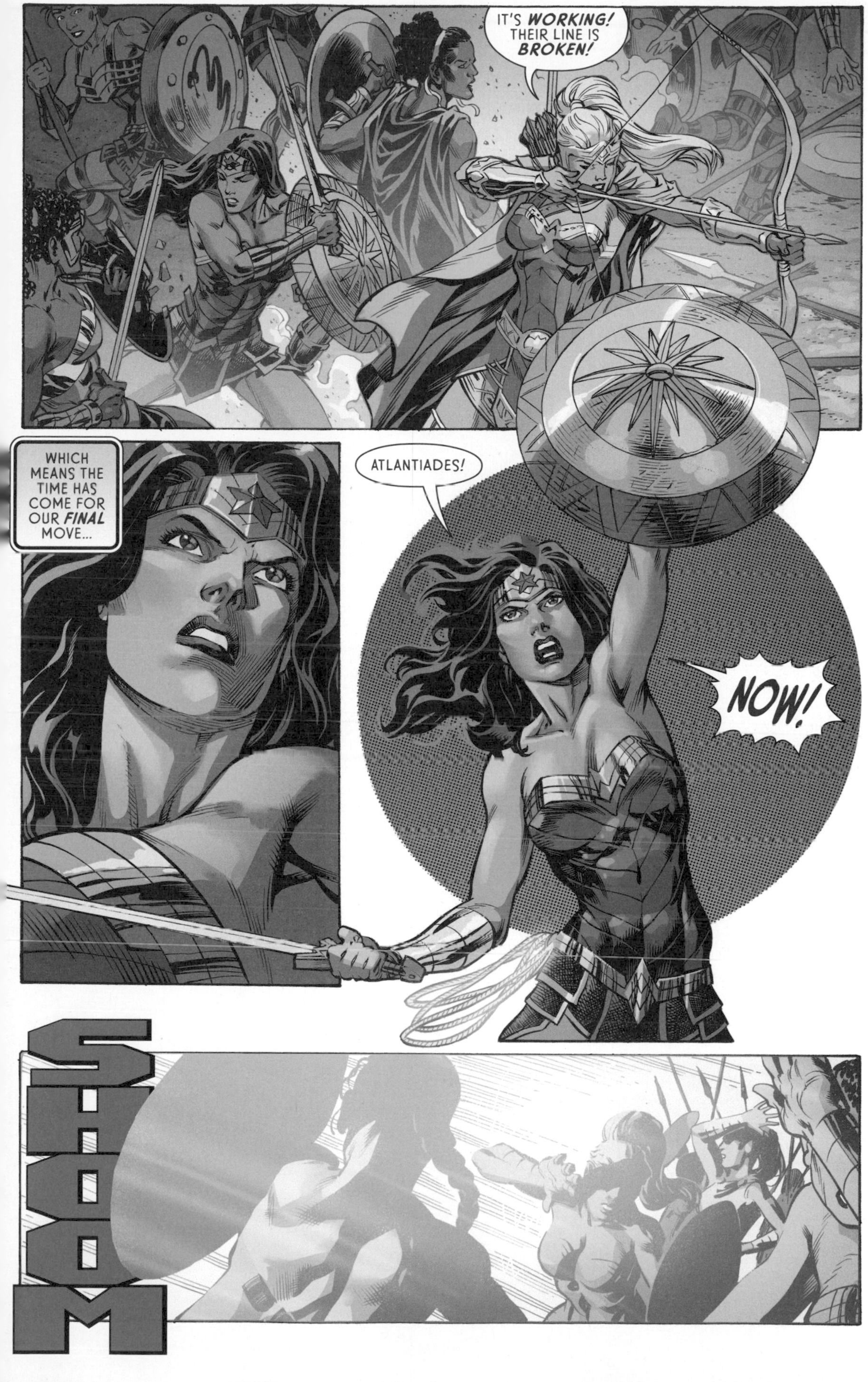
IT'S WORKING! THEIR LINE IS BROKEN!
WHICH MEANS THE TIME HAS COME FOR OUR FINAL MOVE...
ATLANTIADES!
NOW!
SHOOM

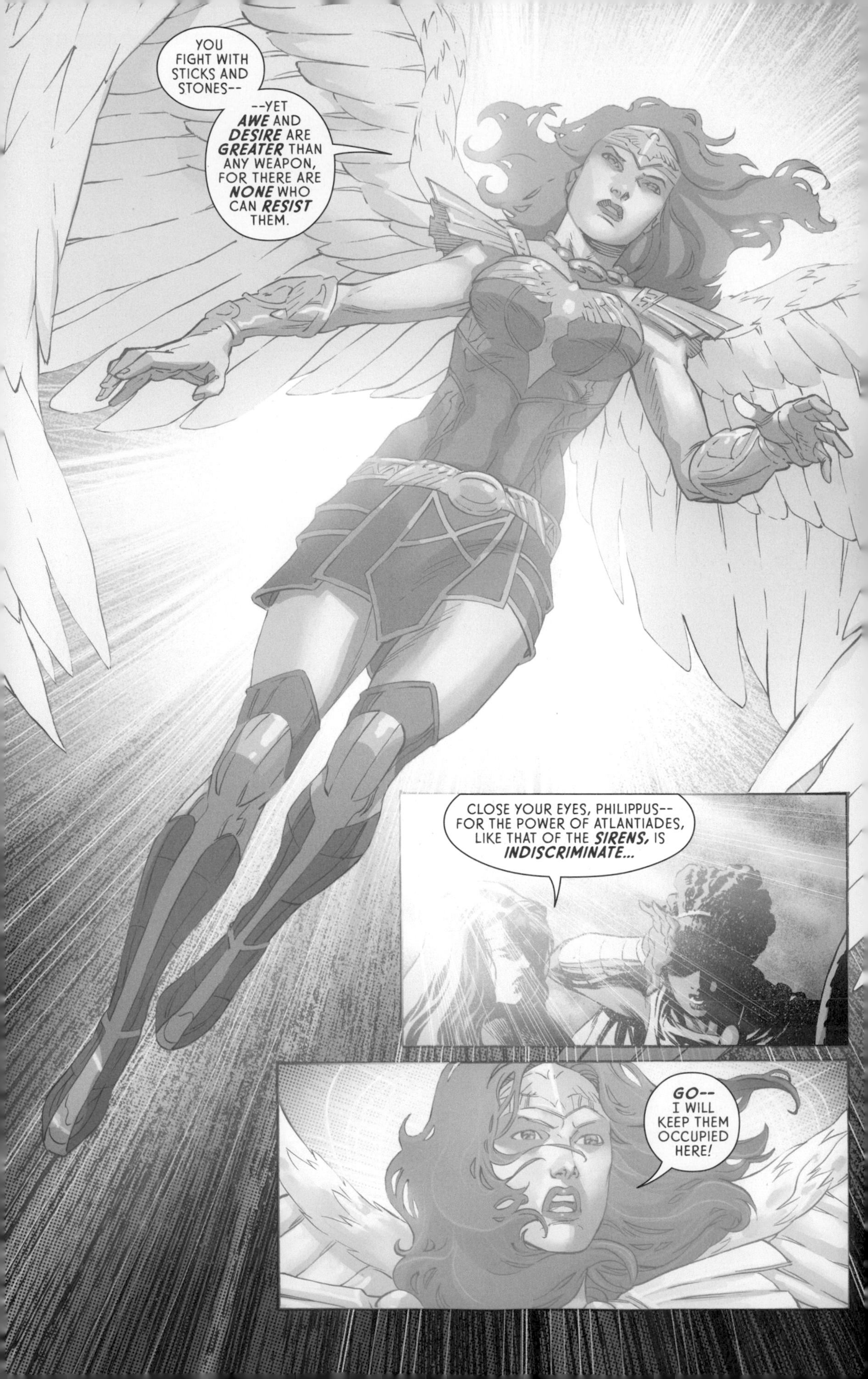
YOU FIGHT WITH STICKS AND STONES--
--YET **AWE** AND **DESIRE** ARE **GREATER** THAN ANY WEAPON, FOR THERE ARE **NONE** WHO CAN **RESIST** THEM.
CLOSE YOUR EYES, PHILIPPUS-- FOR THE POWER OF ATLANTIADES, LIKE THAT OF THE **SIRENS,** IS **INDISCRIMINATE...**
GO-- I WILL KEEP THEM OCCUPIED HERE!

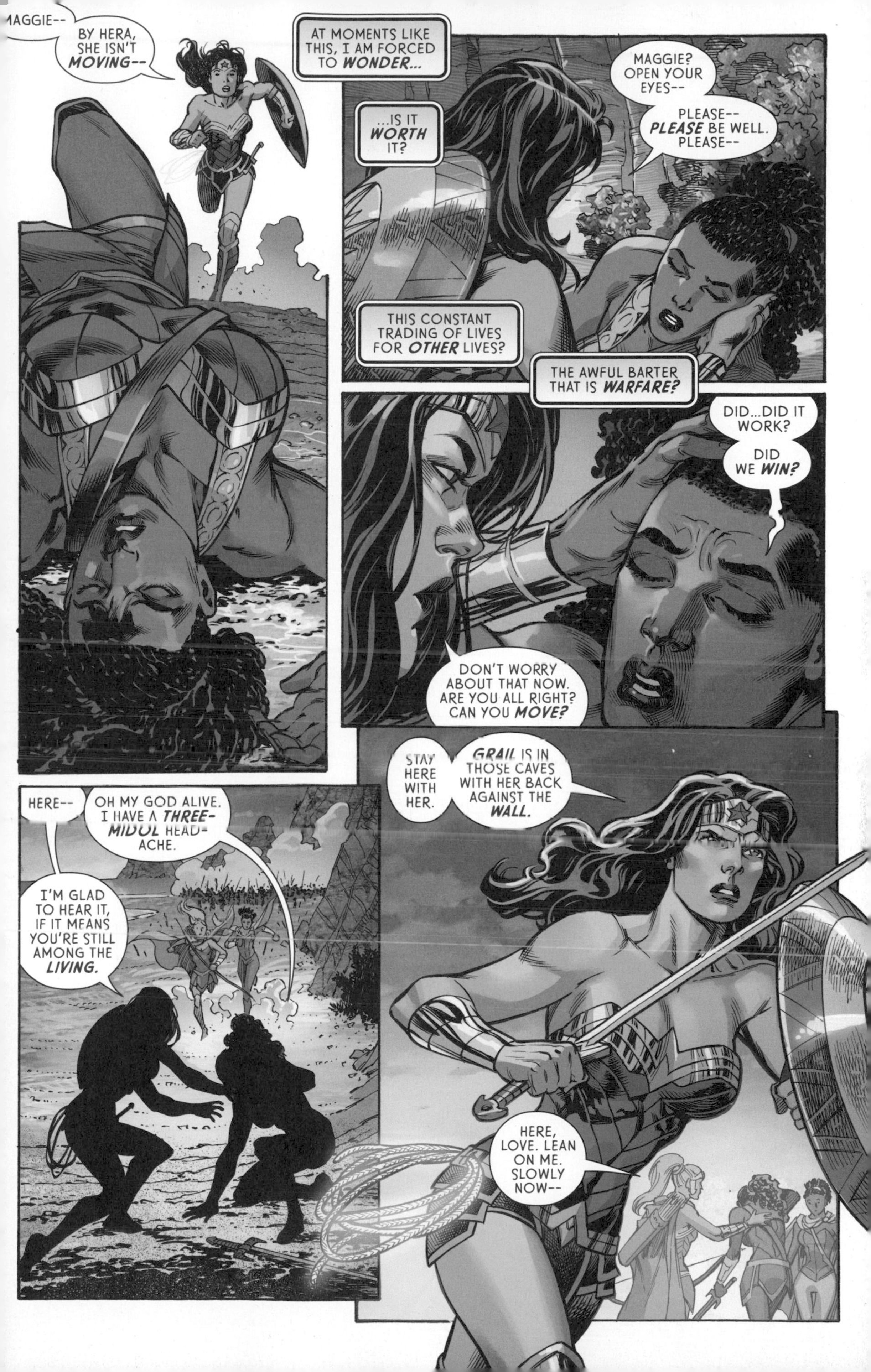
MAGGIE--
BY HERA, SHE ISN'T MOVING--
AT MOMENTS LIKE THIS, I AM FORCED TO WONDER...
...IS IT WORTH IT?
MAGGIE? OPEN YOUR EYES--
PLEASE-- PLEASE BE WELL. PLEASE--
THIS CONSTANT TRADING OF LIVES FOR OTHER LIVES?
THE AWFUL BARTER THAT IS WARFARE?
DID...DID IT WORK?
DID WE WIN?
DON'T WORRY ABOUT THAT NOW. ARE YOU ALL RIGHT? CAN YOU MOVE?
HERE--
OH MY GOD ALIVE. I HAVE A THREE-MIDOL HEAD-ACHE.
I'M GLAD TO HEAR IT, IF IT MEANS YOU'RE STILL AMONG THE LIVING.
STAY HERE WITH HER.
GRAIL IS IN THOSE CAVES WITH HER BACK AGAINST THE WALL.
HERE, LOVE. LEAN ON ME. SLOWLY NOW--

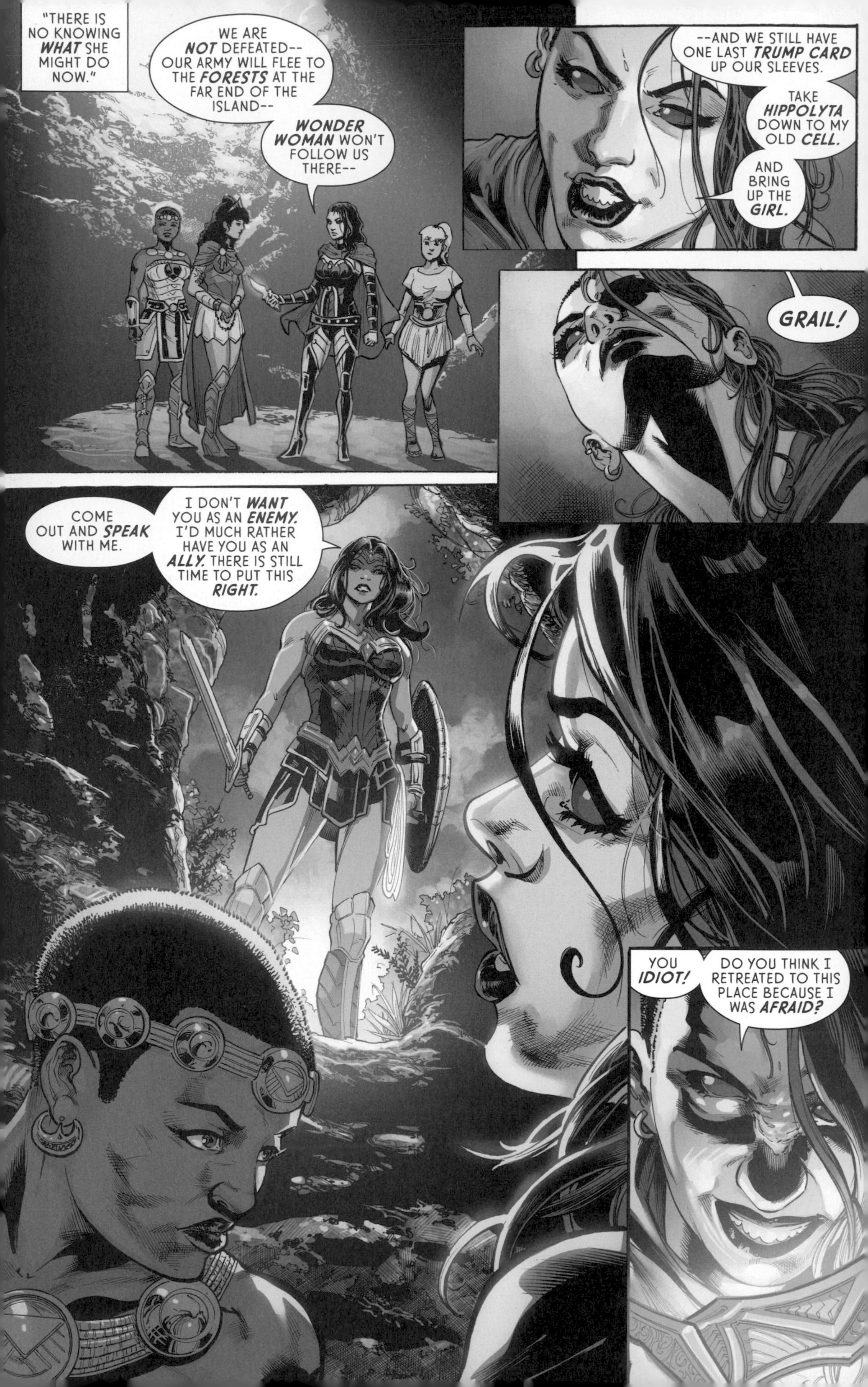
"THERE IS NO KNOWING WHAT SHE MIGHT DO NOW."
WE ARE NOT DEFEATED-- OUR ARMY WILL FLEE TO THE FORESTS AT THE FAR END OF THE ISLAND--
WONDER WOMAN WON'T FOLLOW US THERE--
--AND WE STILL HAVE ONE LAST TRUMP CARD UP OUR SLEEVES.
TAKE HIPPOLYTA DOWN TO MY OLD CELL.
AND BRING UP THE GIRL.
GRAIL!
COME OUT AND SPEAK WITH ME.
I DON'T WANT YOU AS AN ENEMY. I'D MUCH RATHER HAVE YOU AS AN ALLY. THERE IS STILL TIME TO PUT THIS RIGHT.
YOU IDIOT!
DO YOU THINK I RETREATED TO THIS PLACE BECAUSE I WAS AFRAID?

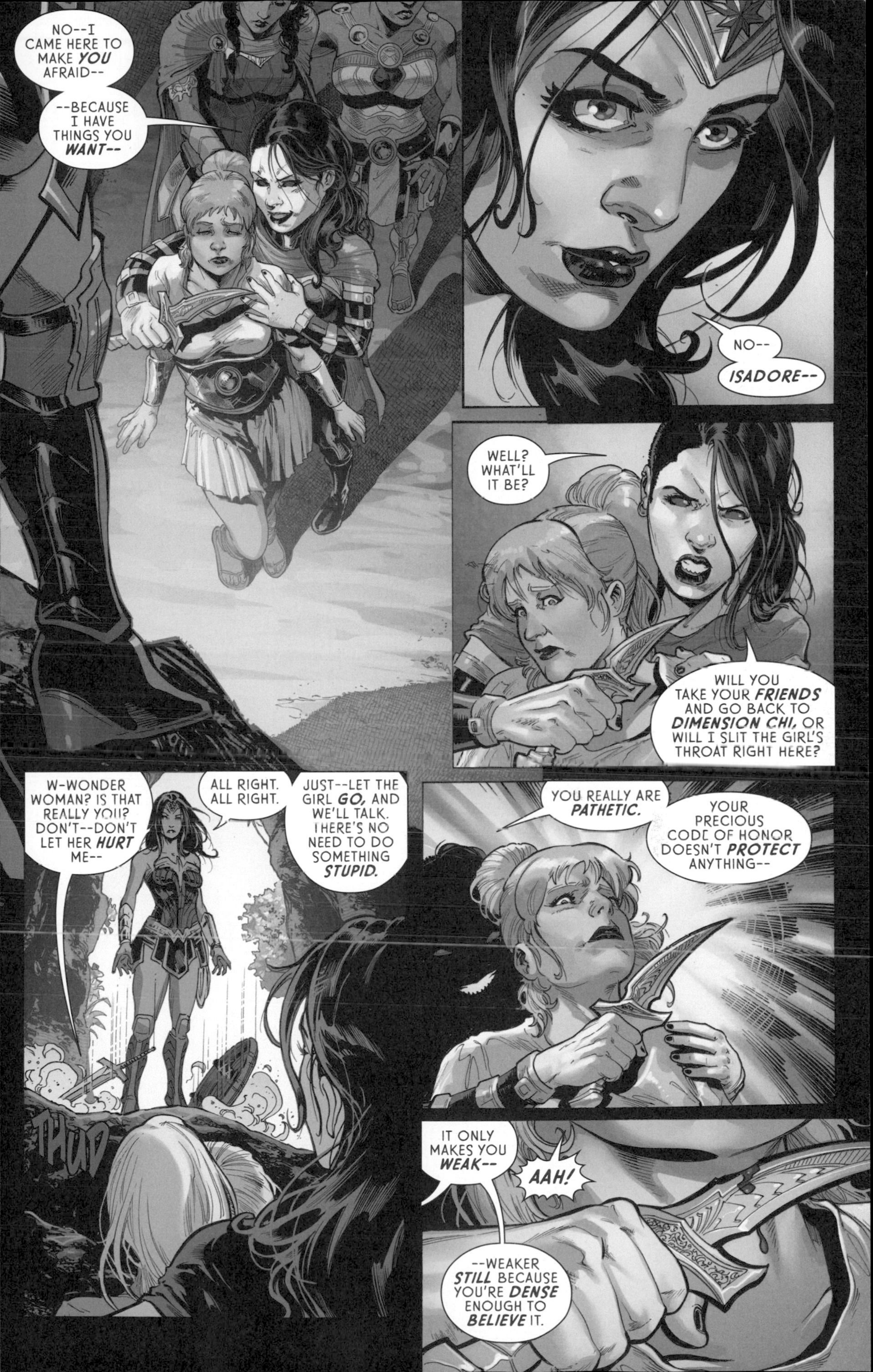
NO--I CAME HERE TO MAKE YOU AFRAID--
--BECAUSE I HAVE THINGS YOU WANT--
NO-- ISADORE--
WELL? WHAT'LL IT BE?
WILL YOU TAKE YOUR FRIENDS AND GO BACK TO DIMENSION CHI, OR WILL I SLIT THE GIRL'S THROAT RIGHT HERE?
W-WONDER WOMAN? IS THAT REALLY YOU? DON'T--DON'T LET HER HURT ME--
ALL RIGHT. ALL RIGHT.
JUST--LET THE GIRL GO, AND WE'LL TALK. THERE'S NO NEED TO DO SOMETHING STUPID.
THUD
YOU REALLY ARE PATHETIC.
YOUR PRECIOUS CODE OF HONOR DOESN'T PROTECT ANYTHING--
IT ONLY MAKES YOU WEAK--
AAH!
--WEAKER STILL BECAUSE YOU'RE DENSE ENOUGH TO BELIEVE IT.

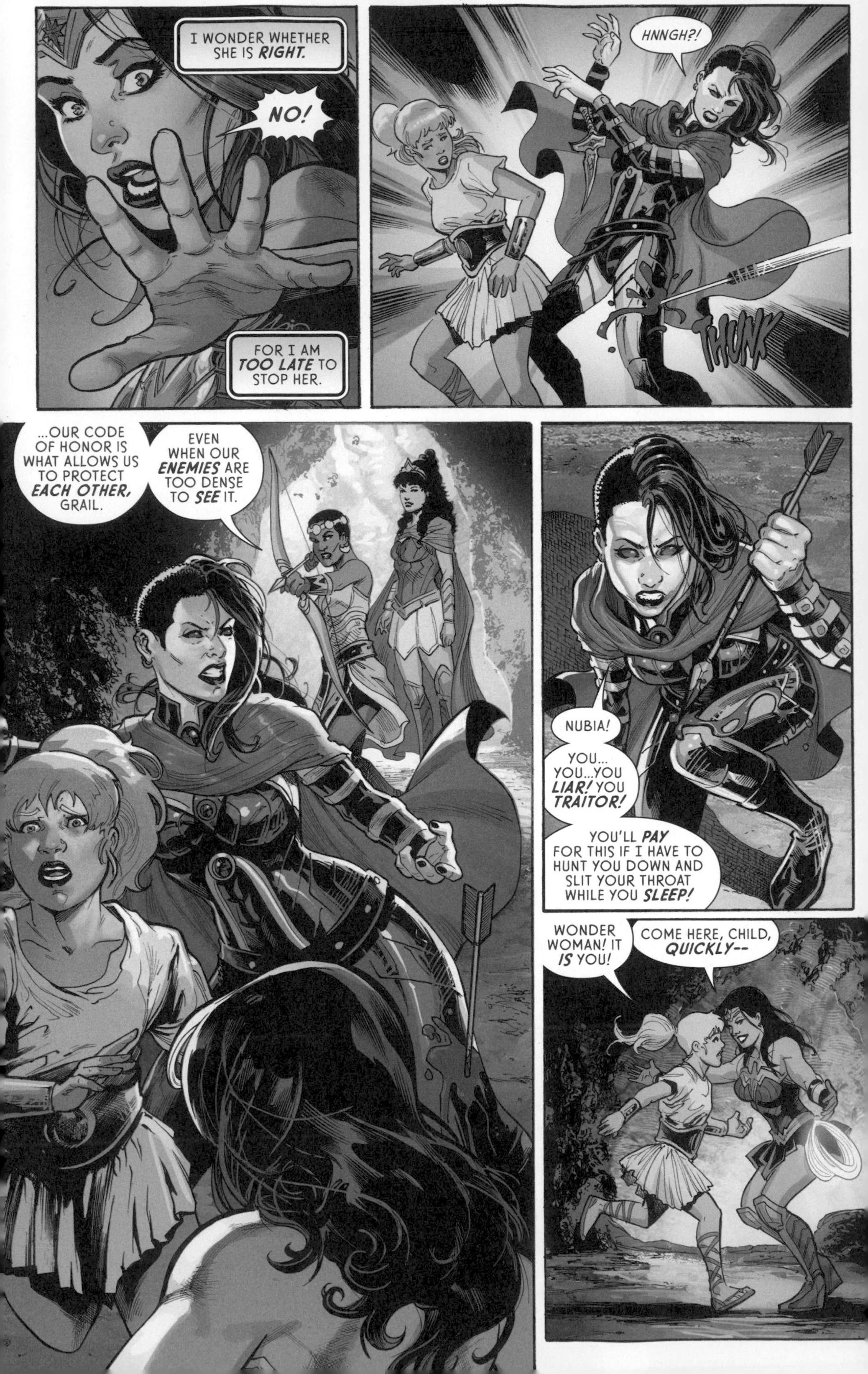
I WONDER WHETHER SHE IS RIGHT.
NO!
FOR I AM TOO LATE TO STOP HER.
HNNGH?!
THUNK
...OUR CODE OF HONOR IS WHAT ALLOWS US TO PROTECT EACH OTHER, GRAIL.
EVEN WHEN OUR ENEMIES ARE TOO DENSE TO SEE IT.
NUBIA!
YOU... YOU...YOU LIAR! YOU TRAITOR!
YOU'LL PAY FOR THIS IF I HAVE TO HUNT YOU DOWN AND SLIT YOUR THROAT WHILE YOU SLEEP!
WONDER WOMAN! IT IS YOU!
COME HERE, CHILD, QUICKLY--

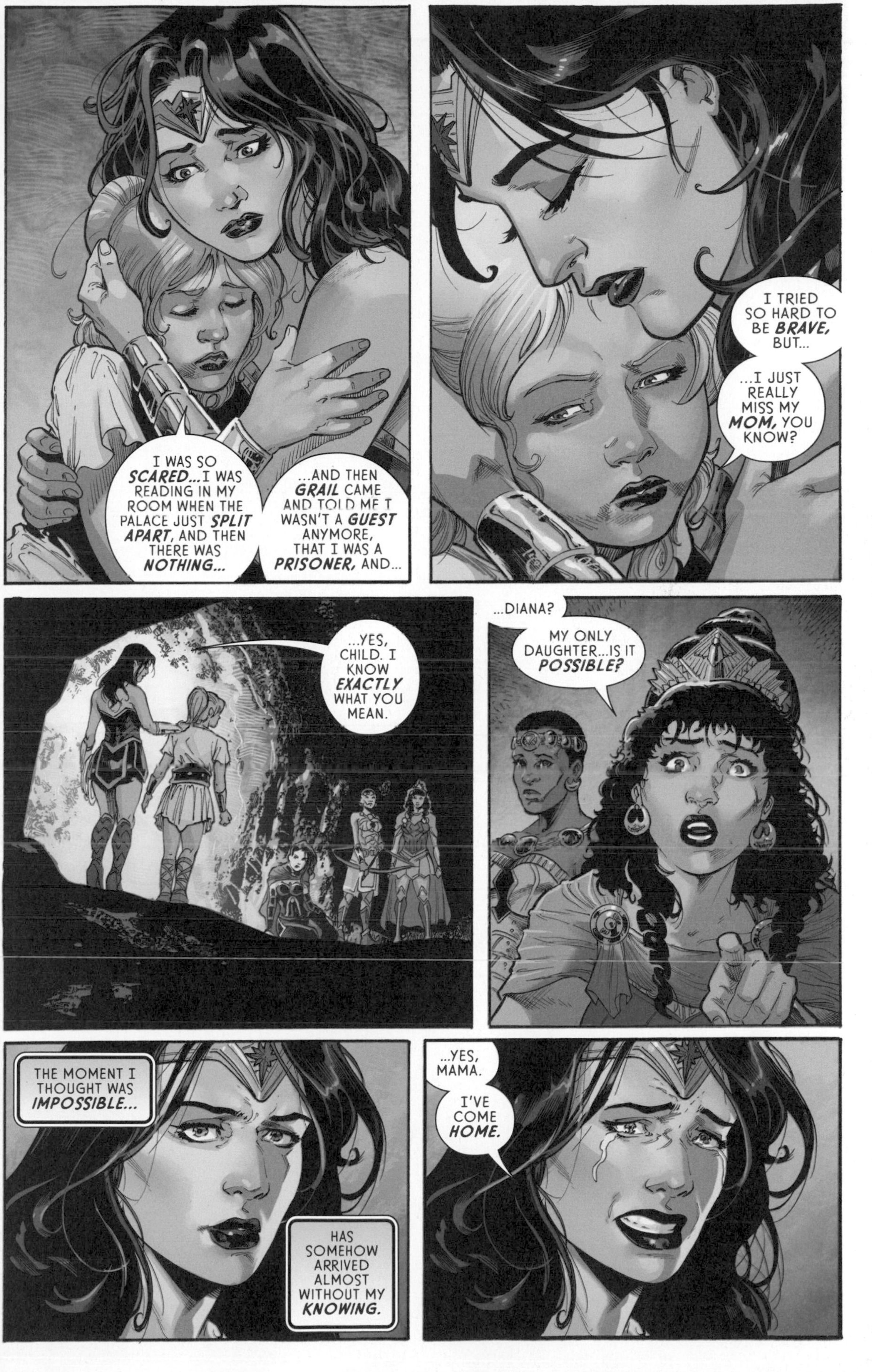
I WAS SO SCARED...I WAS READING IN MY ROOM WHEN THE PALACE JUST SPLIT APART, AND THEN THERE WAS NOTHING...
...AND THEN GRAIL CAME AND TOLD ME I WASN'T A GUEST ANYMORE, THAT I WAS A PRISONER, AND...
I TRIED SO HARD TO BE BRAVE, BUT...
...I JUST REALLY MISS MY MOM, YOU KNOW?
...YES, CHILD. I KNOW EXACTLY WHAT YOU MEAN.
...DIANA?
MY ONLY DAUGHTER...IS IT POSSIBLE?
THE MOMENT I THOUGHT WAS IMPOSSIBLE...
HAS SOMEHOW ARRIVED ALMOST WITHOUT MY KNOWING.
...YES, MAMA.
I'VE COME HOME.

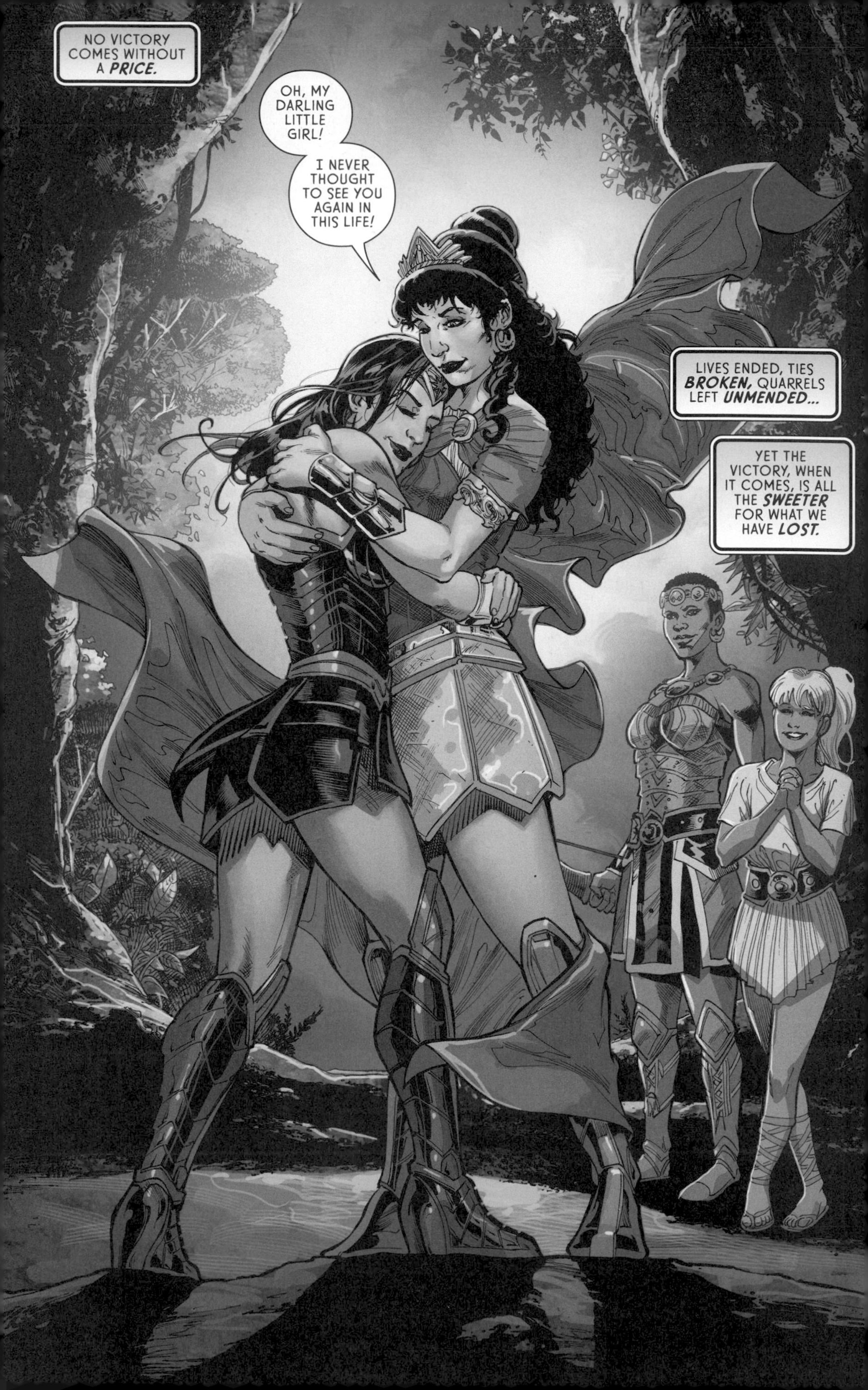
NO VICTORY COMES WITHOUT A ***PRICE.***
OH, MY DARLING LITTLE GIRL!
I NEVER THOUGHT TO SEE YOU AGAIN IN THIS LIFE!
LIVES ENDED, TIES ***BROKEN,*** QUARRELS LEFT ***UNMENDED...***
YET THE VICTORY, WHEN IT COMES, IS ALL THE ***SWEETER*** FOR WHAT WE HAVE ***LOST.***

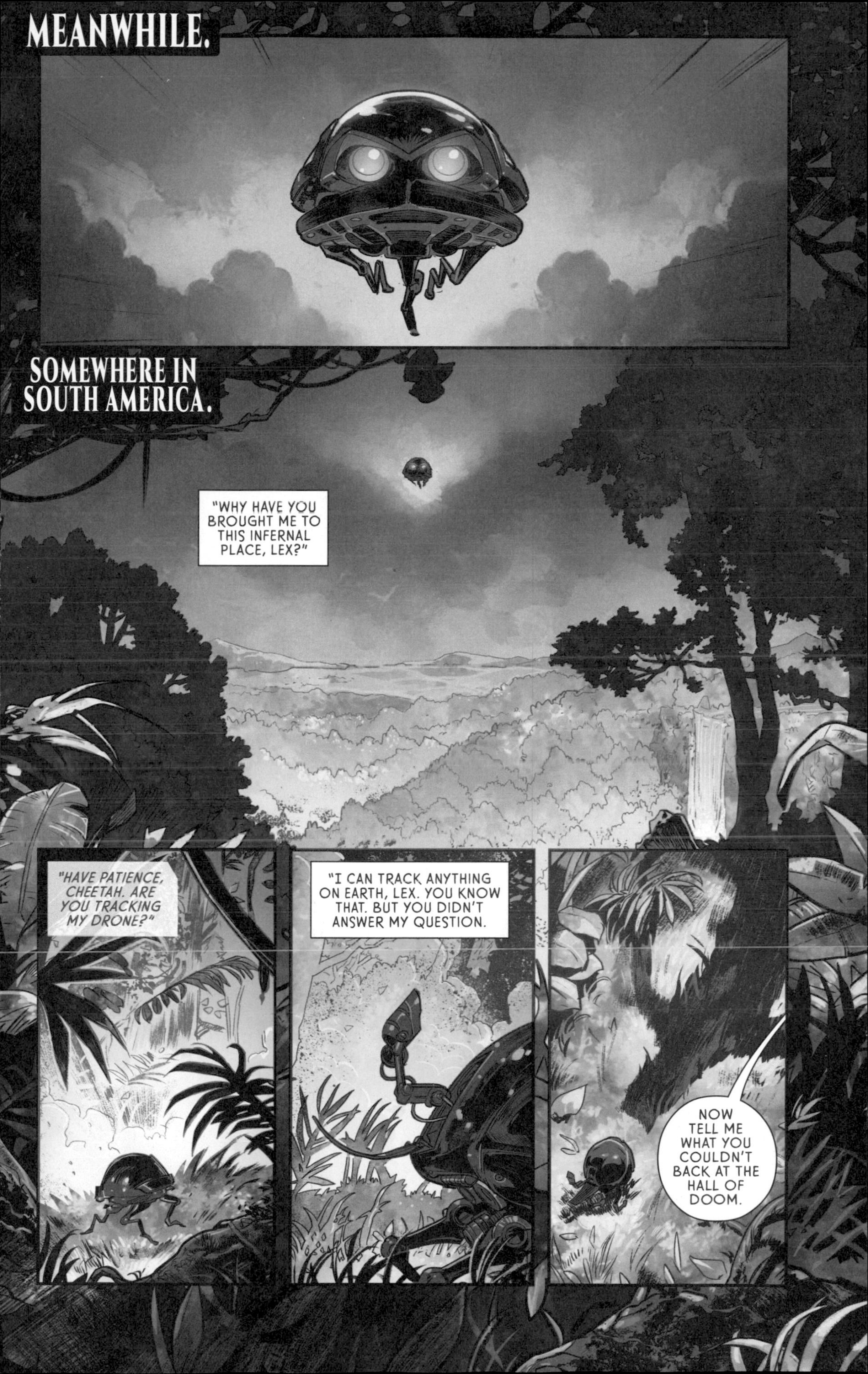
MEANWHILE.
SOMEWHERE IN SOUTH AMERICA.
"WHY HAVE YOU BROUGHT ME TO THIS INFERNAL PLACE, LEX?"
"HAVE PATIENCE, CHEETAH. ARE YOU TRACKING MY DRONE?"
"I CAN TRACK ANYTHING ON EARTH, LEX. YOU KNOW THAT. BUT YOU DIDN'T ANSWER MY QUESTION.
NOW TELL ME WHAT YOU COULDN'T BACK AT THE HALL OF DOOM.

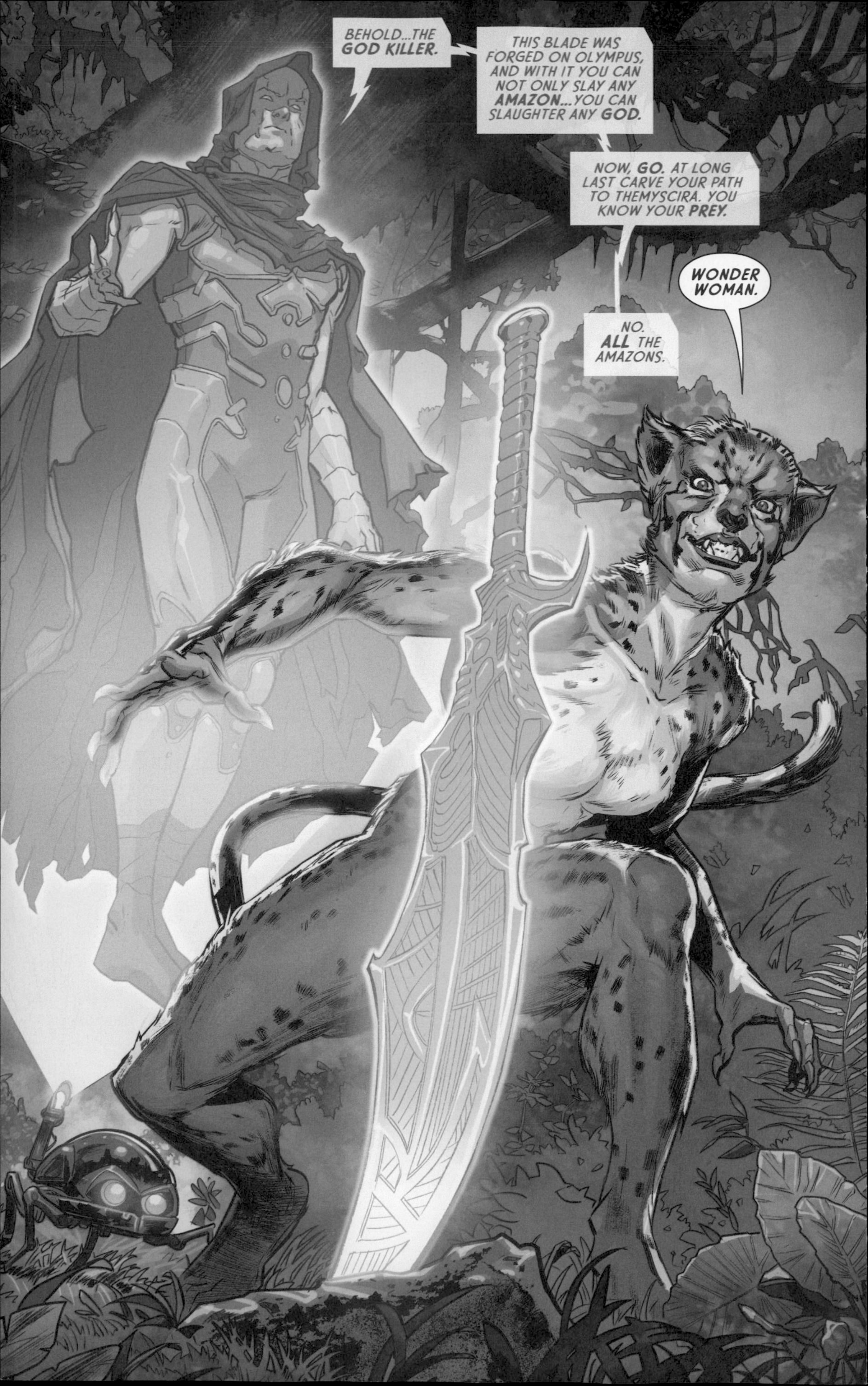
BEHOLD...THE GOD KILLER.
THIS BLADE WAS FORGED ON OLYMPUS, AND WITH IT YOU CAN NOT ONLY SLAY ANY AMAZON...YOU CAN SLAUGHTER ANY GOD.
NOW, GO. AT LONG LAST CARVE YOUR PATH TO THEMYSCIRA. YOU KNOW YOUR PREY.
WONDER WOMAN.
NO. ALL THE AMAZONS.

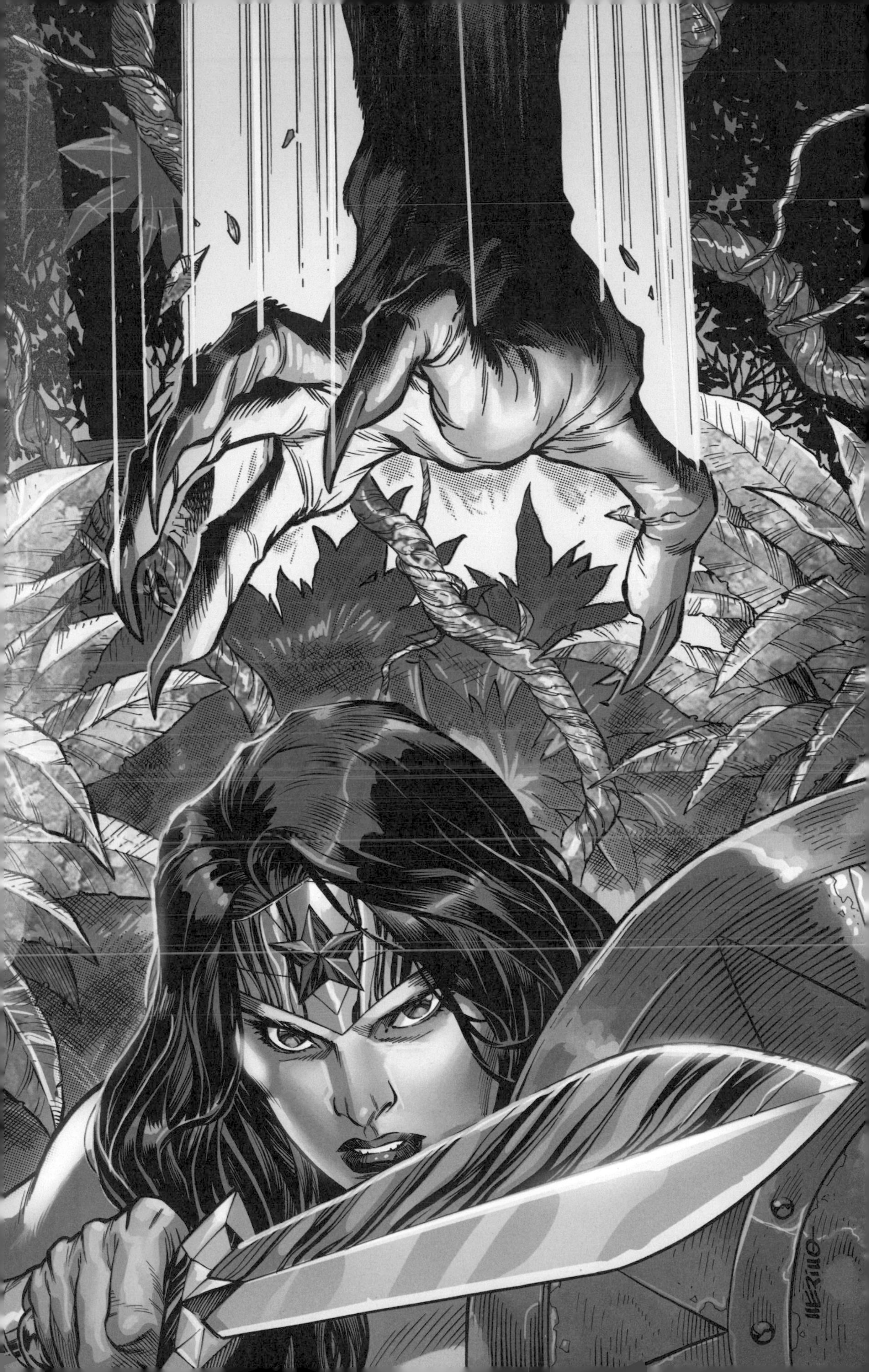

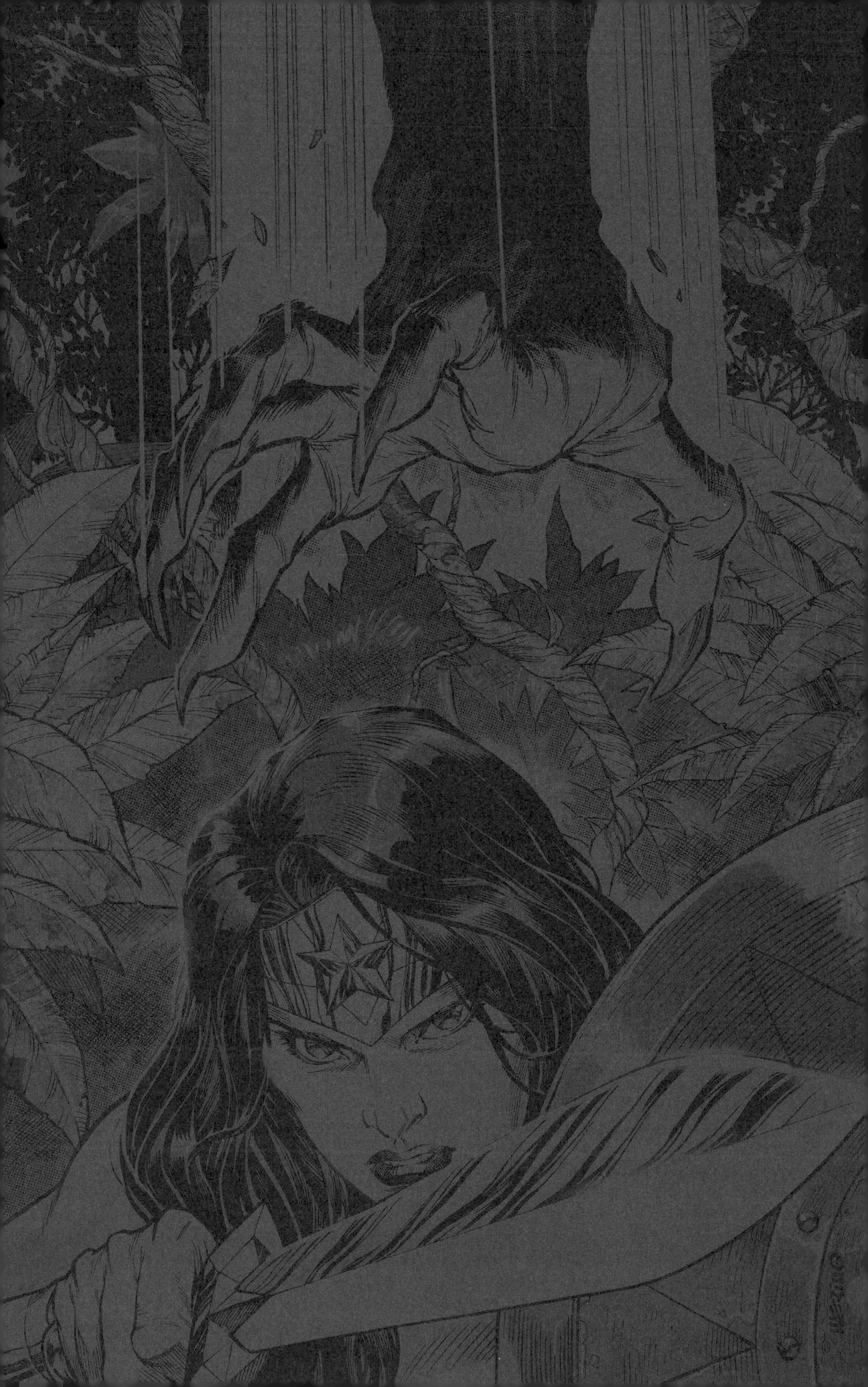

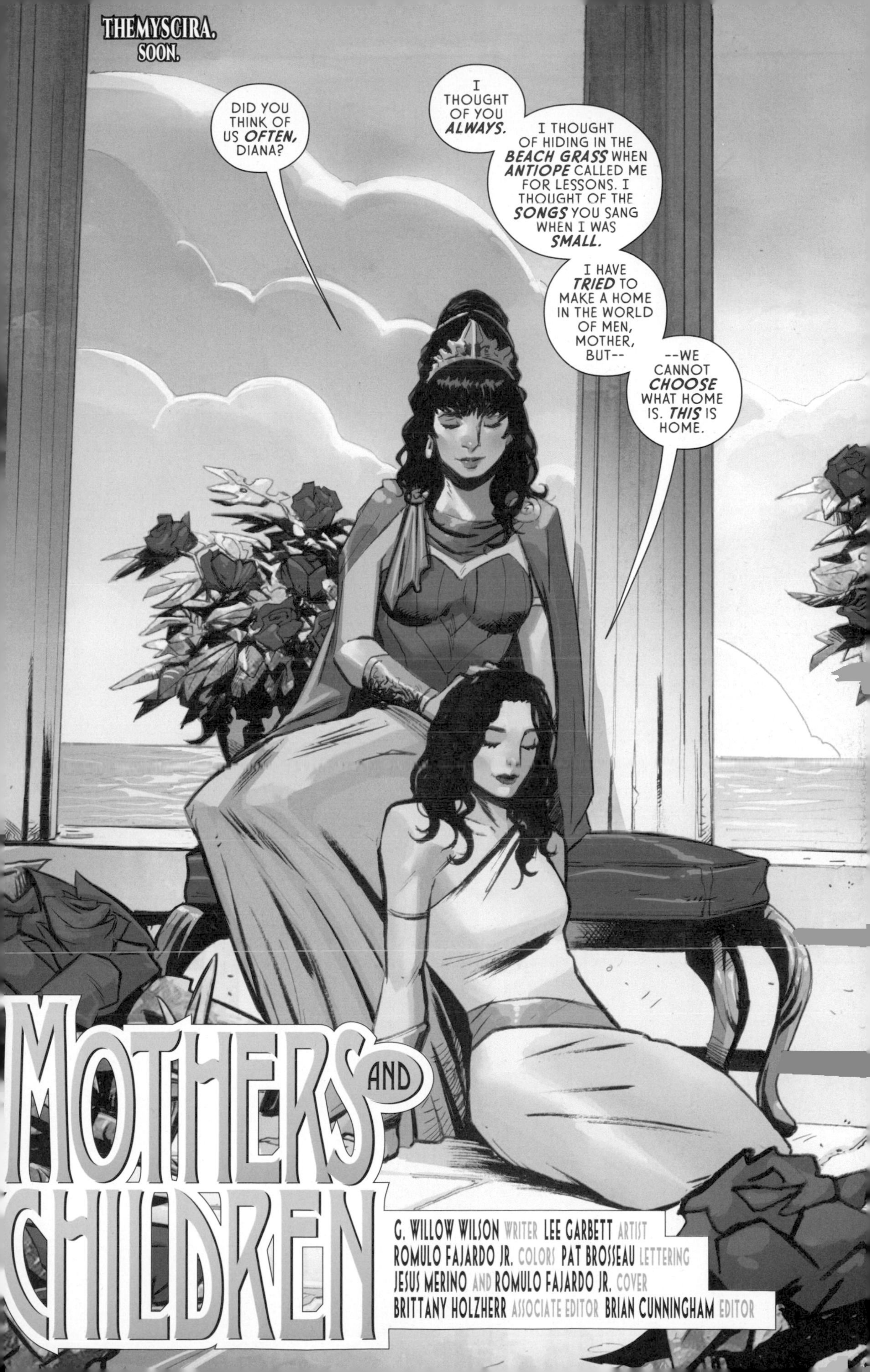
THEMYSCIRA. SOON.
DID YOU THINK OF US OFTEN, DIANA?
I THOUGHT OF YOU ALWAYS.
I THOUGHT OF HIDING IN THE BEACH GRASS WHEN ANTIOPE CALLED ME FOR LESSONS. I THOUGHT OF THE SONGS YOU SANG WHEN I WAS SMALL.
I HAVE TRIED TO MAKE A HOME IN THE WORLD OF MEN, MOTHER, BUT--
--WE CANNOT CHOOSE WHAT HOME IS. THIS IS HOME.
MOTHERS AND CHILDREN
G. WILLOW WILSON WRITER LEE GARBETT ARTIST
ROMULO FAJARDO JR. COLORS PAT BROSSEAU LETTERING
JESUS MERINO AND ROMULO FAJARDO JR. COVER
BRITTANY HOLZHERR ASSOCIATE EDITOR BRIAN CUNNINGHAM EDITOR

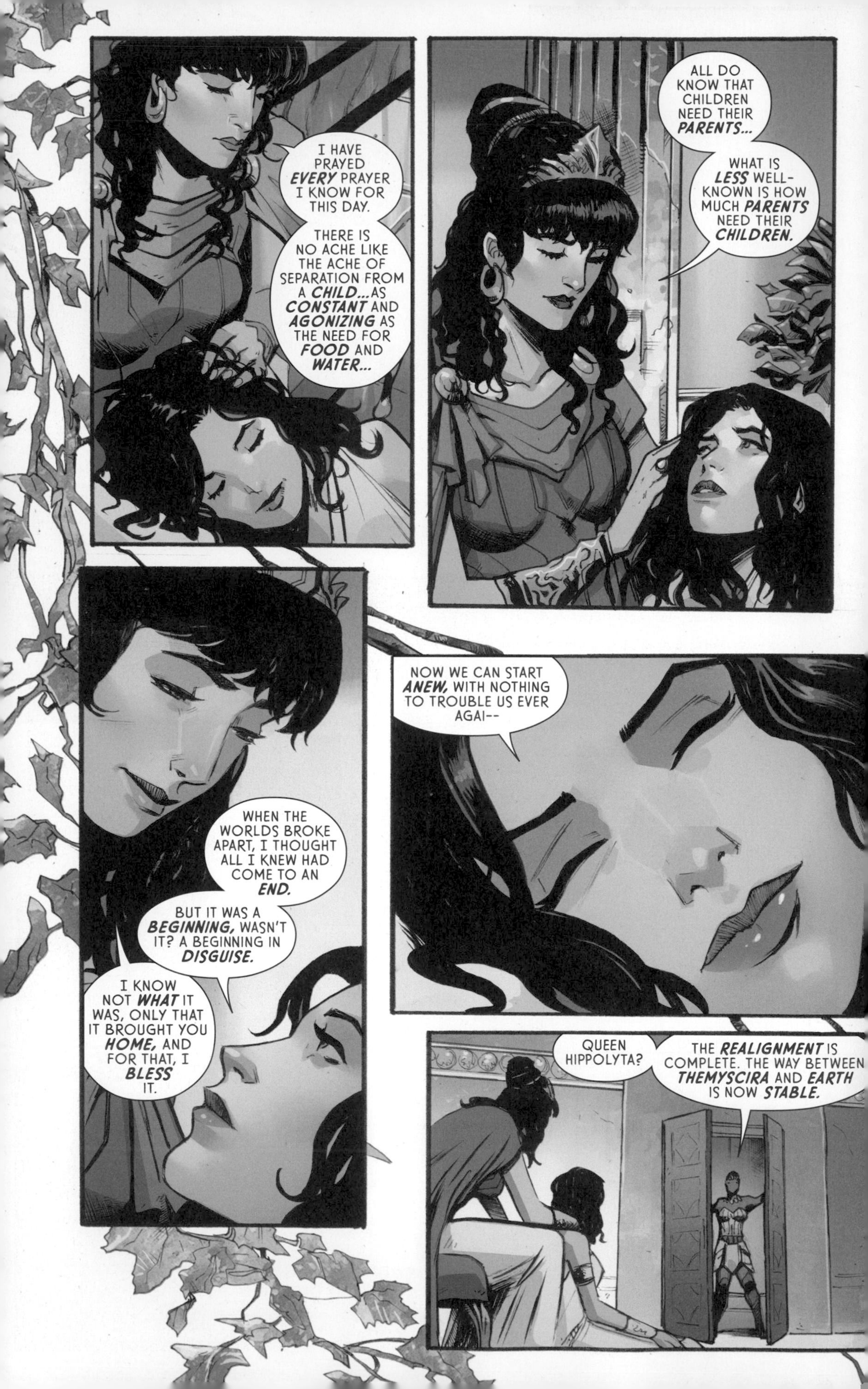
I HAVE PRAYED EVERY PRAYER I KNOW FOR THIS DAY.
THERE IS NO ACHE LIKE THE ACHE OF SEPARATION FROM A CHILD...AS CONSTANT AND AGONIZING AS THE NEED FOR FOOD AND WATER...
ALL DO KNOW THAT CHILDREN NEED THEIR PARENTS...
WHAT IS LESS WELL-KNOWN IS HOW MUCH PARENTS NEED THEIR CHILDREN.
WHEN THE WORLDS BROKE APART, I THOUGHT ALL I KNEW HAD COME TO AN END.
BUT IT WAS A BEGINNING, WASN'T IT? A BEGINNING IN DISGUISE.
I KNOW NOT WHAT IT WAS, ONLY THAT IT BROUGHT YOU HOME, AND FOR THAT, I BLESS IT.
NOW WE CAN START ANEW, WITH NOTHING TO TROUBLE US EVER AGAI--
QUEEN HIPPOLYTA?
THE REALIGNMENT IS COMPLETE. THE WAY BETWEEN THEMYSCIRA AND EARTH IS NOW STABLE.

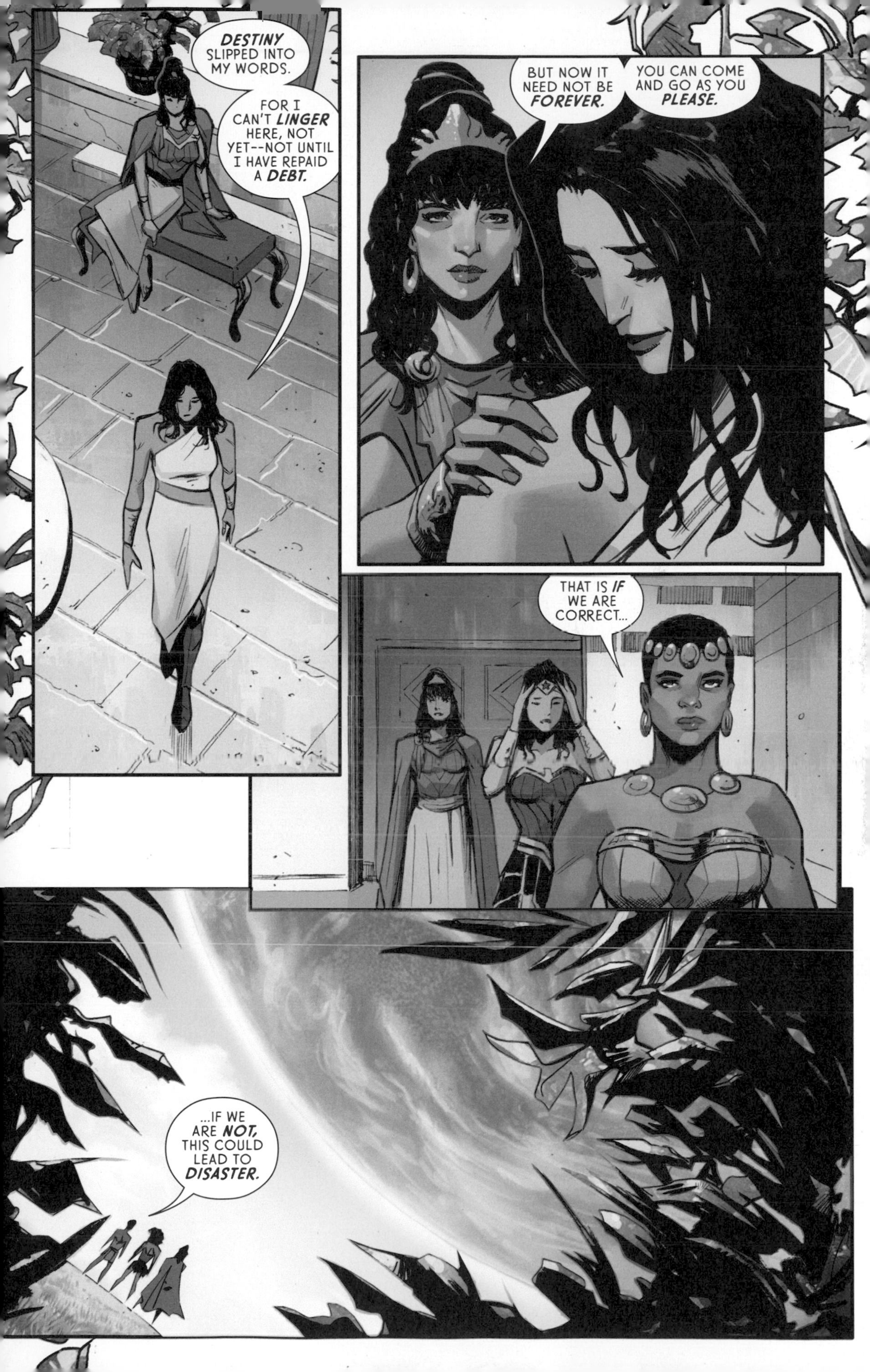
DESTINY SLIPPED INTO MY WORDS.
FOR I CAN'T LINGER HERE, NOT YET--NOT UNTIL I HAVE REPAID A DEBT.
BUT NOW IT NEED NOT BE FOREVER.
YOU CAN COME AND GO AS YOU PLEASE.
THAT IS IF WE ARE CORRECT...
...IF WE ARE NOT, THIS COULD LEAD TO DISASTER.

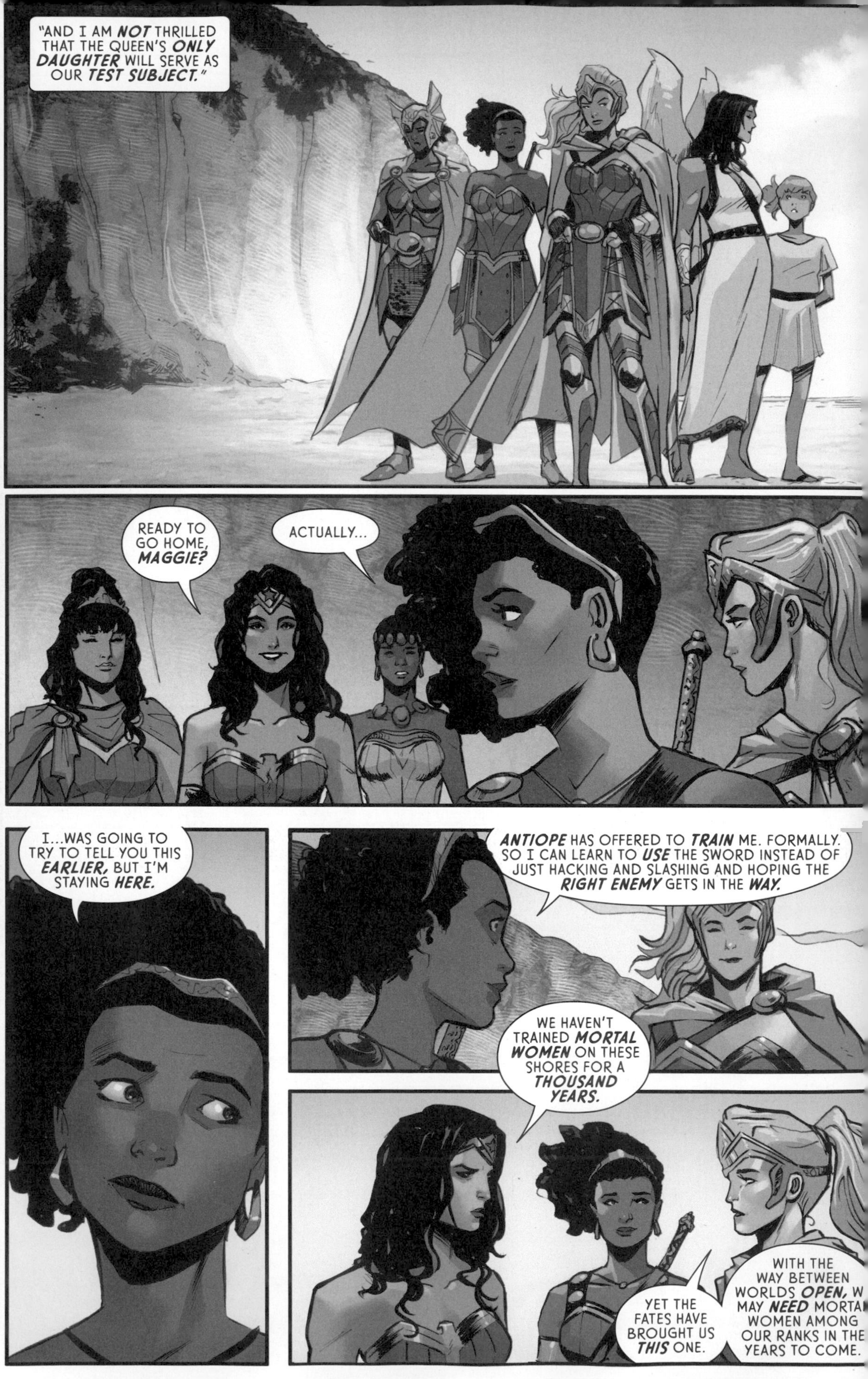
"AND I AM NOT THRILLED THAT THE QUEEN'S ONLY DAUGHTER WILL SERVE AS OUR TEST SUBJECT."
READY TO GO HOME, MAGGIE?
ACTUALLY...
I...WAS GOING TO TRY TO TELL YOU THIS EARLIER, BUT I'M STAYING HERE.
ANTIOPE HAS OFFERED TO TRAIN ME. FORMALLY. SO I CAN LEARN TO USE THE SWORD INSTEAD OF JUST HACKING AND SLASHING AND HOPING THE RIGHT ENEMY GETS IN THE WAY.
WE HAVEN'T TRAINED MORTAL WOMEN ON THESE SHORES FOR A THOUSAND YEARS.
YET THE FATES HAVE BROUGHT US THIS ONE.
WITH THE WAY BETWEEN WORLDS OPEN, W MAY NEED MORTA WOMEN AMONG OUR RANKS IN THE YEARS TO COME.

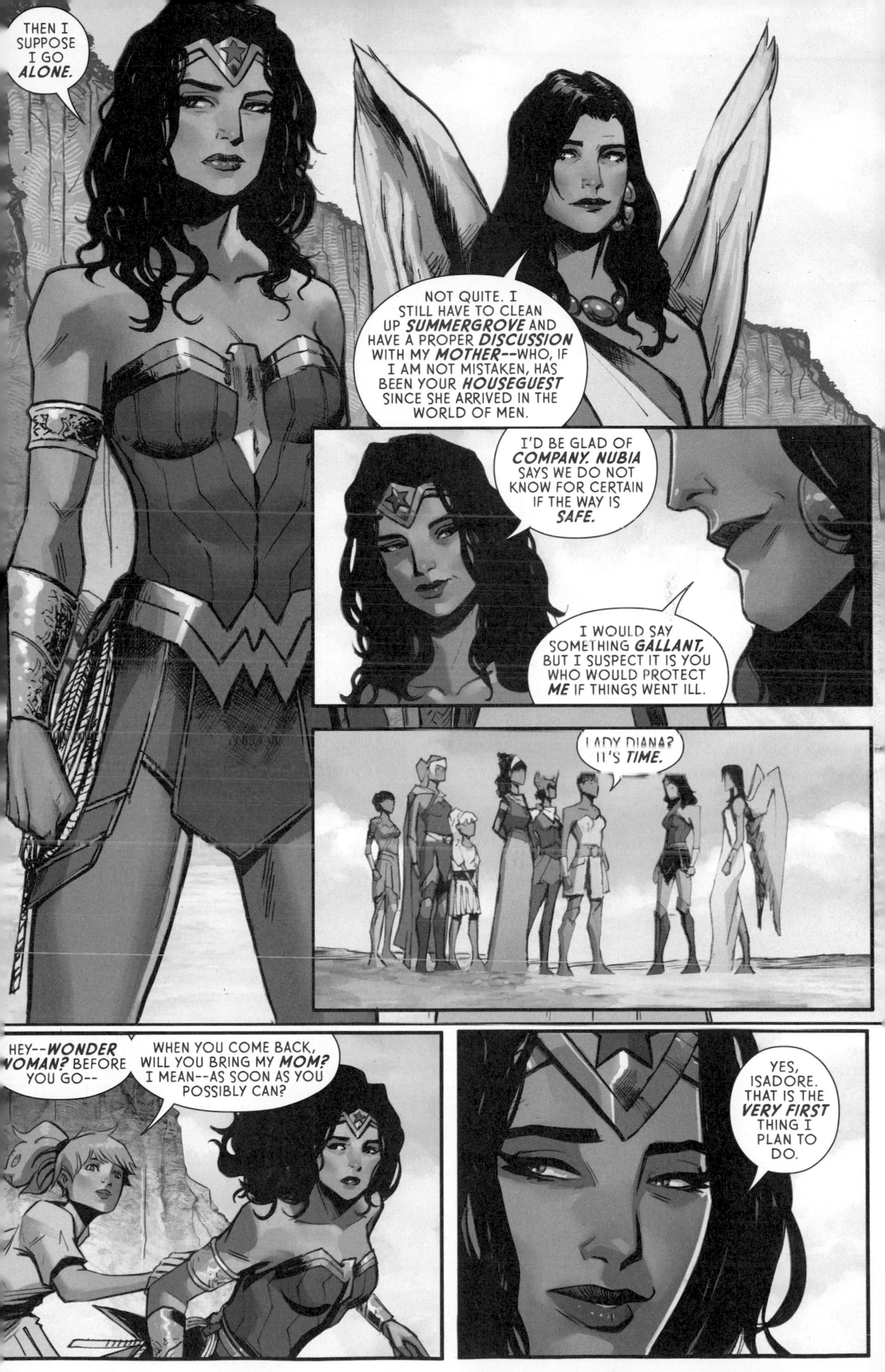
THEN I SUPPOSE I GO ALONE.
NOT QUITE. I STILL HAVE TO CLEAN UP SUMMERGROVE AND HAVE A PROPER DISCUSSION WITH MY MOTHER--WHO, IF I AM NOT MISTAKEN, HAS BEEN YOUR HOUSEGUEST SINCE SHE ARRIVED IN THE WORLD OF MEN.
I'D BE GLAD OF COMPANY. NUBIA SAYS WE DO NOT KNOW FOR CERTAIN IF THE WAY IS SAFE.
I WOULD SAY SOMETHING GALLANT, BUT I SUSPECT IT IS YOU WHO WOULD PROTECT ME IF THINGS WENT ILL.
LADY DIANA? IT'S TIME.
HEY--WONDER WOMAN? BEFORE YOU GO--
WHEN YOU COME BACK, WILL YOU BRING MY MOM? I MEAN--AS SOON AS YOU POSSIBLY CAN?
YES, ISADORE. THAT IS THE VERY FIRST THING I PLAN TO DO.

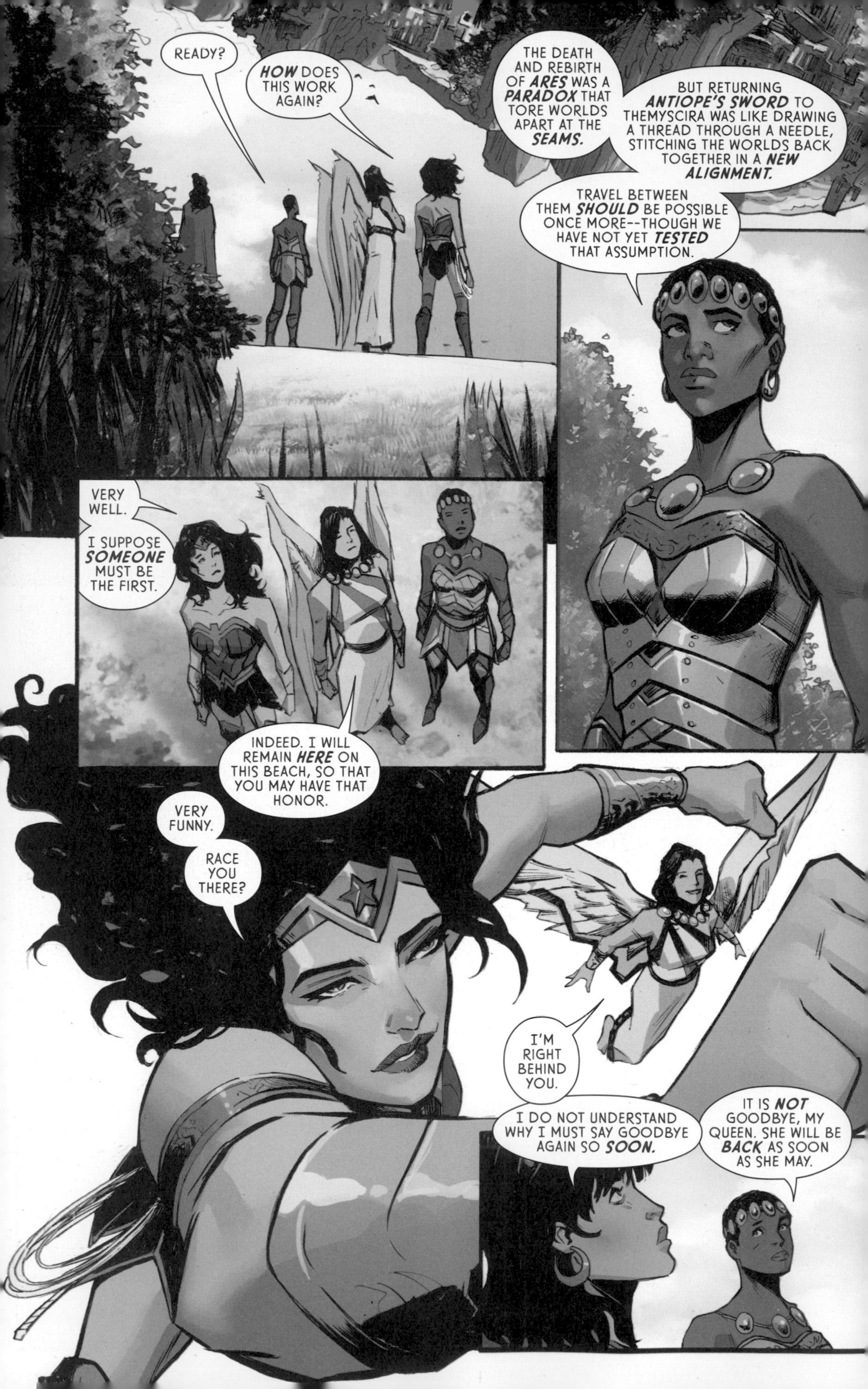
READY?
HOW DOES THIS WORK AGAIN?
THE DEATH AND REBIRTH OF ARES WAS A PARADOX THAT TORE WORLDS APART AT THE SEAMS.
BUT RETURNING ANTIOPE'S SWORD TO THEMYSCIRA WAS LIKE DRAWING A THREAD THROUGH A NEEDLE, STITCHING THE WORLDS BACK TOGETHER IN A NEW ALIGNMENT.
TRAVEL BETWEEN THEM SHOULD BE POSSIBLE ONCE MORE--THOUGH WE HAVE NOT YET TESTED THAT ASSUMPTION.
VERY WELL.
I SUPPOSE SOMEONE MUST BE THE FIRST.
INDEED. I WILL REMAIN HERE ON THIS BEACH, SO THAT YOU MAY HAVE THAT HONOR.
VERY FUNNY.
RACE YOU THERE?
I'M RIGHT BEHIND YOU.
I DO NOT UNDERSTAND WHY I MUST SAY GOODBYE AGAIN SO SOON.
IT IS NOT GOODBYE, MY QUEEN. SHE WILL BE BACK AS SOON AS SHE MAY.

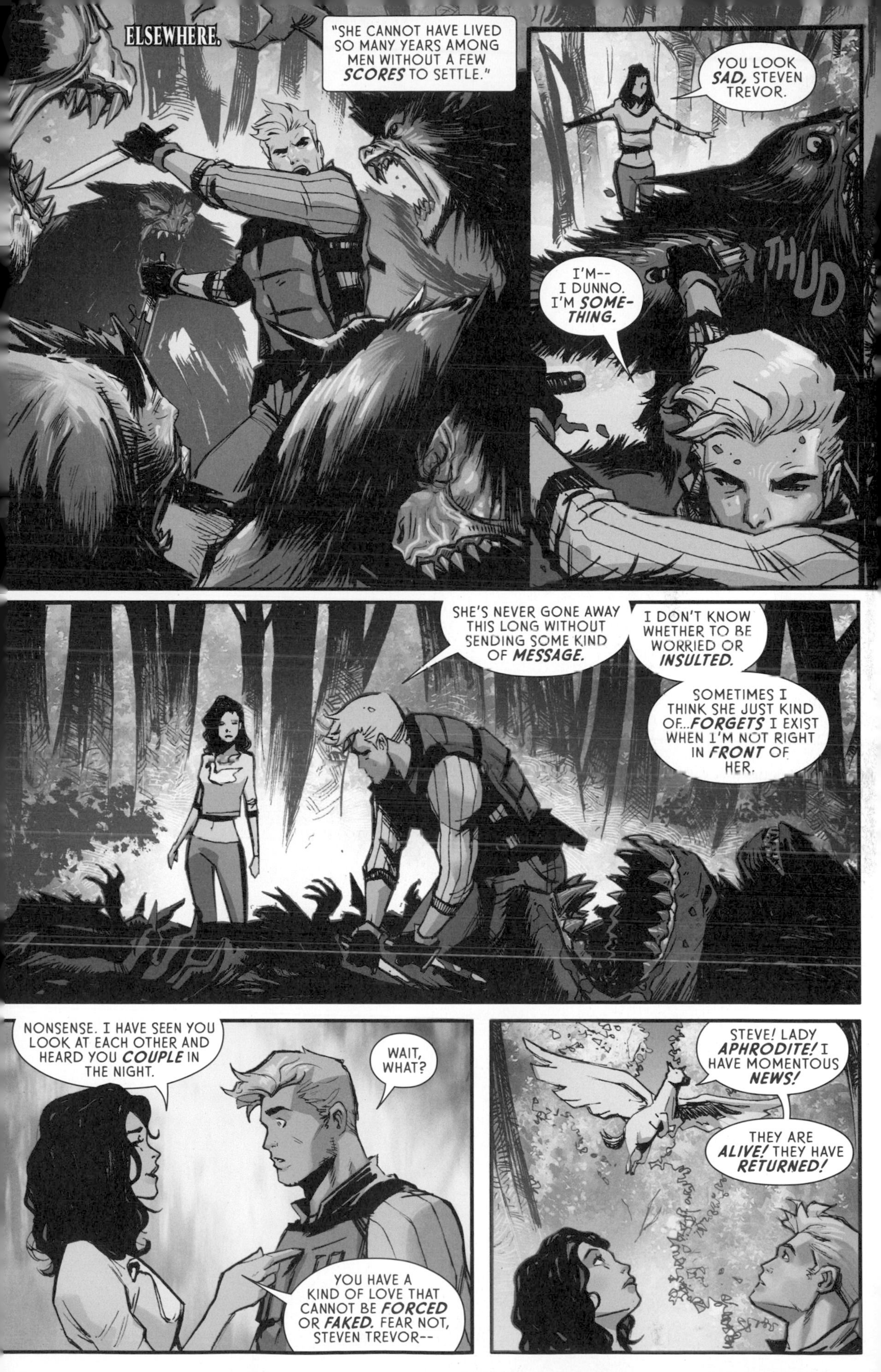

ELSEWHERE.
"SHE CANNOT HAVE LIVED SO MANY YEARS AMONG MEN WITHOUT A FEW SCORES TO SETTLE."
YOU LOOK SAD, STEVEN TREVOR.
I'M-- I DUNNO. I'M SOME-THING.
THUD
SHE'S NEVER GONE AWAY THIS LONG WITHOUT SENDING SOME KIND OF MESSAGE.
I DON'T KNOW WHETHER TO BE WORRIED OR INSULTED.
SOMETIMES I THINK SHE JUST KIND OF...FORGETS I EXIST WHEN I'M NOT RIGHT IN FRONT OF HER.
NONSENSE. I HAVE SEEN YOU LOOK AT EACH OTHER AND HEARD YOU COUPLE IN THE NIGHT.
WAIT, WHAT?
YOU HAVE A KIND OF LOVE THAT CANNOT BE FORCED OR FAKED. FEAR NOT, STEVEN TREVOR--
STEVE! LADY APHRODITE! I HAVE MOMENTOUS NEWS!
THEY ARE ALIVE! THEY HAVE RETURNED!

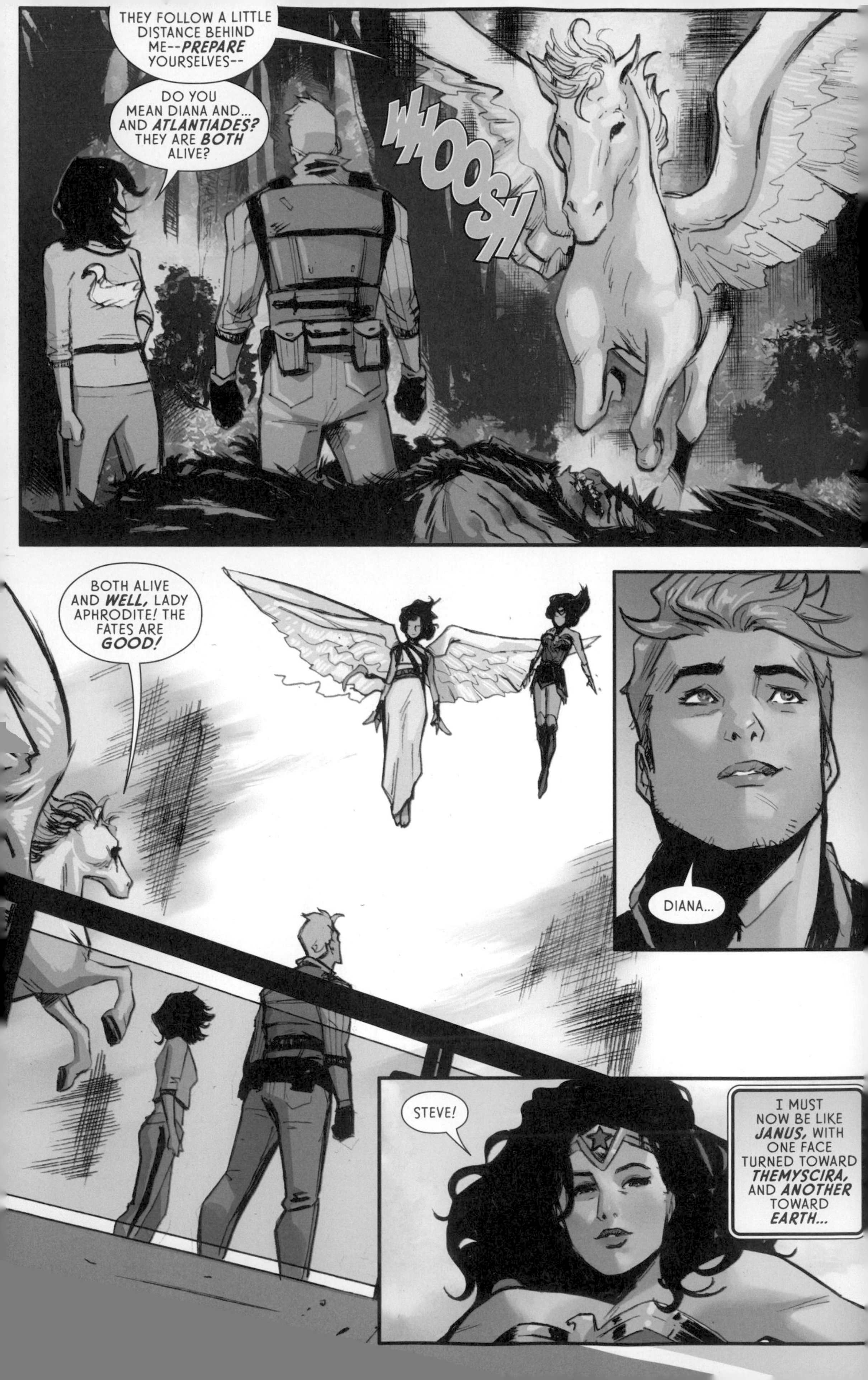
THEY FOLLOW A LITTLE DISTANCE BEHIND ME--PREPARE YOURSELVES--
DO YOU MEAN DIANA AND... AND ATLANTIADES? THEY ARE BOTH ALIVE?
WHOOSH
BOTH ALIVE AND WELL, LADY APHRODITE! THE FATES ARE GOOD!
DIANA...
STEVE!
I MUST NOW BE LIKE JANUS, WITH ONE FACE TURNED TOWARD THEMYSCIRA, AND ANOTHER TOWARD EARTH...

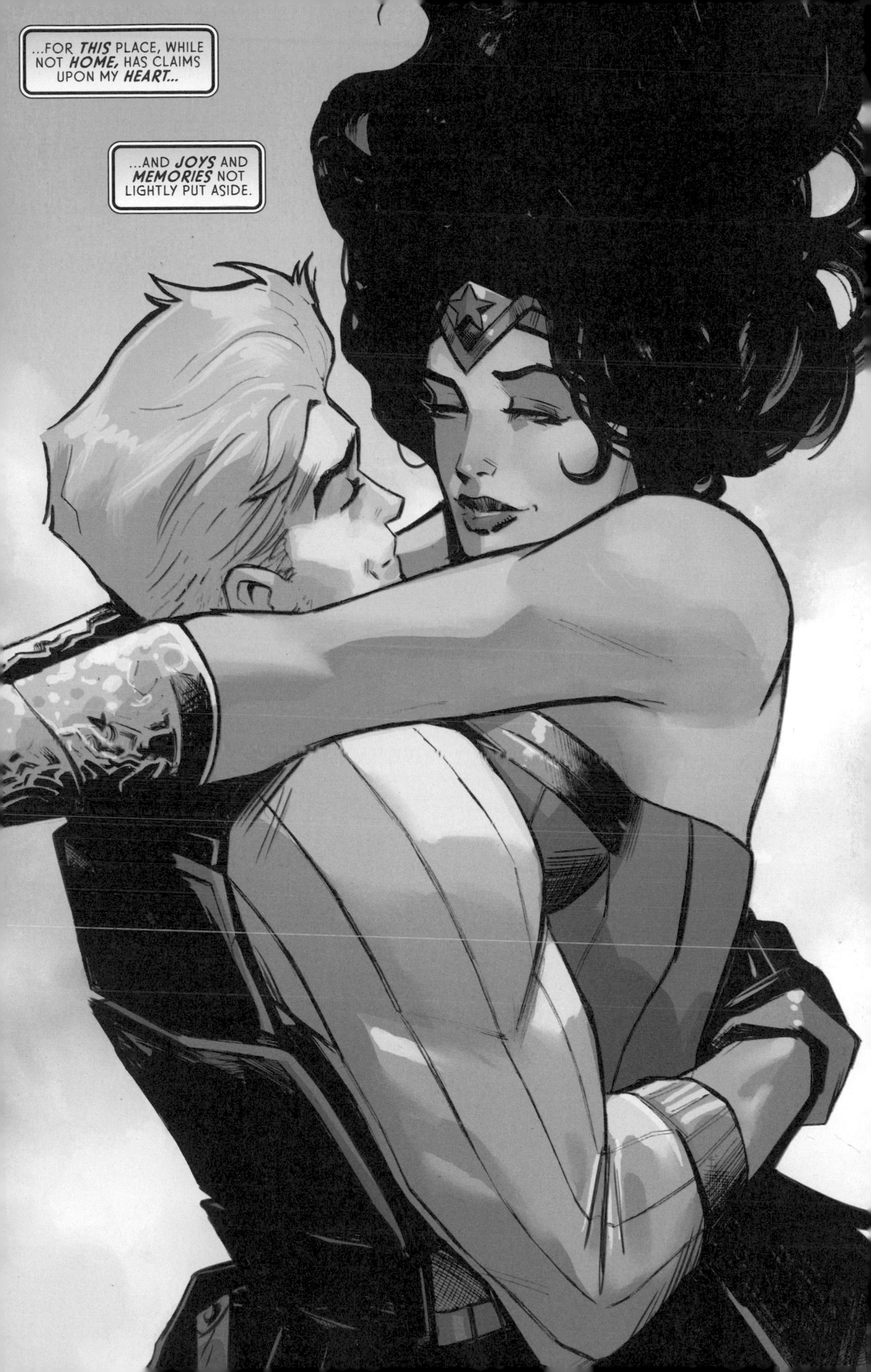
...FOR THIS PLACE, WHILE NOT HOME, HAS CLAIMS UPON MY HEART...
...AND JOYS AND MEMORIES NOT LIGHTLY PUT ASIDE.

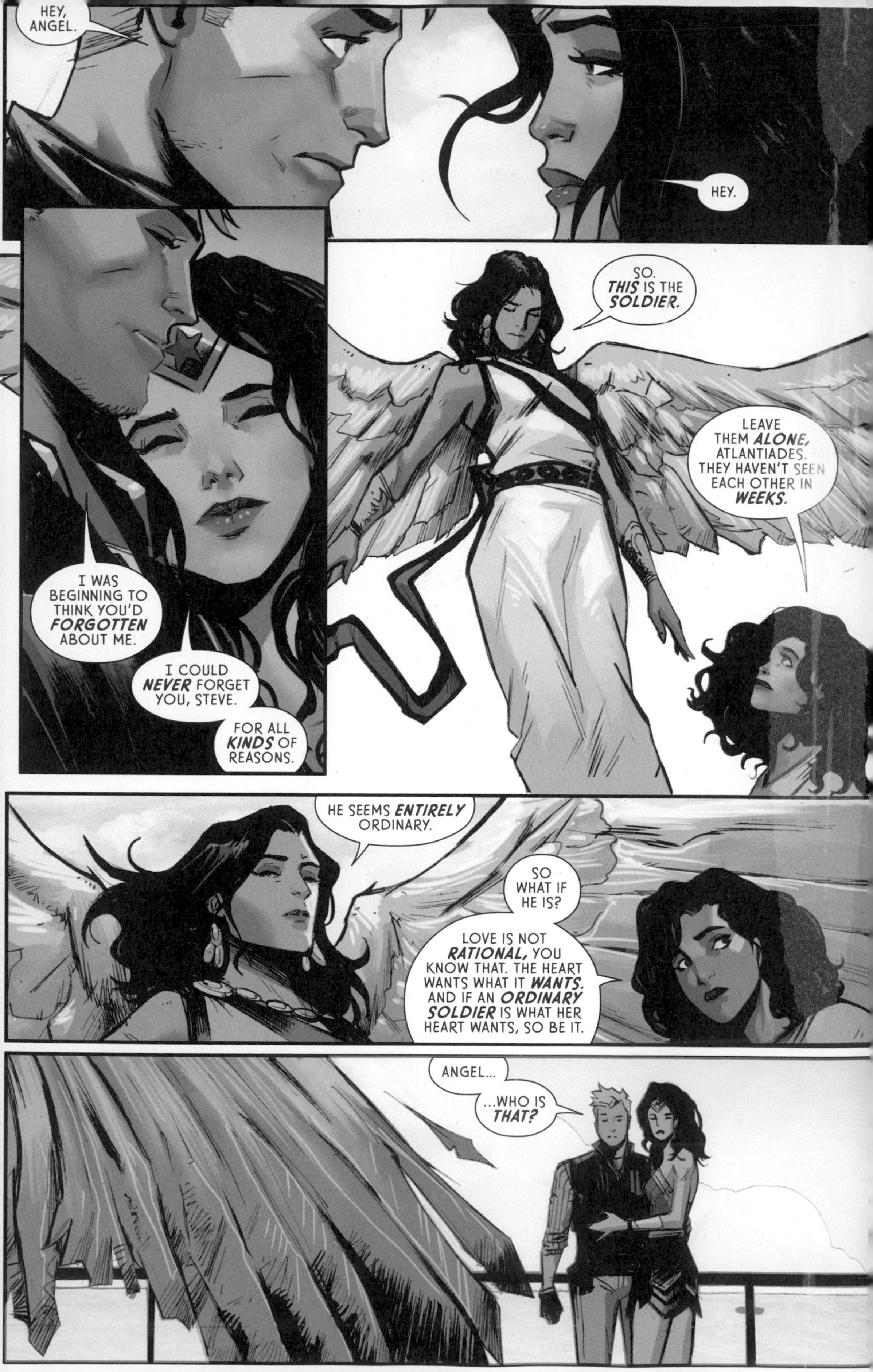
HEY, ANGEL.
HEY.
I WAS BEGINNING TO THINK YOU'D FORGOTTEN ABOUT ME.
I COULD NEVER FORGET YOU, STEVE.
FOR ALL KINDS OF REASONS.
SO. THIS IS THE SOLDIER.
LEAVE THEM ALONE, ATLANTIADES. THEY HAVEN'T SEEN EACH OTHER IN WEEKS.
HE SEEMS ENTIRELY ORDINARY.
SO WHAT IF HE IS?
LOVE IS NOT RATIONAL, YOU KNOW THAT. THE HEART WANTS WHAT IT WANTS. AND IF AN ORDINARY SOLDIER IS WHAT HER HEART WANTS, SO BE IT.
ANGEL...
...WHO IS THAT?

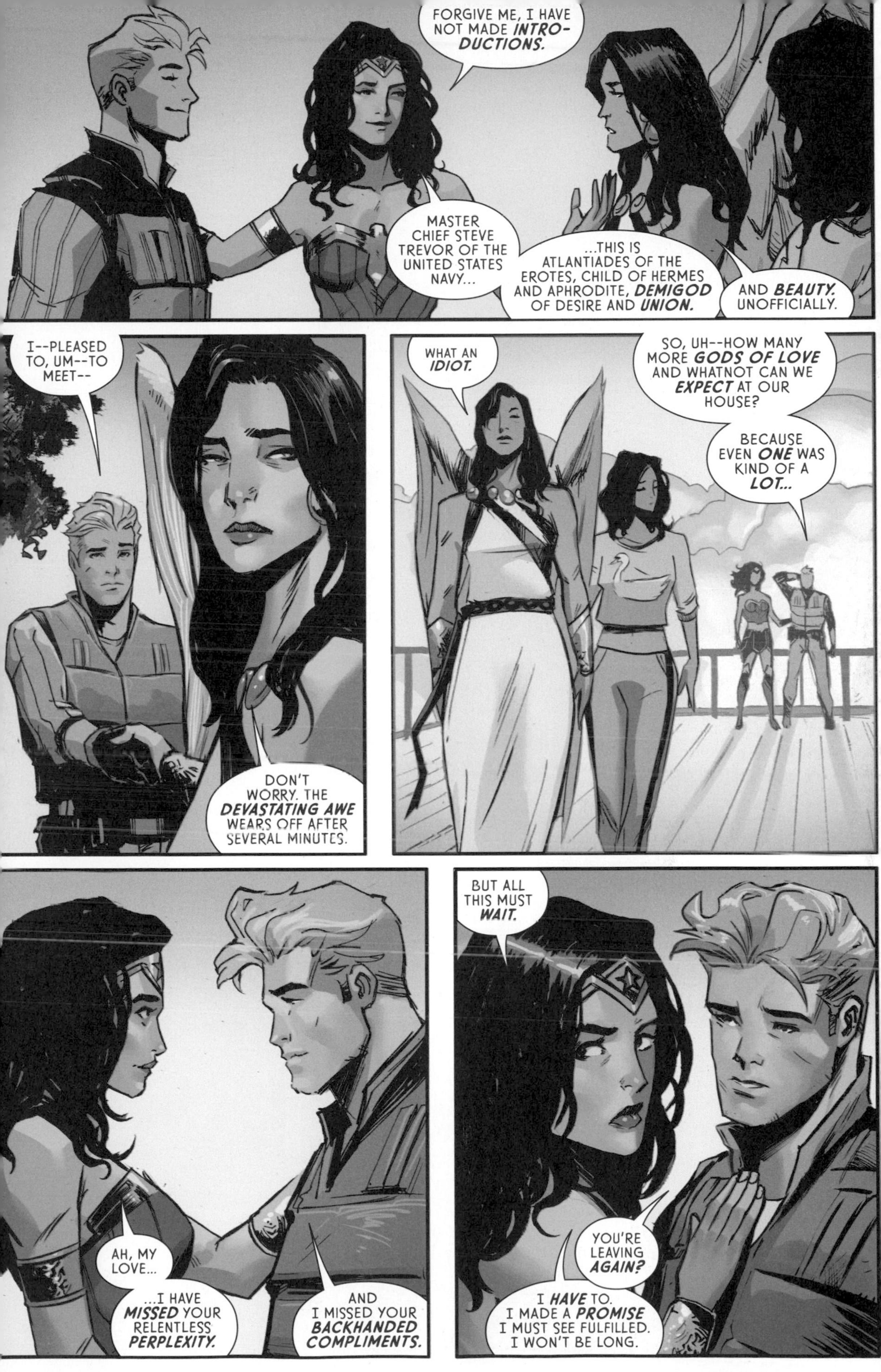
FORGIVE ME, I HAVE NOT MADE *INTRO-DUCTIONS.*
MASTER CHIEF STEVE TREVOR OF THE UNITED STATES NAVY...
...THIS IS ATLANTIADES OF THE EROTES, CHILD OF HERMES AND APHRODITE, *DEMIGOD* OF DESIRE AND *UNION.*
AND *BEAUTY.* UNOFFICIALLY.
I--PLEASED TO, UM--TO MEET--
DON'T WORRY. THE *DEVASTATING AWE* WEARS OFF AFTER SEVERAL MINUTES.
WHAT AN *IDIOT.*
SO, UH--HOW MANY MORE *GODS OF LOVE* AND WHATNOT CAN WE *EXPECT* AT OUR HOUSE?
BECAUSE EVEN *ONE* WAS KIND OF A *LOT...*
AH, MY LOVE...
...I HAVE *MISSED* YOUR RELENTLESS *PERPLEXITY.*
AND I MISSED YOUR *BACKHANDED COMPLIMENTS.*
BUT ALL THIS MUST *WAIT.*
YOU'RE LEAVING *AGAIN?*
I *HAVE* TO. I MADE A *PROMISE* I MUST SEE FULFILLED. I WON'T BE LONG.

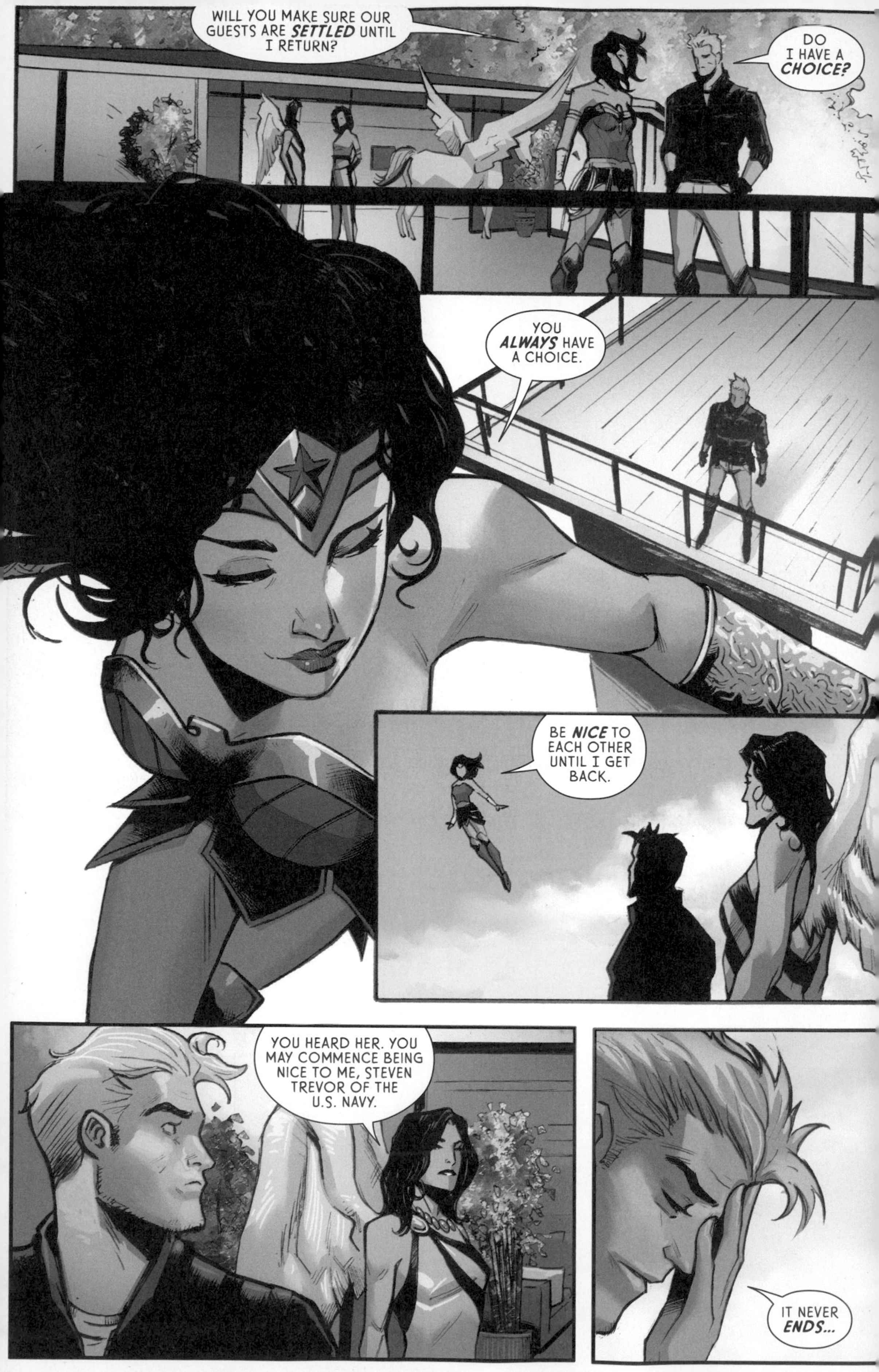
WILL YOU MAKE SURE OUR GUESTS ARE **SETTLED** UNTIL I RETURN?
DO I HAVE A **CHOICE?**
YOU **ALWAYS** HAVE A CHOICE.
BE **NICE** TO EACH OTHER UNTIL I GET BACK.
YOU HEARD HER. YOU MAY COMMENCE BEING NICE TO ME, STEVEN TREVOR OF THE U.S. NAVY.
IT NEVER **ENDS...**

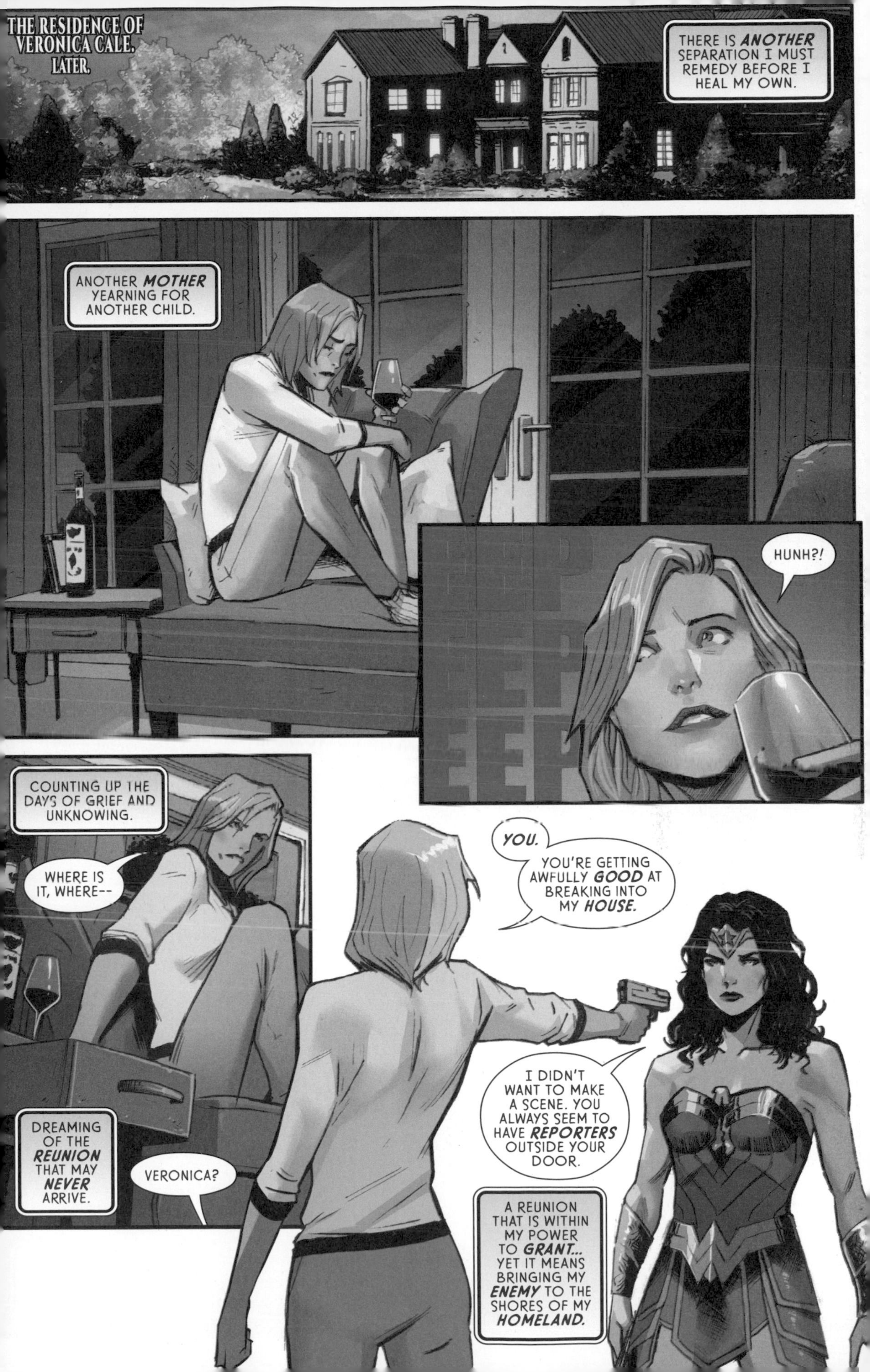
THE RESIDENCE OF VERONICA CALE. LATER.
THERE IS ANOTHER SEPARATION I MUST REMEDY BEFORE I HEAL MY OWN.
ANOTHER MOTHER YEARNING FOR ANOTHER CHILD.
HUNH?!
COUNTING UP THE DAYS OF GRIEF AND UNKNOWING.
WHERE IS IT, WHERE--
DREAMING OF THE REUNION THAT MAY NEVER ARRIVE.
VERONICA?
YOU.
YOU'RE GETTING AWFULLY GOOD AT BREAKING INTO MY HOUSE.
I DIDN'T WANT TO MAKE A SCENE. YOU ALWAYS SEEM TO HAVE REPORTERS OUTSIDE YOUR DOOR.
A REUNION THAT IS WITHIN MY POWER TO GRANT... YET IT MEANS BRINGING MY ENEMY TO THE SHORES OF MY HOMELAND.

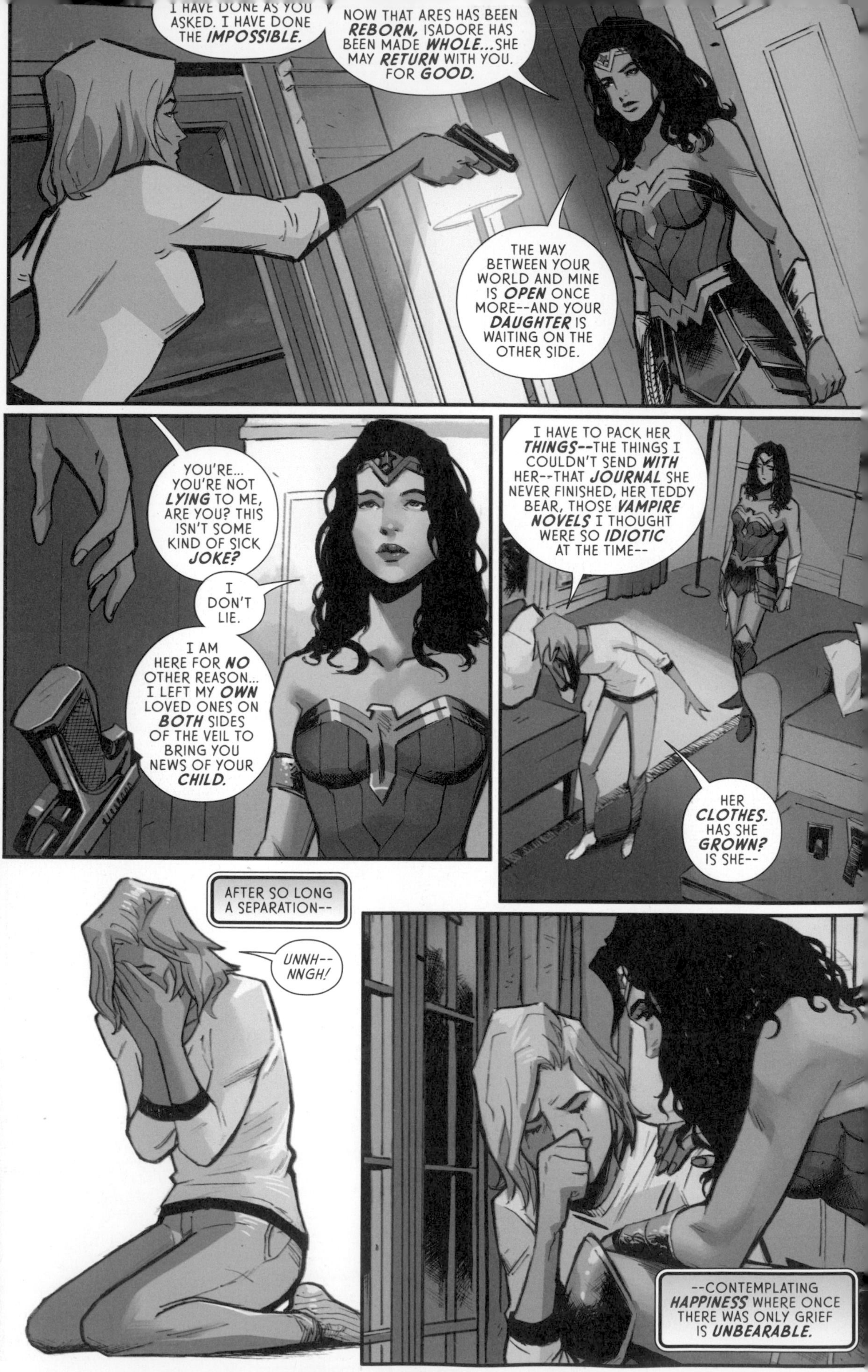
I HAVE DONE AS YOU ASKED. I HAVE DONE THE IMPOSSIBLE.
NOW THAT ARES HAS BEEN REBORN, ISADORE HAS BEEN MADE WHOLE...SHE MAY RETURN WITH YOU. FOR GOOD.
THE WAY BETWEEN YOUR WORLD AND MINE IS OPEN ONCE MORE--AND YOUR DAUGHTER IS WAITING ON THE OTHER SIDE.
YOU'RE... YOU'RE NOT LYING TO ME, ARE YOU? THIS ISN'T SOME KIND OF SICK JOKE?
I DON'T LIE.
I AM HERE FOR NO OTHER REASON... I LEFT MY OWN LOVED ONES ON BOTH SIDES OF THE VEIL TO BRING YOU NEWS OF YOUR CHILD.
I HAVE TO PACK HER THINGS--THE THINGS I COULDN'T SEND WITH HER--THAT JOURNAL SHE NEVER FINISHED, HER TEDDY BEAR, THOSE VAMPIRE NOVELS I THOUGHT WERE SO IDIOTIC AT THE TIME--
HER CLOTHES. HAS SHE GROWN? IS SHE--
AFTER SO LONG A SEPARATION--
UNNH--NNGH!
--CONTEMPLATING HAPPINESS WHERE ONCE THERE WAS ONLY GRIEF IS UNBEARABLE.

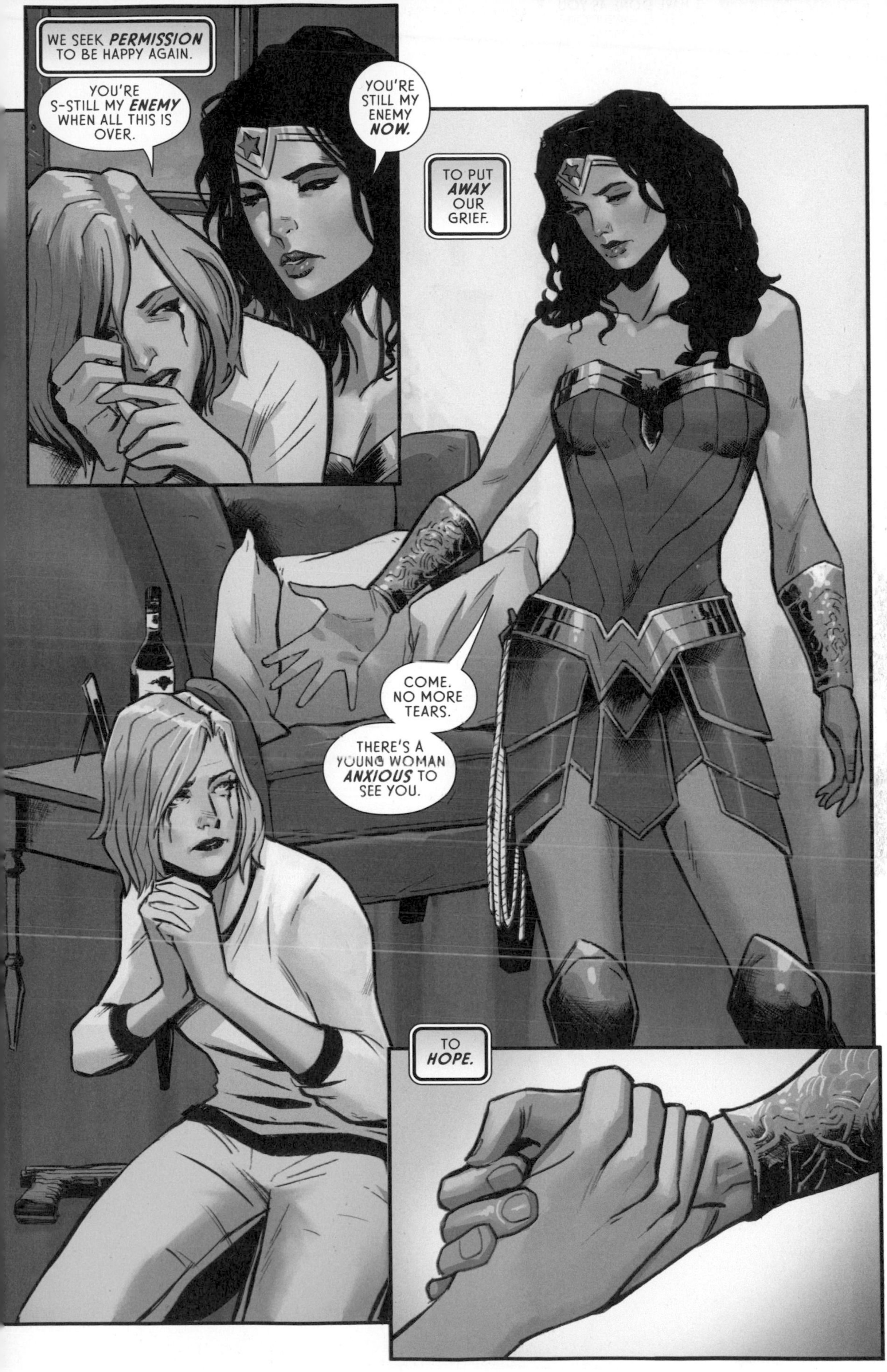

WE SEEK *PERMISSION* TO BE HAPPY AGAIN.
YOU'RE S-STILL MY *ENEMY* WHEN ALL THIS IS OVER.
YOU'RE STILL MY ENEMY *NOW.*
TO PUT *AWAY* OUR GRIEF.
COME. NO MORE TEARS.
THERE'S A YOUNG WOMAN *ANXIOUS* TO SEE YOU.
TO *HOPE.*

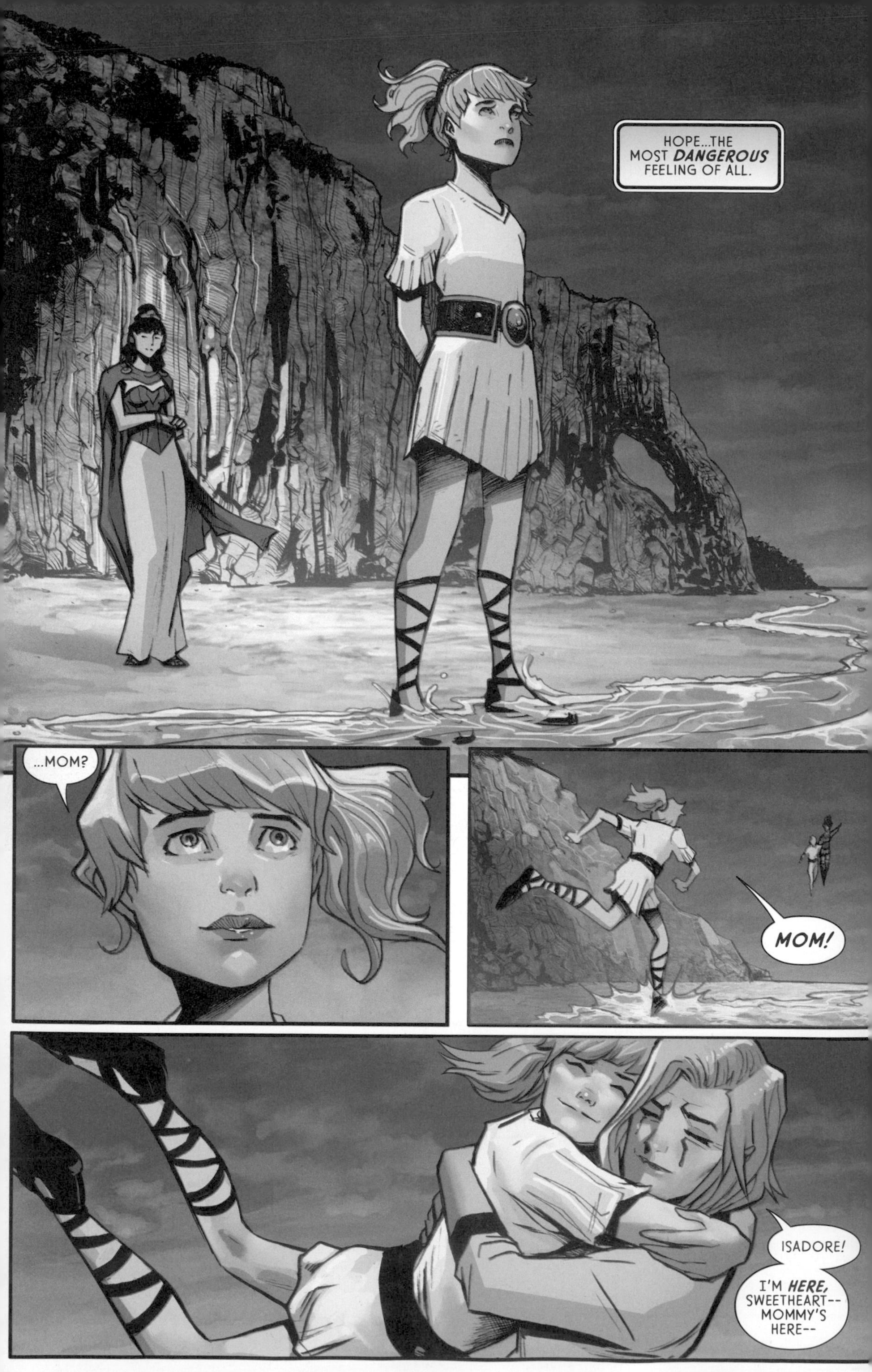
HOPE...THE MOST ***DANGEROUS*** FEELING OF ALL.
...MOM?
MOM!
ISADORE!
I'M ***HERE,*** SWEETHEART-- MOMMY'S HERE--

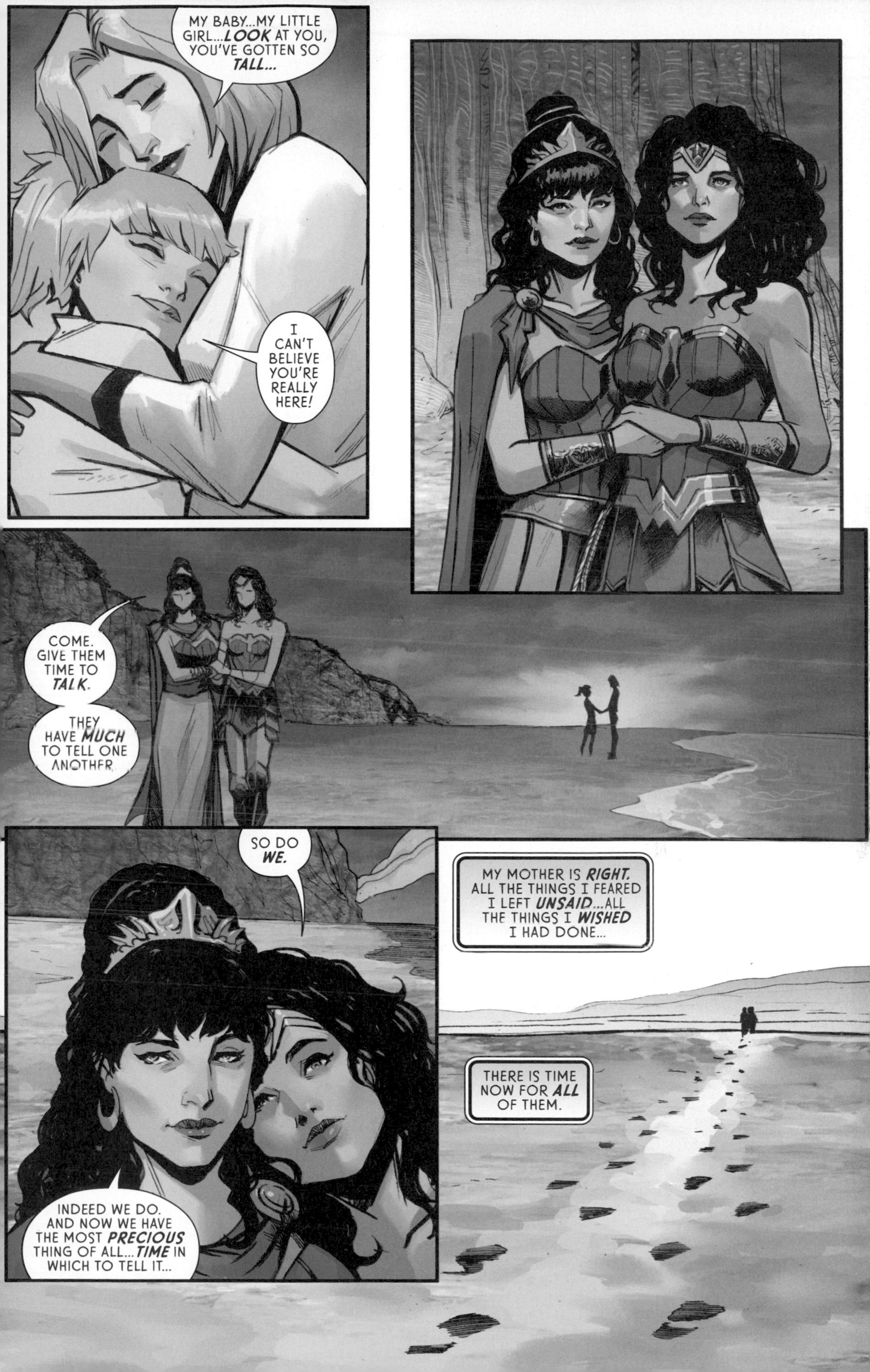
MY BABY...MY LITTLE GIRL...LOOK AT YOU, YOU'VE GOTTEN SO TALL...
I CAN'T BELIEVE YOU'RE REALLY HERE!
COME. GIVE THEM TIME TO TALK.
THEY HAVE MUCH TO TELL ONE ANOTHER.
SO DO WE.
INDEED WE DO. AND NOW WE HAVE THE MOST PRECIOUS THING OF ALL...TIME IN WHICH TO TELL IT...
MY MOTHER IS RIGHT. ALL THE THINGS I FEARED I LEFT UNSAID...ALL THE THINGS I WISHED I HAD DONE...
THERE IS TIME NOW FOR ALL OF THEM.

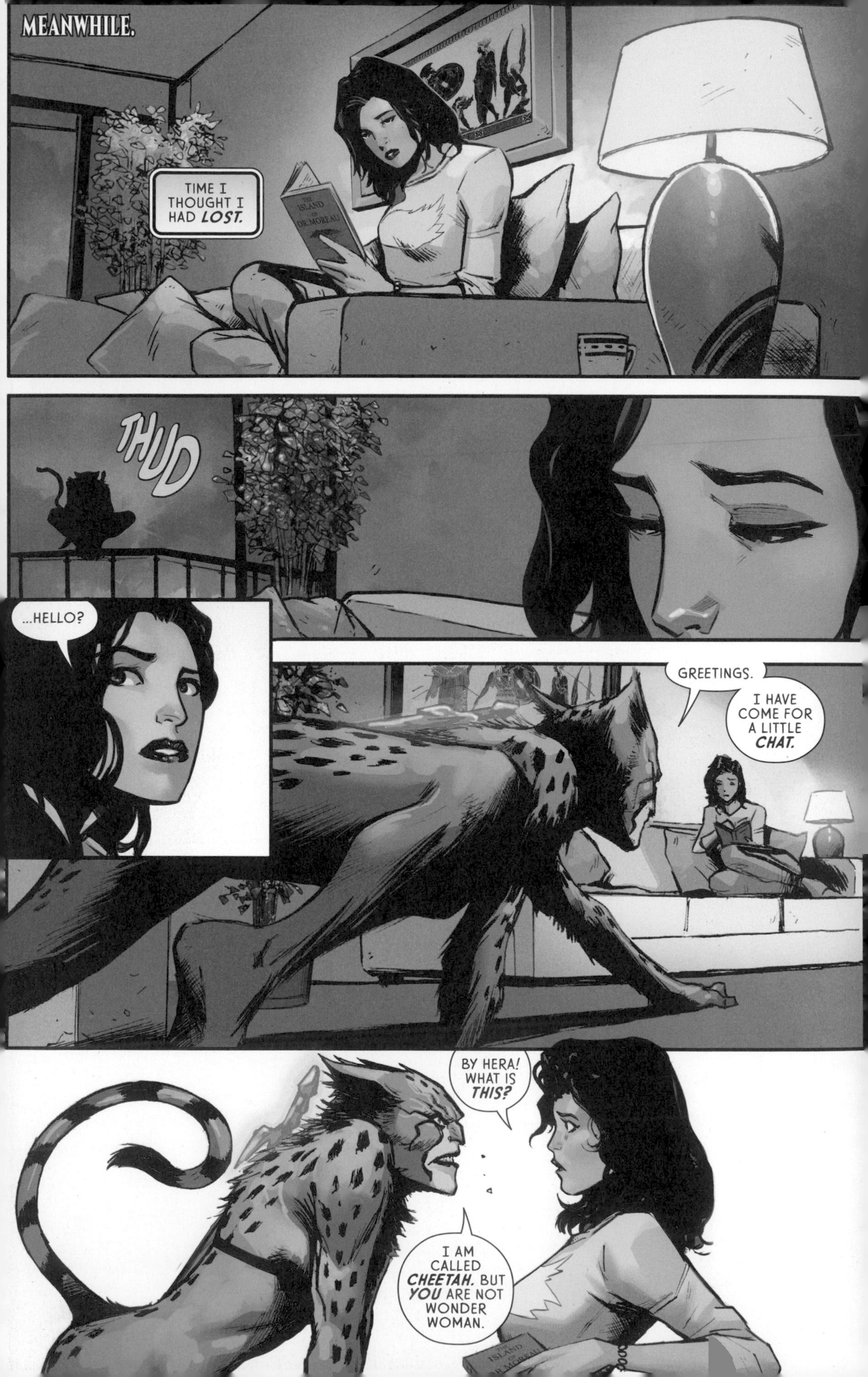
MEANWHILE.
TIME I THOUGHT I HAD *LOST.*
THE ISLAND OF DR. MOREAU
THUD
...HELLO?
GREETINGS.
I HAVE COME FOR A LITTLE *CHAT.*
BY HERA! WHAT IS *THIS?*
I AM CALLED *CHEETAH.* BUT *YOU* ARE NOT WONDER WOMAN.

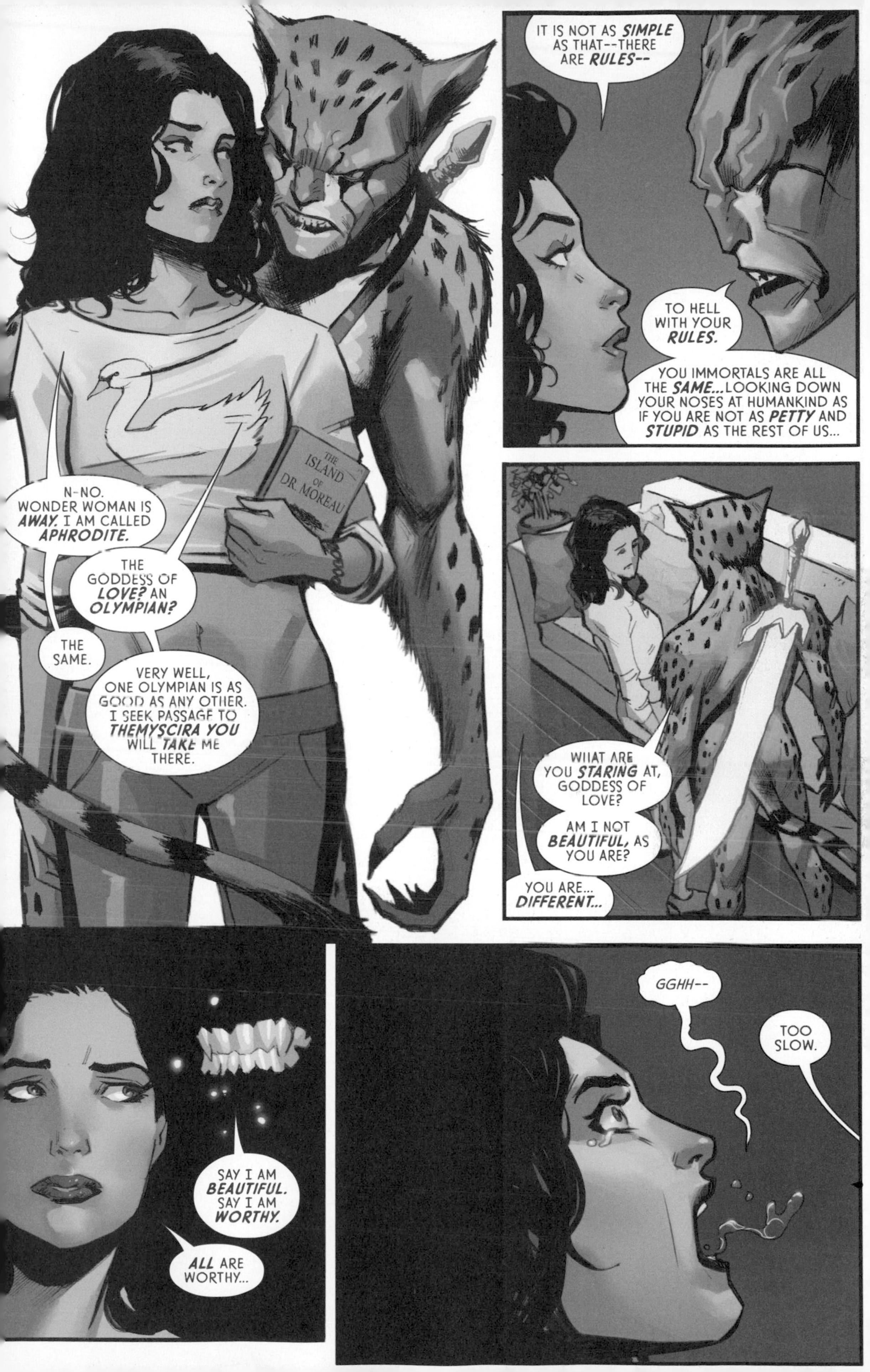

N-NO. WONDER WOMAN IS AWAY. I AM CALLED APHRODITE.
THE GODDESS OF LOVE? AN OLYMPIAN?
THE SAME.
VERY WELL, ONE OLYMPIAN IS AS GOOD AS ANY OTHER. I SEEK PASSAGE TO THEMYSCIRA YOU WILL TAKE ME THERE.
THE ISLAND OF DR. MOREAU
IT IS NOT AS SIMPLE AS THAT--THERE ARE RULES--
TO HELL WITH YOUR RULES.
YOU IMMORTALS ARE ALL THE SAME...LOOKING DOWN YOUR NOSES AT HUMANKIND AS IF YOU ARE NOT AS PETTY AND STUPID AS THE REST OF US...
WHAT ARE YOU STARING AT, GODDESS OF LOVE?
AM I NOT BEAUTIFUL, AS YOU ARE?
YOU ARE... DIFFERENT...
SAY I AM BEAUTIFUL. SAY I AM WORTHY.
ALL ARE WORTHY...
GGHH--
TOO SLOW.

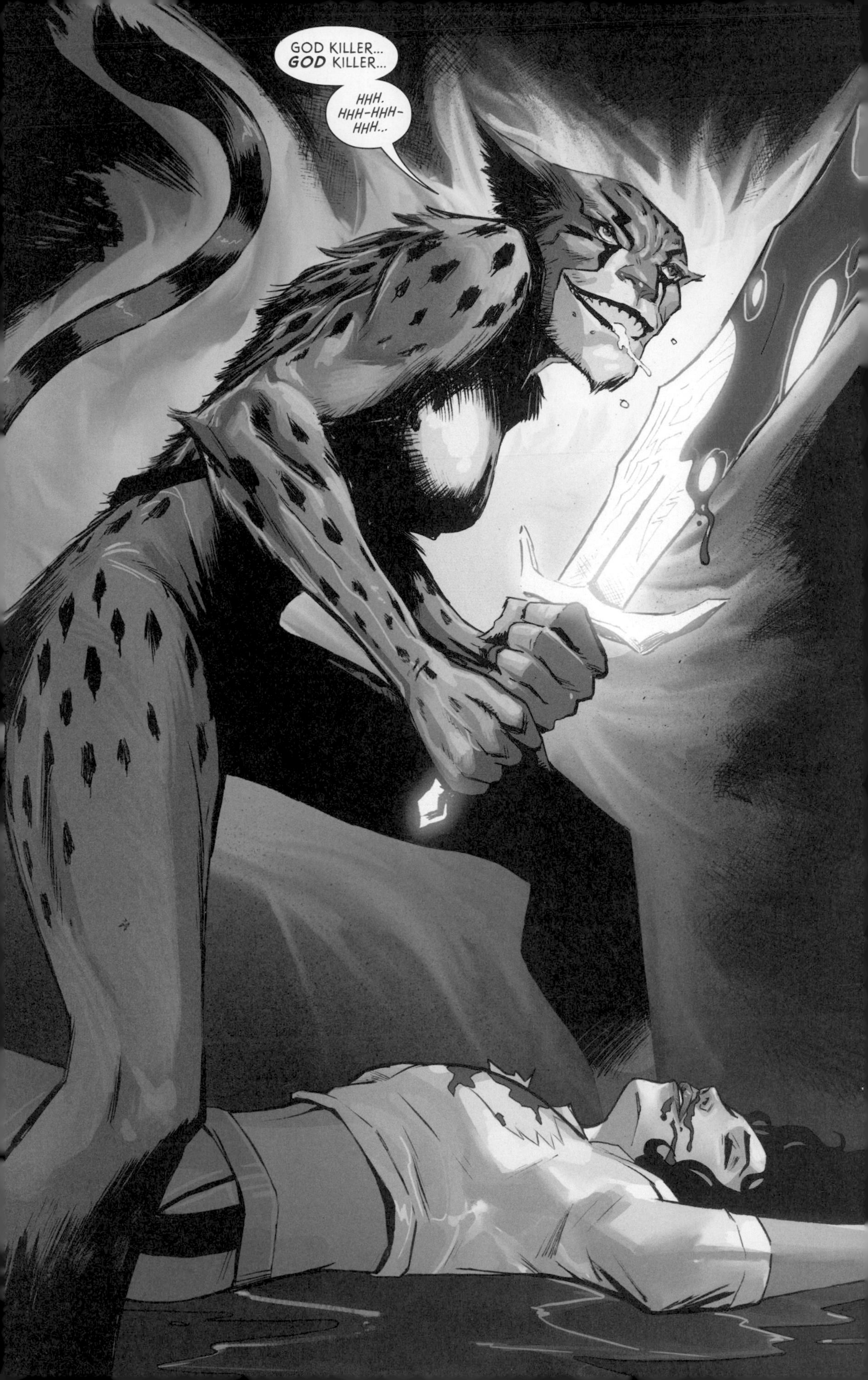
GOD KILLER... GOD KILLER...
HHH. HHH-HHH-HHH...

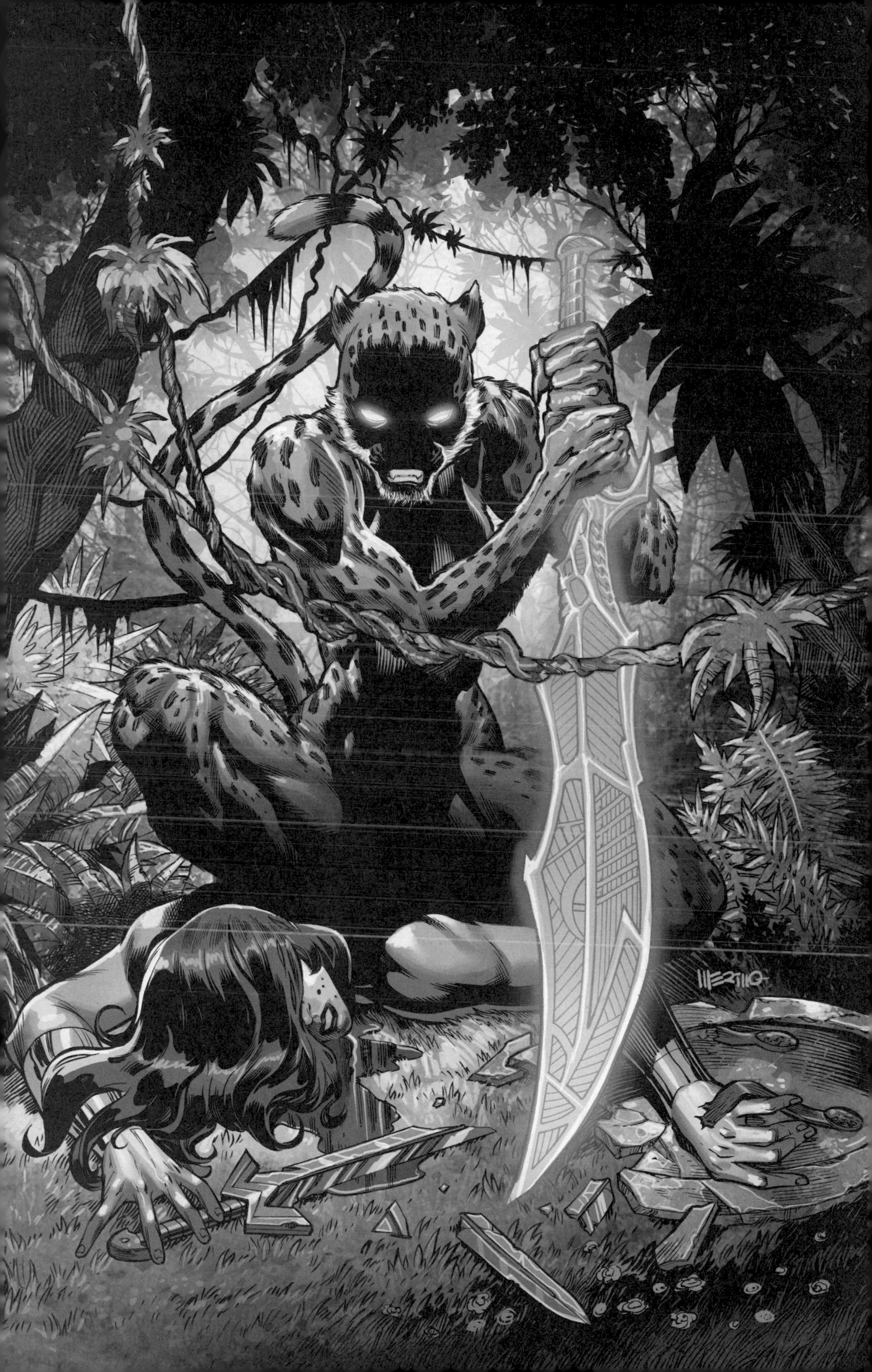

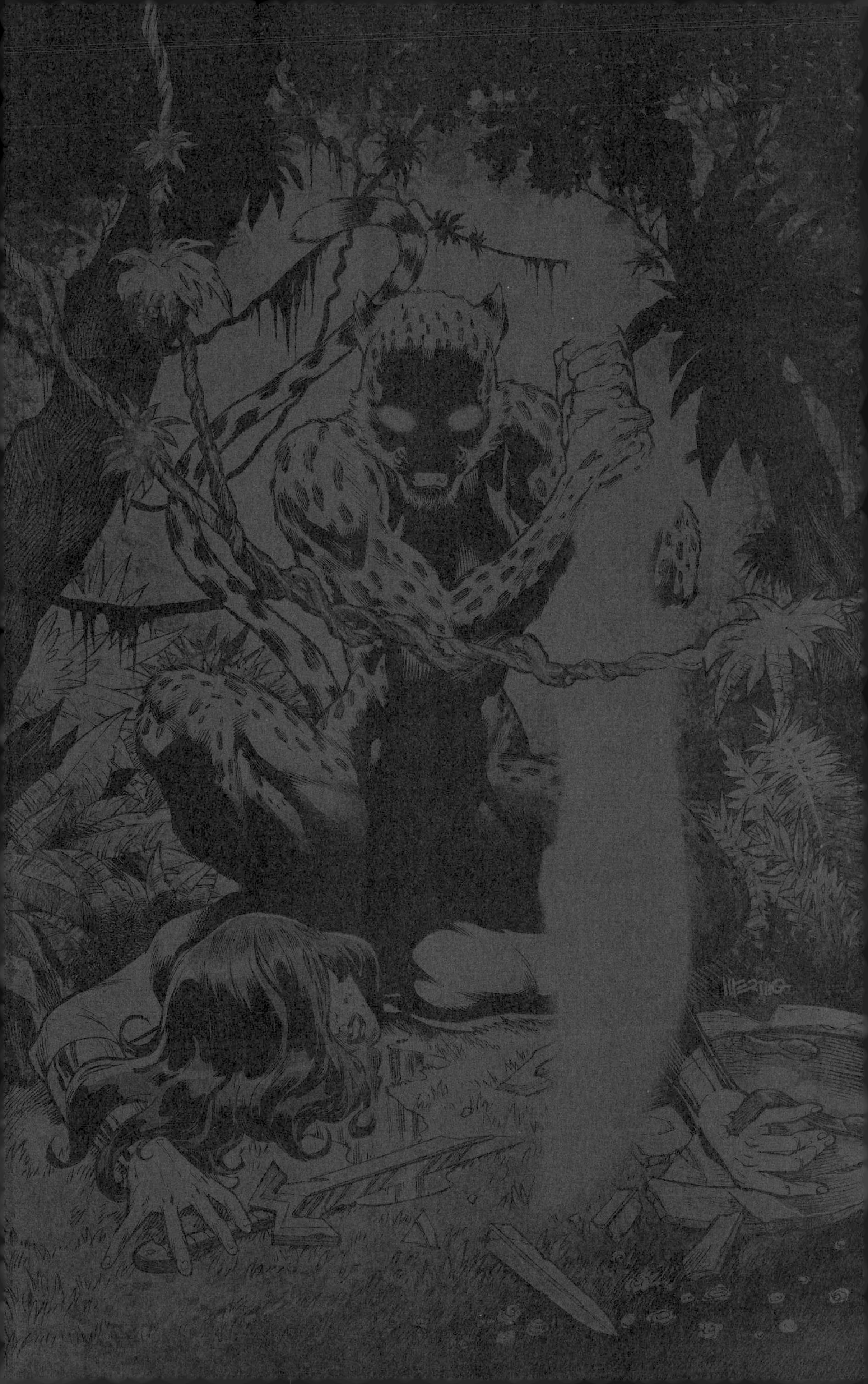

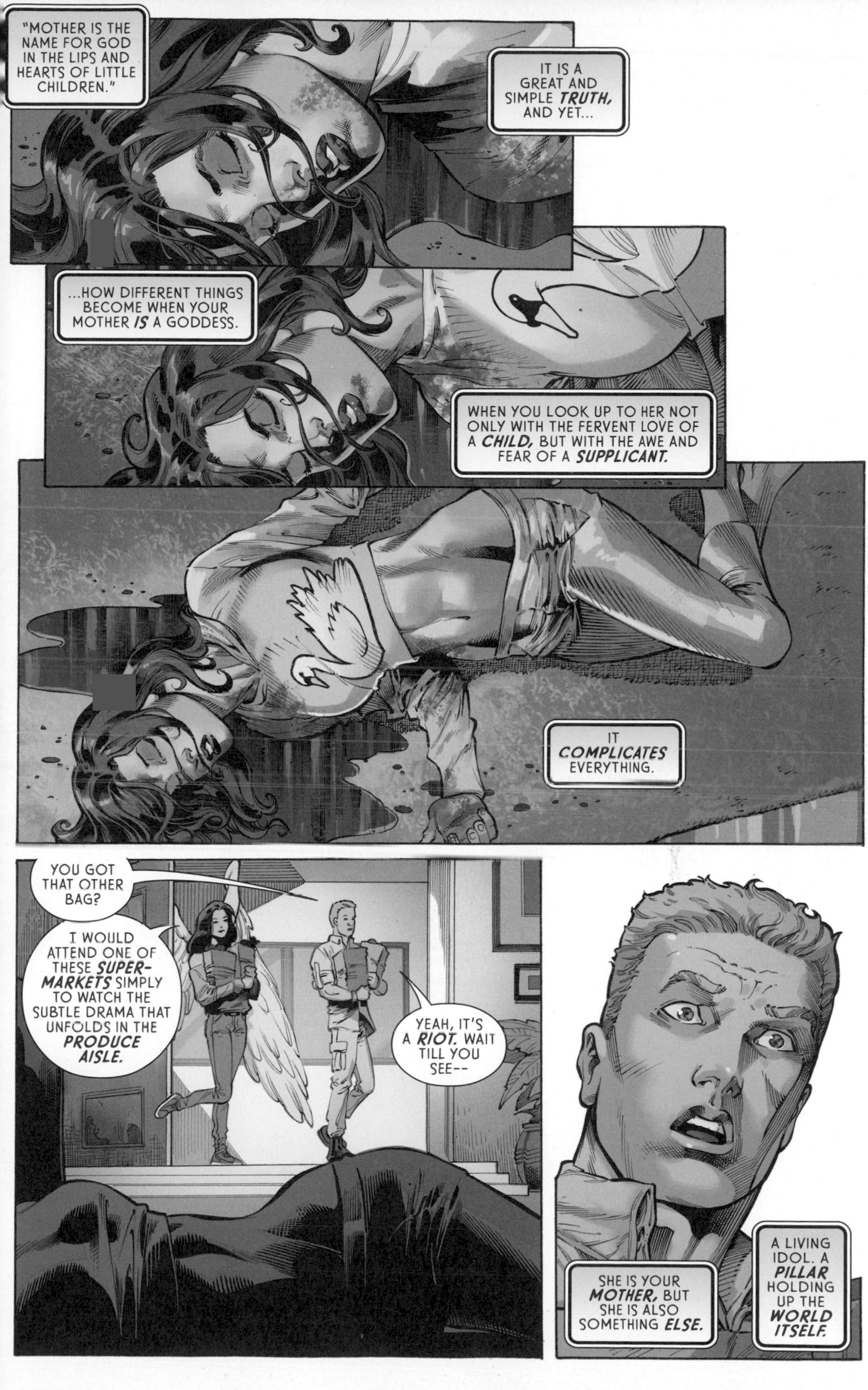
"MOTHER IS THE NAME FOR GOD IN THE LIPS AND HEARTS OF LITTLE CHILDREN."
IT IS A GREAT AND SIMPLE TRUTH, AND YET...
...HOW DIFFERENT THINGS BECOME WHEN YOUR MOTHER IS A GODDESS.
WHEN YOU LOOK UP TO HER NOT ONLY WITH THE FERVENT LOVE OF A CHILD, BUT WITH THE AWE AND FEAR OF A SUPPLICANT.
IT COMPLICATES EVERYTHING.
YOU GOT THAT OTHER BAG?
I WOULD ATTEND ONE OF THESE SUPER-MARKETS SIMPLY TO WATCH THE SUBTLE DRAMA THAT UNFOLDS IN THE PRODUCE AISLE.
YEAH, IT'S A RIOT. WAIT TILL YOU SEE--
SHE IS YOUR MOTHER, BUT SHE IS ALSO SOMETHING ELSE.
A LIVING IDOL. A PILLAR HOLDING UP THE WORLD ITSELF.

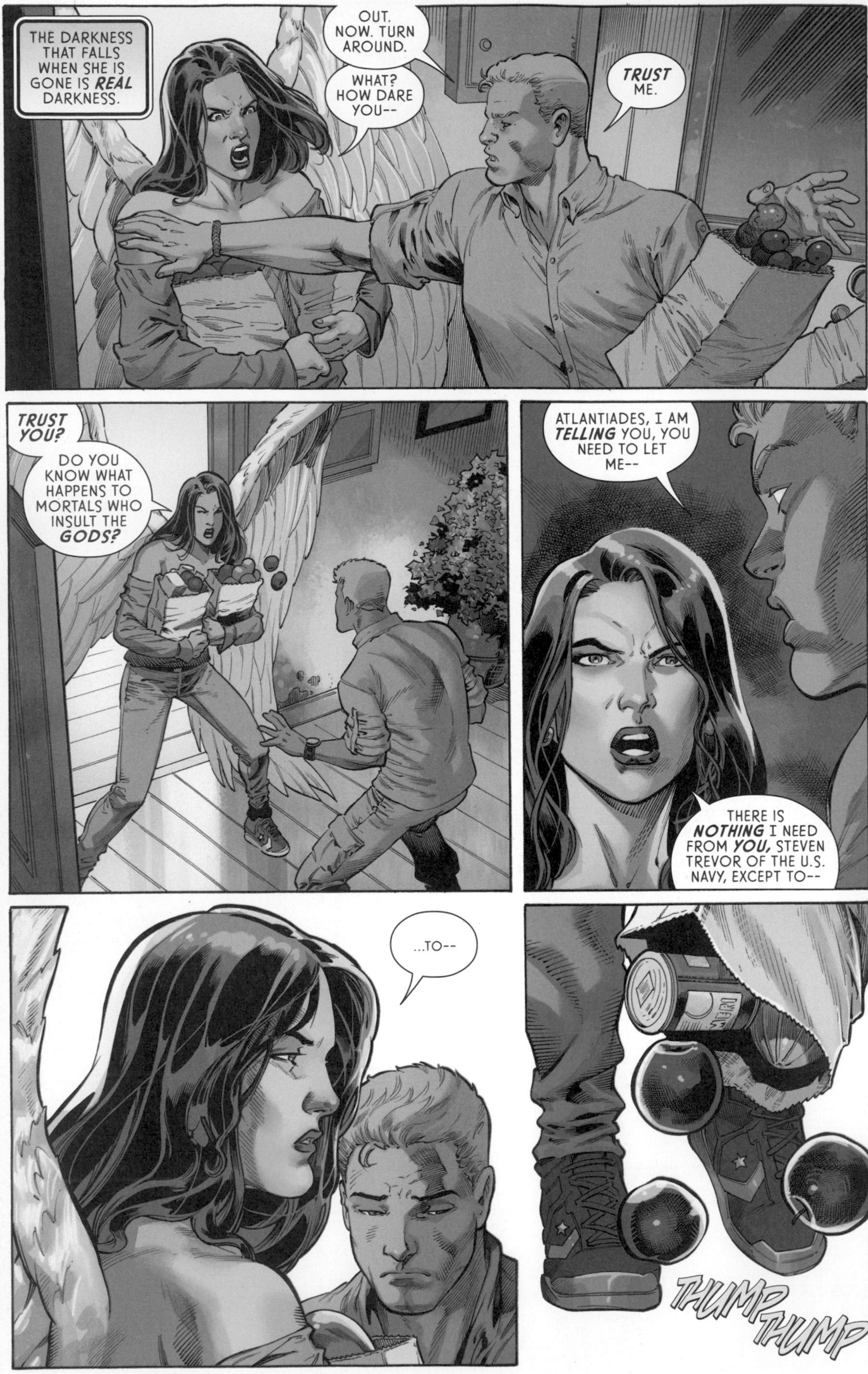
THE DARKNESS THAT FALLS WHEN SHE IS GONE IS *REAL* DARKNESS.
OUT. NOW. TURN AROUND.
WHAT? HOW DARE YOU--
TRUST ME.
TRUST YOU?
DO YOU KNOW WHAT HAPPENS TO MORTALS WHO INSULT THE *GODS?*
ATLANTIADES, I AM *TELLING* YOU, YOU NEED TO LET ME--
THERE IS *NOTHING* I NEED FROM *YOU,* STEVEN TREVOR OF THE U.S. NAVY, EXCEPT TO--
...TO--
THUMP THUMP

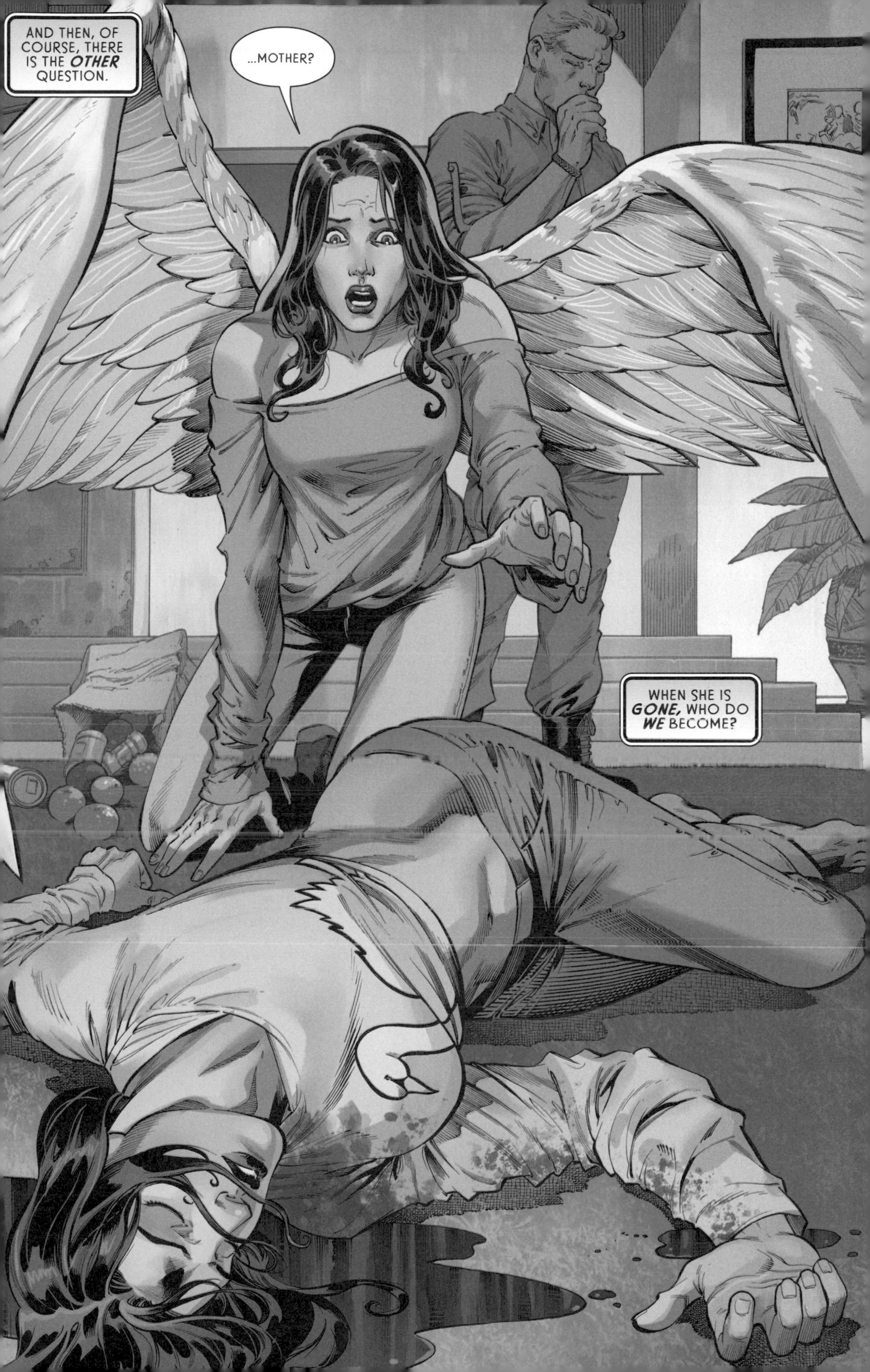
AND THEN, OF COURSE, THERE IS THE OTHER QUESTION.
...MOTHER?
WHEN SHE IS GONE, WHO DO WE BECOME?

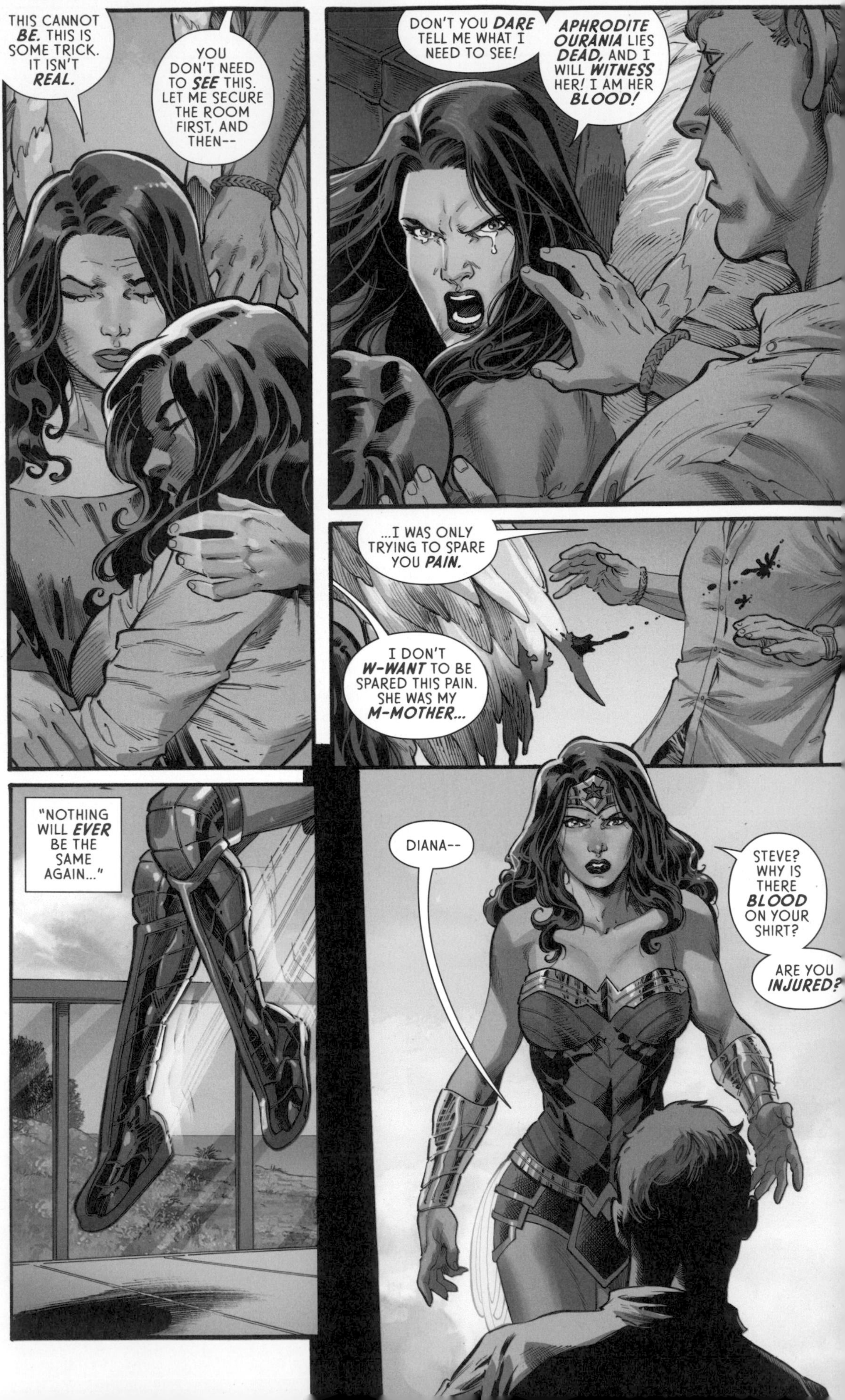

THIS CANNOT BE. THIS IS SOME TRICK. IT ISN'T REAL.
YOU DON'T NEED TO SEE THIS. LET ME SECURE THE ROOM FIRST, AND THEN--
DON'T YOU DARE TELL ME WHAT I NEED TO SEE!
APHRODITE OURANIA LIES DEAD, AND I WILL WITNESS HER! I AM HER BLOOD!
...I WAS ONLY TRYING TO SPARE YOU PAIN.
I DON'T W-WANT TO BE SPARED THIS PAIN. SHE WAS MY M-MOTHER...
"NOTHING WILL EVER BE THE SAME AGAIN..."
DIANA--
STEVE? WHY IS THERE BLOOD ON YOUR SHIRT?
ARE YOU INJURED?

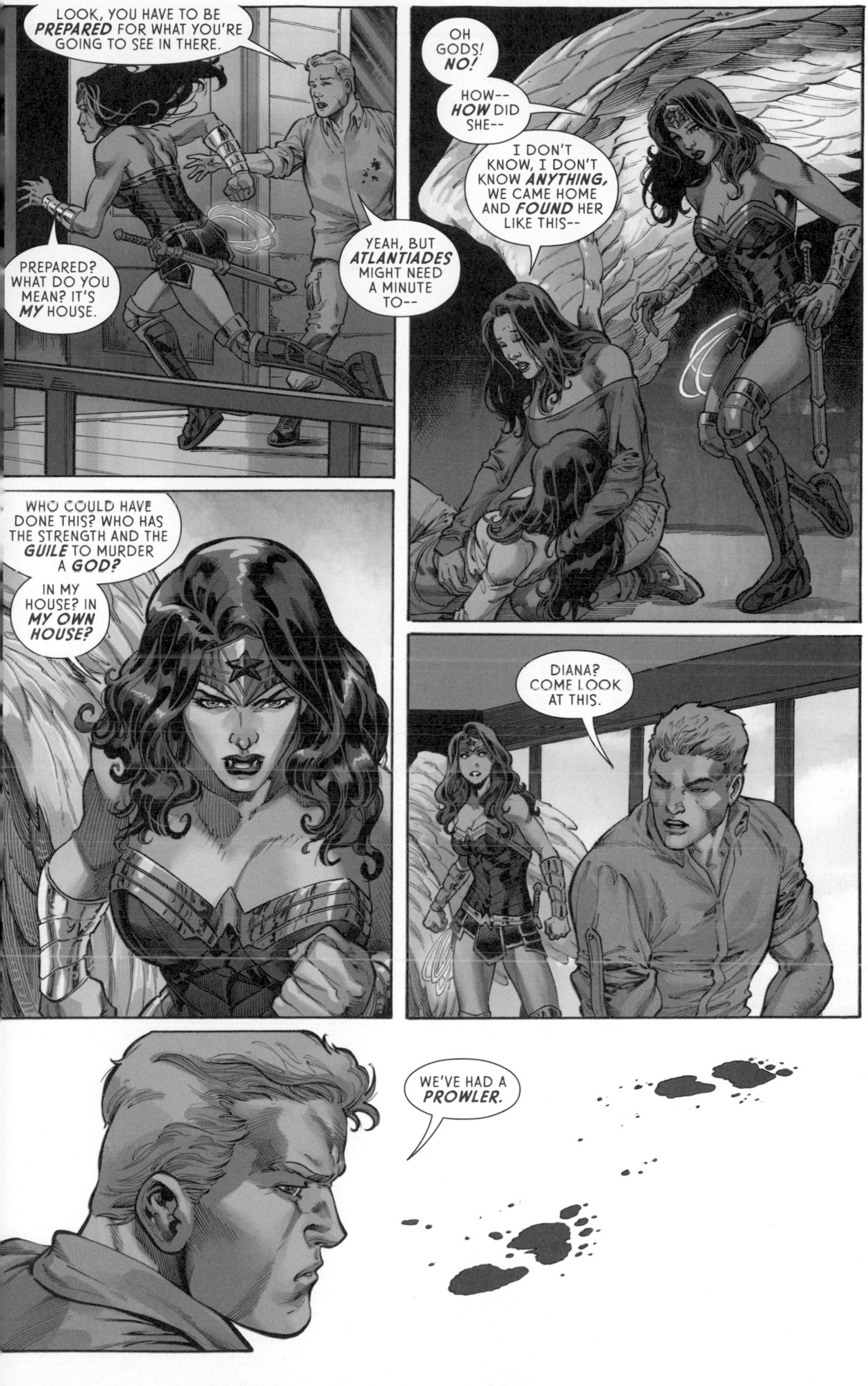
LOOK, YOU HAVE TO BE PREPARED FOR WHAT YOU'RE GOING TO SEE IN THERE.
PREPARED? WHAT DO YOU MEAN? IT'S MY HOUSE.
YEAH, BUT ATLANTIADES MIGHT NEED A MINUTE TO--
OH GODS! NO!
HOW-- HOW DID SHE--
I DON'T KNOW, I DON'T KNOW ANYTHING, WE CAME HOME AND FOUND HER LIKE THIS--
WHO COULD HAVE DONE THIS? WHO HAS THE STRENGTH AND THE GUILE TO MURDER A GOD?
IN MY HOUSE? IN MY OWN HOUSE?
DIANA? COME LOOK AT THIS.
WE'VE HAD A PROWLER.

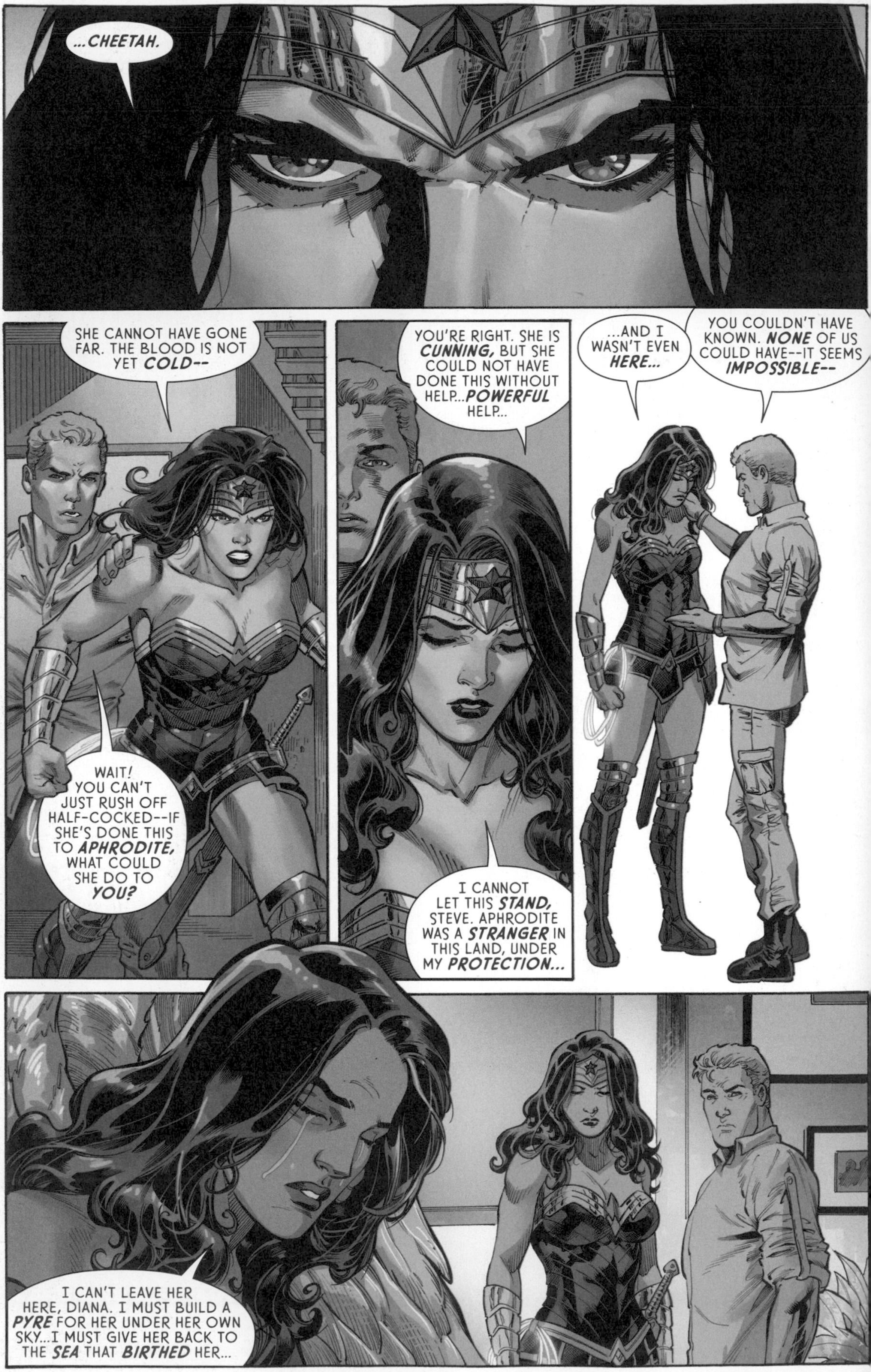
...CHEETAH.
SHE CANNOT HAVE GONE FAR. THE BLOOD IS NOT YET COLD--
WAIT! YOU CAN'T JUST RUSH OFF HALF-COCKED--IF SHE'S DONE THIS TO APHRODITE, WHAT COULD SHE DO TO YOU?
YOU'RE RIGHT. SHE IS CUNNING, BUT SHE COULD NOT HAVE DONE THIS WITHOUT HELP...POWERFUL HELP...
I CANNOT LET THIS STAND, STEVE. APHRODITE WAS A STRANGER IN THIS LAND, UNDER MY PROTECTION...
...AND I WASN'T EVEN HERE...
YOU COULDN'T HAVE KNOWN. NONE OF US COULD HAVE--IT SEEMS IMPOSSIBLE--
I CAN'T LEAVE HER HERE, DIANA. I MUST BUILD A PYRE FOR HER UNDER HER OWN SKY...I MUST GIVE HER BACK TO THE SEA THAT BIRTHED HER...

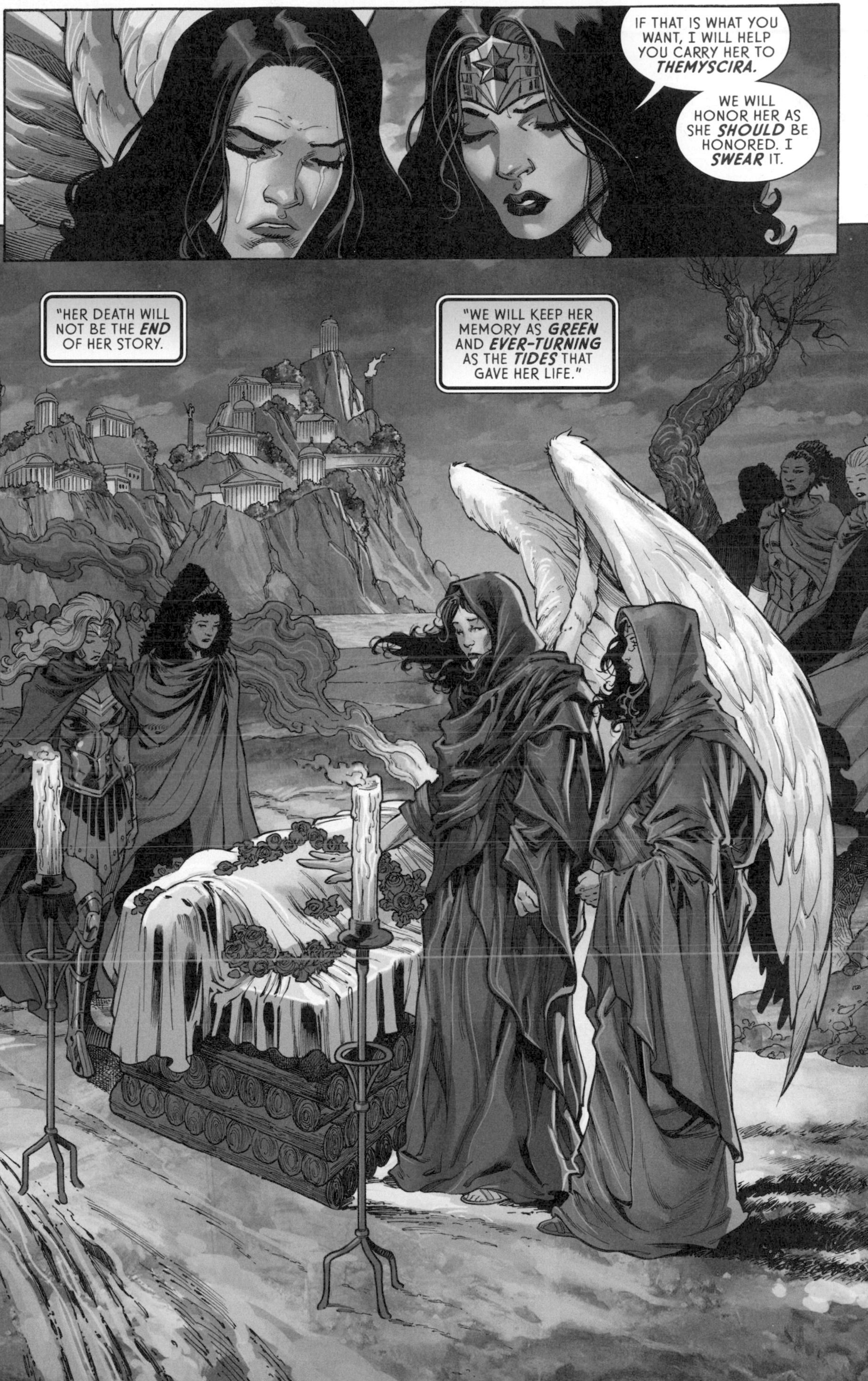

IF THAT IS WHAT YOU WANT, I WILL HELP YOU CARRY HER TO THEMYSCIRA.
WE WILL HONOR HER AS SHE SHOULD BE HONORED. I SWEAR IT.
"HER DEATH WILL NOT BE THE END OF HER STORY.
"WE WILL KEEP HER MEMORY AS GREEN AND EVER-TURNING AS THE TIDES THAT GAVE HER LIFE."

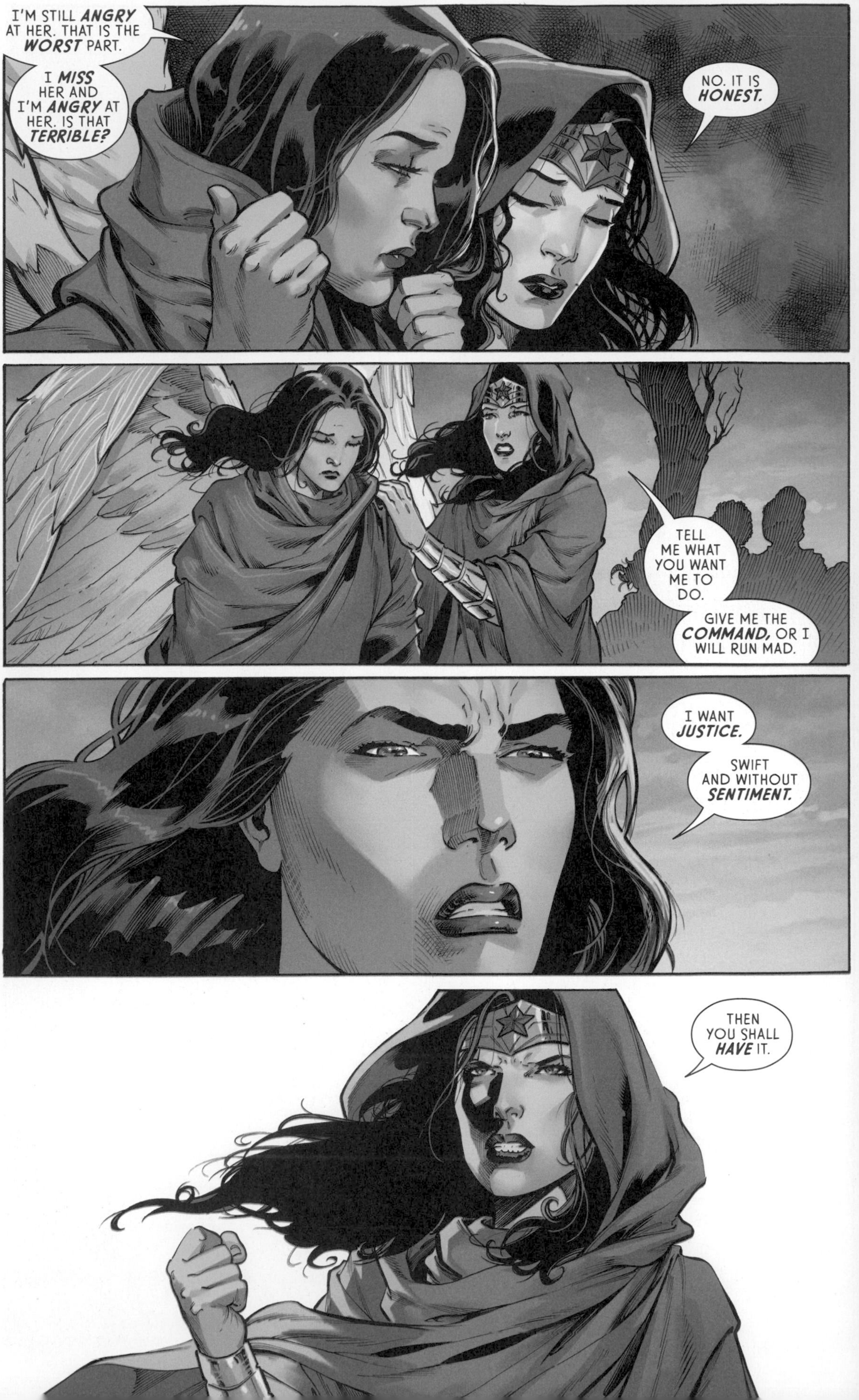
I'M STILL ANGRY AT HER. THAT IS THE WORST PART.
I MISS HER AND I'M ANGRY AT HER. IS THAT TERRIBLE?
NO. IT IS HONEST.
TELL ME WHAT YOU WANT ME TO DO.
GIVE ME THE COMMAND, OR I WILL RUN MAD.
I WANT JUSTICE.
SWIFT AND WITHOUT SENTIMENT.
THEN YOU SHALL HAVE IT.

I DO NOT SPARE A SINGLE MOMENT.

I AM *DIANA OF THE HUNT* NOW.

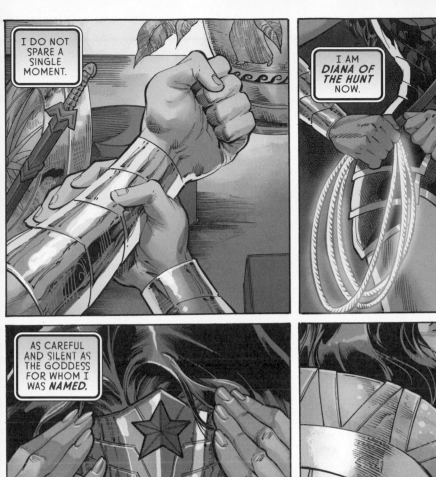

AS CAREFUL AND SILENT AS THE GODDESS FOR WHOM I WAS *NAMED.*

AND LIKE HER, I SEE ONLY MY *QUARRY.*

YOU JUST GOT BACK AND NOW YOU'RE *LEAVING* AGAIN?

CHEETAH'S TRAIL IS ALREADY GOING *COLD.* I MUST MOVE *QUICKLY.*

CAN I ASK YOU A QUESTION?

YES, IF IT'S *BRIEF.*

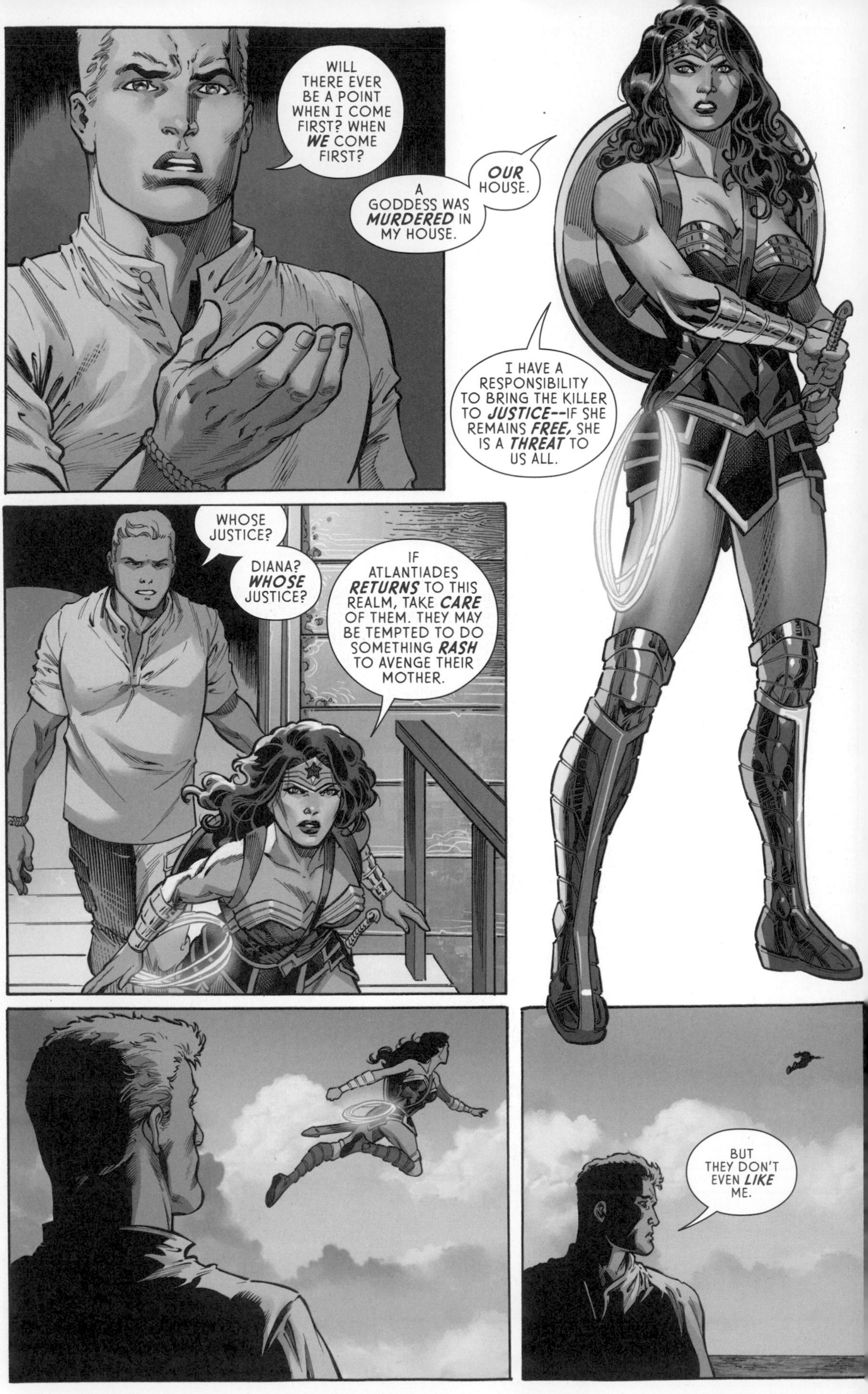
WILL THERE EVER BE A POINT WHEN I COME FIRST? WHEN ***WE*** COME FIRST?
A GODDESS WAS ***MURDERED*** IN MY HOUSE.
OUR HOUSE.
I HAVE A RESPONSIBILITY TO BRING THE KILLER TO ***JUSTICE--***IF SHE REMAINS ***FREE,*** SHE IS A ***THREAT*** TO US ALL.
WHOSE JUSTICE?
DIANA? ***WHOSE*** JUSTICE?
IF ATLANTIADES ***RETURNS*** TO THIS REALM, TAKE ***CARE*** OF THEM. THEY MAY BE TEMPTED TO DO SOMETHING ***RASH*** TO AVENGE THEIR MOTHER.
BUT THEY DON'T EVEN ***LIKE*** ME.

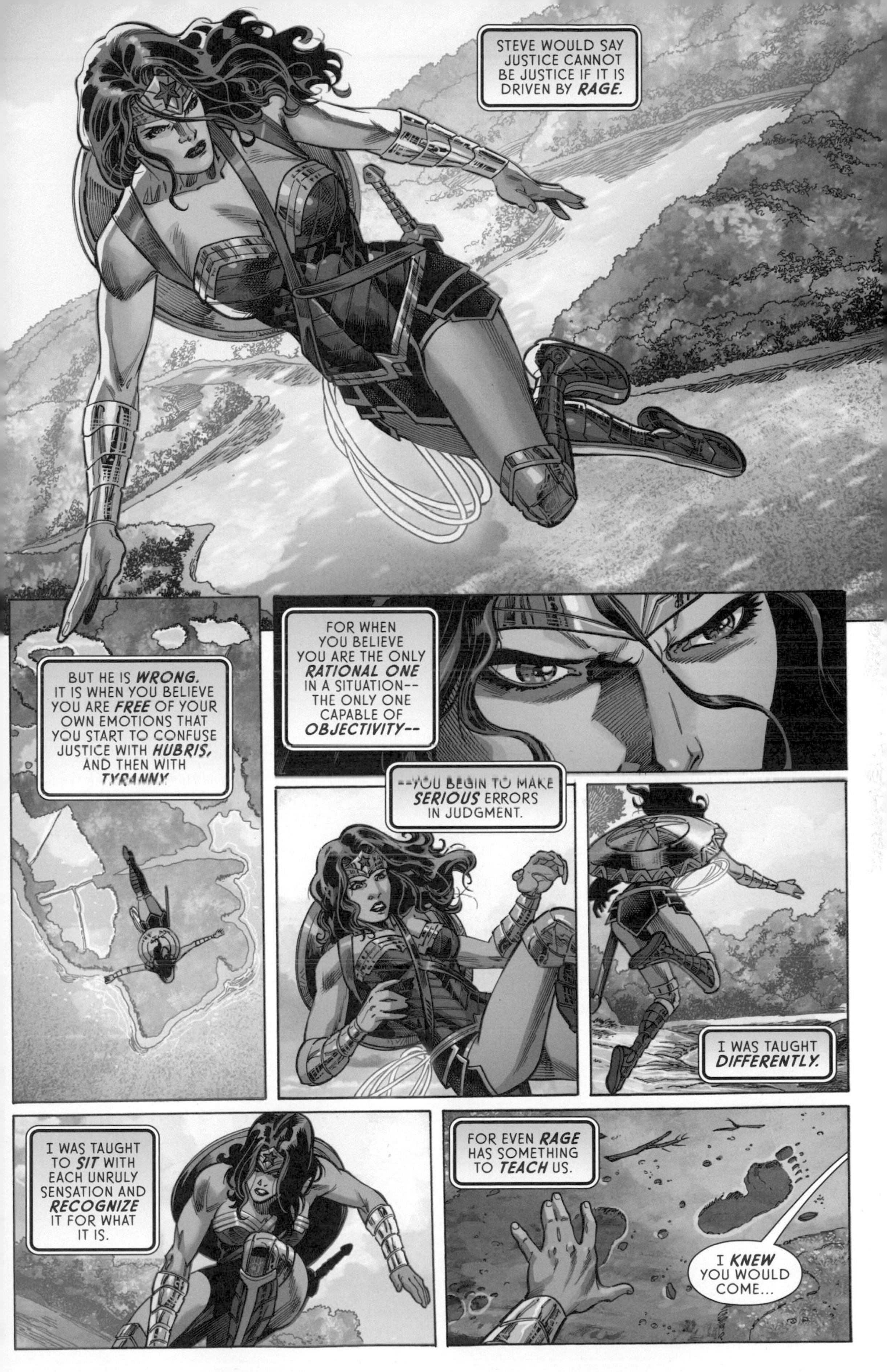
STEVE WOULD SAY JUSTICE CANNOT BE JUSTICE IF IT IS DRIVEN BY RAGE.
BUT HE IS WRONG. IT IS WHEN YOU BELIEVE YOU ARE FREE OF YOUR OWN EMOTIONS THAT YOU START TO CONFUSE JUSTICE WITH HUBRIS, AND THEN WITH TYRANNY.
FOR WHEN YOU BELIEVE YOU ARE THE ONLY RATIONAL ONE IN A SITUATION-- THE ONLY ONE CAPABLE OF OBJECTIVITY--
--YOU BEGIN TO MAKE SERIOUS ERRORS IN JUDGMENT.
I WAS TAUGHT DIFFERENTLY.
I WAS TAUGHT TO SIT WITH EACH UNRULY SENSATION AND RECOGNIZE IT FOR WHAT IT IS.
FOR EVEN RAGE HAS SOMETHING TO TEACH US.
I KNEW YOU WOULD COME...

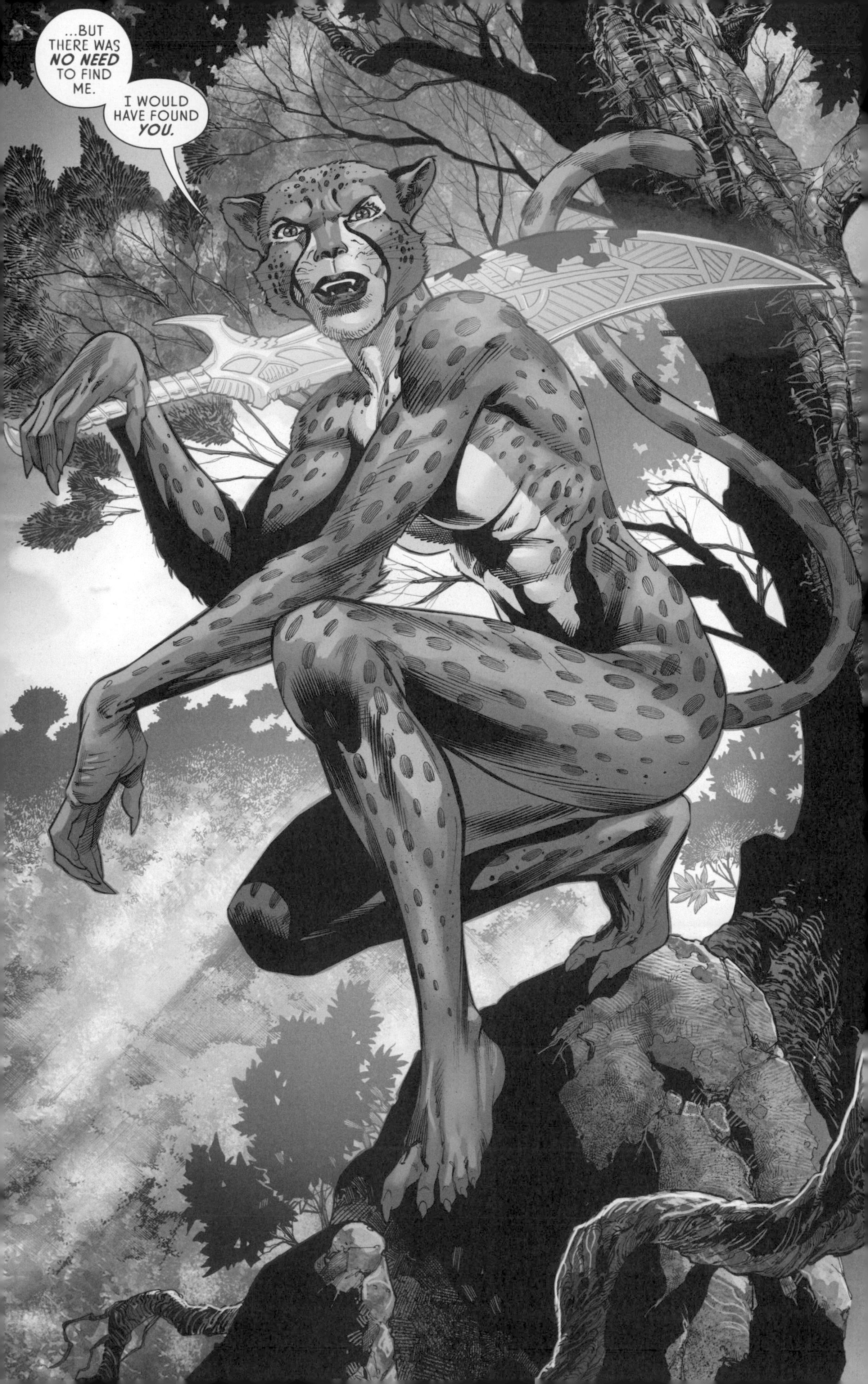
...BUT THERE WAS **NO NEED** TO FIND ME.
I WOULD HAVE FOUND ***YOU.***

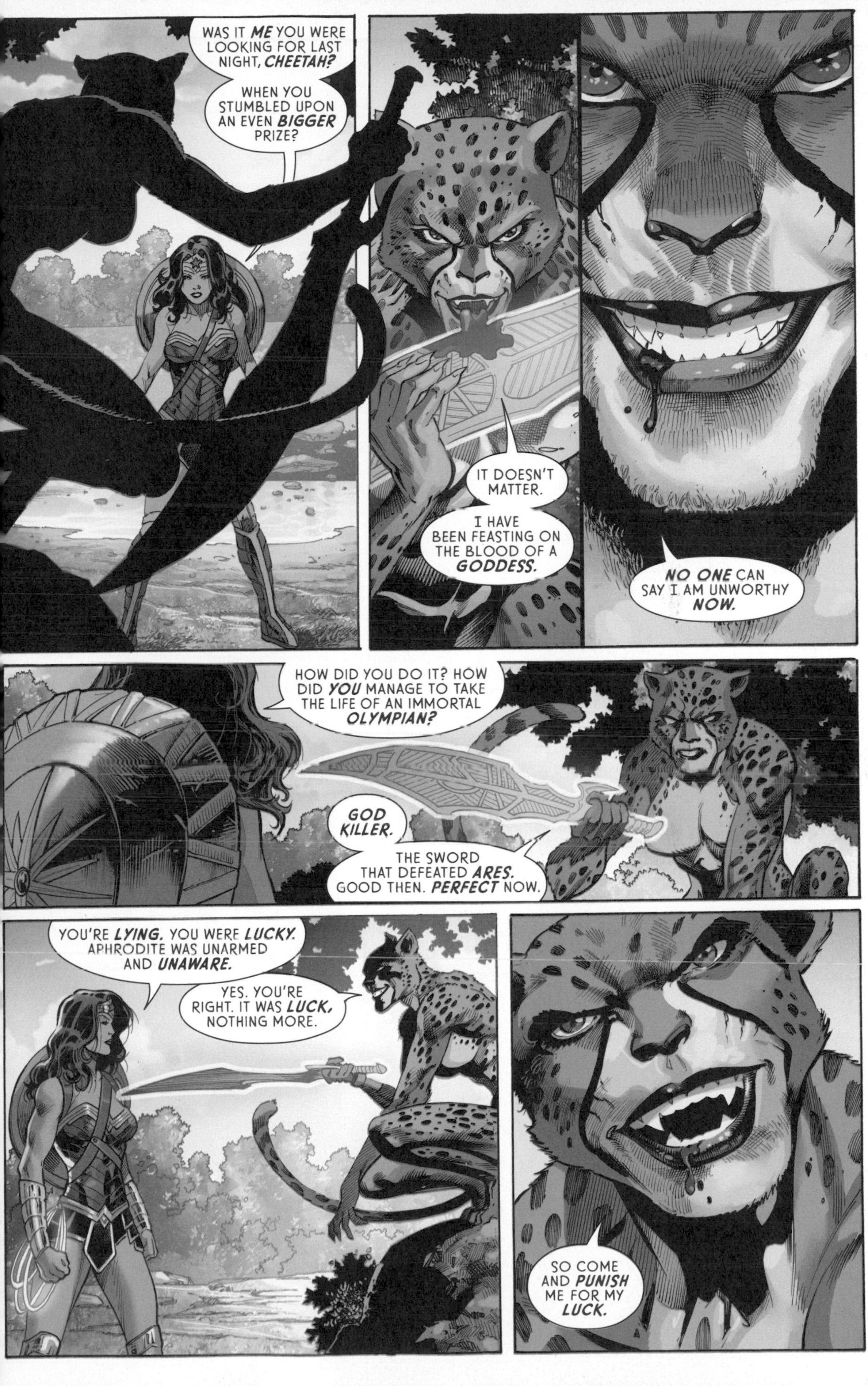
WAS IT ME YOU WERE LOOKING FOR LAST NIGHT, CHEETAH?
WHEN YOU STUMBLED UPON AN EVEN BIGGER PRIZE?
IT DOESN'T MATTER.
I HAVE BEEN FEASTING ON THE BLOOD OF A GODDESS.
NO ONE CAN SAY I AM UNWORTHY NOW.
HOW DID YOU DO IT? HOW DID YOU MANAGE TO TAKE THE LIFE OF AN IMMORTAL OLYMPIAN?
GOD KILLER.
THE SWORD THAT DEFEATED ARES. GOOD THEN. PERFECT NOW.
YOU'RE LYING. YOU WERE LUCKY. APHRODITE WAS UNARMED AND UNAWARE.
YES. YOU'RE RIGHT. IT WAS LUCK, NOTHING MORE.
SO COME AND PUNISH ME FOR MY LUCK.

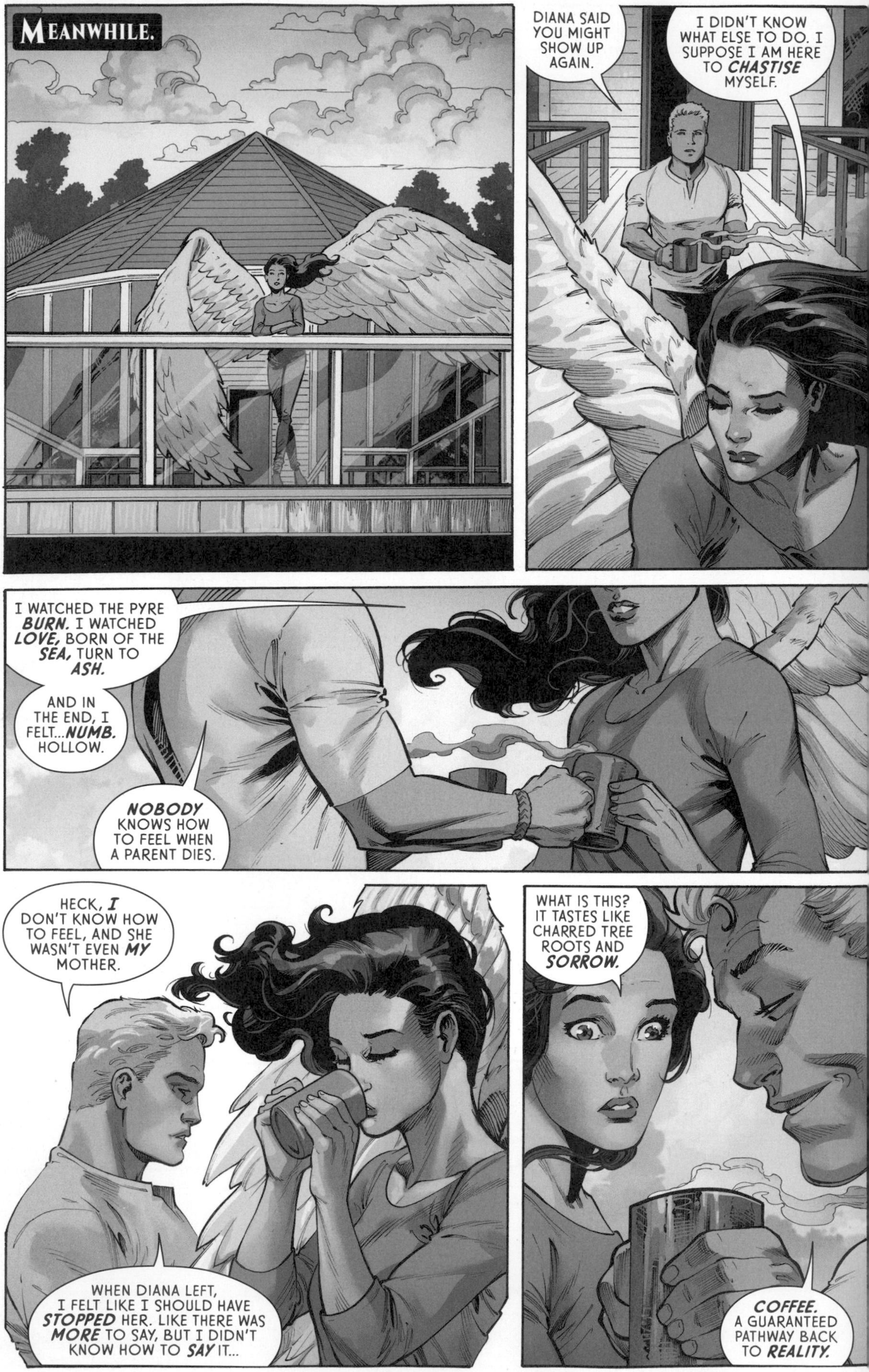
MEANWHILE.
DIANA SAID YOU MIGHT SHOW UP AGAIN.
I DIDN'T KNOW WHAT ELSE TO DO. I SUPPOSE I AM HERE TO CHASTISE MYSELF.
I WATCHED THE PYRE BURN. I WATCHED LOVE, BORN OF THE SEA, TURN TO ASH.
AND IN THE END, I FELT...NUMB. HOLLOW.
NOBODY KNOWS HOW TO FEEL WHEN A PARENT DIES.
HECK, I DON'T KNOW HOW TO FEEL, AND SHE WASN'T EVEN MY MOTHER.
WHEN DIANA LEFT, I FELT LIKE I SHOULD HAVE STOPPED HER. LIKE THERE WAS MORE TO SAY, BUT I DIDN'T KNOW HOW TO SAY IT...
WHAT IS THIS? IT TASTES LIKE CHARRED TREE ROOTS AND SORROW.
COFFEE. A GUARANTEED PATHWAY BACK TO REALITY.

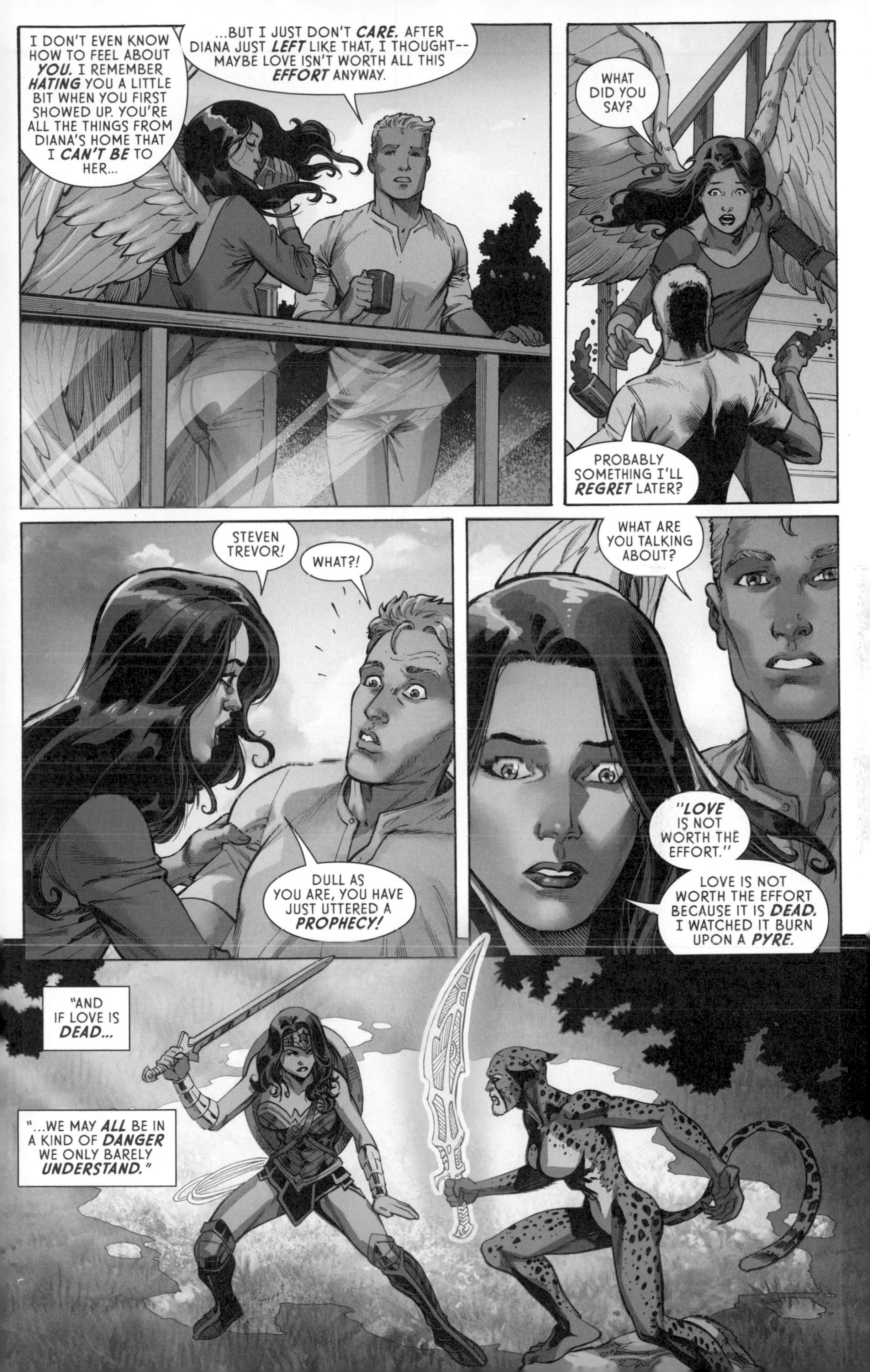
I DON'T EVEN KNOW HOW TO FEEL ABOUT YOU. I REMEMBER HATING YOU A LITTLE BIT WHEN YOU FIRST SHOWED UP. YOU'RE ALL THE THINGS FROM DIANA'S HOME THAT I CAN'T BE TO HER...
...BUT I JUST DON'T CARE. AFTER DIANA JUST LEFT LIKE THAT, I THOUGHT-- MAYBE LOVE ISN'T WORTH ALL THIS EFFORT ANYWAY.
WHAT DID YOU SAY?
PROBABLY SOMETHING I'LL REGRET LATER?
STEVEN TREVOR!
WHAT?!
DULL AS YOU ARE, YOU HAVE JUST UTTERED A PROPHECY!
WHAT ARE YOU TALKING ABOUT?
"LOVE IS NOT WORTH THE EFFORT."
LOVE IS NOT WORTH THE EFFORT BECAUSE IT IS DEAD. I WATCHED IT BURN UPON A PYRE.
"AND IF LOVE IS DEAD...
"...WE MAY ALL BE IN A KIND OF DANGER WE ONLY BARELY UNDERSTAND."

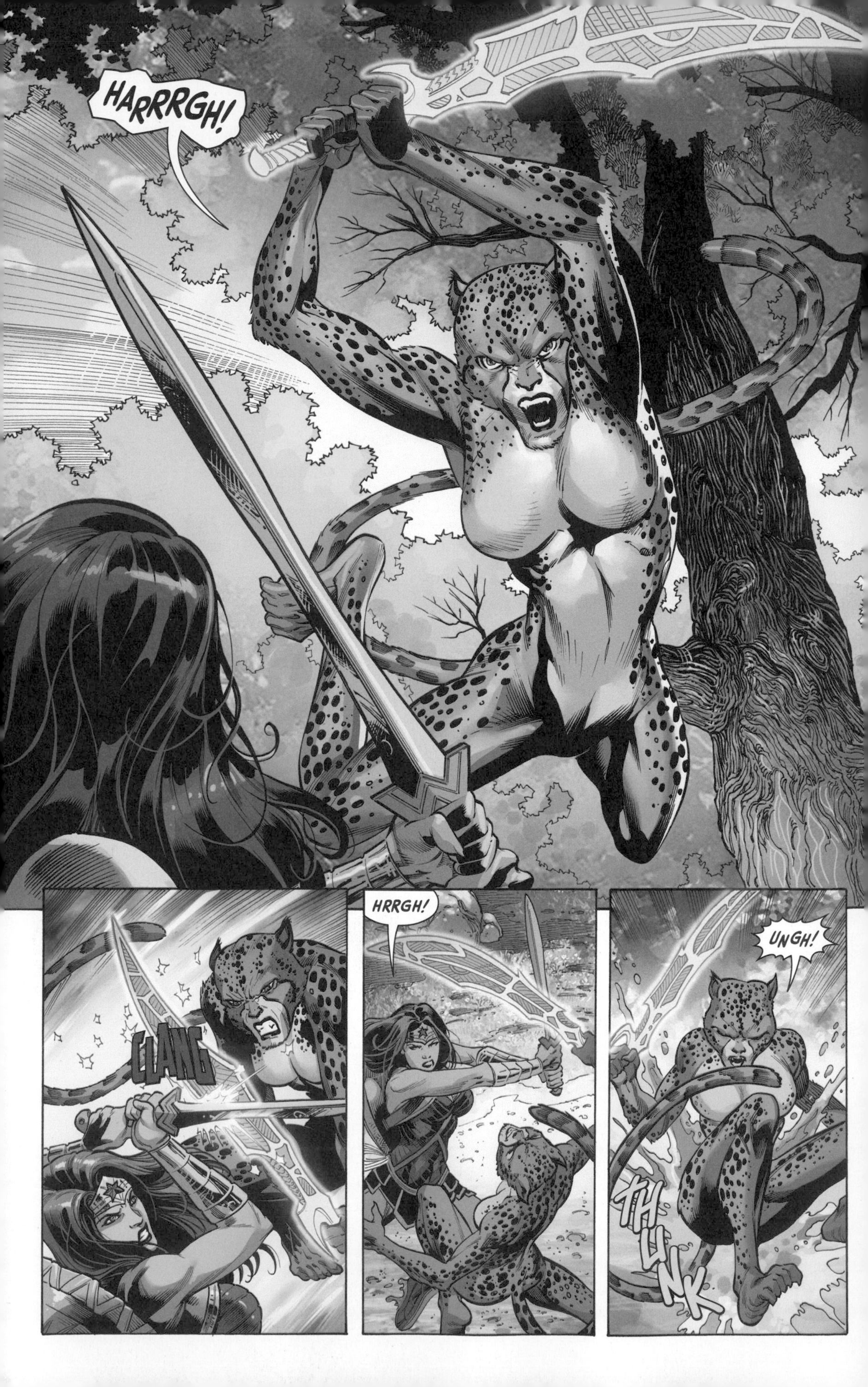
HARRRGH!
CLANG
HRRGH!
UNGH!
THUNK

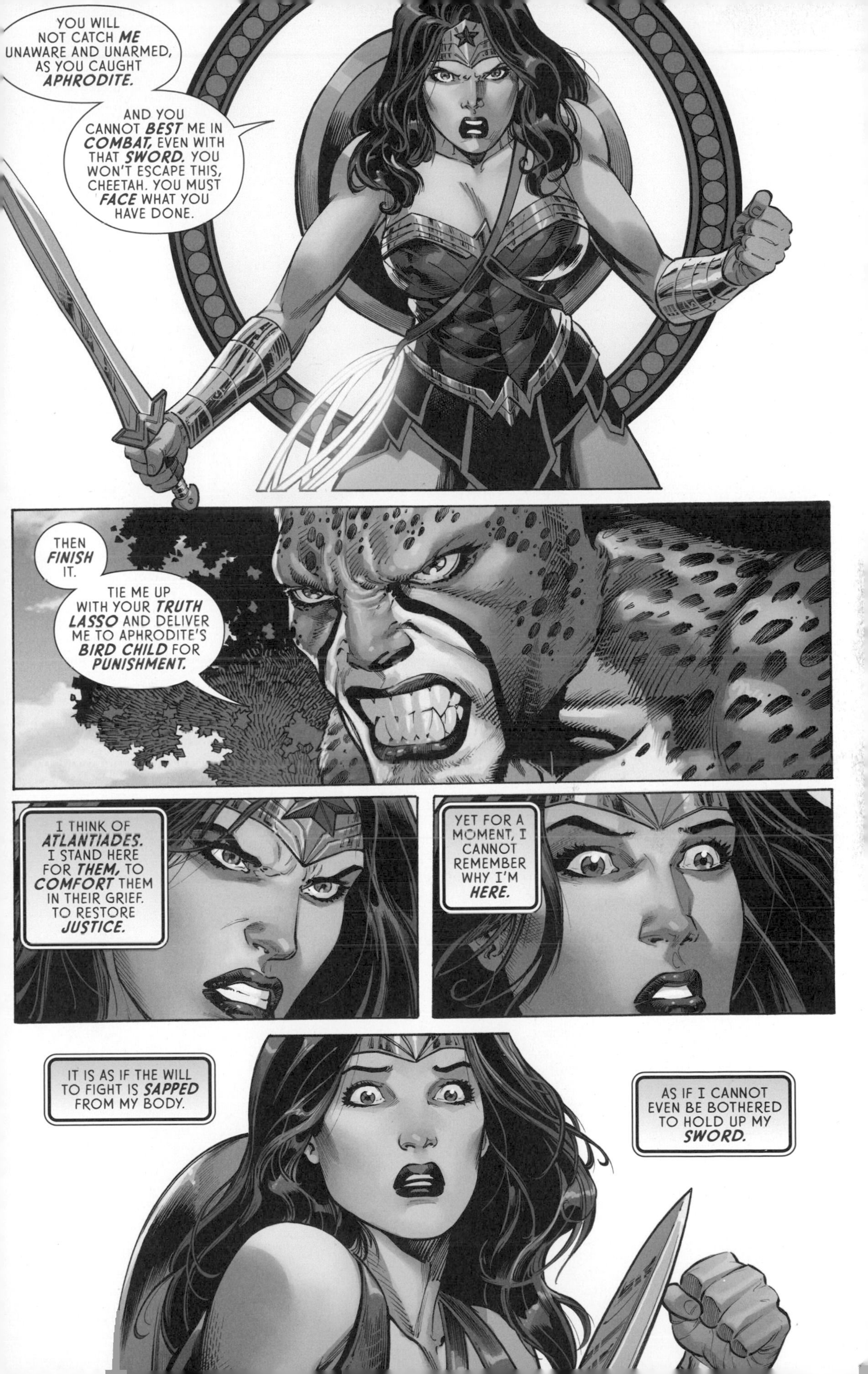
YOU WILL NOT CATCH ME UNAWARE AND UNARMED, AS YOU CAUGHT APHRODITE.
AND YOU CANNOT BEST ME IN COMBAT, EVEN WITH THAT SWORD. YOU WON'T ESCAPE THIS, CHEETAH. YOU MUST FACE WHAT YOU HAVE DONE.
THEN FINISH IT.
TIE ME UP WITH YOUR TRUTH LASSO AND DELIVER ME TO APHRODITE'S BIRD CHILD FOR PUNISHMENT.
I THINK OF ATLANTIADES. I STAND HERE FOR THEM, TO COMFORT THEM IN THEIR GRIEF. TO RESTORE JUSTICE.
YET FOR A MOMENT, I CANNOT REMEMBER WHY I'M HERE.
IT IS AS IF THE WILL TO FIGHT IS SAPPED FROM MY BODY.
AS IF I CANNOT EVEN BE BOTHERED TO HOLD UP MY SWORD.

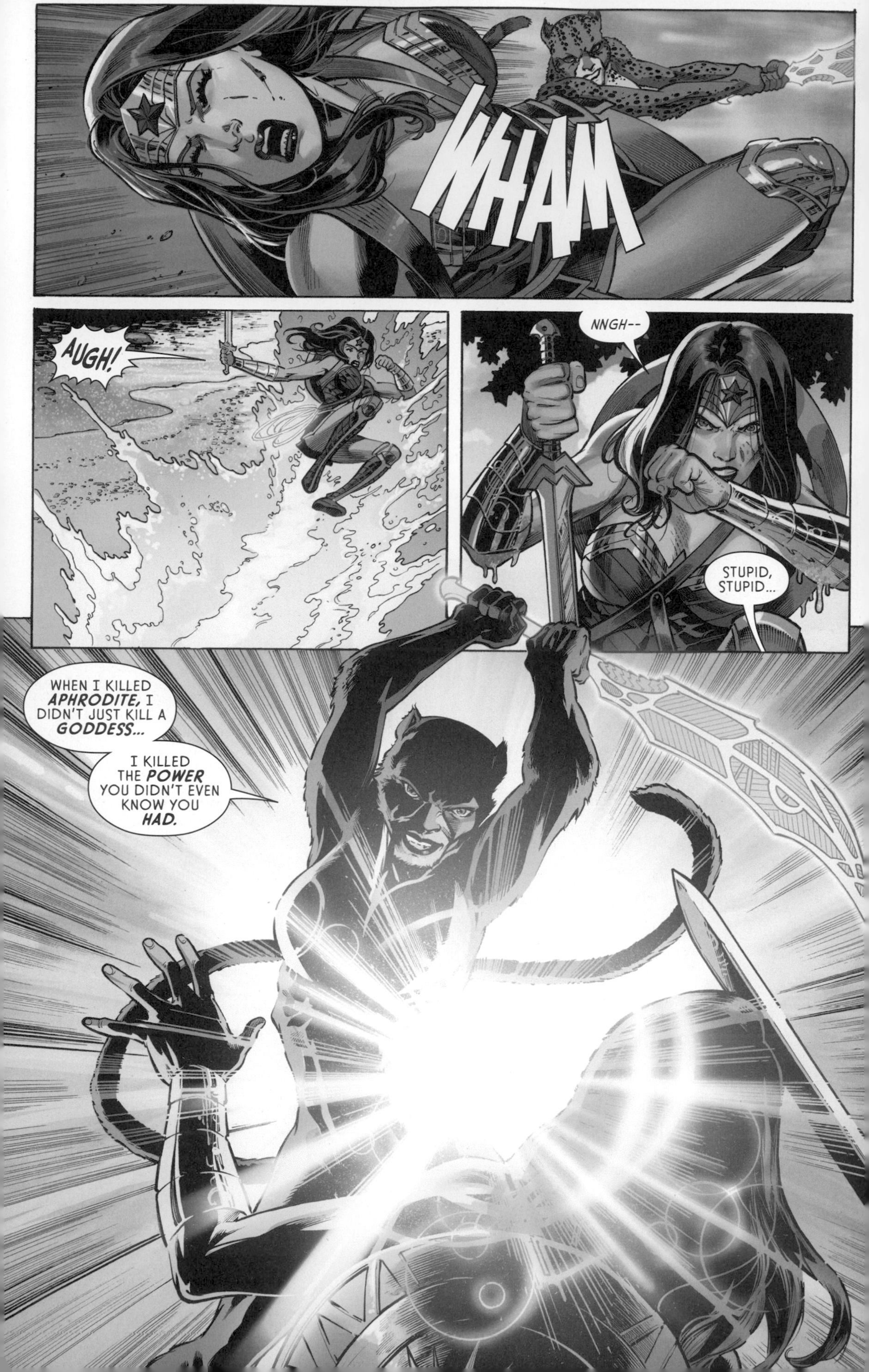
WHAM
AUGH!
NNGH--
STUPID, STUPID...
WHEN I KILLED APHRODITE, I DIDN'T JUST KILL A GODDESS...
I KILLED THE POWER YOU DIDN'T EVEN KNOW YOU HAD.

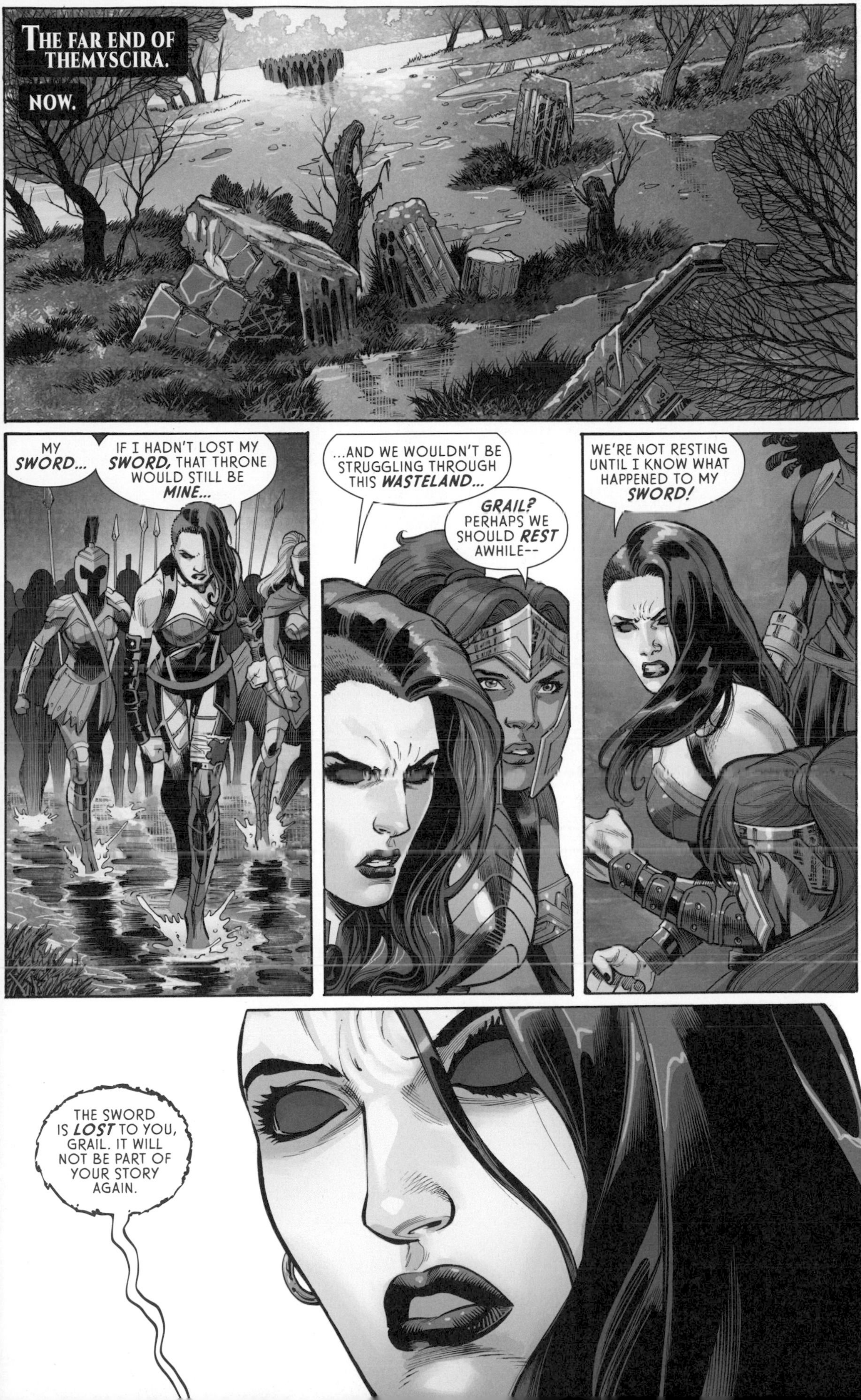
THE FAR END OF THEMYSCIRA.
NOW.
MY SWORD...
IF I HADN'T LOST MY SWORD, THAT THRONE WOULD STILL BE MINE...
...AND WE WOULDN'T BE STRUGGLING THROUGH THIS WASTELAND...
GRAIL? PERHAPS WE SHOULD REST AWHILE--
WE'RE NOT RESTING UNTIL I KNOW WHAT HAPPENED TO MY SWORD!
THE SWORD IS LOST TO YOU, GRAIL. IT WILL NOT BE PART OF YOUR STORY AGAIN.

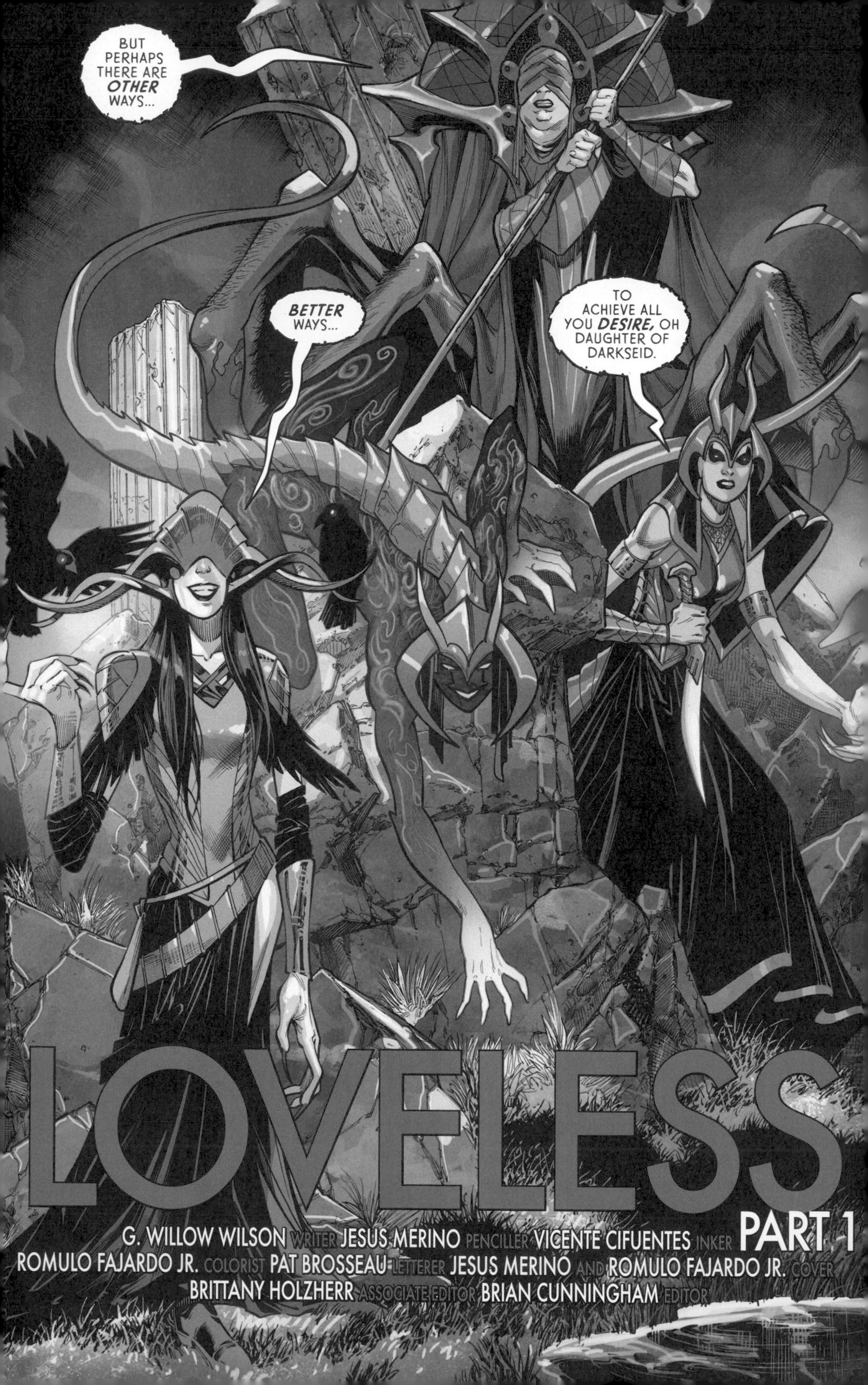
BUT PERHAPS THERE ARE OTHER WAYS...
BETTER WAYS...
TO ACHIEVE ALL YOU DESIRE, OH DAUGHTER OF DARKSEID.
LOVELESS PART 1
G. WILLOW WILSON WRITER JESUS MERINO PENCILLER VICENTE CIFUENTES INKER
ROMULO FAJARDO JR. COLORIST PAT BROSSEAU LETTERER JESUS MERINO AND ROMULO FAJARDO JR. COVER
BRITTANY HOLZHERR ASSOCIATE EDITOR BRIAN CUNNINGHAM EDITOR

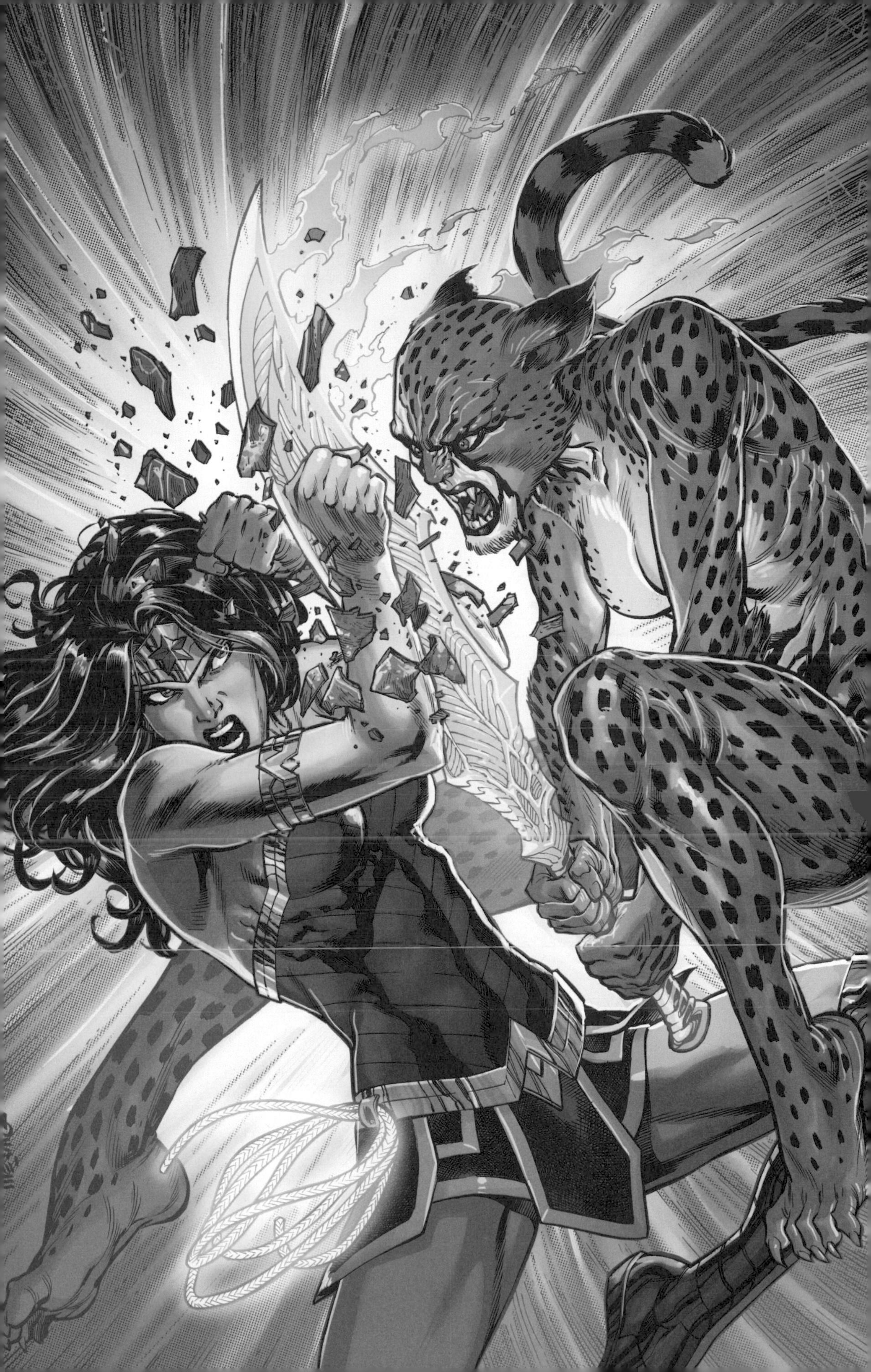

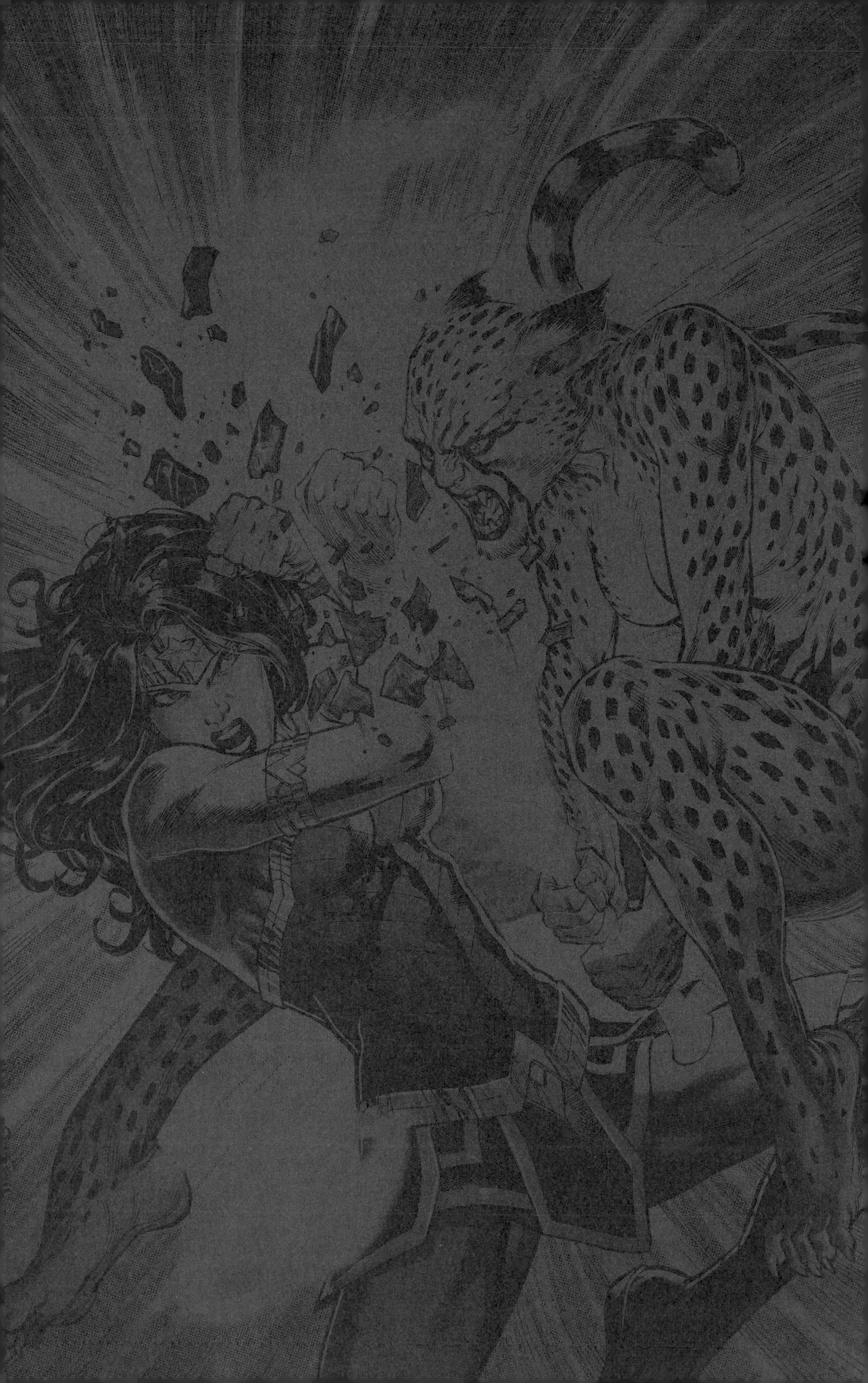

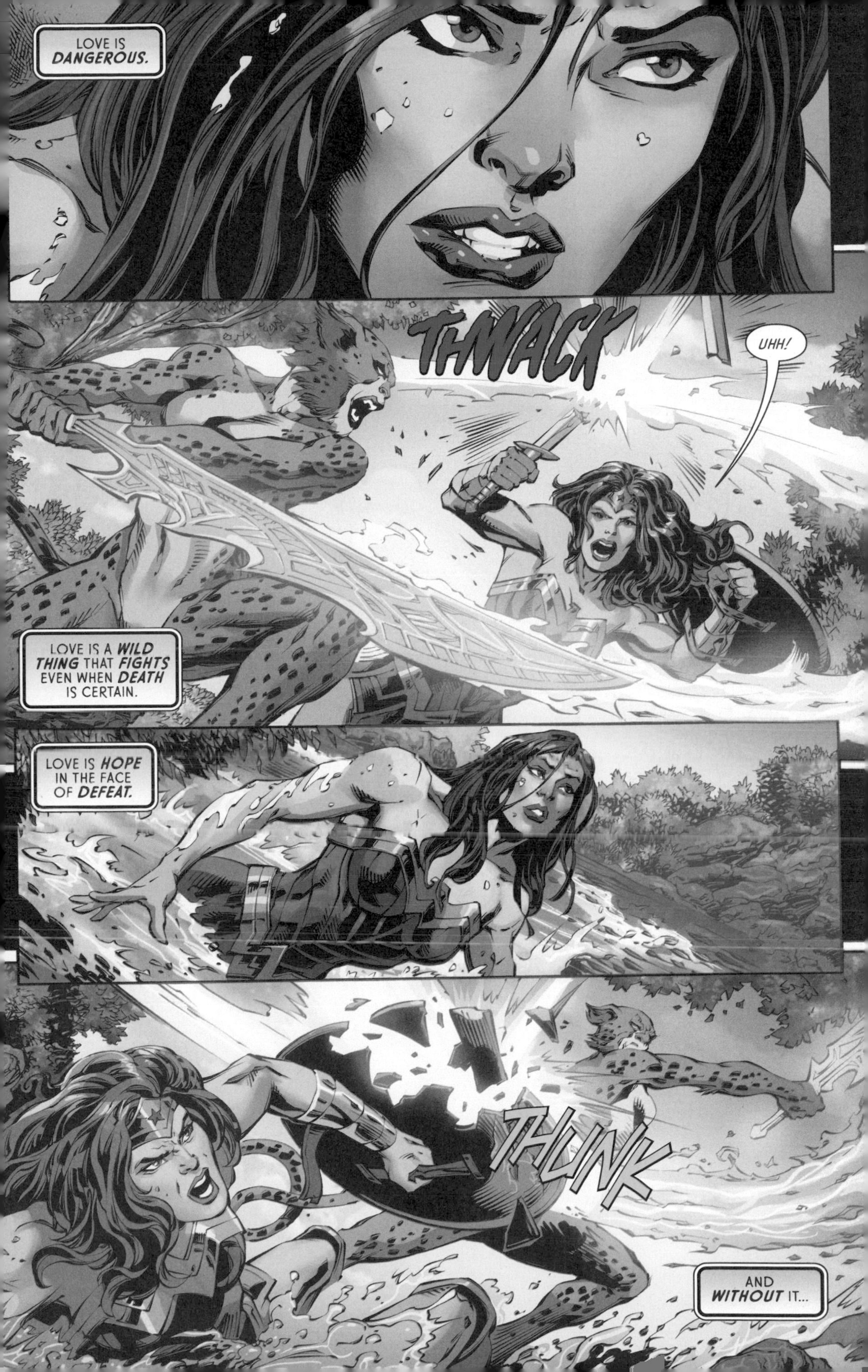
LOVE IS DANGEROUS.
THWACK
UHH!
LOVE IS A WILD THING THAT FIGHTS EVEN WHEN DEATH IS CERTAIN.
LOVE IS HOPE IN THE FACE OF DEFEAT.
THUNK
AND WITHOUT IT...

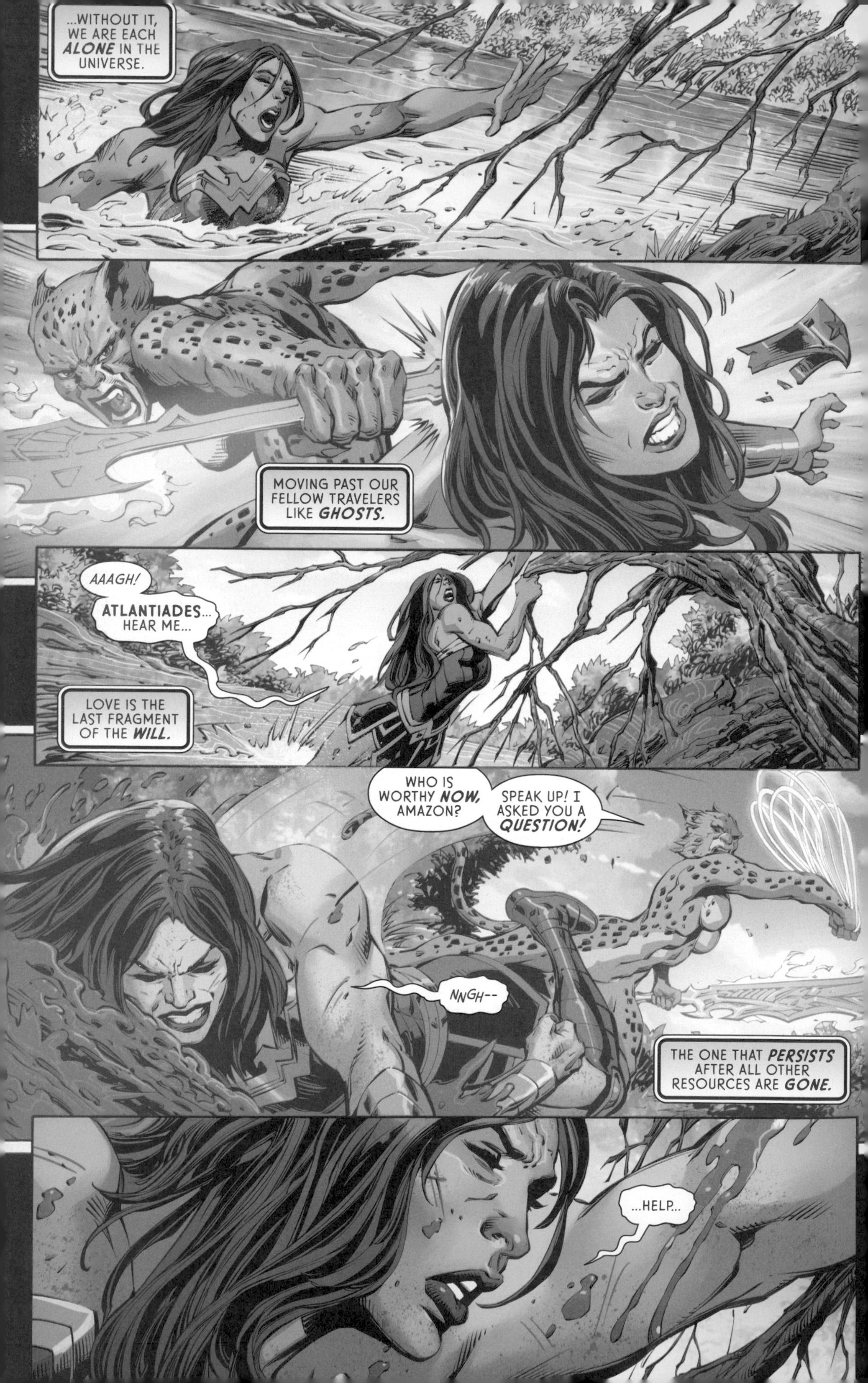
...WITHOUT IT, WE ARE EACH ALONE IN THE UNIVERSE.
MOVING PAST OUR FELLOW TRAVELERS LIKE GHOSTS.
AAAGH!
ATLANTIADES... HEAR ME...
LOVE IS THE LAST FRAGMENT OF THE WILL.
WHO IS WORTHY NOW, AMAZON?
SPEAK UP! I ASKED YOU A QUESTION!
NNGH--
THE ONE THAT PERSISTS AFTER ALL OTHER RESOURCES ARE GONE.
...HELP...

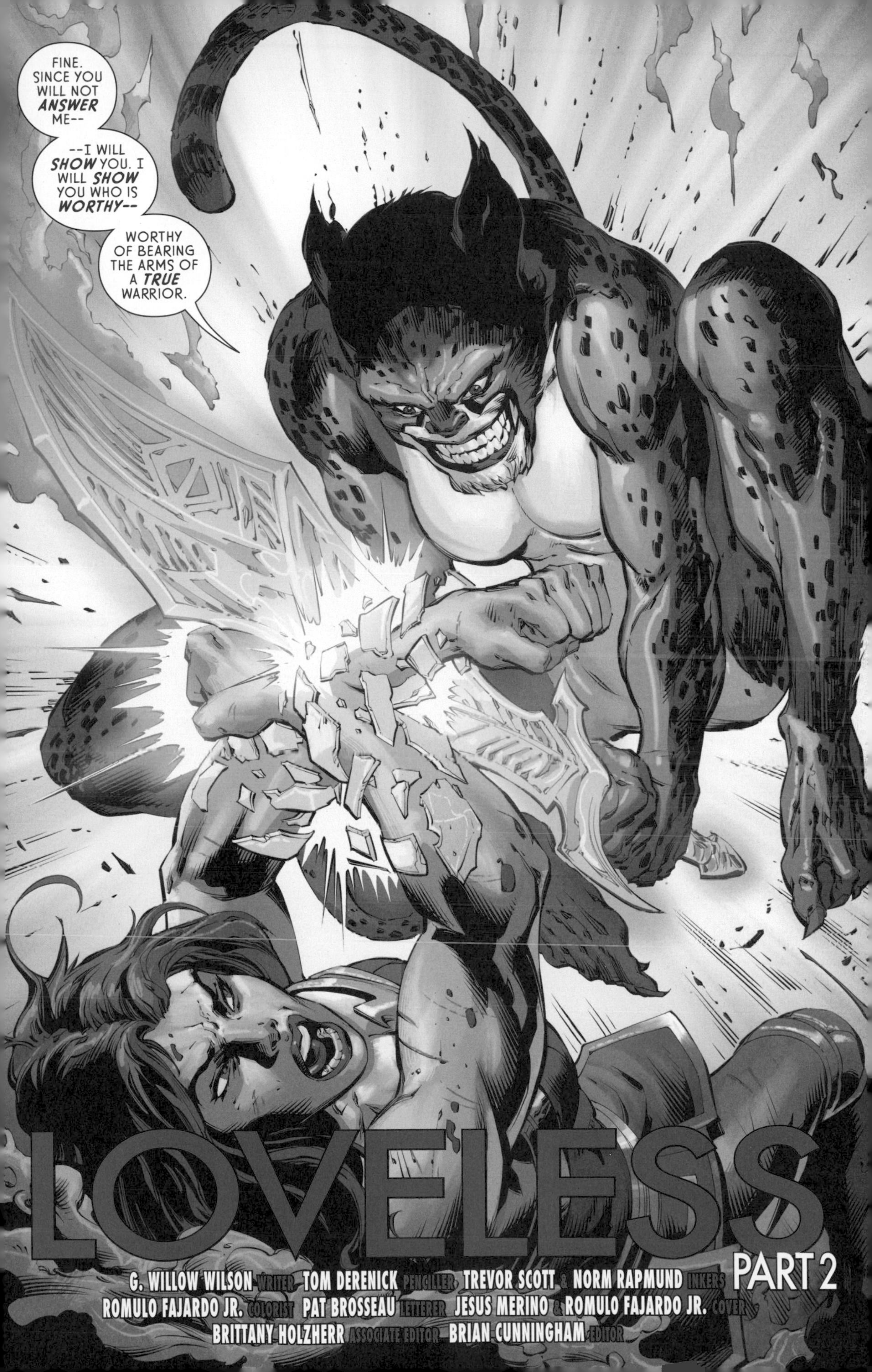
FINE. SINCE YOU WILL NOT ANSWER ME--
--I WILL SHOW YOU. I WILL SHOW YOU WHO IS WORTHY--
WORTHY OF BEARING THE ARMS OF A TRUE WARRIOR.
LOVELESS PART 2
G. WILLOW WILSON WRITER TOM DERENICK PENCILLER TREVOR SCOTT & NORM RAPMUND INKERS
ROMULO FAJARDO JR. COLORIST PAT BROSSEAU LETTERER JESUS MERINO & ROMULO FAJARDO JR. COVER
BRITTANY HOLZHERR ASSOCIATE EDITOR BRIAN CUNNINGHAM EDITOR

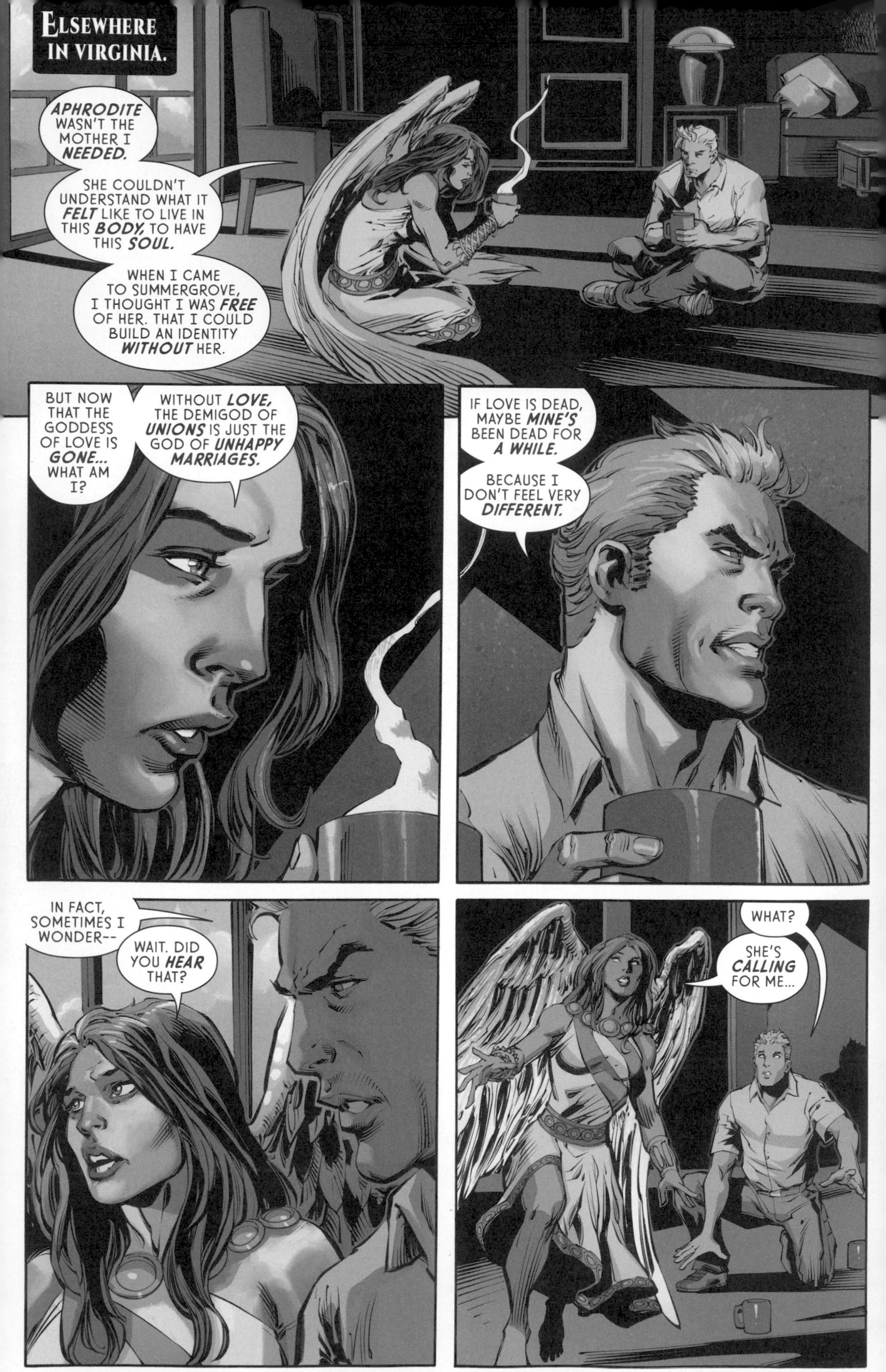
ELSEWHERE IN VIRGINIA.
APHRODITE WASN'T THE MOTHER I NEEDED.
SHE COULDN'T UNDERSTAND WHAT IT FELT LIKE TO LIVE IN THIS BODY, TO HAVE THIS SOUL.
WHEN I CAME TO SUMMERGROVE, I THOUGHT I WAS FREE OF HER. THAT I COULD BUILD AN IDENTITY WITHOUT HER.
BUT NOW THAT THE GODDESS OF LOVE IS GONE... WHAT AM I?
WITHOUT LOVE, THE DEMIGOD OF UNIONS IS JUST THE GOD OF UNHAPPY MARRIAGES.
IF LOVE IS DEAD, MAYBE MINE'S BEEN DEAD FOR A WHILE.
BECAUSE I DON'T FEEL VERY DIFFERENT.
IN FACT, SOMETIMES I WONDER--
WAIT. DID YOU HEAR THAT?
WHAT?
SHE'S CALLING FOR ME...

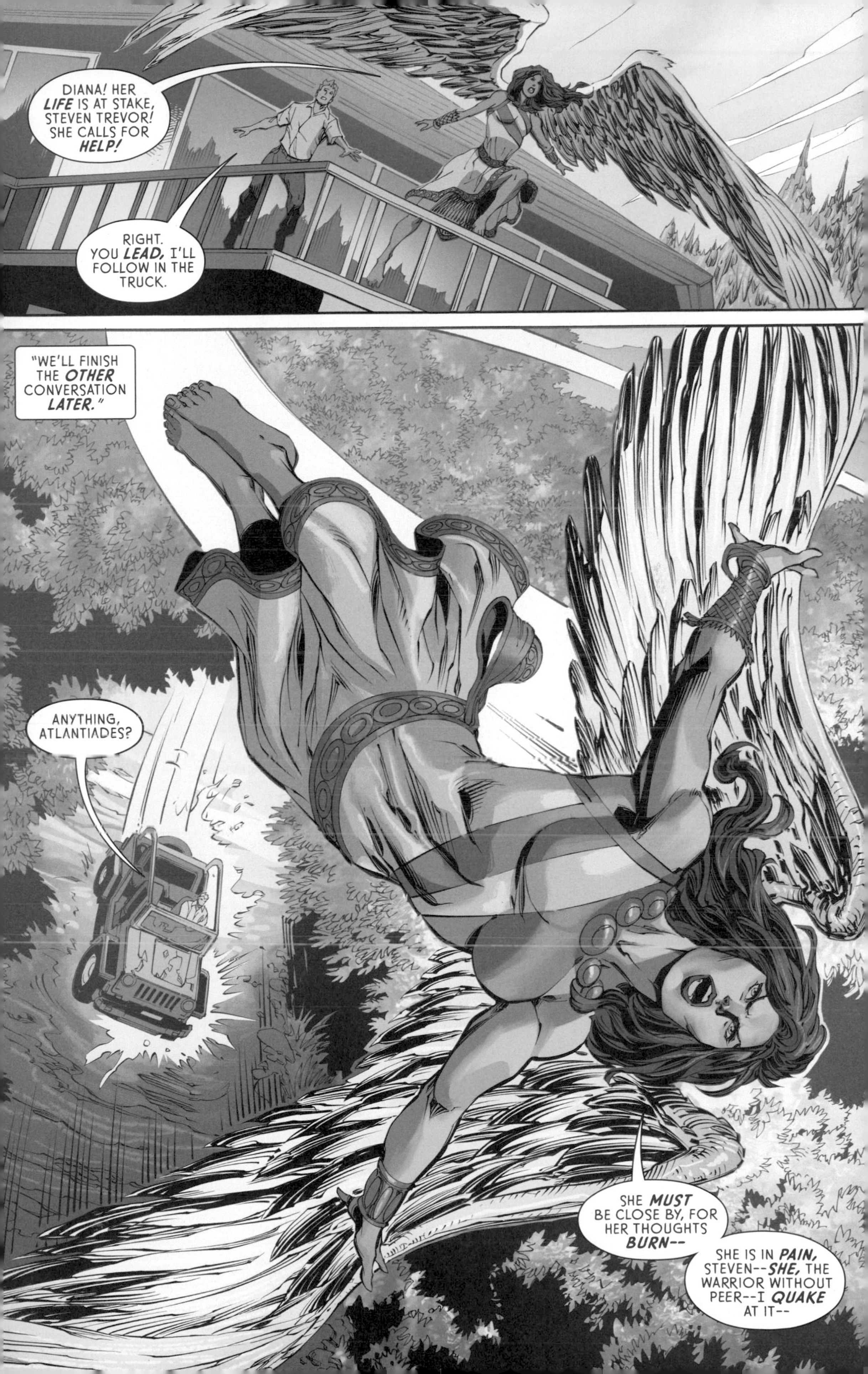
DIANA! HER LIFE IS AT STAKE, STEVEN TREVOR! SHE CALLS FOR HELP!
RIGHT. YOU LEAD, I'LL FOLLOW IN THE TRUCK.
"WE'LL FINISH THE OTHER CONVERSATION LATER."
ANYTHING, ATLANTIADES?
SHE MUST BE CLOSE BY, FOR HER THOUGHTS BURN--
SHE IS IN PAIN, STEVEN--SHE, THE WARRIOR WITHOUT PEER--I QUAKE AT IT--

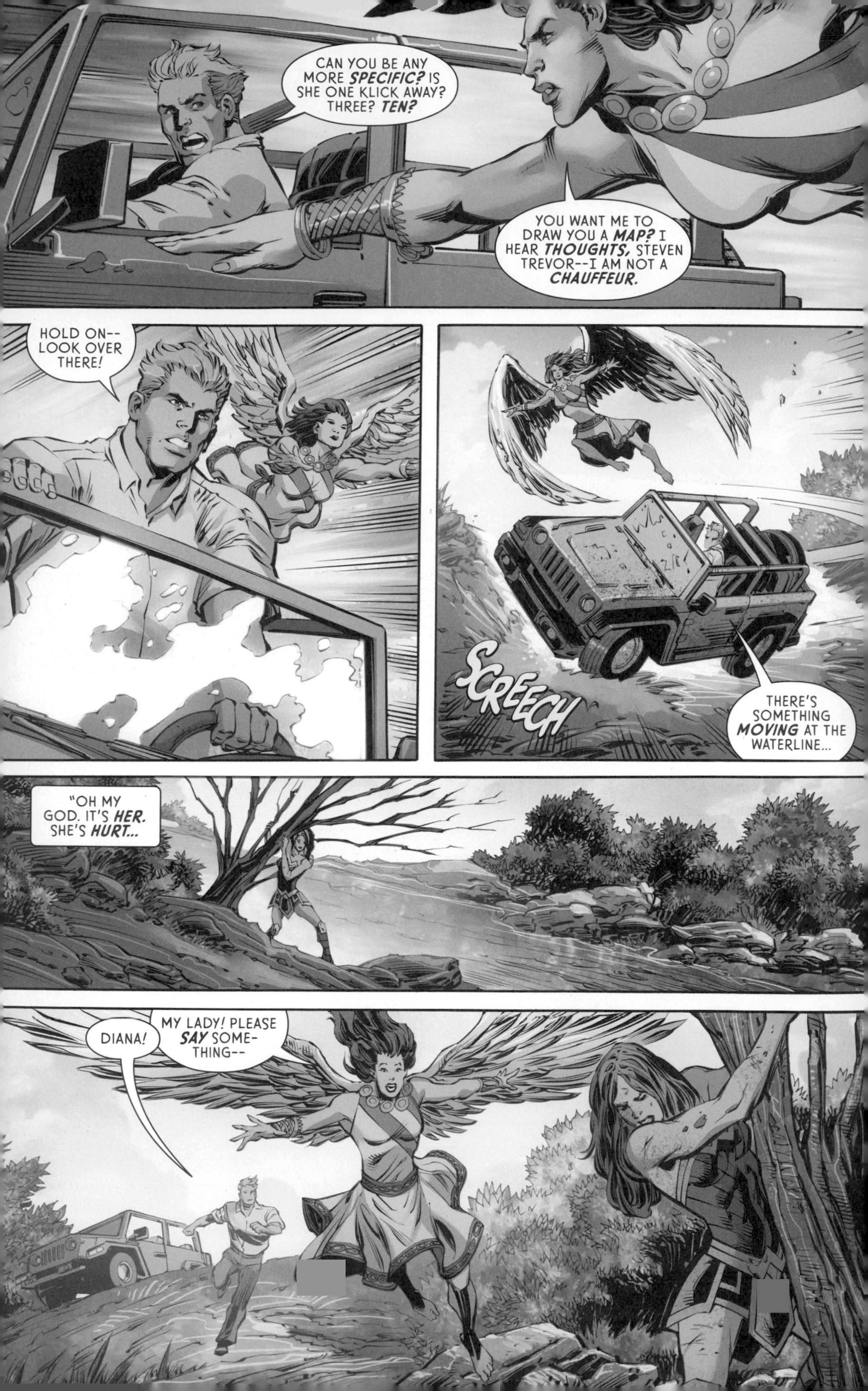
CAN YOU BE ANY MORE SPECIFIC? IS SHE ONE KLICK AWAY? THREE? TEN?
YOU WANT ME TO DRAW YOU A MAP? I HEAR THOUGHTS, STEVEN TREVOR--I AM NOT A CHAUFFEUR.
HOLD ON-- LOOK OVER THERE!
SCREECH
THERE'S SOMETHING MOVING AT THE WATERLINE...
"OH MY GOD. IT'S HER. SHE'S HURT...
DIANA!
MY LADY! PLEASE SAY SOME-THING--

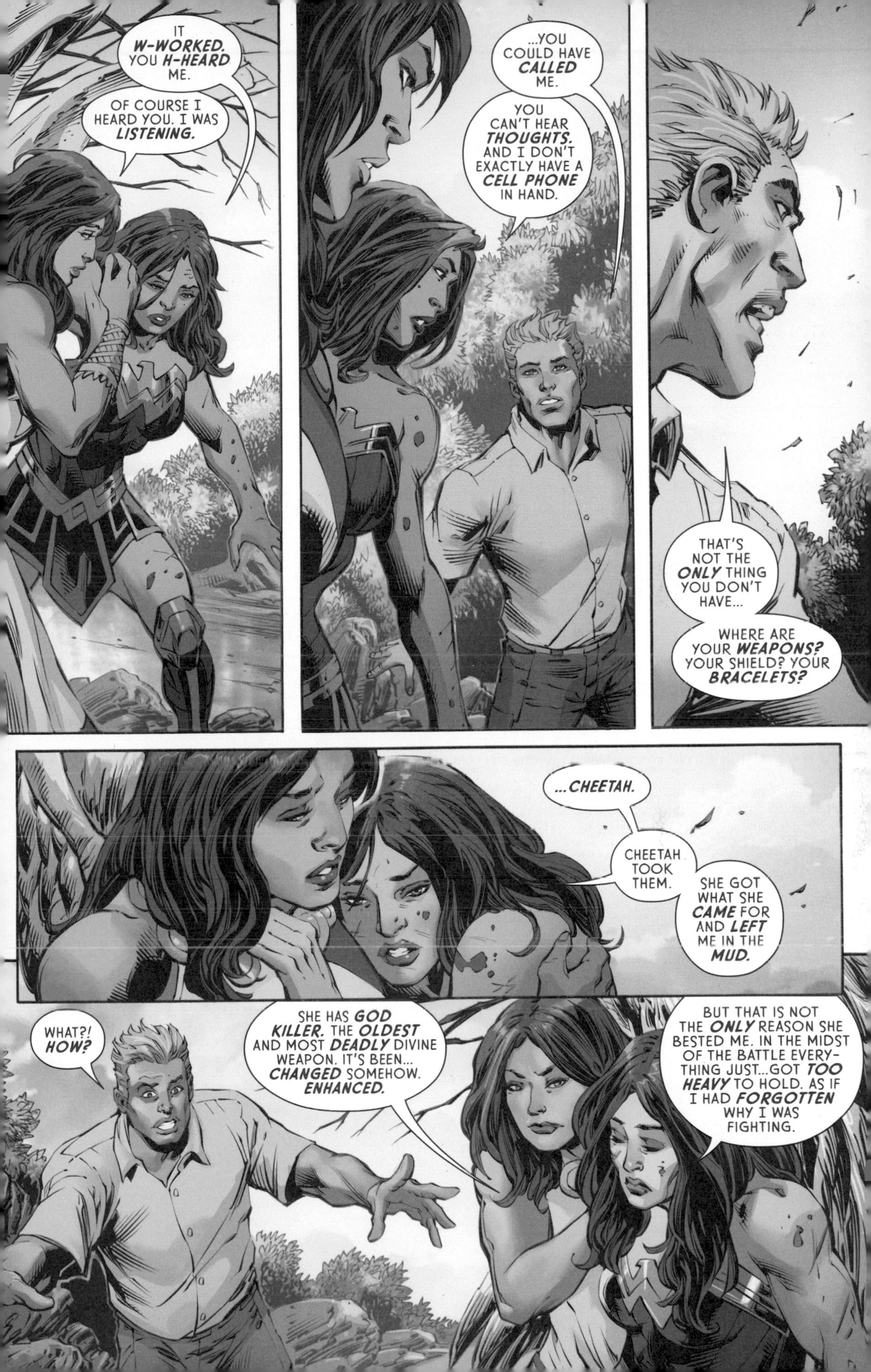
IT W-WORKED. YOU H-HEARD ME.
OF COURSE I HEARD YOU. I WAS LISTENING.
...YOU COULD HAVE CALLED ME.
YOU CAN'T HEAR THOUGHTS. AND I DON'T EXACTLY HAVE A CELL PHONE IN HAND.
THAT'S NOT THE ONLY THING YOU DON'T HAVE...
WHERE ARE YOUR WEAPONS? YOUR SHIELD? YOUR BRACELETS?
...CHEETAH.
CHEETAH TOOK THEM.
SHE GOT WHAT SHE CAME FOR AND LEFT ME IN THE MUD.
WHAT?! HOW?
SHE HAS GOD KILLER. THE OLDEST AND MOST DEADLY DIVINE WEAPON. IT'S BEEN... CHANGED SOMEHOW. ENHANCED.
BUT THAT IS NOT THE ONLY REASON SHE BESTED ME. IN THE MIDST OF THE BATTLE EVERY-THING JUST...GOT TOO HEAVY TO HOLD. AS IF I HAD FORGOTTEN WHY I WAS FIGHTING.

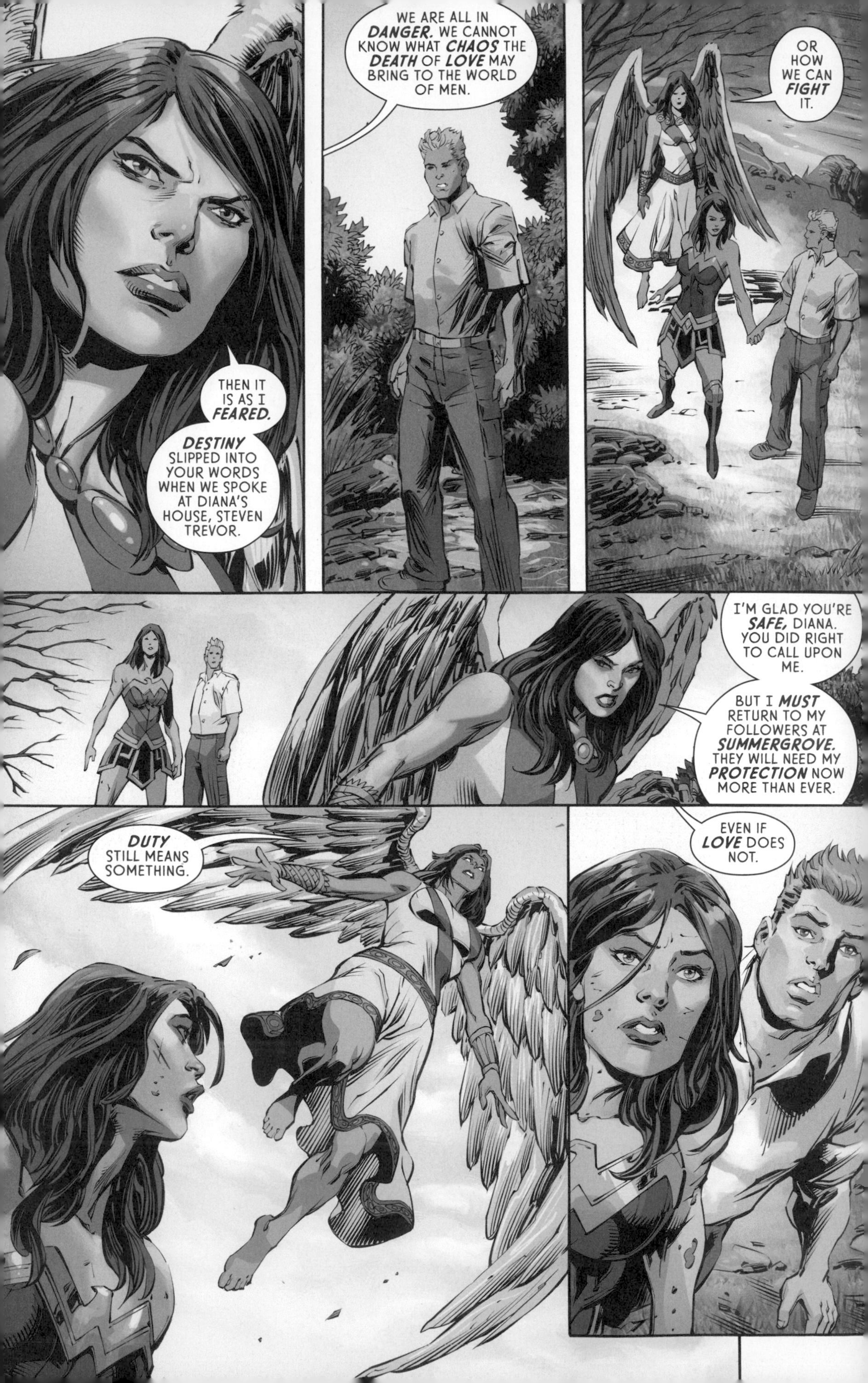
THEN IT IS AS I FEARED.
DESTINY SLIPPED INTO YOUR WORDS WHEN WE SPOKE AT DIANA'S HOUSE, STEVEN TREVOR.
WE ARE ALL IN DANGER. WE CANNOT KNOW WHAT CHAOS THE DEATH OF LOVE MAY BRING TO THE WORLD OF MEN.
OR HOW WE CAN FIGHT IT.
I'M GLAD YOU'RE SAFE, DIANA. YOU DID RIGHT TO CALL UPON ME.
BUT I MUST RETURN TO MY FOLLOWERS AT SUMMERGROVE. THEY WILL NEED MY PROTECTION NOW MORE THAN EVER.
DUTY STILL MEANS SOMETHING.
EVEN IF LOVE DOES NOT.

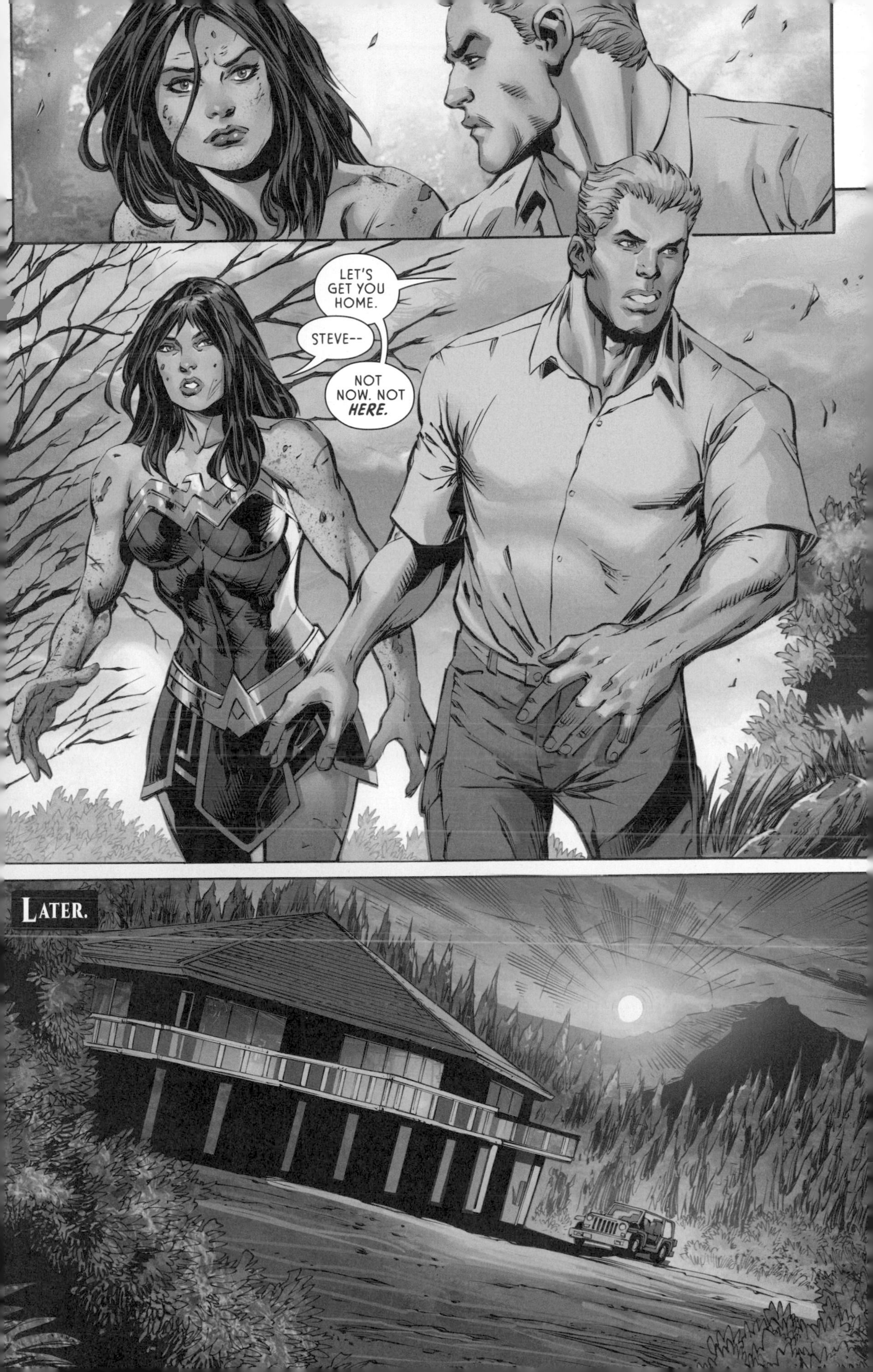

LET'S GET YOU HOME.
STEVE--
NOT NOW. NOT HERE.
LATER.

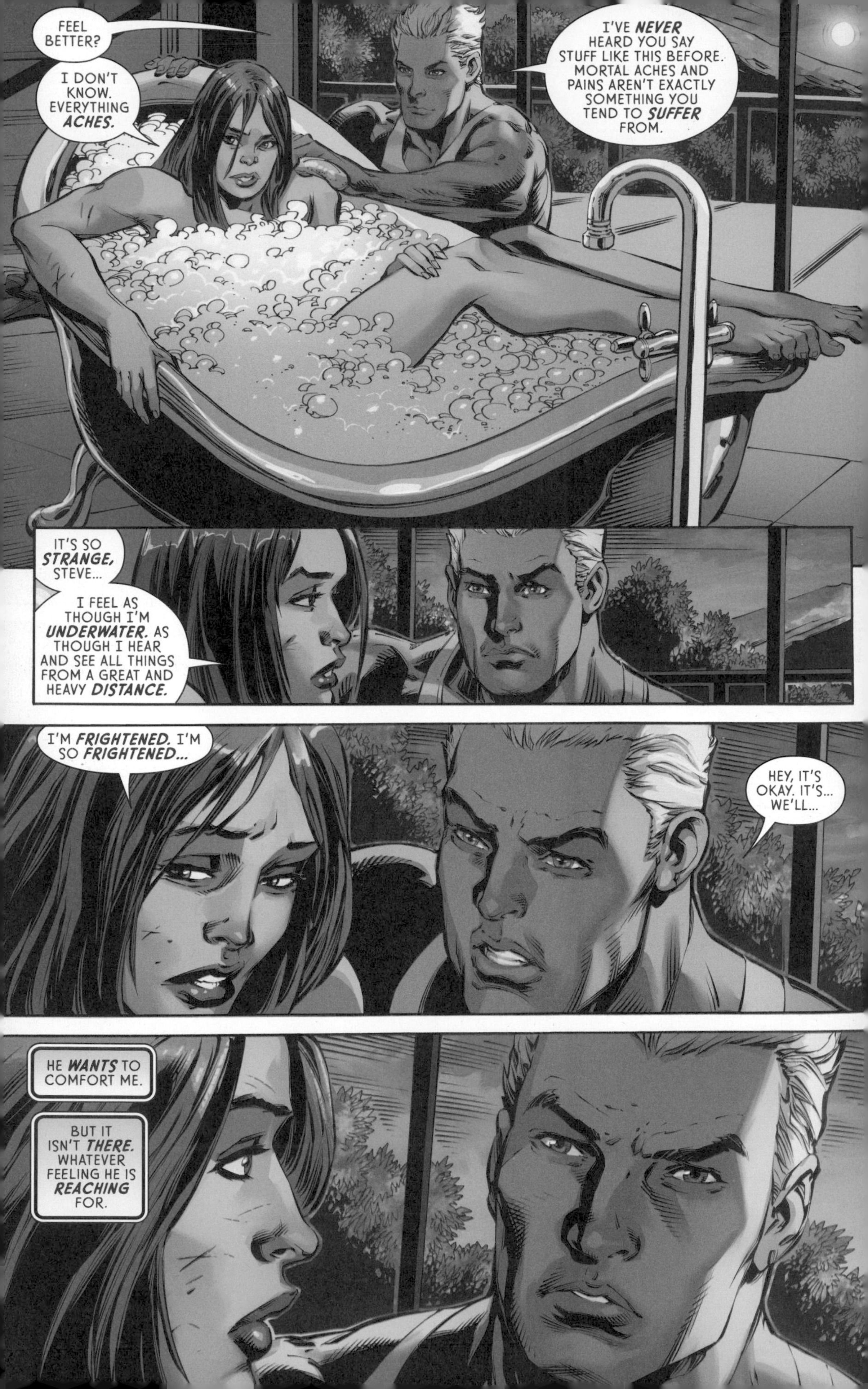
FEEL BETTER?
I DON'T KNOW. EVERYTHING ACHES.
I'VE NEVER HEARD YOU SAY STUFF LIKE THIS BEFORE. MORTAL ACHES AND PAINS AREN'T EXACTLY SOMETHING YOU TEND TO SUFFER FROM.
IT'S SO STRANGE, STEVE...
I FEEL AS THOUGH I'M UNDERWATER. AS THOUGH I HEAR AND SEE ALL THINGS FROM A GREAT AND HEAVY DISTANCE.
I'M FRIGHTENED. I'M SO FRIGHTENED...
HEY, IT'S OKAY. IT'S... WE'LL...
HE WANTS TO COMFORT ME.
BUT IT ISN'T THERE. WHATEVER FEELING HE IS REACHING FOR.

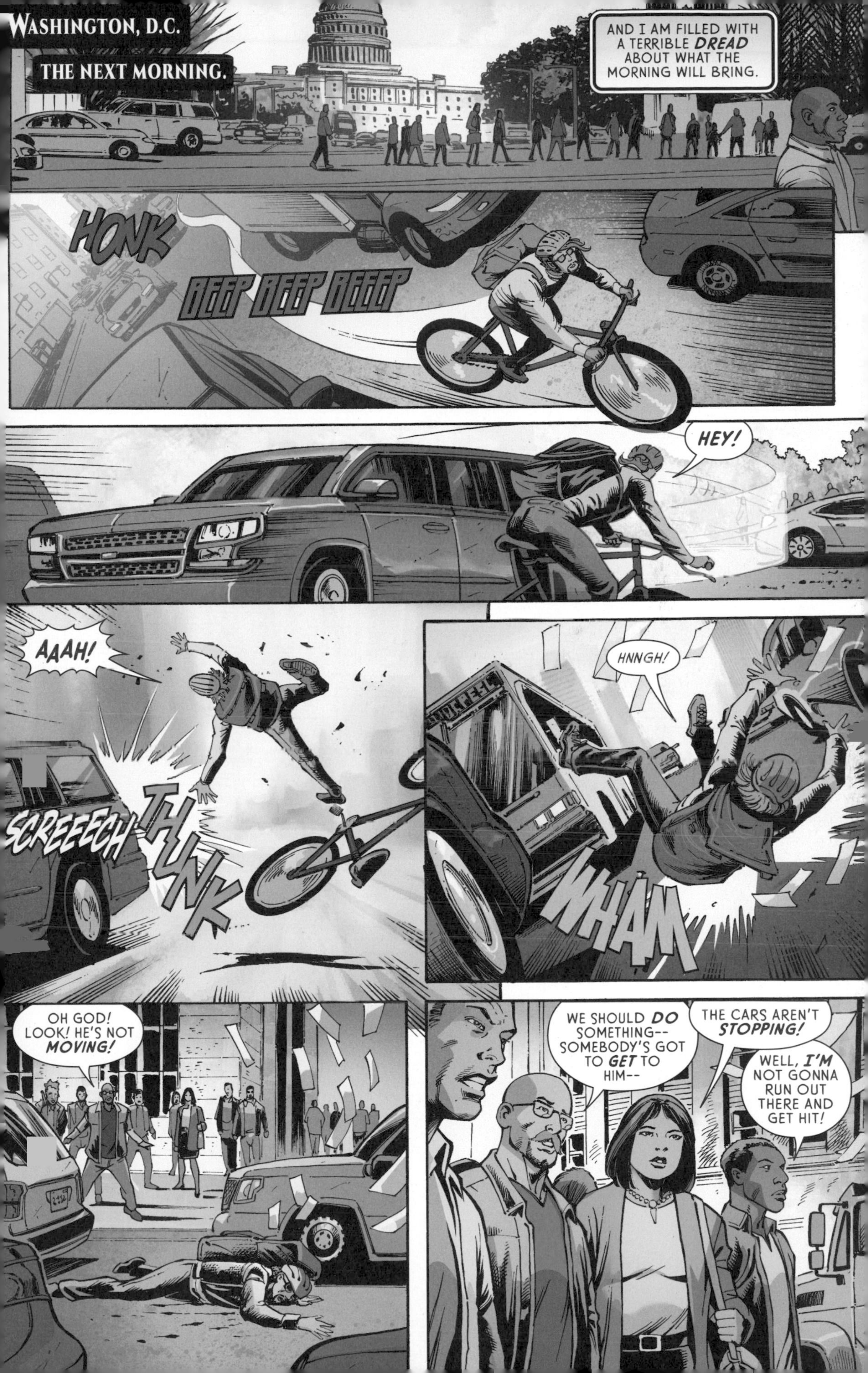
WASHINGTON, D.C.
THE NEXT MORNING.
AND I AM FILLED WITH A TERRIBLE DREAD ABOUT WHAT THE MORNING WILL BRING.
HONK
BEEP BEEP BEEEP
HEY!
AAAH!
SCREEECH
THUNK
HNNGH!
WHAM
OH GOD! LOOK! HE'S NOT MOVING!
WE SHOULD DO SOMETHING-- SOMEBODY'S GOT TO GET TO HIM--
THE CARS AREN'T STOPPING!
WELL, I'M NOT GONNA RUN OUT THERE AND GET HIT!

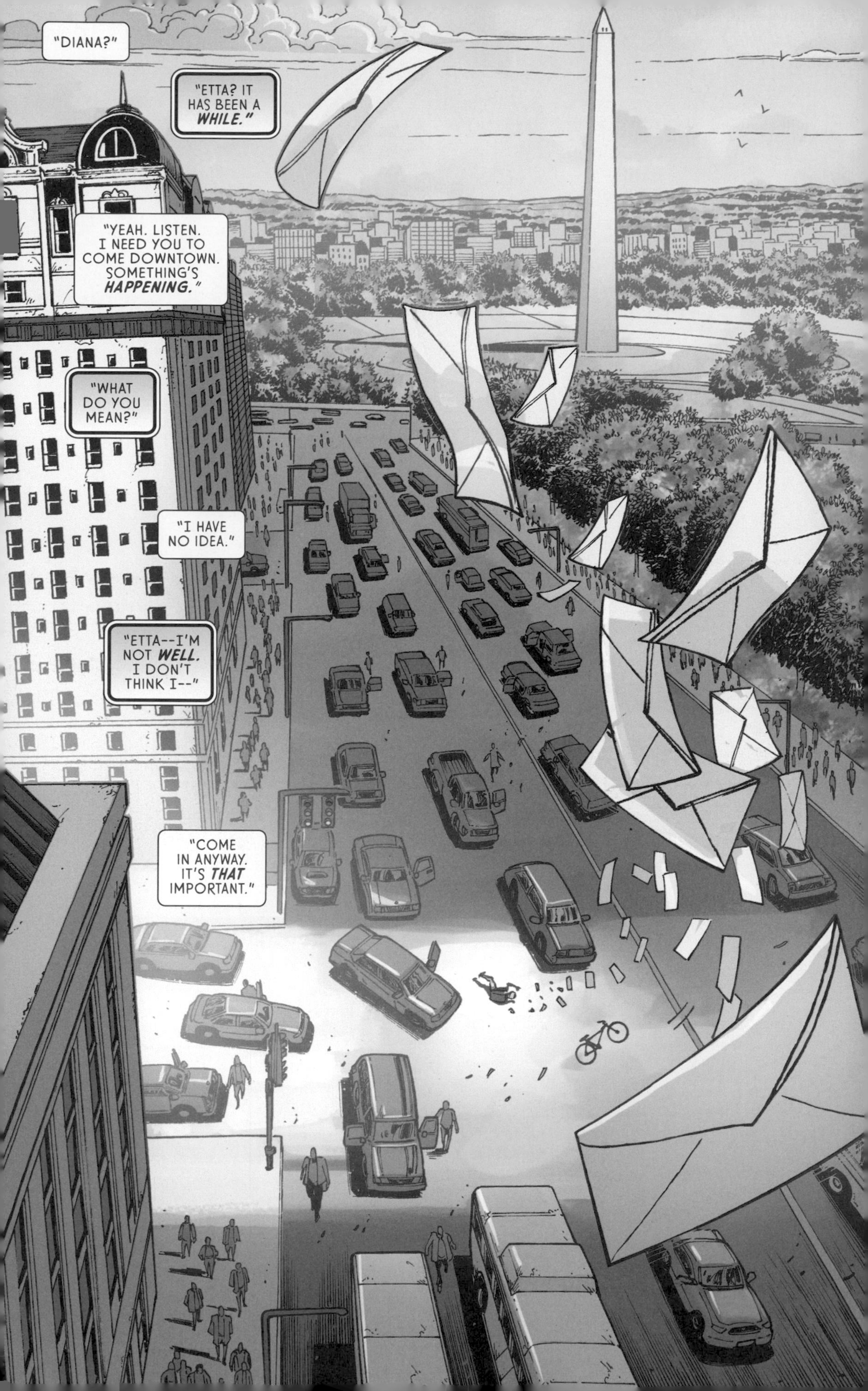
"DIANA?"
"ETTA? IT HAS BEEN A *WHILE.*"
"YEAH. LISTEN. I NEED YOU TO COME DOWNTOWN. SOMETHING'S *HAPPENING.*"
"WHAT DO YOU MEAN?"
"I HAVE NO IDEA."
"ETTA--I'M NOT *WELL.* I DON'T THINK I--"
"COME IN ANYWAY. IT'S *THAT* IMPORTANT."

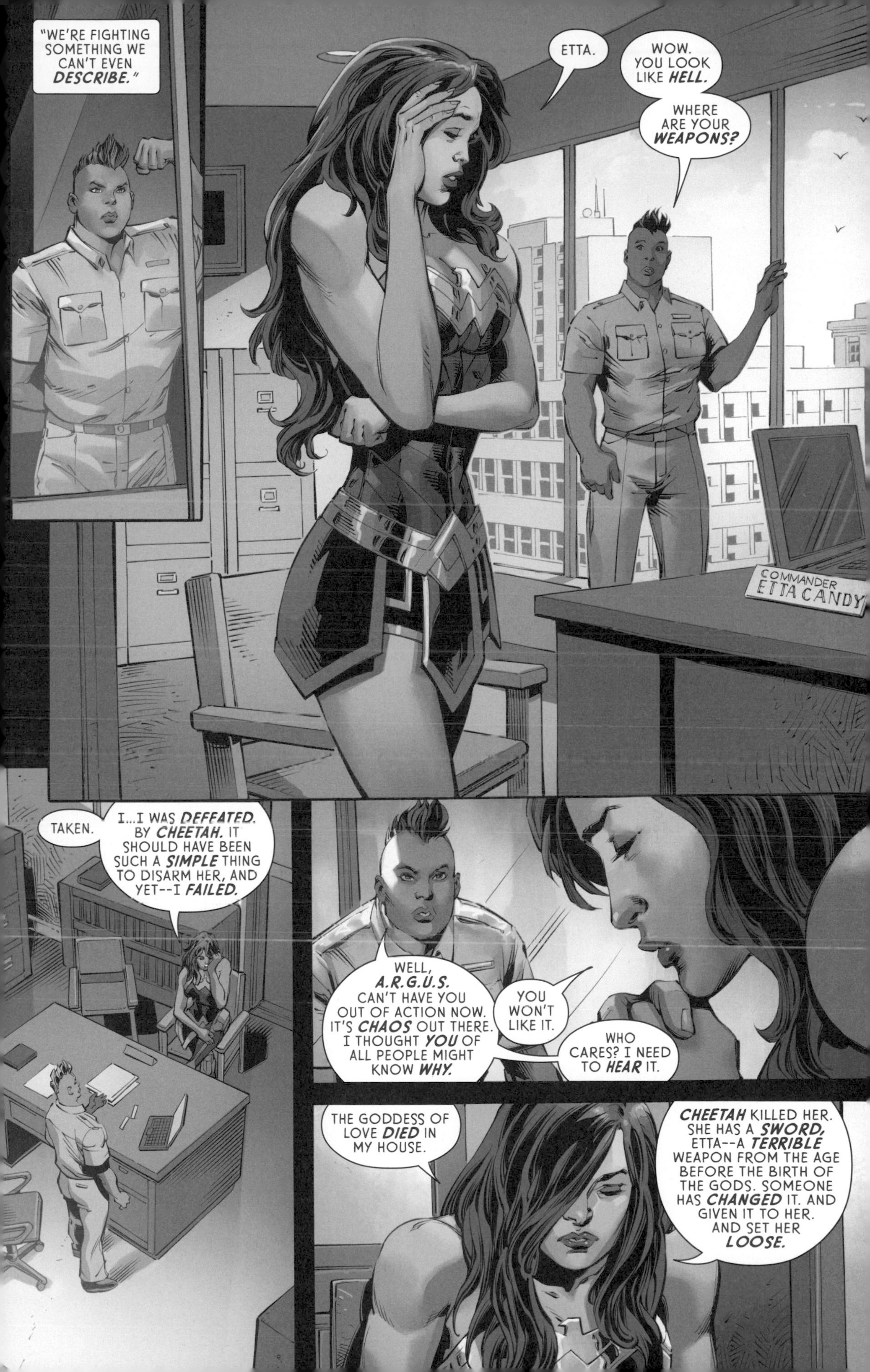
"WE'RE FIGHTING SOMETHING WE CAN'T EVEN DESCRIBE."
ETTA.
WOW. YOU LOOK LIKE HELL.
WHERE ARE YOUR WEAPONS?
COMMANDER ETTA CANDY
TAKEN.
I...I WAS DEFEATED. BY CHEETAH. IT SHOULD HAVE BEEN SUCH A SIMPLE THING TO DISARM HER, AND YET--I FAILED.
WELL, A.R.G.U.S. CAN'T HAVE YOU OUT OF ACTION NOW. IT'S CHAOS OUT THERE. I THOUGHT YOU OF ALL PEOPLE MIGHT KNOW WHY.
YOU WON'T LIKE IT.
WHO CARES? I NEED TO HEAR IT.
THE GODDESS OF LOVE DIED IN MY HOUSE.
CHEETAH KILLED HER. SHE HAS A SWORD, ETTA--A TERRIBLE WEAPON FROM THE AGE BEFORE THE BIRTH OF THE GODS. SOMEONE HAS CHANGED IT. AND GIVEN IT TO HER. AND SET HER LOOSE.

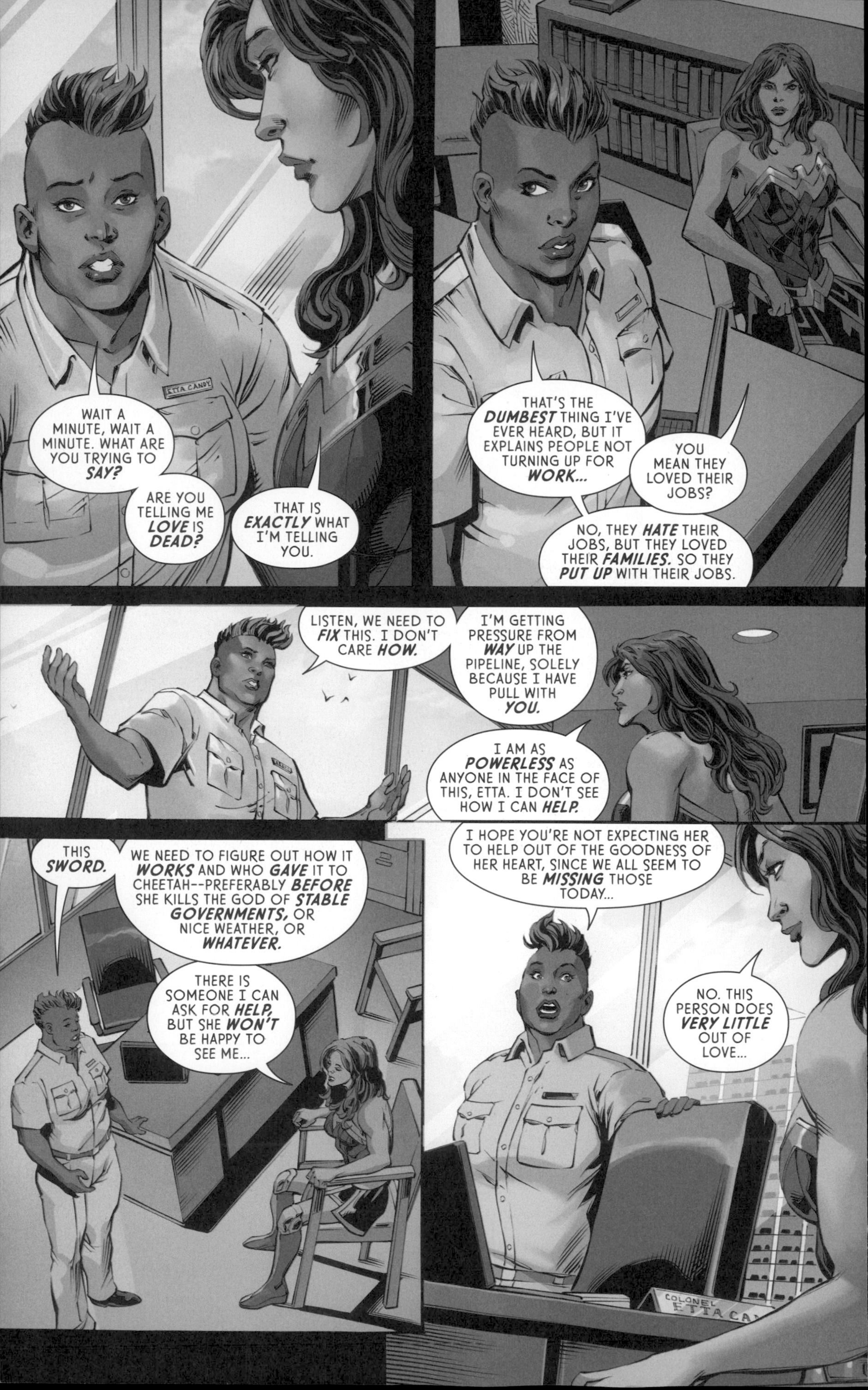
ETTA CANDY
WAIT A MINUTE, WAIT A MINUTE. WHAT ARE YOU TRYING TO SAY?
ARE YOU TELLING ME LOVE IS DEAD?
THAT IS EXACTLY WHAT I'M TELLING YOU.
THAT'S THE DUMBEST THING I'VE EVER HEARD, BUT IT EXPLAINS PEOPLE NOT TURNING UP FOR WORK...
YOU MEAN THEY LOVED THEIR JOBS?
NO, THEY HATE THEIR JOBS, BUT THEY LOVED THEIR FAMILIES. SO THEY PUT UP WITH THEIR JOBS.
LISTEN, WE NEED TO FIX THIS. I DON'T CARE HOW.
I'M GETTING PRESSURE FROM WAY UP THE PIPELINE, SOLELY BECAUSE I HAVE PULL WITH YOU.
I AM AS POWERLESS AS ANYONE IN THE FACE OF THIS, ETTA. I DON'T SEE HOW I CAN HELP.
THIS SWORD.
WE NEED TO FIGURE OUT HOW IT WORKS AND WHO GAVE IT TO CHEETAH--PREFERABLY BEFORE SHE KILLS THE GOD OF STABLE GOVERNMENTS, OR NICE WEATHER, OR WHATEVER.
THERE IS SOMEONE I CAN ASK FOR HELP, BUT SHE WON'T BE HAPPY TO SEE ME...
I HOPE YOU'RE NOT EXPECTING HER TO HELP OUT OF THE GOODNESS OF HER HEART, SINCE WE ALL SEEM TO BE MISSING THOSE TODAY...
NO. THIS PERSON DOES VERY LITTLE OUT OF LOVE...
COLONEL ETTA CAN

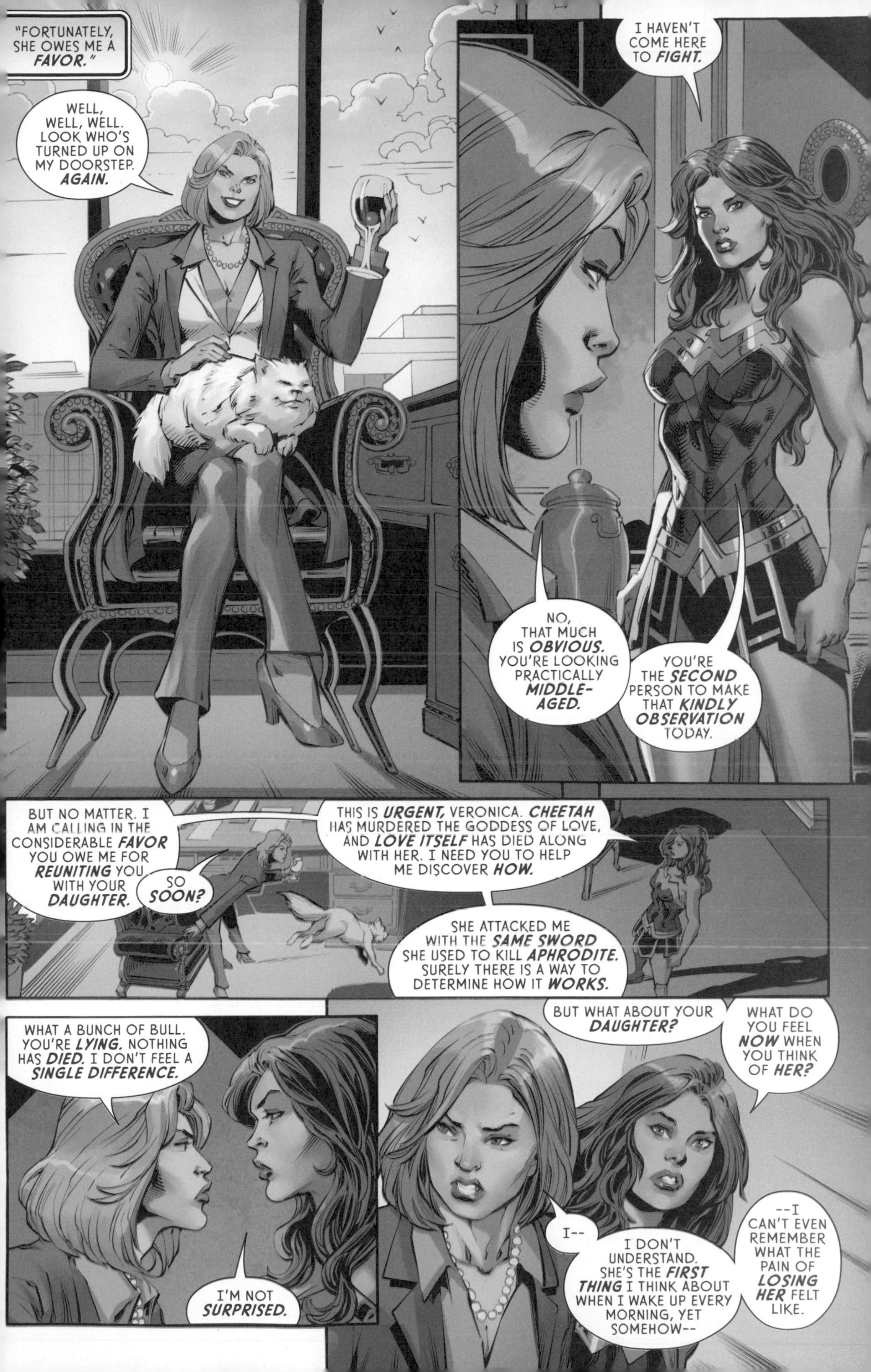
"FORTUNATELY, SHE OWES ME A FAVOR."
WELL, WELL, WELL. LOOK WHO'S TURNED UP ON MY DOORSTEP. AGAIN.
I HAVEN'T COME HERE TO FIGHT.
NO, THAT MUCH IS OBVIOUS. YOU'RE LOOKING PRACTICALLY MIDDLE-AGED.
YOU'RE THE SECOND PERSON TO MAKE THAT KINDLY OBSERVATION TODAY.
BUT NO MATTER. I AM CALLING IN THE CONSIDERABLE FAVOR YOU OWE ME FOR REUNITING YOU WITH YOUR DAUGHTER.
SO SOON?
THIS IS URGENT, VERONICA. CHEETAH HAS MURDERED THE GODDESS OF LOVE, AND LOVE ITSELF HAS DIED ALONG WITH HER. I NEED YOU TO HELP ME DISCOVER HOW.
SHE ATTACKED ME WITH THE SAME SWORD SHE USED TO KILL APHRODITE. SURELY THERE IS A WAY TO DETERMINE HOW IT WORKS.
WHAT A BUNCH OF BULL. YOU'RE LYING. NOTHING HAS DIED. I DON'T FEEL A SINGLE DIFFERENCE.
I'M NOT SURPRISED.
BUT WHAT ABOUT YOUR DAUGHTER?
WHAT DO YOU FEEL NOW WHEN YOU THINK OF HER?
I--
I DON'T UNDERSTAND. SHE'S THE FIRST THING I THINK ABOUT WHEN I WAKE UP EVERY MORNING, YET SOMEHOW--
--I CAN'T EVEN REMEMBER WHAT THE PAIN OF LOSING HER FELT LIKE.

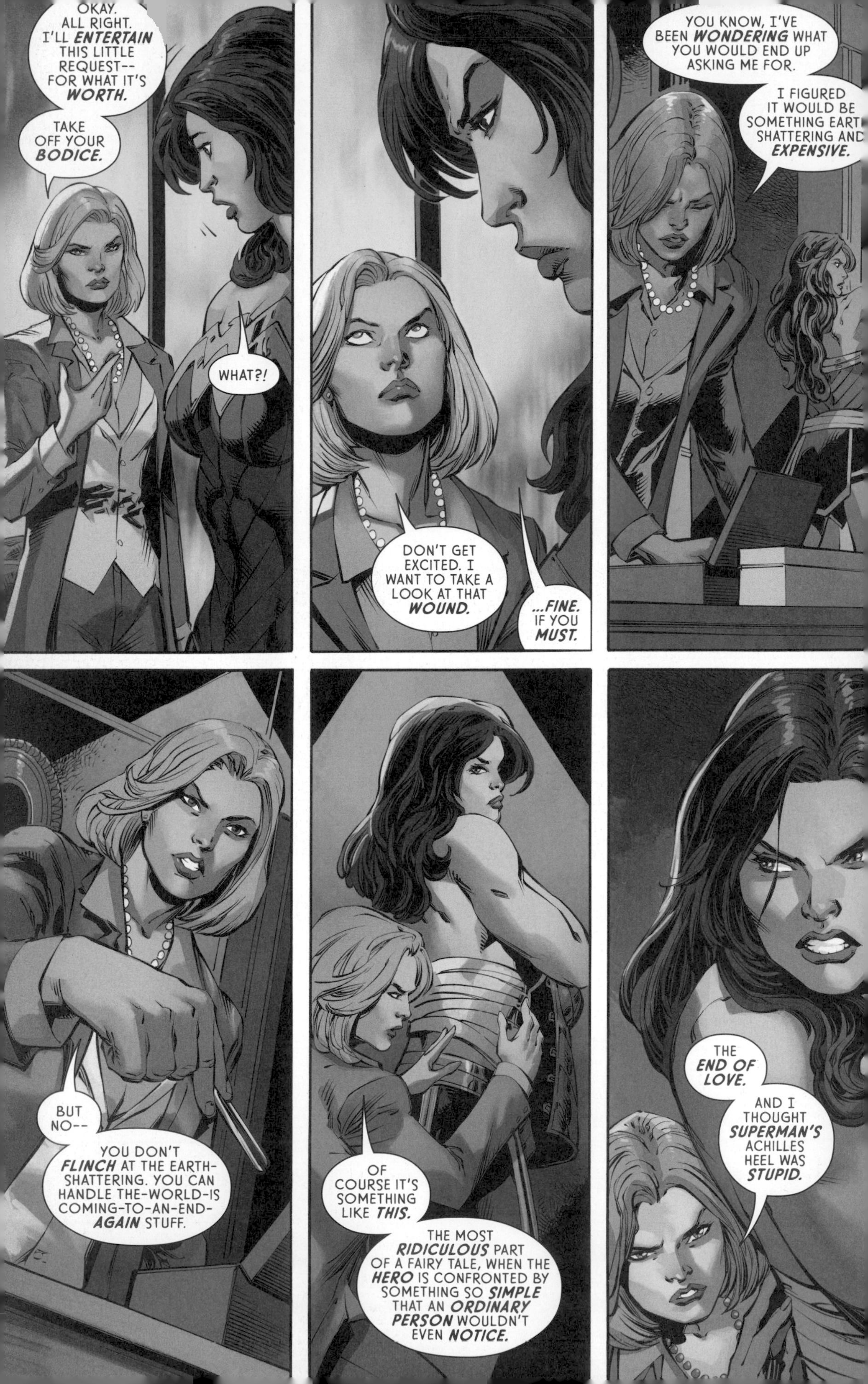

OKAY. ALL RIGHT. I'LL ENTERTAIN THIS LITTLE REQUEST-- FOR WHAT IT'S WORTH.
TAKE OFF YOUR BODICE.
WHAT?!
DON'T GET EXCITED. I WANT TO TAKE A LOOK AT THAT WOUND.
...FINE. IF YOU MUST.
YOU KNOW, I'VE BEEN WONDERING WHAT YOU WOULD END UP ASKING ME FOR.
I FIGURED IT WOULD BE SOMETHING EARTH SHATTERING AND EXPENSIVE.
BUT NO--
YOU DON'T FLINCH AT THE EARTH-SHATTERING. YOU CAN HANDLE THE-WORLD-IS COMING-TO-AN-END-AGAIN STUFF.
OF COURSE IT'S SOMETHING LIKE THIS.
THE MOST RIDICULOUS PART OF A FAIRY TALE, WHEN THE HERO IS CONFRONTED BY SOMETHING SO SIMPLE THAT AN ORDINARY PERSON WOULDN'T EVEN NOTICE.
THE END OF LOVE.
AND I THOUGHT SUPERMAN'S ACHILLES HEEL WAS STUPID.

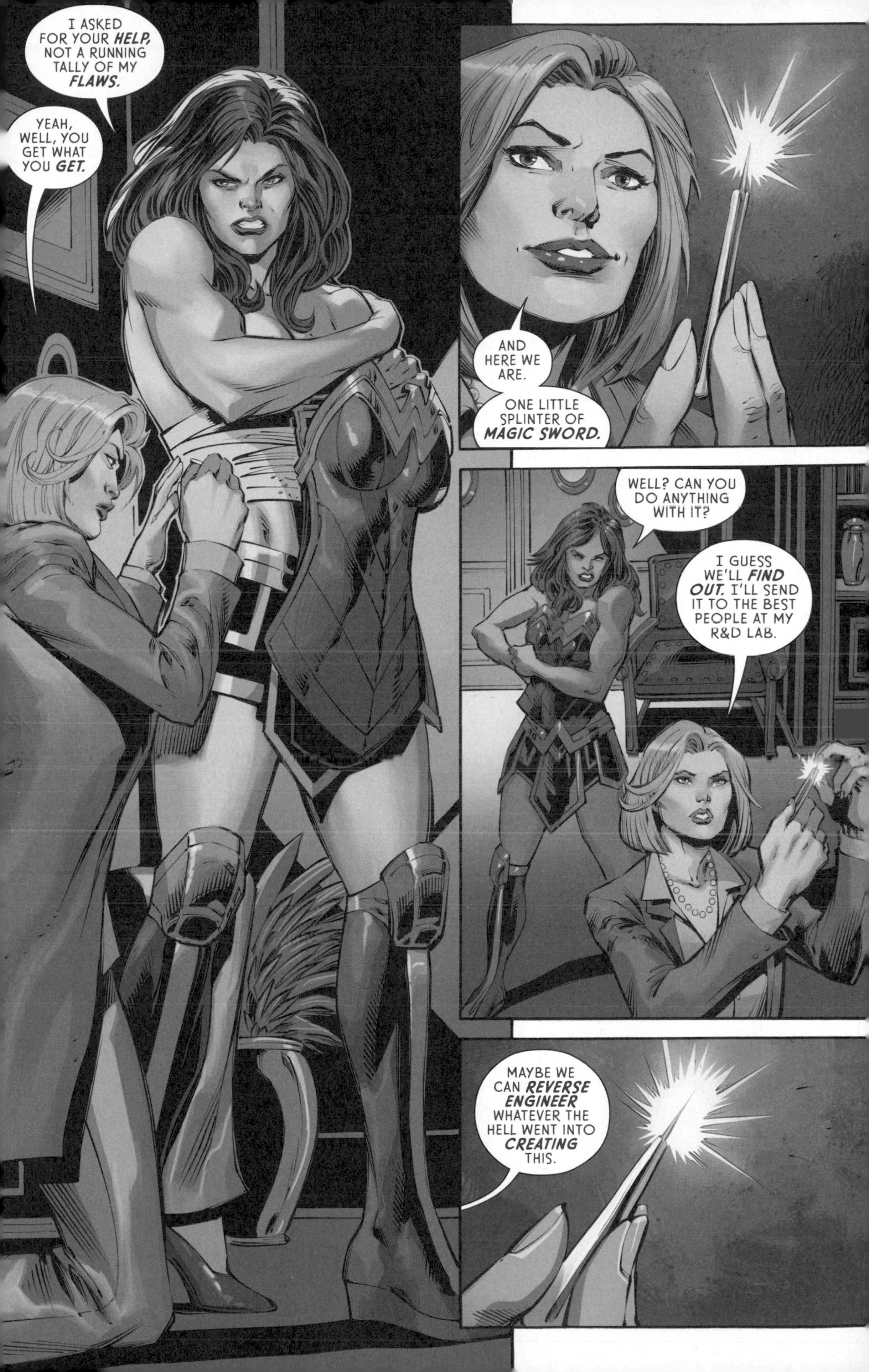

I ASKED FOR YOUR HELP, NOT A RUNNING TALLY OF MY FLAWS.
YEAH, WELL, YOU GET WHAT YOU GET.
AND HERE WE ARE.
ONE LITTLE SPLINTER OF MAGIC SWORD.
WELL? CAN YOU DO ANYTHING WITH IT?
I GUESS WE'LL FIND OUT. I'LL SEND IT TO THE BEST PEOPLE AT MY R&D LAB.
MAYBE WE CAN REVERSE ENGINEER WHATEVER THE HELL WENT INTO CREATING THIS.

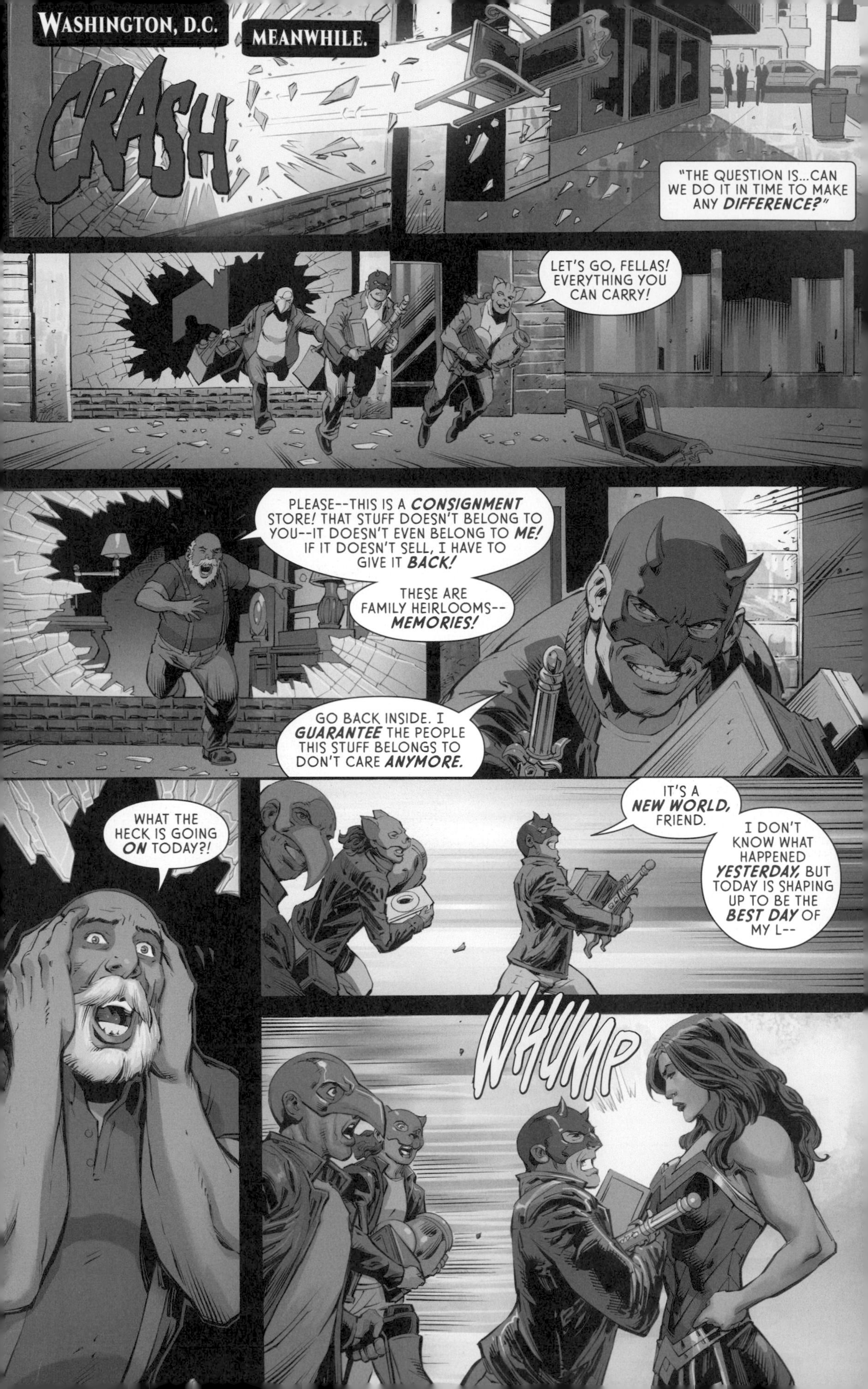

WASHINGTON, D.C.
MEANWHILE.
CRASH
"THE QUESTION IS...CAN WE DO IT IN TIME TO MAKE ANY DIFFERENCE?"
LET'S GO, FELLAS! EVERYTHING YOU CAN CARRY!
PLEASE--THIS IS A CONSIGNMENT STORE! THAT STUFF DOESN'T BELONG TO YOU--IT DOESN'T EVEN BELONG TO ME! IF IT DOESN'T SELL, I HAVE TO GIVE IT BACK!
THESE ARE FAMILY HEIRLOOMS--MEMORIES!
GO BACK INSIDE. I GUARANTEE THE PEOPLE THIS STUFF BELONGS TO DON'T CARE ANYMORE.
WHAT THE HECK IS GOING ON TODAY?!
IT'S A NEW WORLD, FRIEND.
I DON'T KNOW WHAT HAPPENED YESTERDAY, BUT TODAY IS SHAPING UP TO BE THE BEST DAY OF MY L--
WHUMP

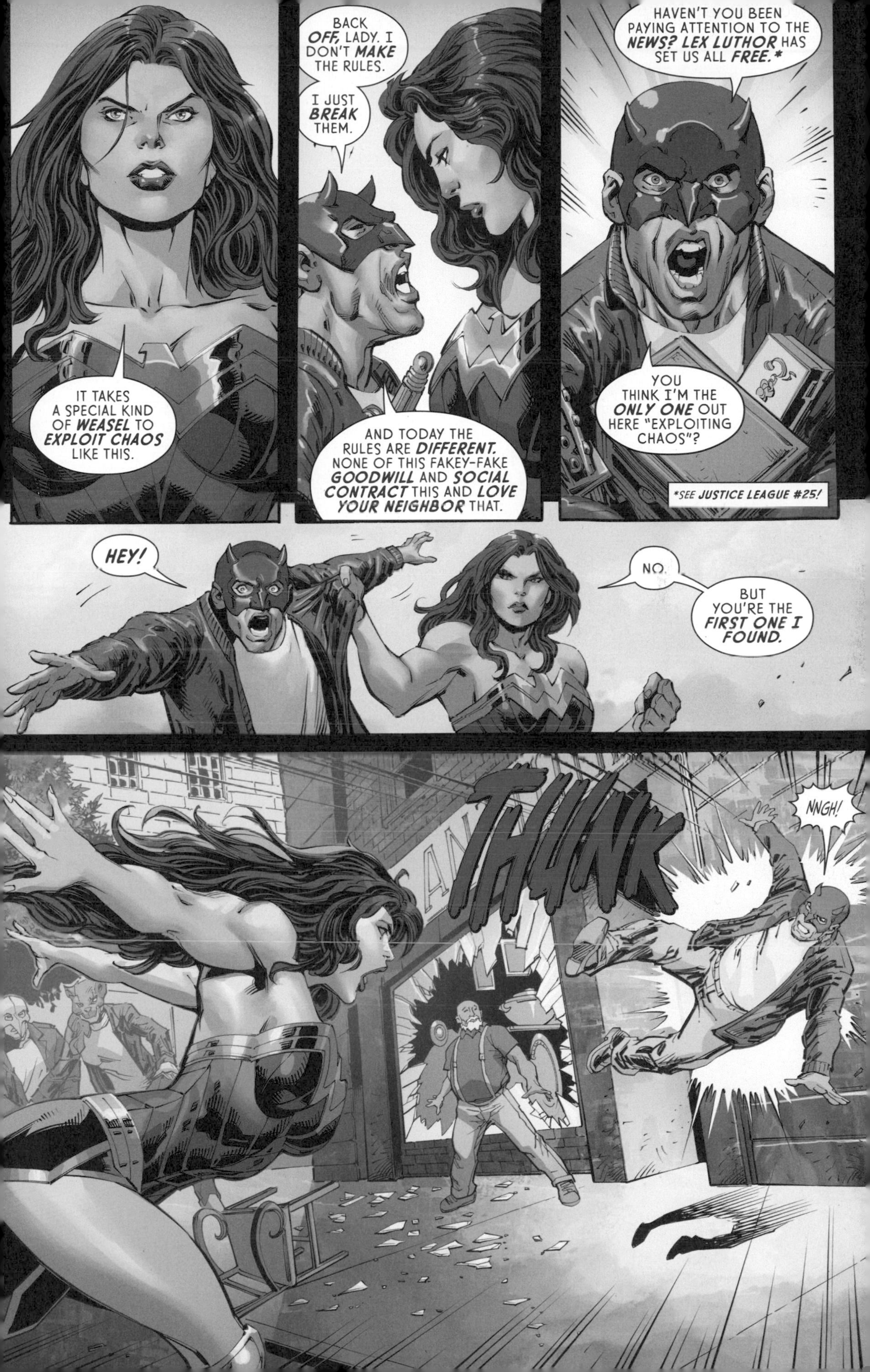
IT TAKES A SPECIAL KIND OF WEASEL TO EXPLOIT CHAOS LIKE THIS.
BACK OFF, LADY. I DON'T MAKE THE RULES.
I JUST BREAK THEM.
AND TODAY THE RULES ARE DIFFERENT. NONE OF THIS FAKEY-FAKE GOODWILL AND SOCIAL CONTRACT THIS AND LOVE YOUR NEIGHBOR THAT.
HAVEN'T YOU BEEN PAYING ATTENTION TO THE NEWS? LEX LUTHOR HAS SET US ALL FREE.*
YOU THINK I'M THE ONLY ONE OUT HERE "EXPLOITING CHAOS"?
*SEE JUSTICE LEAGUE #25!
HEY!
NO.
BUT YOU'RE THE FIRST ONE I FOUND.
THUNK
NNGH!

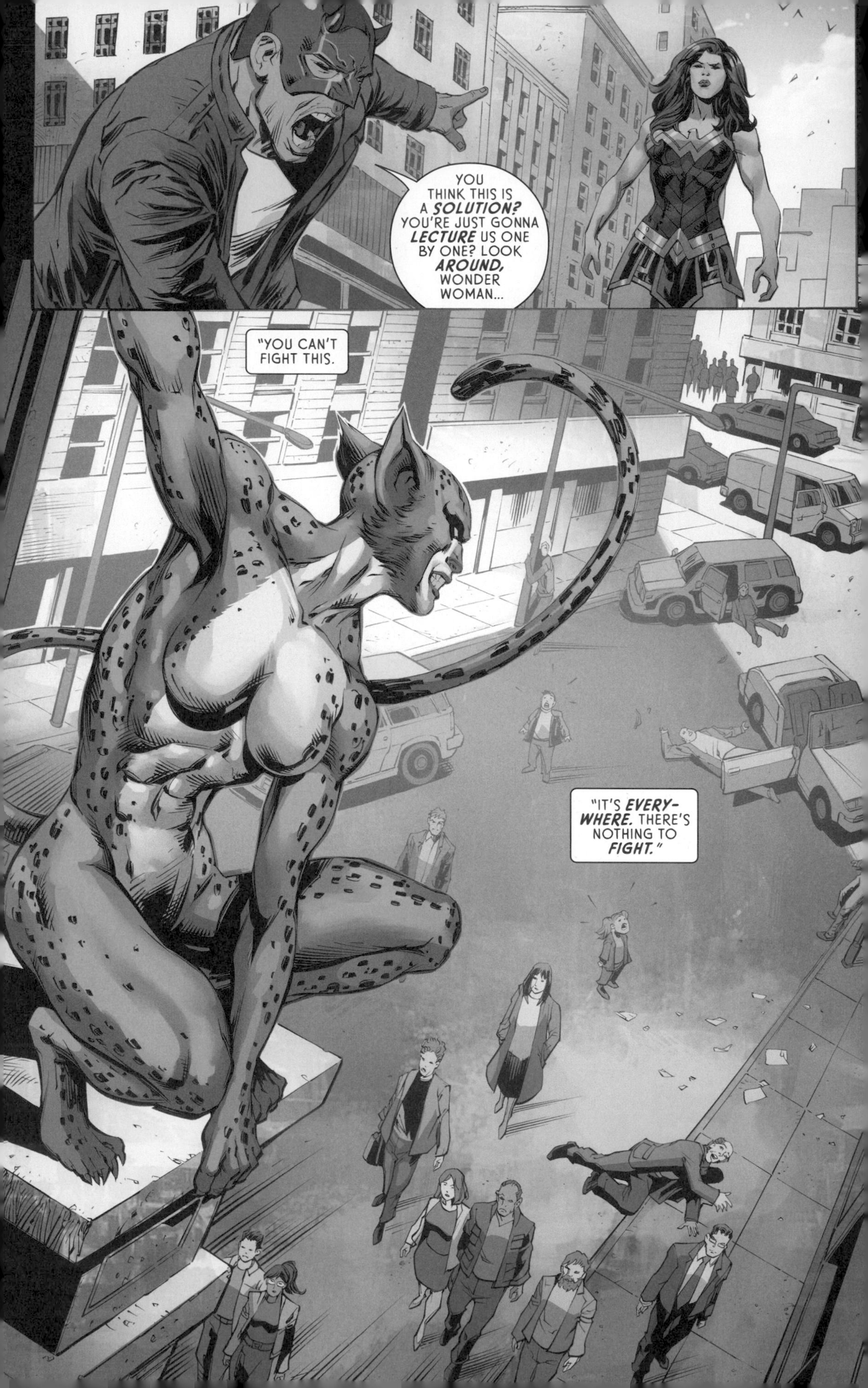
YOU THINK THIS IS A SOLUTION? YOU'RE JUST GONNA LECTURE US ONE BY ONE? LOOK AROUND, WONDER WOMAN...
"YOU CAN'T FIGHT THIS.
"IT'S EVERY-WHERE. THERE'S NOTHING TO FIGHT."

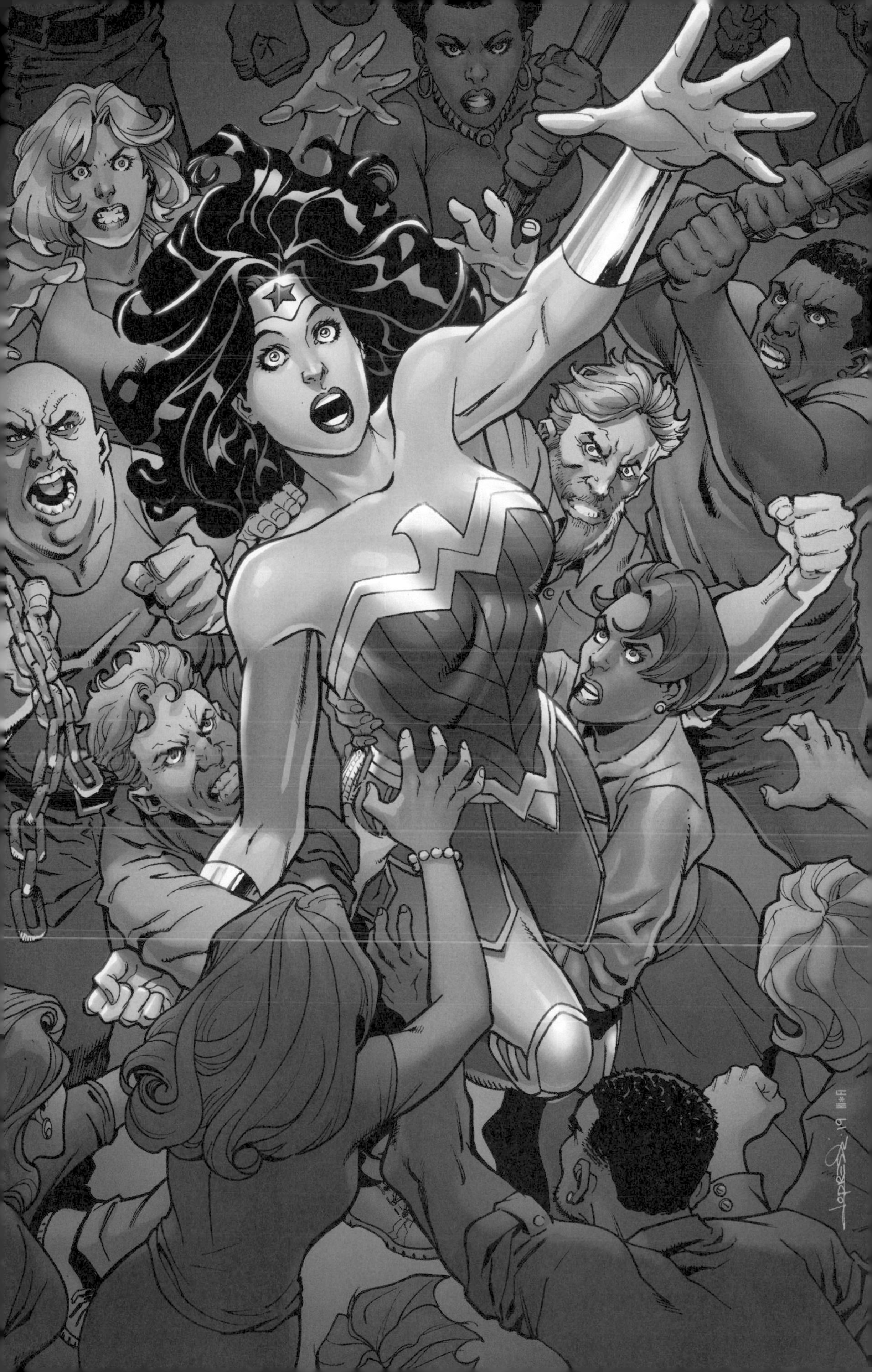

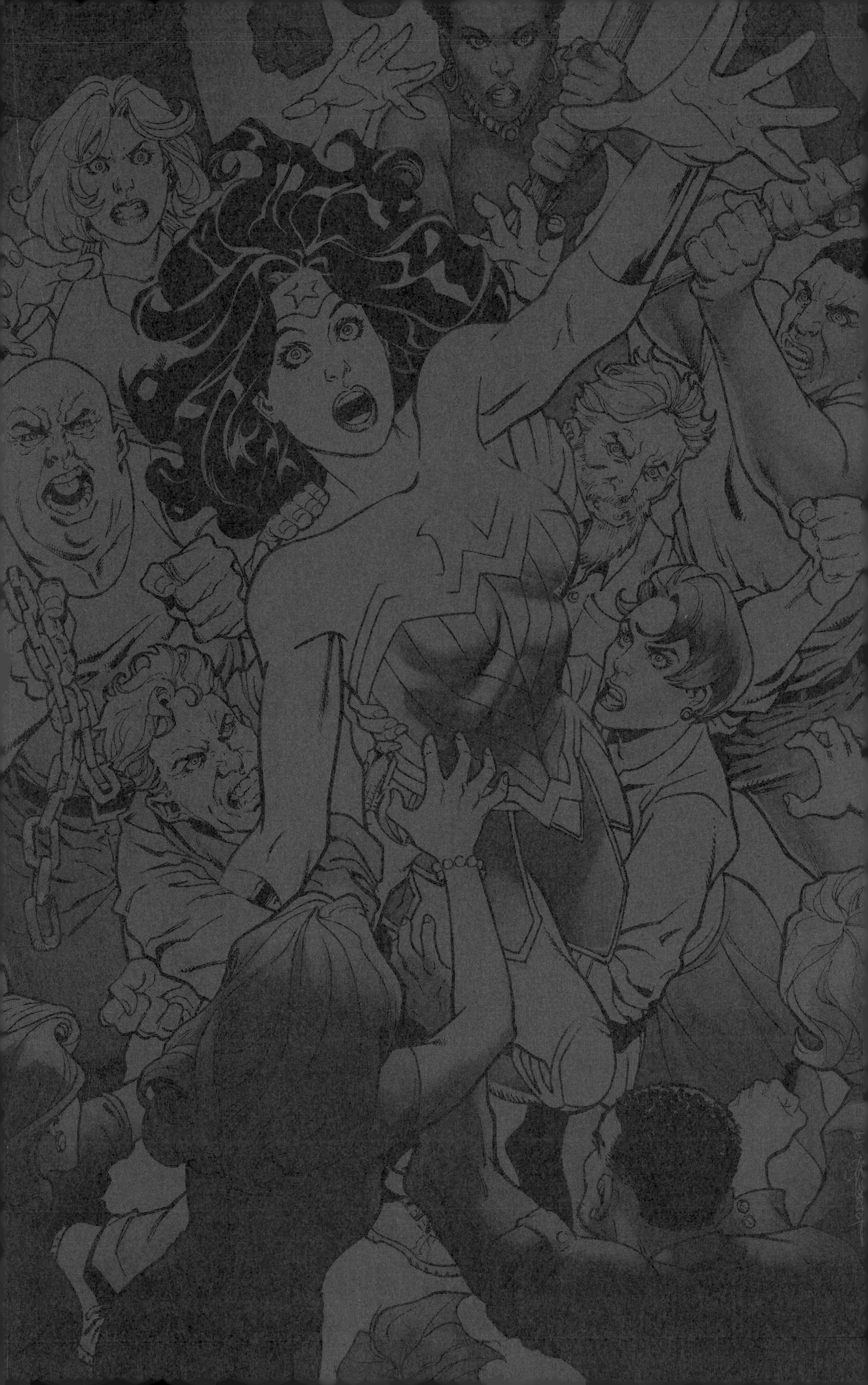

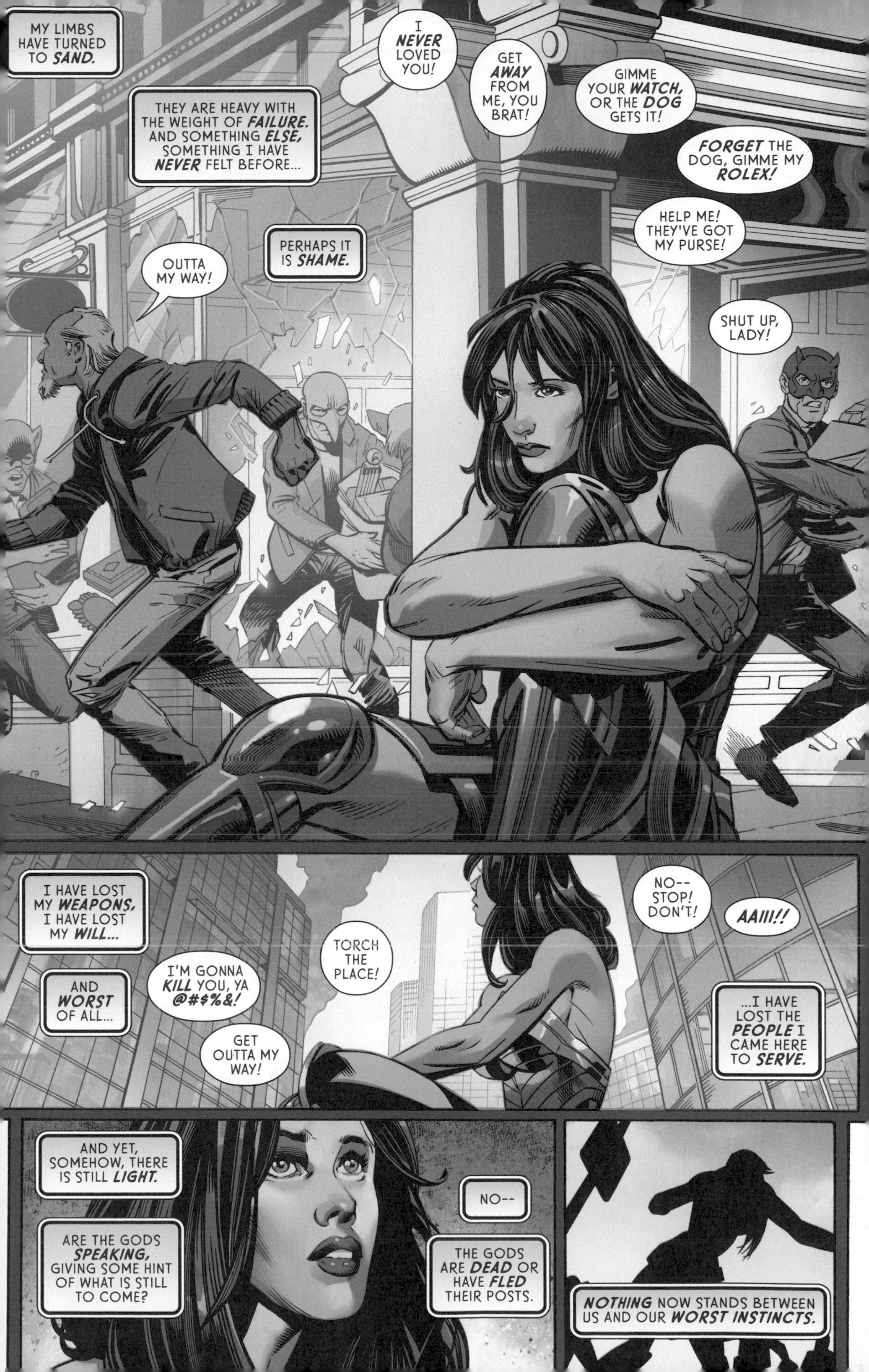
MY LIMBS HAVE TURNED TO SAND.
THEY ARE HEAVY WITH THE WEIGHT OF FAILURE. AND SOMETHING ELSE, SOMETHING I HAVE NEVER FELT BEFORE...
I NEVER LOVED YOU!
GET AWAY FROM ME, YOU BRAT!
GIMME YOUR WATCH, OR THE DOG GETS IT!
FORGET THE DOG, GIMME MY ROLEX!
OUTTA MY WAY!
PERHAPS IT IS SHAME.
HELP ME! THEY'VE GOT MY PURSE!
SHUT UP, LADY!
I HAVE LOST MY WEAPONS, I HAVE LOST MY WILL...
AND WORST OF ALL...
I'M GONNA KILL YOU, YA @#$%&!
TORCH THE PLACE!
GET OUTTA MY WAY!
NO-- STOP! DON'T!
AAIII!!
...I HAVE LOST THE PEOPLE I CAME HERE TO SERVE.
AND YET, SOMEHOW, THERE IS STILL LIGHT.
ARE THE GODS SPEAKING, GIVING SOME HINT OF WHAT IS STILL TO COME?
NO--
THE GODS ARE DEAD OR HAVE FLED THEIR POSTS.
NOTHING NOW STANDS BETWEEN US AND OUR WORST INSTINCTS.

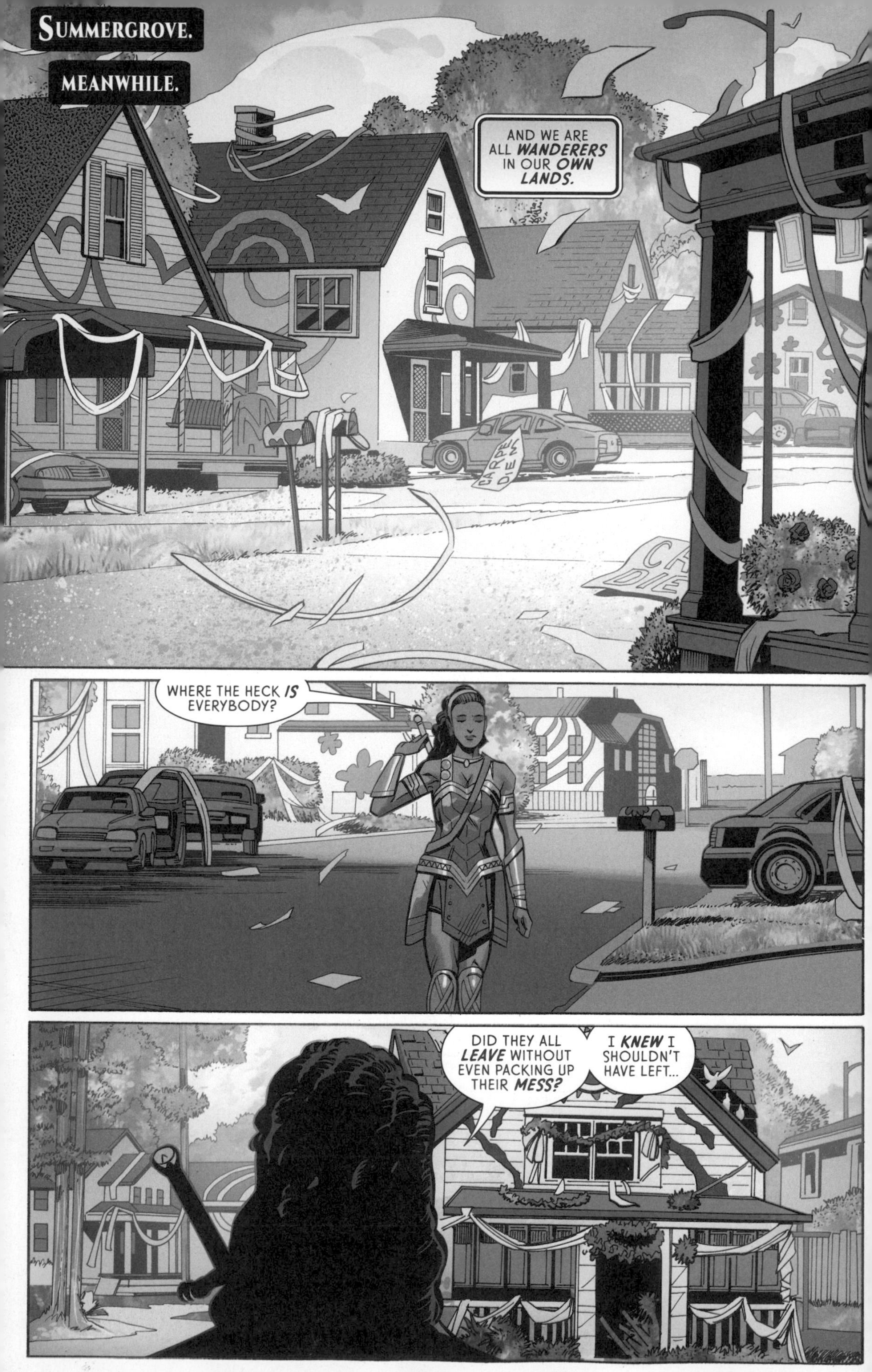
SUMMERGROVE.
MEANWHILE.
AND WE ARE ALL *WANDERERS* IN OUR *OWN* LANDS.
CARPE DIEM
WHERE THE HECK *IS* EVERYBODY?
DID THEY ALL *LEAVE* WITHOUT EVEN PACKING UP THEIR *MESS?*
I *KNEW* I SHOULDN'T HAVE LEFT...

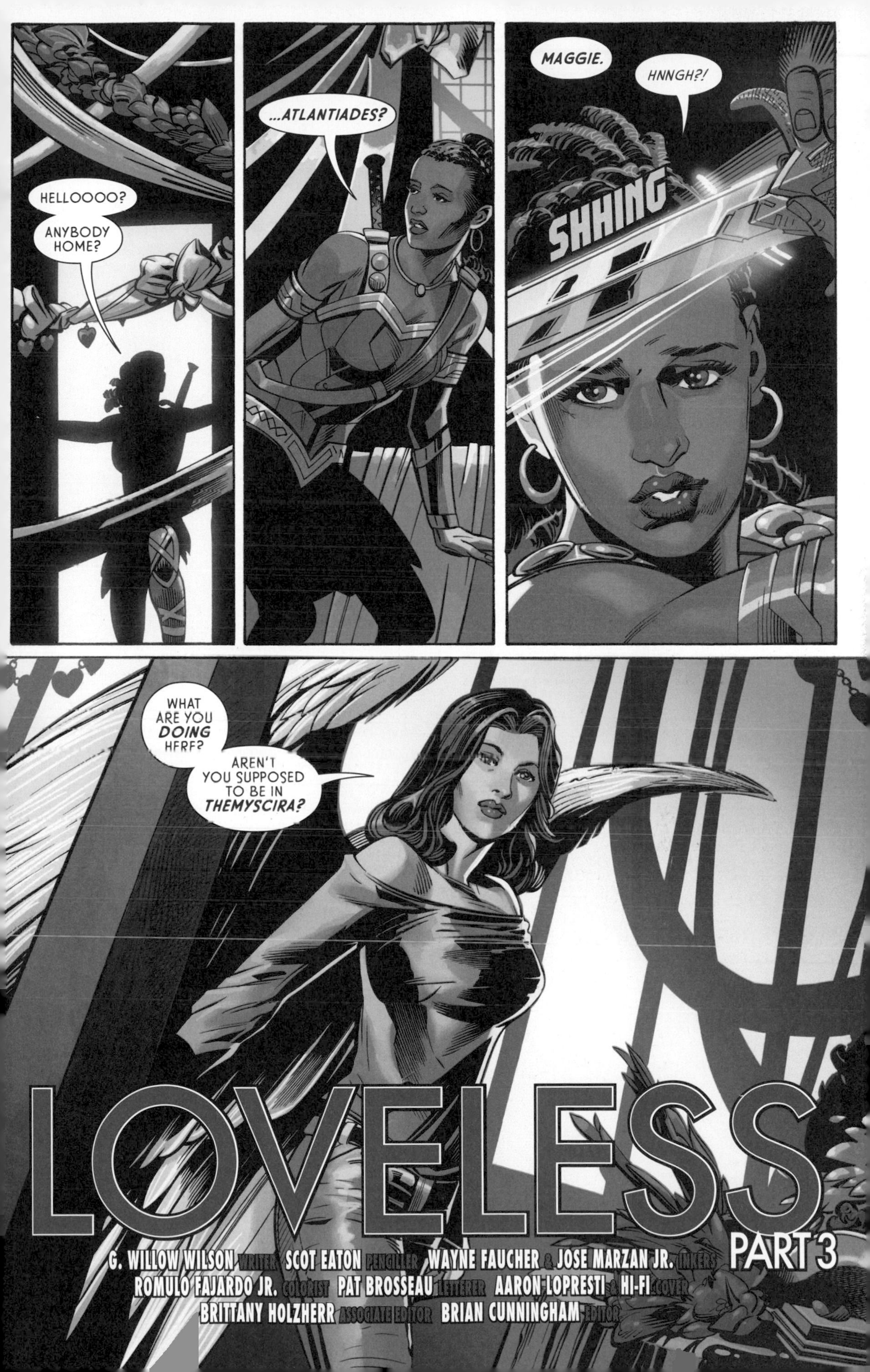
HELLOOOO?
ANYBODY HOME?
...ATLANTIADES?
MAGGIE.
HNNGH?!
SHHING
WHAT ARE YOU DOING HERE?
AREN'T YOU SUPPOSED TO BE IN THEMYSCIRA?
LOVELESS
PART 3
G. WILLOW WILSON WRITER SCOT EATON PENCILLER WAYNE FAUCHER & JOSE MARZAN JR. INKERS
ROMULO FAJARDO JR. COLORIST PAT BROSSEAU LETTERER AARON LOPRESTI & HI-FI COVER
BRITTANY HOLZHERR ASSOCIATE EDITOR BRIAN CUNNINGHAM EDITOR

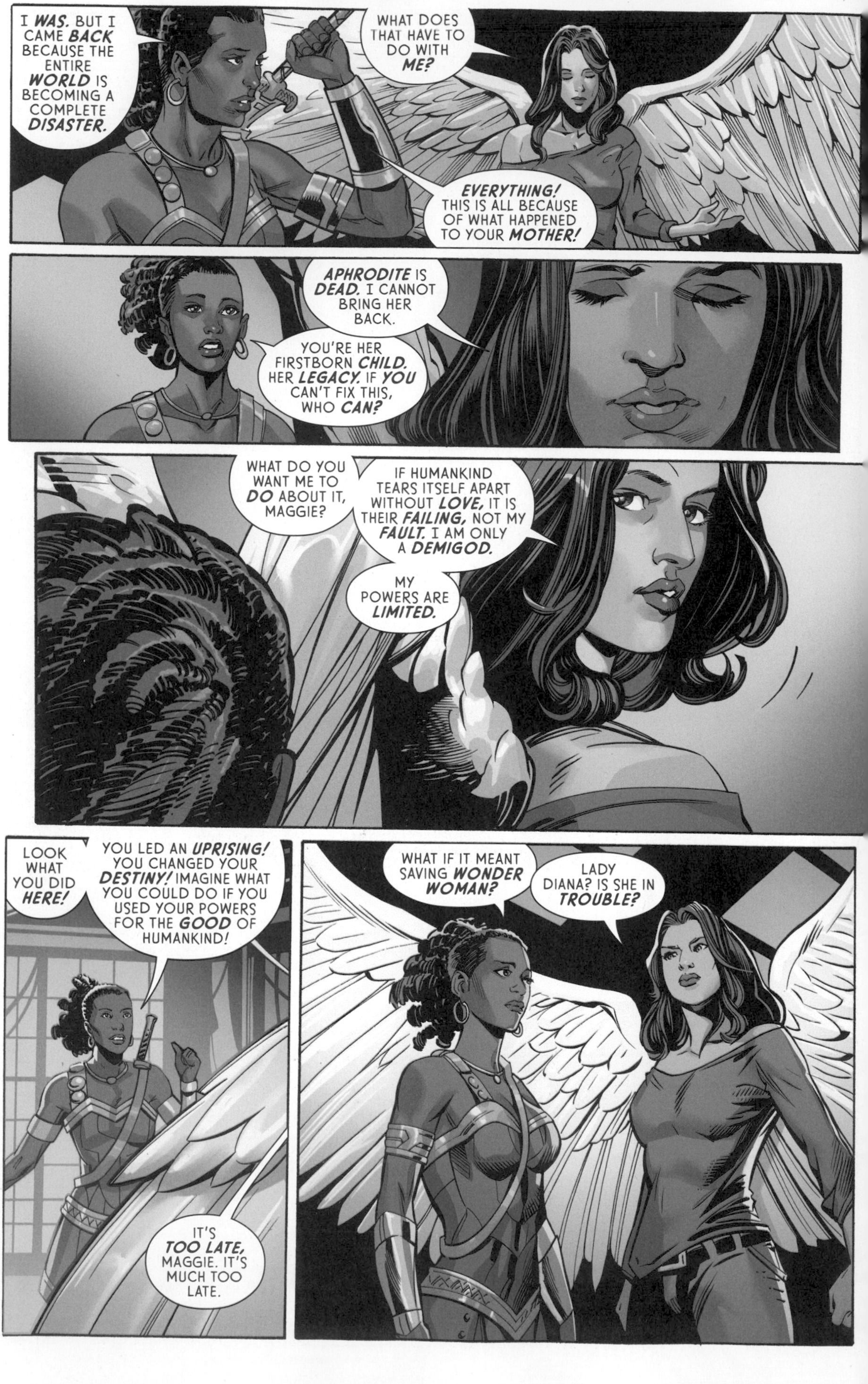

I WAS. BUT I CAME BACK BECAUSE THE ENTIRE WORLD IS BECOMING A COMPLETE DISASTER.
WHAT DOES THAT HAVE TO DO WITH ME?
EVERYTHING! THIS IS ALL BECAUSE OF WHAT HAPPENED TO YOUR MOTHER!
APHRODITE IS DEAD. I CANNOT BRING HER BACK.
YOU'RE HER FIRSTBORN CHILD. HER LEGACY. IF YOU CAN'T FIX THIS, WHO CAN?
WHAT DO YOU WANT ME TO DO ABOUT IT, MAGGIE?
IF HUMANKIND TEARS ITSELF APART WITHOUT LOVE, IT IS THEIR FAILING, NOT MY FAULT. I AM ONLY A DEMIGOD.
MY POWERS ARE LIMITED.
LOOK WHAT YOU DID HERE!
YOU LED AN UPRISING! YOU CHANGED YOUR DESTINY! IMAGINE WHAT YOU COULD DO IF YOU USED YOUR POWERS FOR THE GOOD OF HUMANKIND!
IT'S TOO LATE, MAGGIE. IT'S MUCH TOO LATE.
WHAT IF IT MEANT SAVING WONDER WOMAN?
LADY DIANA? IS SHE IN TROUBLE?

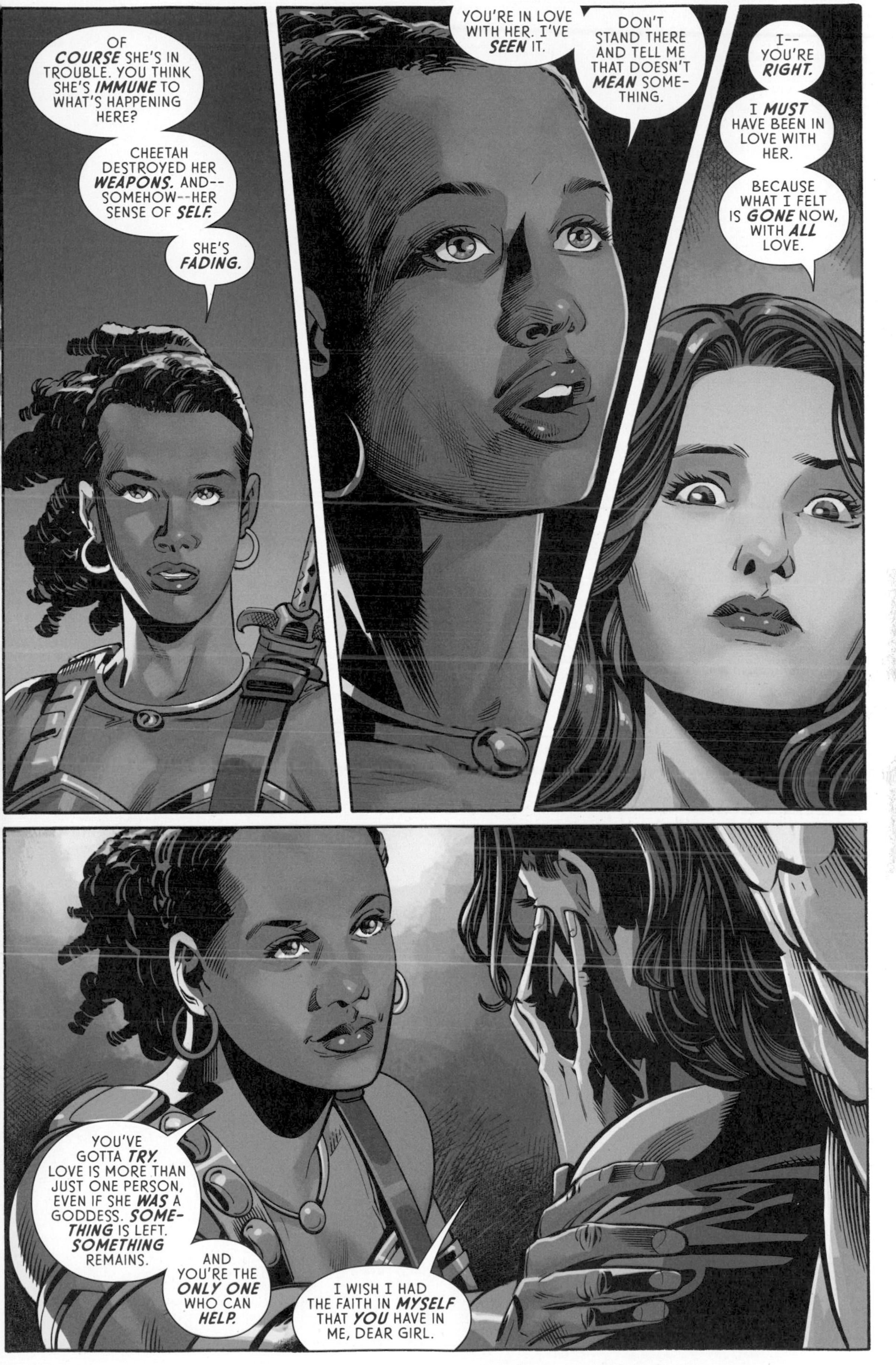
OF COURSE SHE'S IN TROUBLE. YOU THINK SHE'S IMMUNE TO WHAT'S HAPPENING HERE?
CHEETAH DESTROYED HER WEAPONS. AND-- SOMEHOW--HER SENSE OF SELF.
SHE'S FADING.
YOU'RE IN LOVE WITH HER. I'VE SEEN IT.
DON'T STAND THERE AND TELL ME THAT DOESN'T MEAN SOME-THING.
I-- YOU'RE RIGHT.
I MUST HAVE BEEN IN LOVE WITH HER.
BECAUSE WHAT I FELT IS GONE NOW, WITH ALL LOVE.
YOU'VE GOTTA TRY. LOVE IS MORE THAN JUST ONE PERSON, EVEN IF SHE WAS A GODDESS. SOME-THING IS LEFT. SOMETHING REMAINS.
AND YOU'RE THE ONLY ONE WHO CAN HELP.
I WISH I HAD THE FAITH IN MYSELF THAT YOU HAVE IN ME, DEAR GIRL.

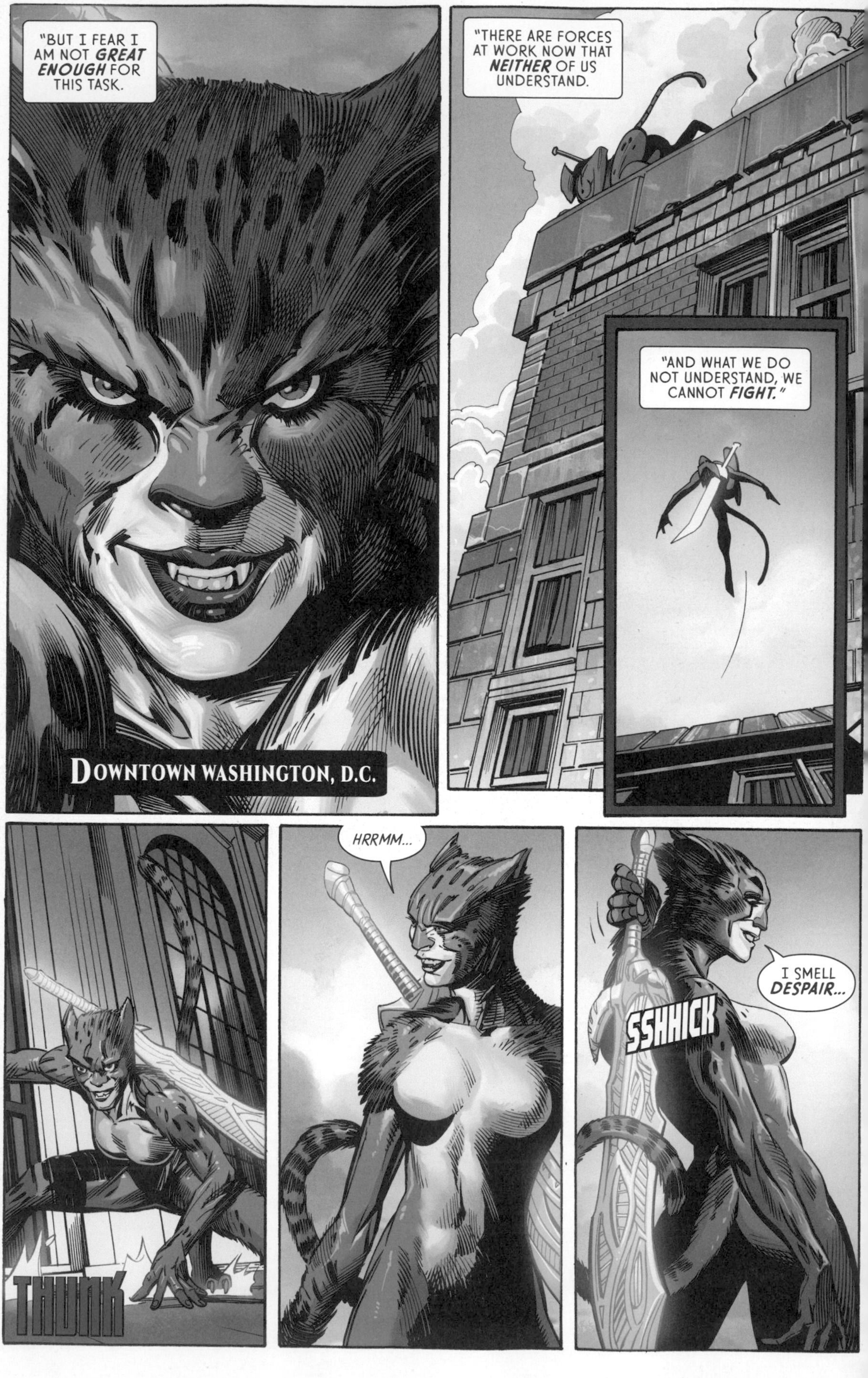
"BUT I FEAR I AM NOT GREAT ENOUGH FOR THIS TASK.
DOWNTOWN WASHINGTON, D.C.
"THERE ARE FORCES AT WORK NOW THAT NEITHER OF US UNDERSTAND.
"AND WHAT WE DO NOT UNDERSTAND, WE CANNOT FIGHT."
THUNK
HRRMM...
SSHHICK
I SMELL DESPAIR...

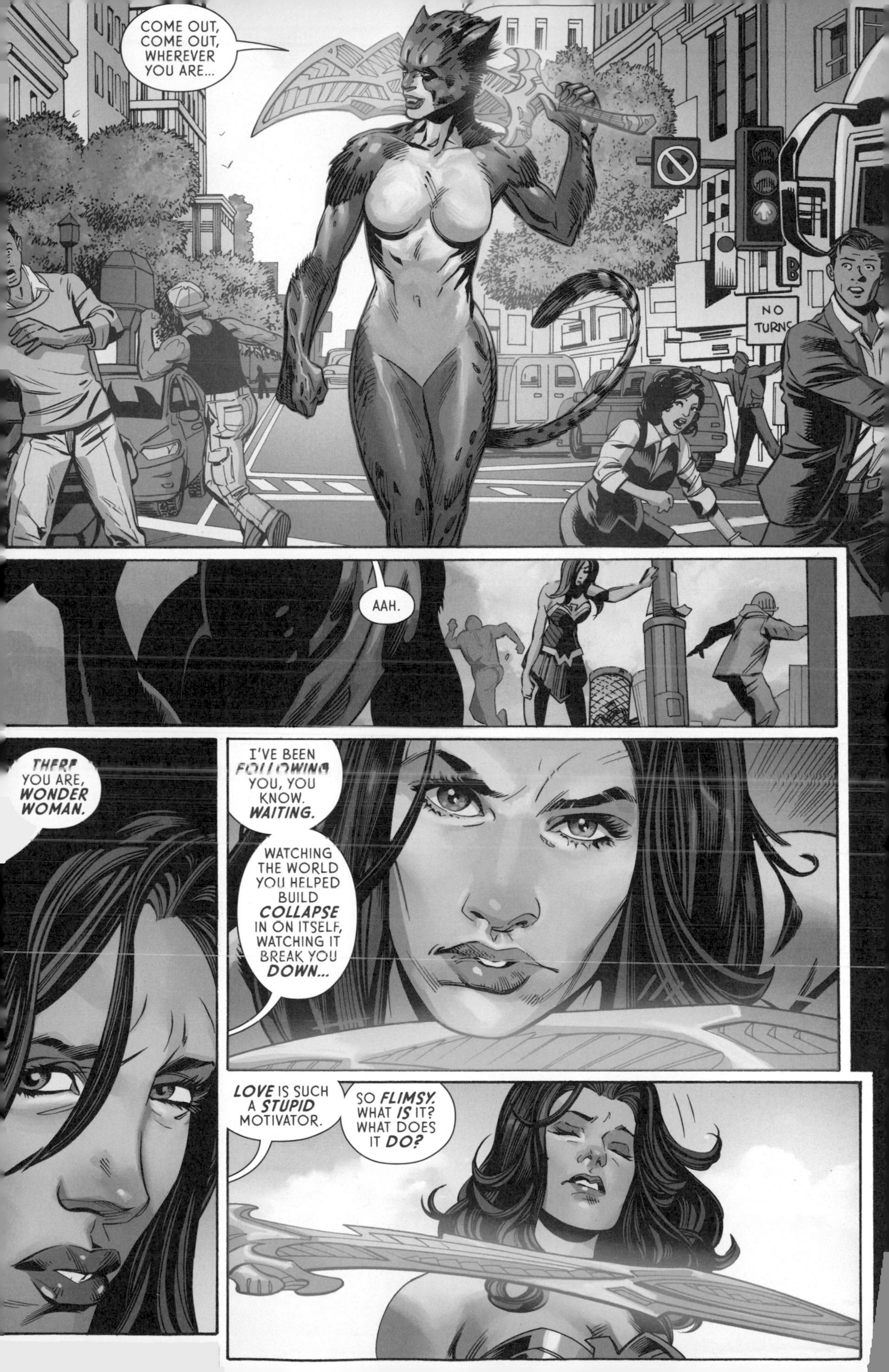
COME OUT, COME OUT, WHEREVER YOU ARE...
NO TURNS
AAH.
THERE YOU ARE, WONDER WOMAN.
I'VE BEEN FOLLOWING YOU, YOU KNOW. WAITING.
WATCHING THE WORLD YOU HELPED BUILD COLLAPSE IN ON ITSELF, WATCHING IT BREAK YOU DOWN...
LOVE IS SUCH A STUPID MOTIVATOR.
SO FLIMSY. WHAT IS IT? WHAT DOES IT DO?

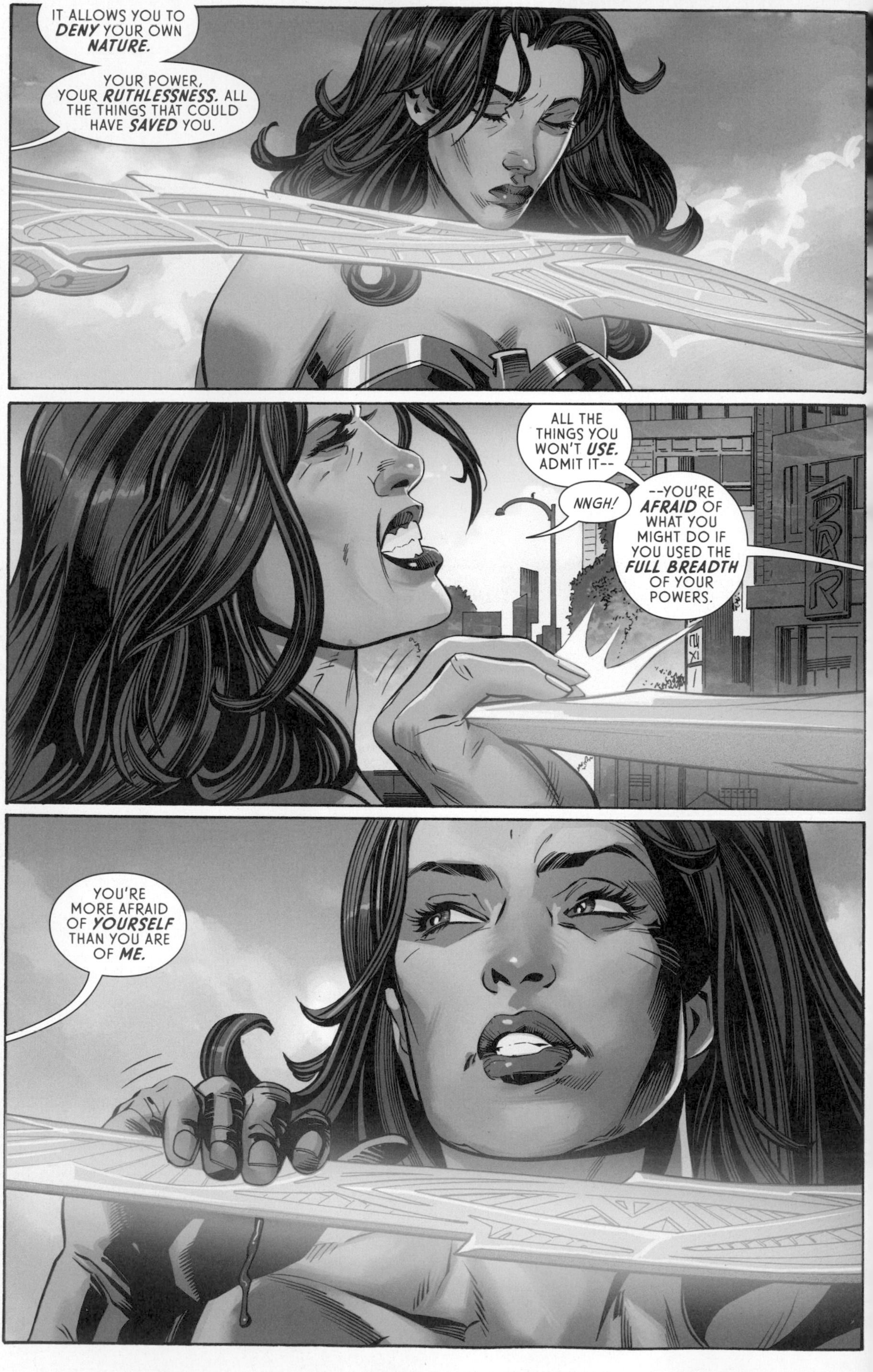
IT ALLOWS YOU TO DENY YOUR OWN NATURE.
YOUR POWER, YOUR RUTHLESSNESS. ALL THE THINGS THAT COULD HAVE SAVED YOU.
ALL THE THINGS YOU WON'T USE. ADMIT IT--
NNGH!
--YOU'RE AFRAID OF WHAT YOU MIGHT DO IF YOU USED THE FULL BREADTH OF YOUR POWERS.
YOU'RE MORE AFRAID OF YOURSELF THAN YOU ARE OF ME.

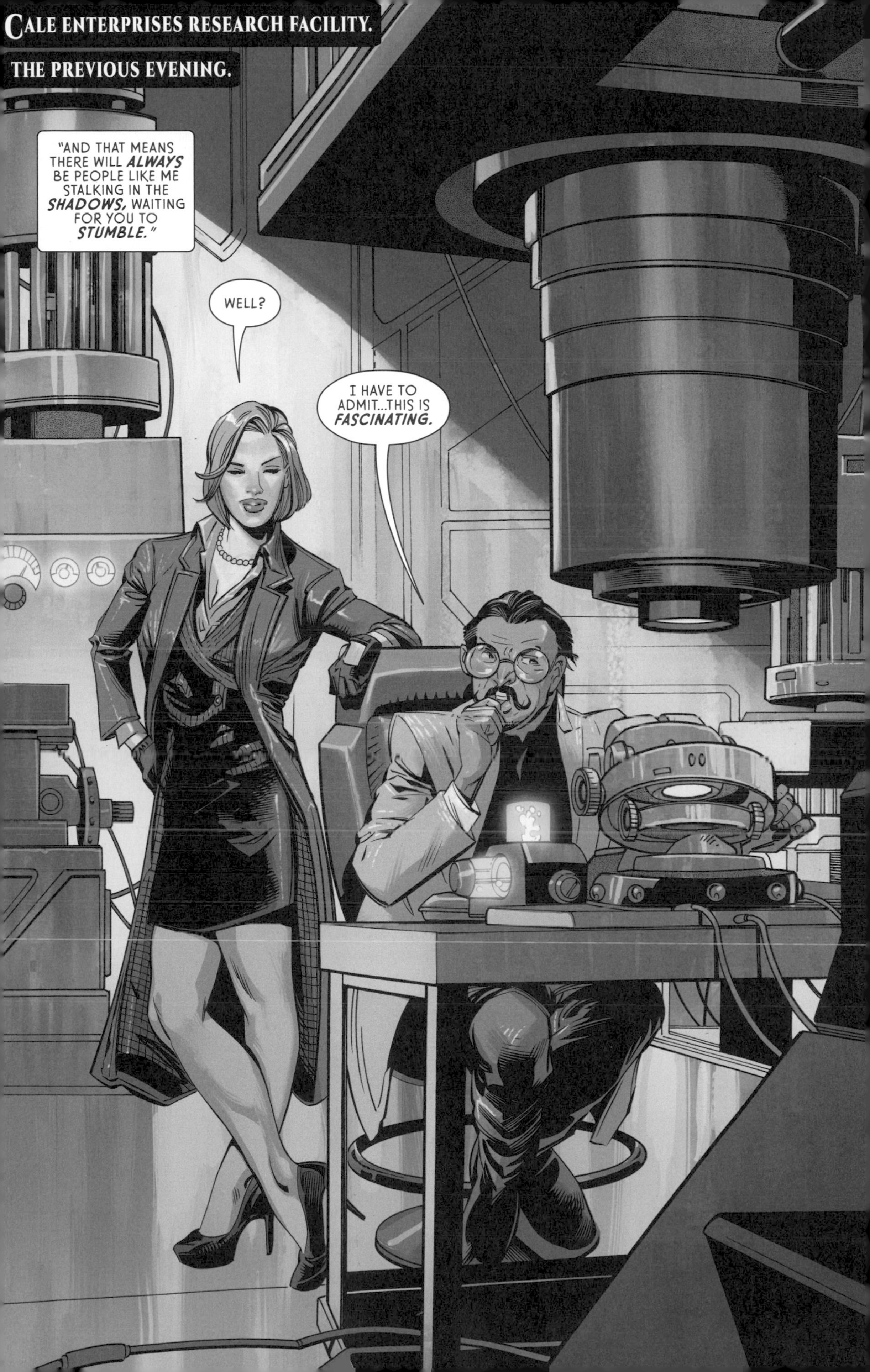
CALE ENTERPRISES RESEARCH FACILITY.
THE PREVIOUS EVENING.
"AND THAT MEANS THERE WILL ALWAYS BE PEOPLE LIKE ME STALKING IN THE SHADOWS, WAITING FOR YOU TO STUMBLE."
WELL?
I HAVE TO ADMIT...THIS IS FASCINATING.

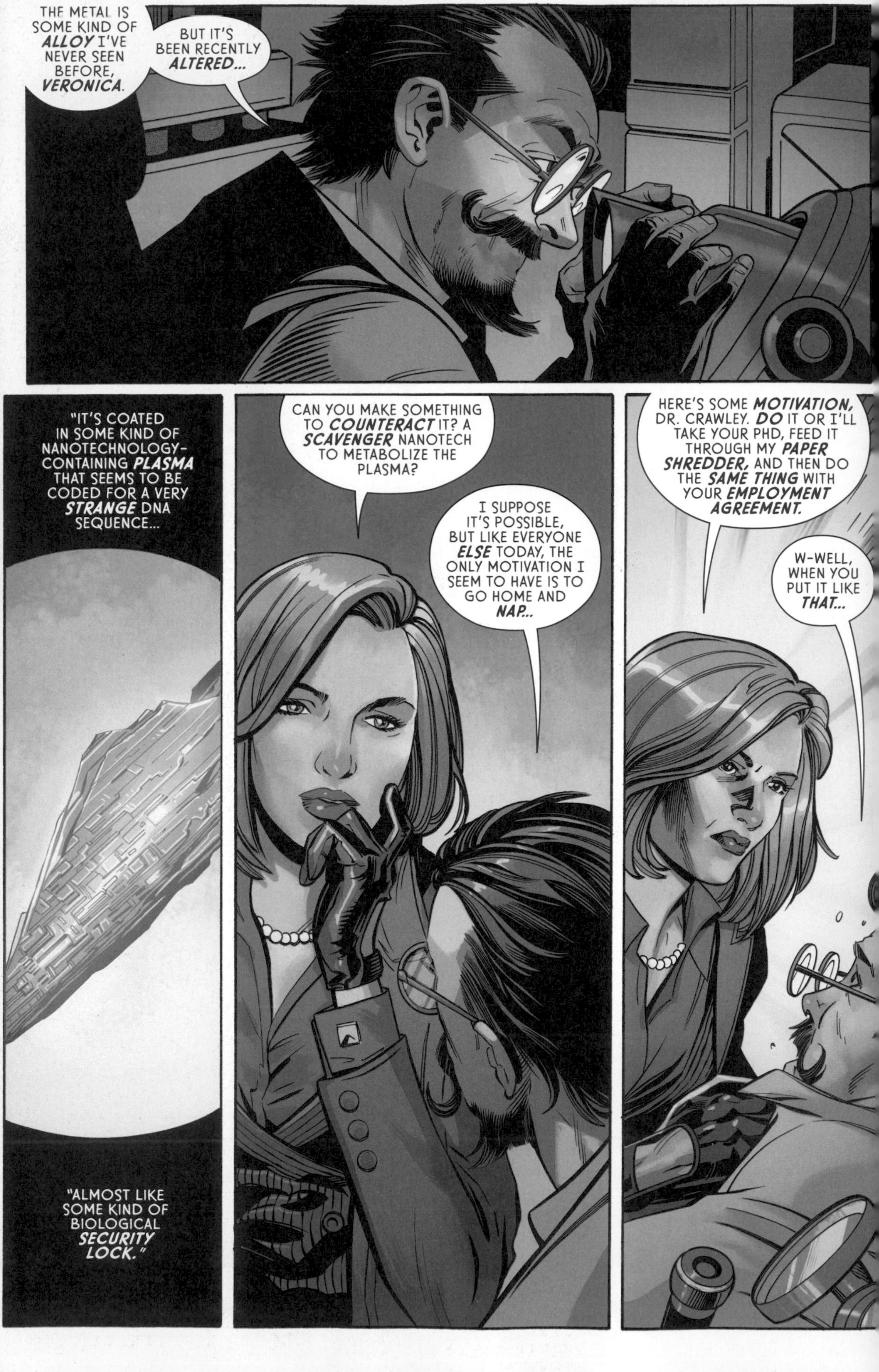
THE METAL IS SOME KIND OF ALLOY I'VE NEVER SEEN BEFORE, VERONICA.
BUT IT'S BEEN RECENTLY ALTERED...
"IT'S COATED IN SOME KIND OF NANOTECHNOLOGY-CONTAINING PLASMA THAT SEEMS TO BE CODED FOR A VERY STRANGE DNA SEQUENCE...
"ALMOST LIKE SOME KIND OF BIOLOGICAL SECURITY LOCK."
CAN YOU MAKE SOMETHING TO COUNTERACT IT? A SCAVENGER NANOTECH TO METABOLIZE THE PLASMA?
I SUPPOSE IT'S POSSIBLE, BUT LIKE EVERYONE ELSE TODAY, THE ONLY MOTIVATION I SEEM TO HAVE IS TO GO HOME AND NAP...
HERE'S SOME MOTIVATION, DR. CRAWLEY. DO IT OR I'LL TAKE YOUR PHD, FEED IT THROUGH MY PAPER SHREDDER, AND THEN DO THE SAME THING WITH YOUR EMPLOYMENT AGREEMENT.
W-WELL, WHEN YOU PUT IT LIKE THAT...

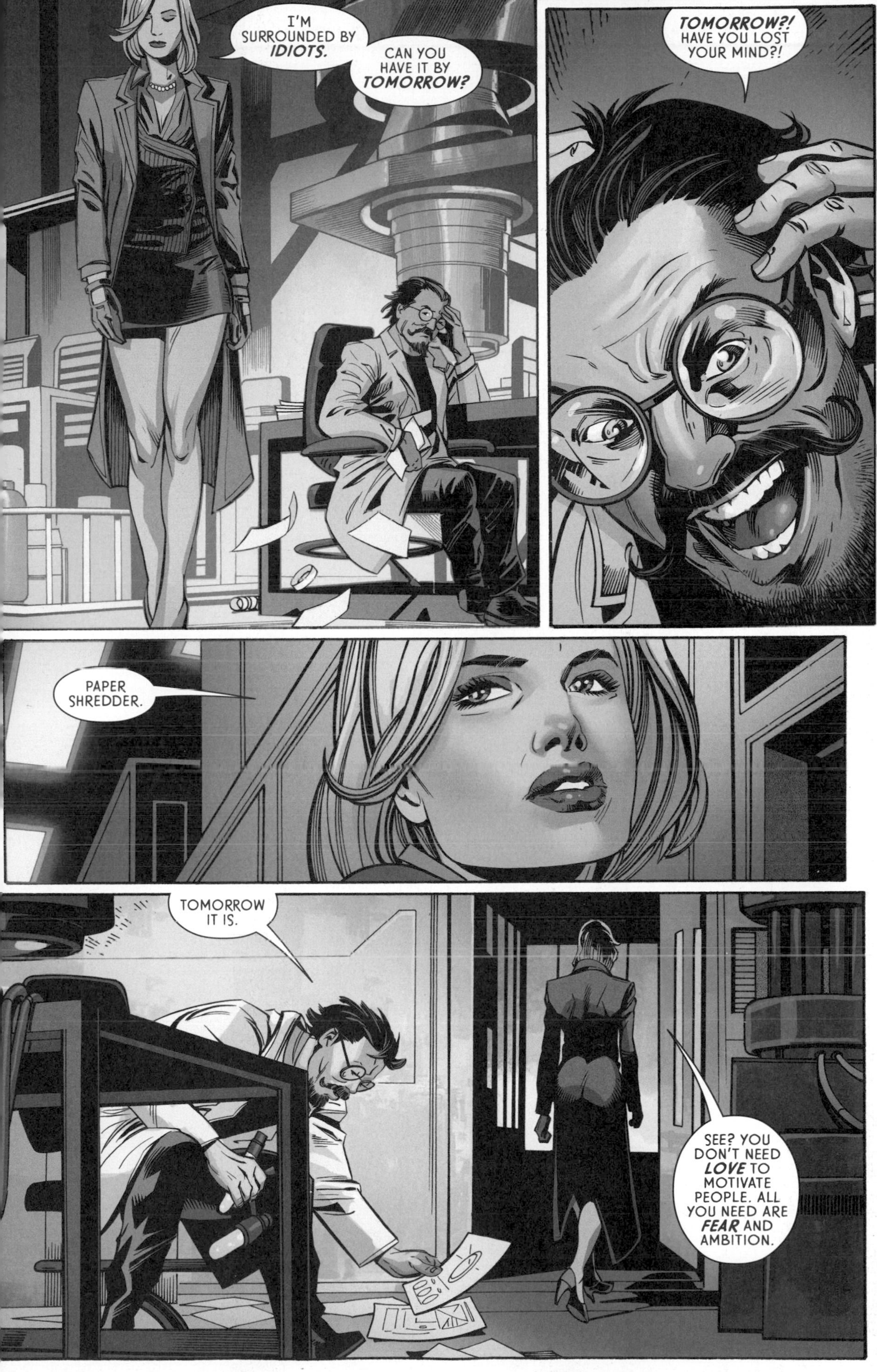
I'M SURROUNDED BY IDIOTS.
CAN YOU HAVE IT BY TOMORROW?
TOMORROW?! HAVE YOU LOST YOUR MIND?!
PAPER SHREDDER.
TOMORROW IT IS.
SEE? YOU DON'T NEED LOVE TO MOTIVATE PEOPLE. ALL YOU NEED ARE FEAR AND AMBITION.

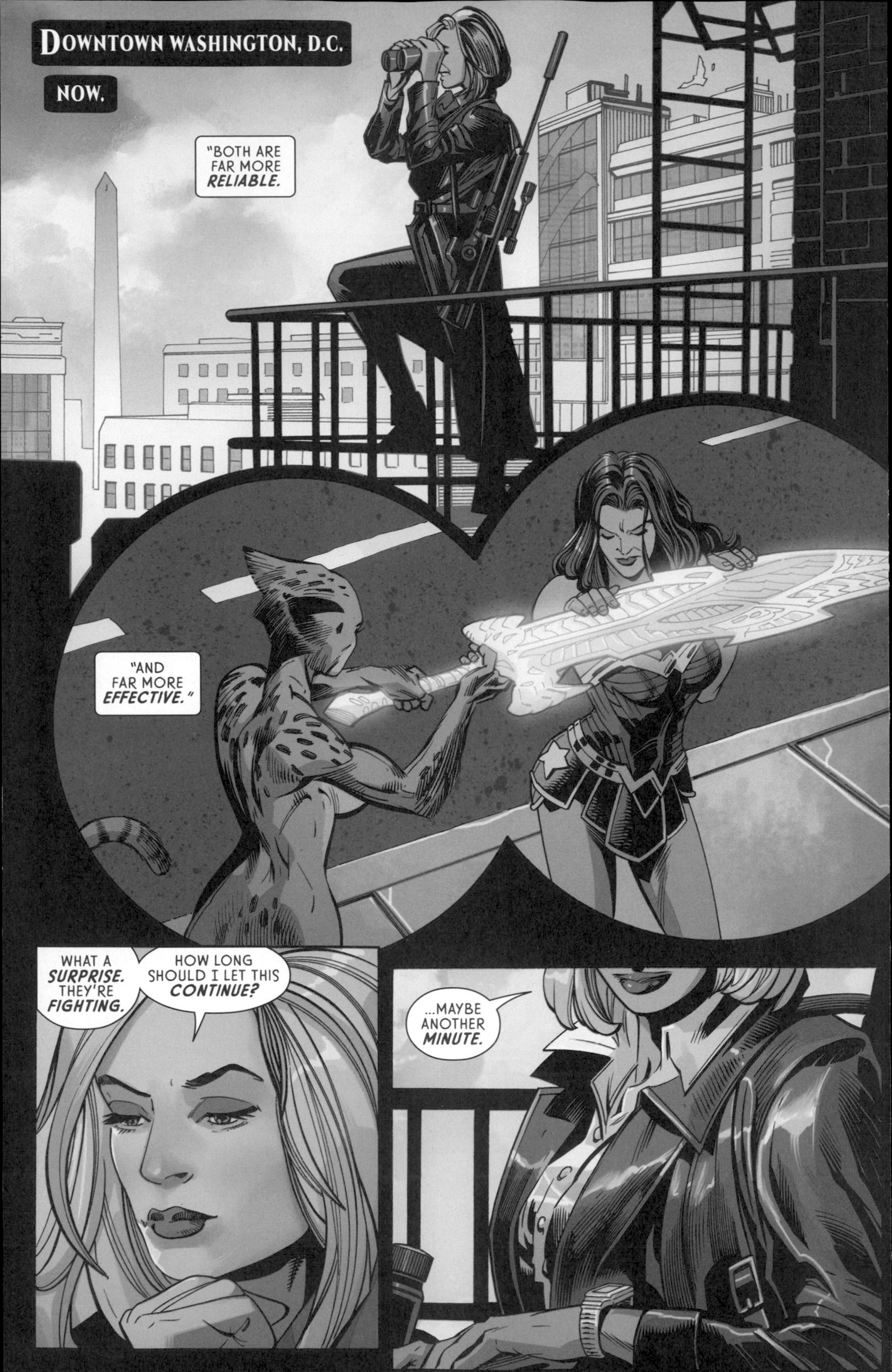
DOWNTOWN WASHINGTON, D.C.
NOW.
"BOTH ARE FAR MORE RELIABLE.
"AND FAR MORE EFFECTIVE."
WHAT A SURPRISE. THEY'RE FIGHTING.
HOW LONG SHOULD I LET THIS CONTINUE?
...MAYBE ANOTHER MINUTE.

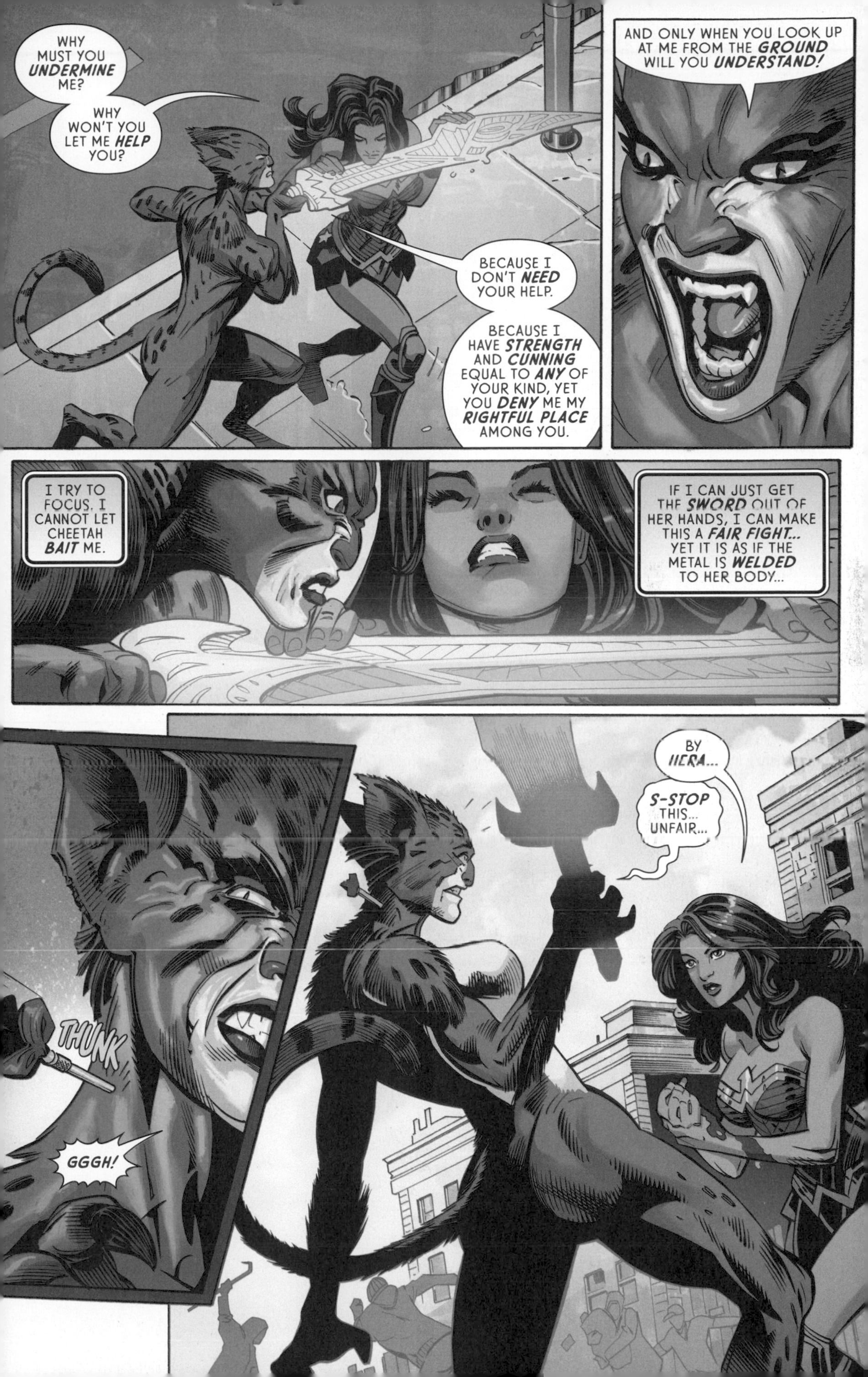
WHY MUST YOU *UNDERMINE* ME?
WHY WON'T YOU LET ME *HELP* YOU?
BECAUSE I DON'T *NEED* YOUR HELP.
BECAUSE I HAVE *STRENGTH* AND *CUNNING* EQUAL TO *ANY* OF YOUR KIND, YET YOU *DENY* ME MY *RIGHTFUL PLACE* AMONG YOU.
AND ONLY WHEN YOU LOOK UP AT ME FROM THE *GROUND* WILL YOU *UNDERSTAND!*
I TRY TO FOCUS. I CANNOT LET CHEETAH *BAIT* ME.
IF I CAN JUST GET THE *SWORD* OUT OF HER HANDS, I CAN MAKE THIS A *FAIR FIGHT...* YET IT IS AS IF THE METAL IS *WELDED* TO HER BODY...
BY *HERA...*
S-STOP THIS... UNFAIR...
THUNK
GGGH!

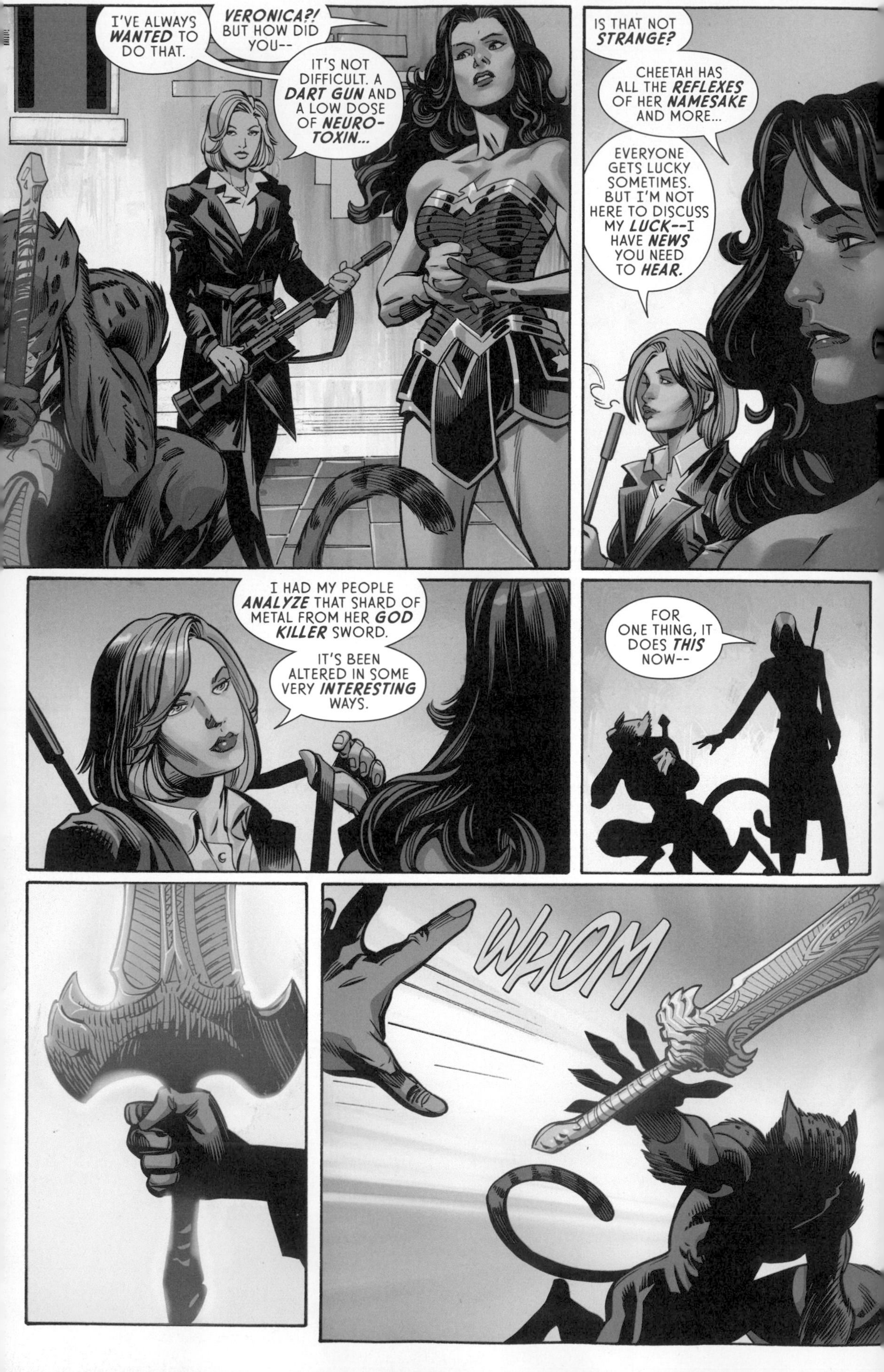
I'VE ALWAYS WANTED TO DO THAT.
VERONICA?! BUT HOW DID YOU--
IT'S NOT DIFFICULT. A DART GUN AND A LOW DOSE OF NEURO-TOXIN...
IS THAT NOT STRANGE?
CHEETAH HAS ALL THE REFLEXES OF HER NAMESAKE AND MORE...
EVERYONE GETS LUCKY SOMETIMES. BUT I'M NOT HERE TO DISCUSS MY LUCK--I HAVE NEWS YOU NEED TO HEAR.
I HAD MY PEOPLE ANALYZE THAT SHARD OF METAL FROM HER GOD KILLER SWORD.
IT'S BEEN ALTERED IN SOME VERY INTERESTING WAYS.
FOR ONE THING, IT DOES THIS NOW--
WHOM

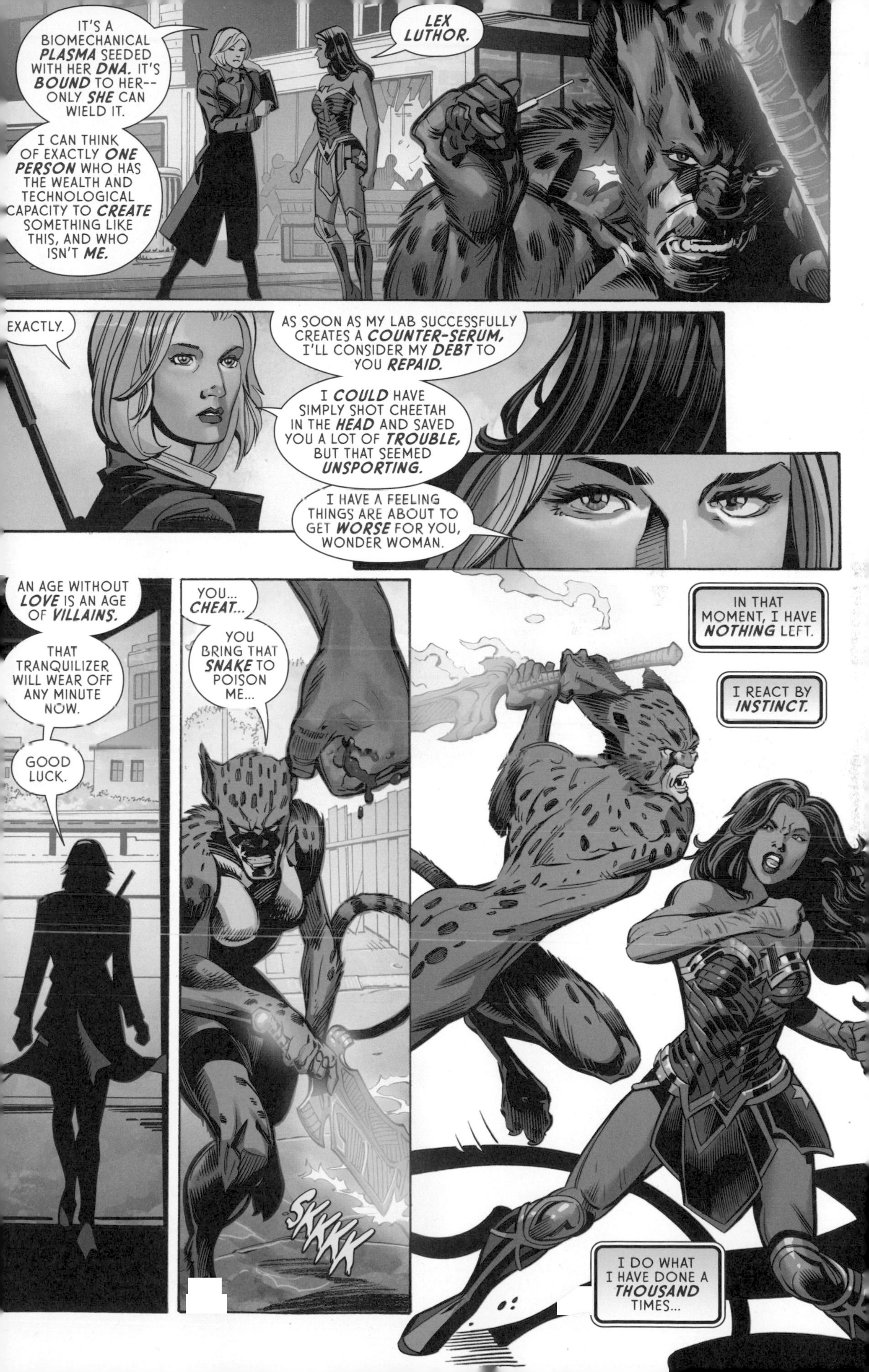

IT'S A BIOMECHANICAL PLASMA SEEDED WITH HER DNA. IT'S BOUND TO HER-- ONLY SHE CAN WIELD IT.
I CAN THINK OF EXACTLY ONE PERSON WHO HAS THE WEALTH AND TECHNOLOGICAL CAPACITY TO CREATE SOMETHING LIKE THIS, AND WHO ISN'T ME.
LEX LUTHOR.
EXACTLY.
AS SOON AS MY LAB SUCCESSFULLY CREATES A COUNTER-SERUM, I'LL CONSIDER MY DEBT TO YOU REPAID.
I COULD HAVE SIMPLY SHOT CHEETAH IN THE HEAD AND SAVED YOU A LOT OF TROUBLE, BUT THAT SEEMED UNSPORTING.
I HAVE A FEELING THINGS ARE ABOUT TO GET WORSE FOR YOU, WONDER WOMAN.
AN AGE WITHOUT LOVE IS AN AGE OF VILLAINS.
THAT TRANQUILIZER WILL WEAR OFF ANY MINUTE NOW.
GOOD LUCK.
YOU... CHEAT...
YOU BRING THAT SNAKE TO POISON ME...
SKKKK
IN THAT MOMENT, I HAVE NOTHING LEFT.
I REACT BY INSTINCT.
I DO WHAT I HAVE DONE A THOUSAND TIMES...

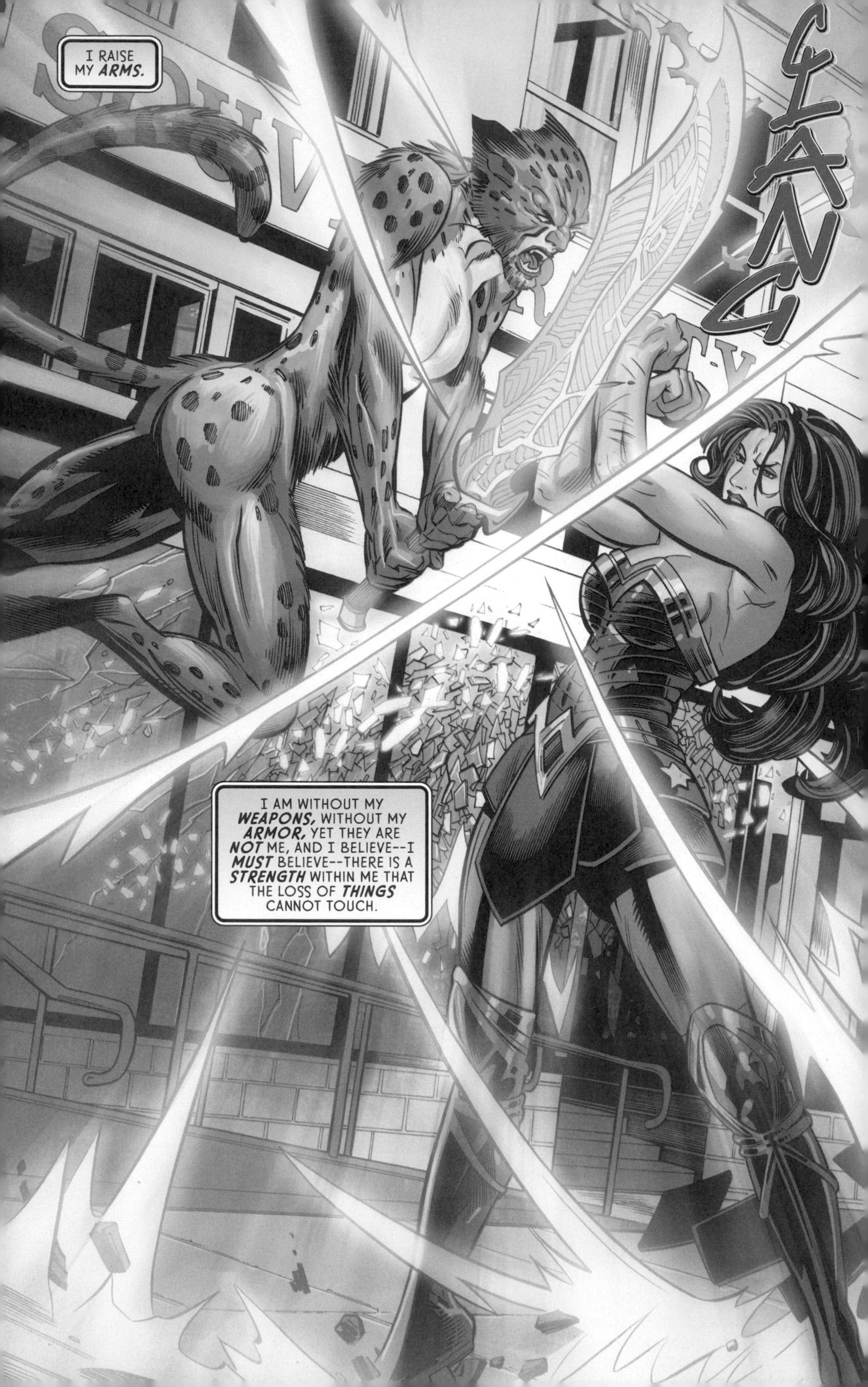
I RAISE MY ARMS.
CLANG
I AM WITHOUT MY WEAPONS, WITHOUT MY ARMOR, YET THEY ARE NOT ME, AND I BELIEVE--I MUST BELIEVE--THERE IS A STRENGTH WITHIN ME THAT THE LOSS OF THINGS CANNOT TOUCH.

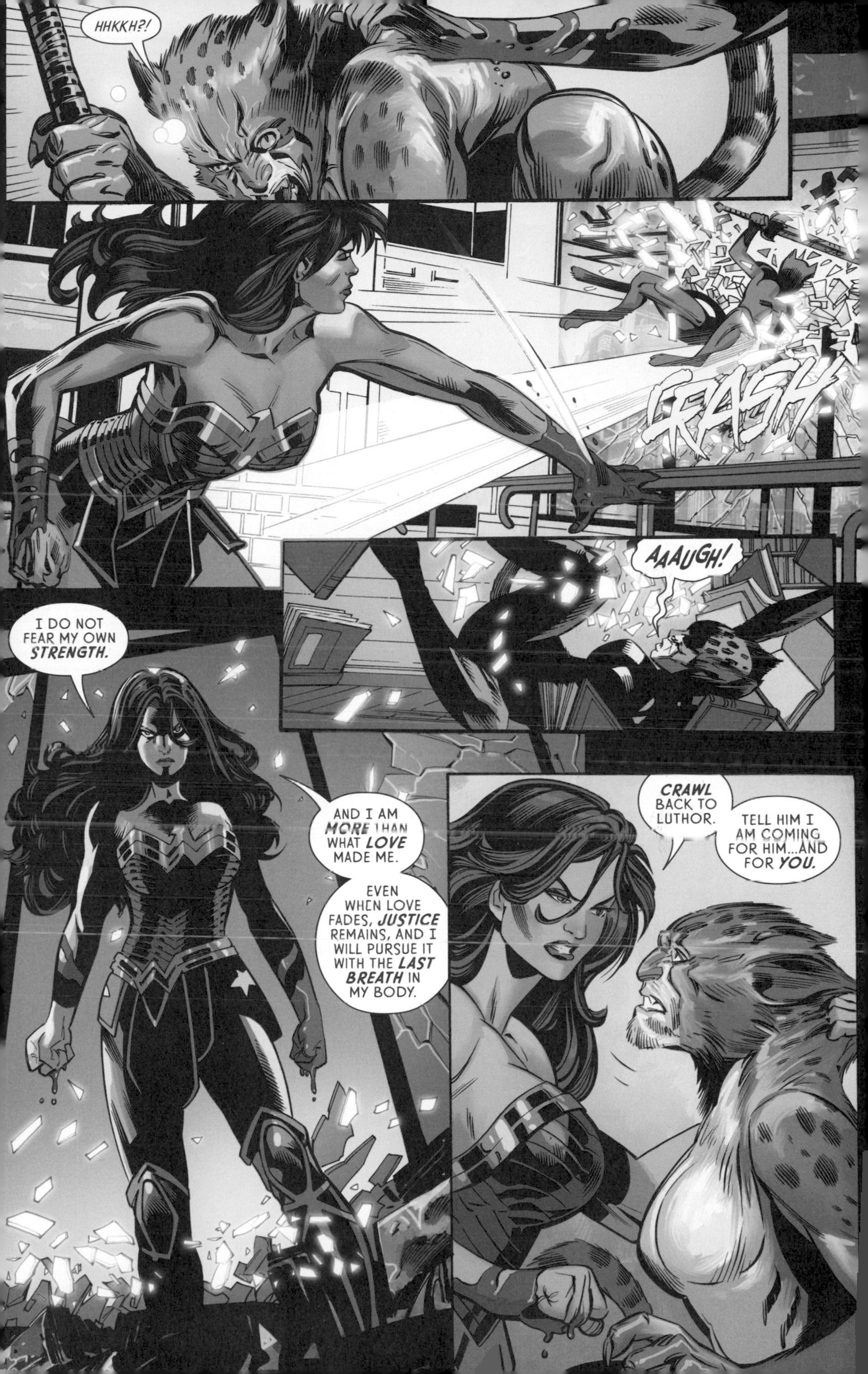
HHKKH?!
CRASH
AAAUGH!
I DO NOT FEAR MY OWN STRENGTH.
AND I AM MORE THAN WHAT LOVE MADE ME.
EVEN WHEN LOVE FADES, JUSTICE REMAINS, AND I WILL PURSUE IT WITH THE LAST BREATH IN MY BODY.
CRAWL BACK TO LUTHOR.
TELL HIM I AM COMING FOR HIM...AND FOR YOU.

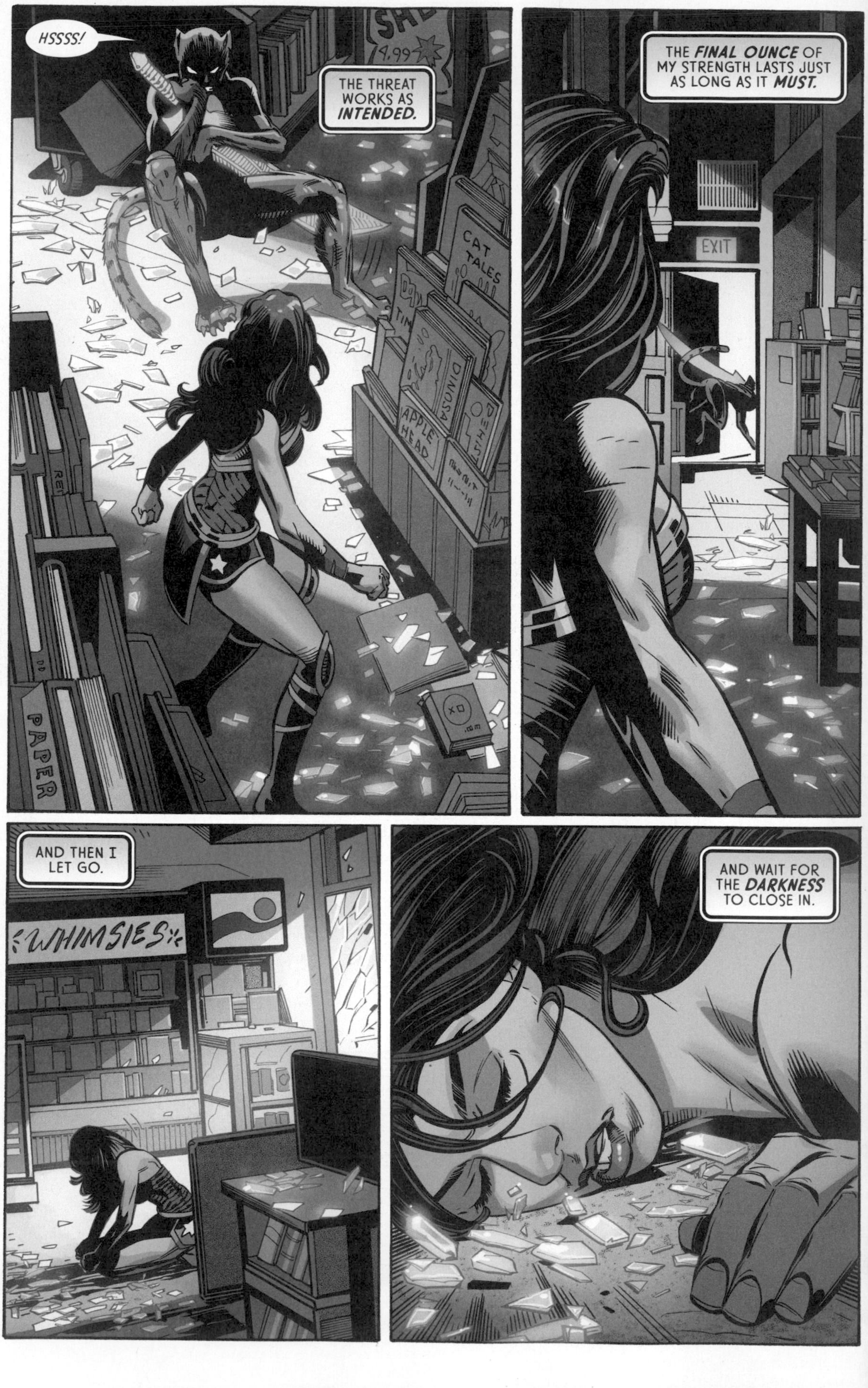
HSSSS!
THE THREAT WORKS AS *INTENDED.*
CAT TALES
APPLE HEAD
PAPER
THE *FINAL OUNCE* OF MY STRENGTH LASTS JUST AS LONG AS IT *MUST.*
EXIT
AND THEN I LET GO.
WHIMSIES
AND WAIT FOR THE *DARKNESS* TO CLOSE IN.

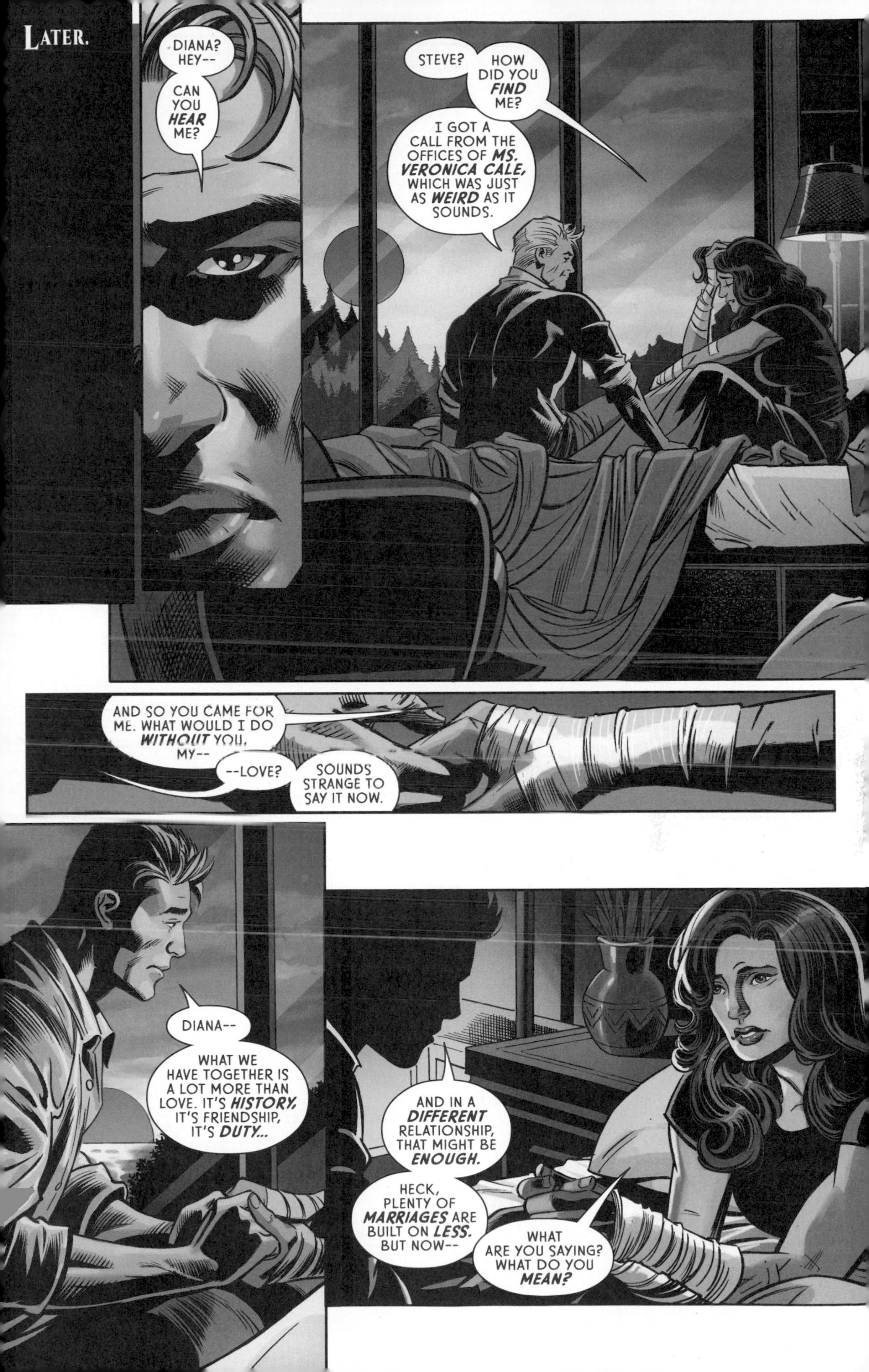
LATER.
DIANA? HEY--
CAN YOU HEAR ME?
STEVE?
HOW DID YOU FIND ME?
I GOT A CALL FROM THE OFFICES OF MS. VERONICA CALE, WHICH WAS JUST AS WEIRD AS IT SOUNDS.
AND SO YOU CAME FOR ME. WHAT WOULD I DO WITHOUT YOU, MY--
--LOVE?
SOUNDS STRANGE TO SAY IT NOW.
DIANA--
WHAT WE HAVE TOGETHER IS A LOT MORE THAN LOVE. IT'S HISTORY, IT'S FRIENDSHIP, IT'S DUTY...
AND IN A DIFFERENT RELATIONSHIP, THAT MIGHT BE ENOUGH.
HECK, PLENTY OF MARRIAGES ARE BUILT ON LESS. BUT NOW--
WHAT ARE YOU SAYING? WHAT DO YOU MEAN?

AND THEN I SEE IT.

AND I UNDERSTAND.

STEVE! YOU'RE NOT--YOU *CAN'T*--

IT'S NOT *JUST* SINCE APHRODITE. IF YOU WERE AROUND MORE, YOU'D HAVE *NOTICED* THAT THINGS HAVE BEEN ROCKY BETWEEN US FOR *A WHILE.*

BUT NOW--IT SEEMS LIKE THE *LAST REASON* TO STAY IS *GONE.*

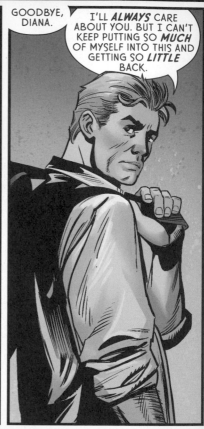

GOODBYE, DIANA.

I'LL *ALWAYS* CARE ABOUT YOU. BUT I CAN'T KEEP PUTTING SO *MUCH* OF MYSELF INTO THIS AND GETTING SO *LITTLE* BACK.

IT IS ONLY IN THAT MOMENT THAT I REALIZE *VERONICA* WAS *RIGHT.*

IT CAN ALWAYS GET *WORSE.* MUCH, MUCH WORSE...

THERE IS NO LOVE SO GREAT THAT IT CANNOT BE *STRIPPED AWAY,* LEAVING YOU *BARE* BEFORE YOUR *ENEMIES.*

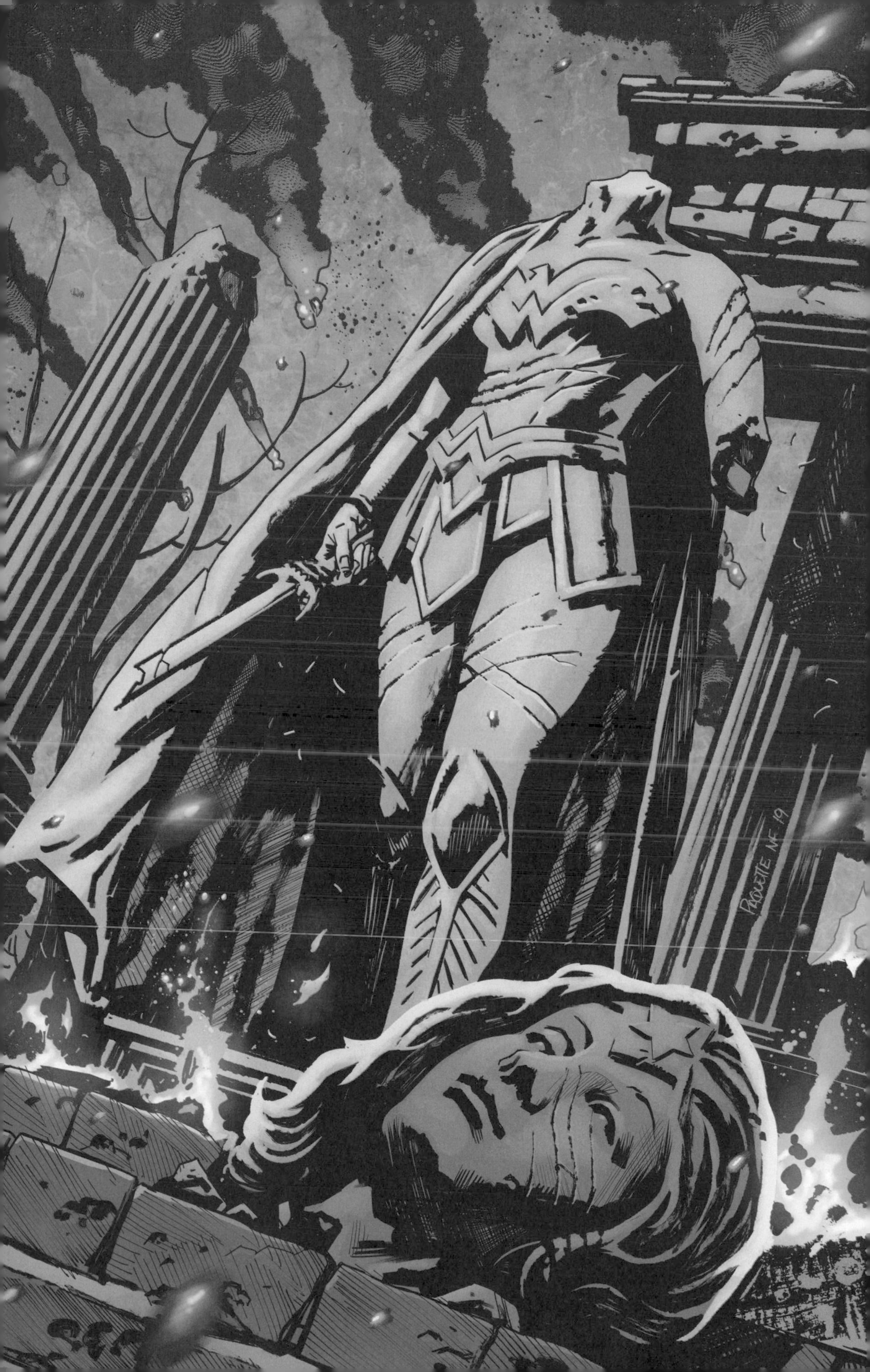
PAQUETTE NF 19

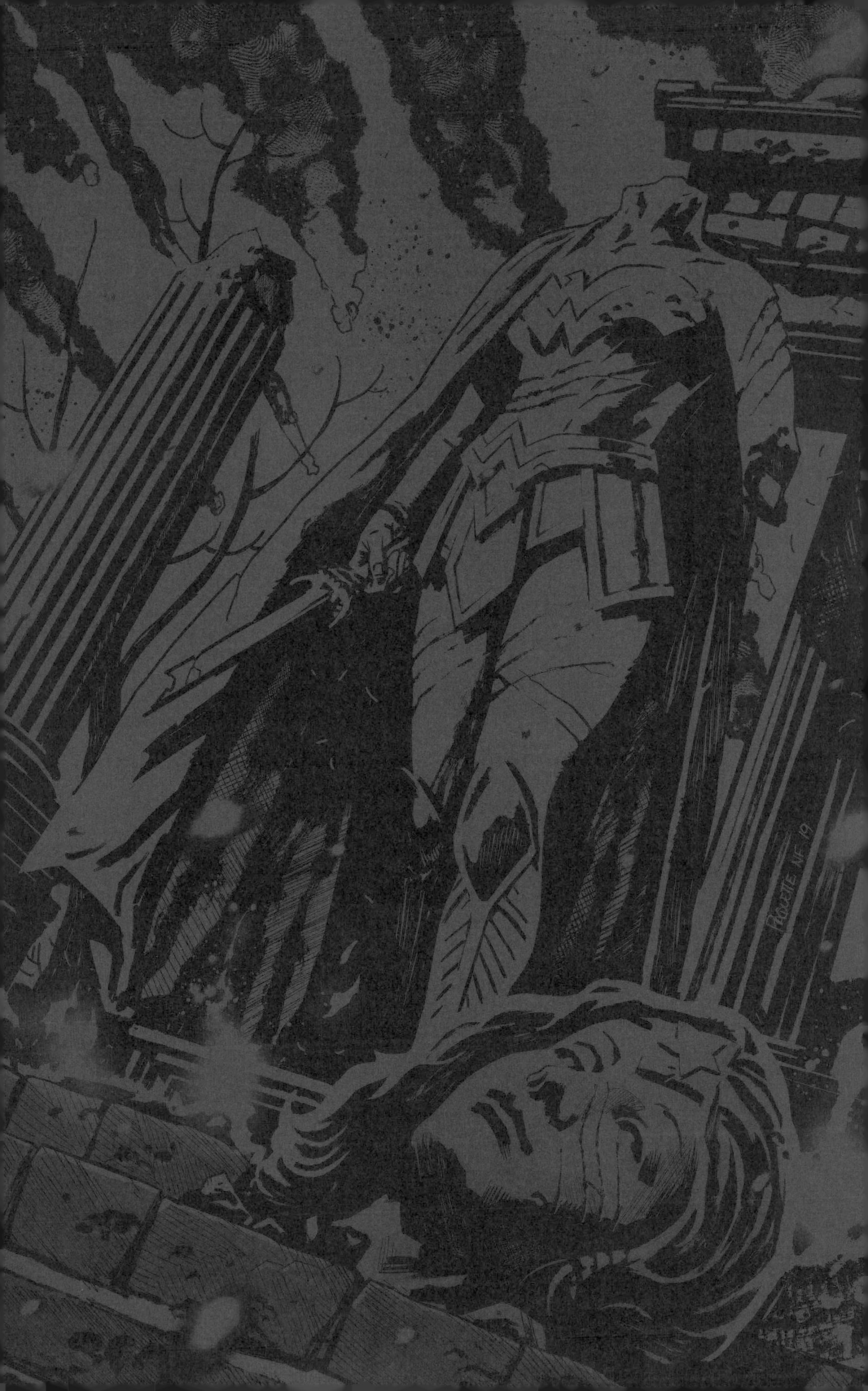

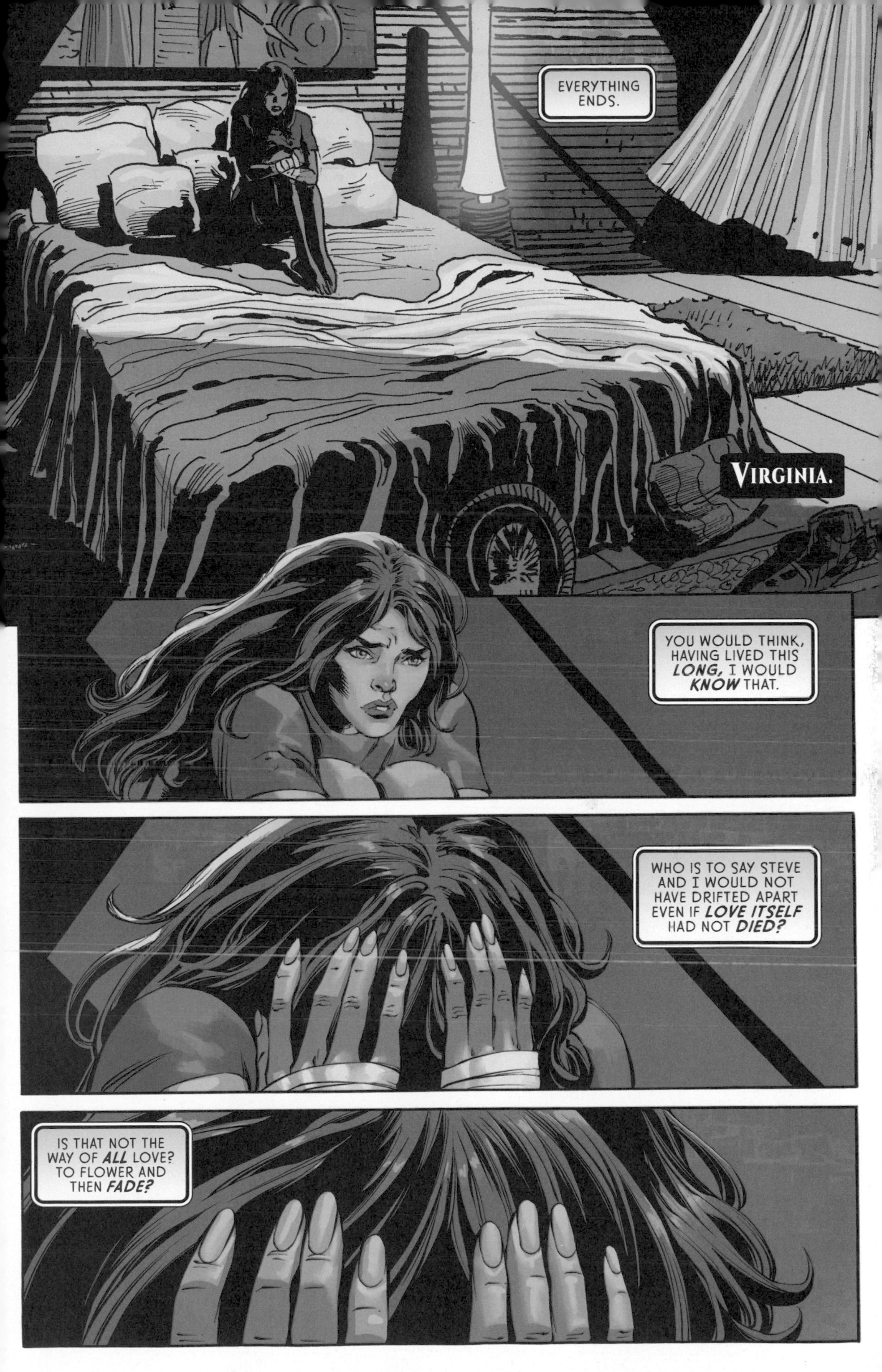
EVERYTHING ENDS.
VIRGINIA.
YOU WOULD THINK, HAVING LIVED THIS LONG, I WOULD KNOW THAT.
WHO IS TO SAY STEVE AND I WOULD NOT HAVE DRIFTED APART EVEN IF LOVE ITSELF HAD NOT DIED?
IS THAT NOT THE WAY OF ALL LOVE? TO FLOWER AND THEN FADE?

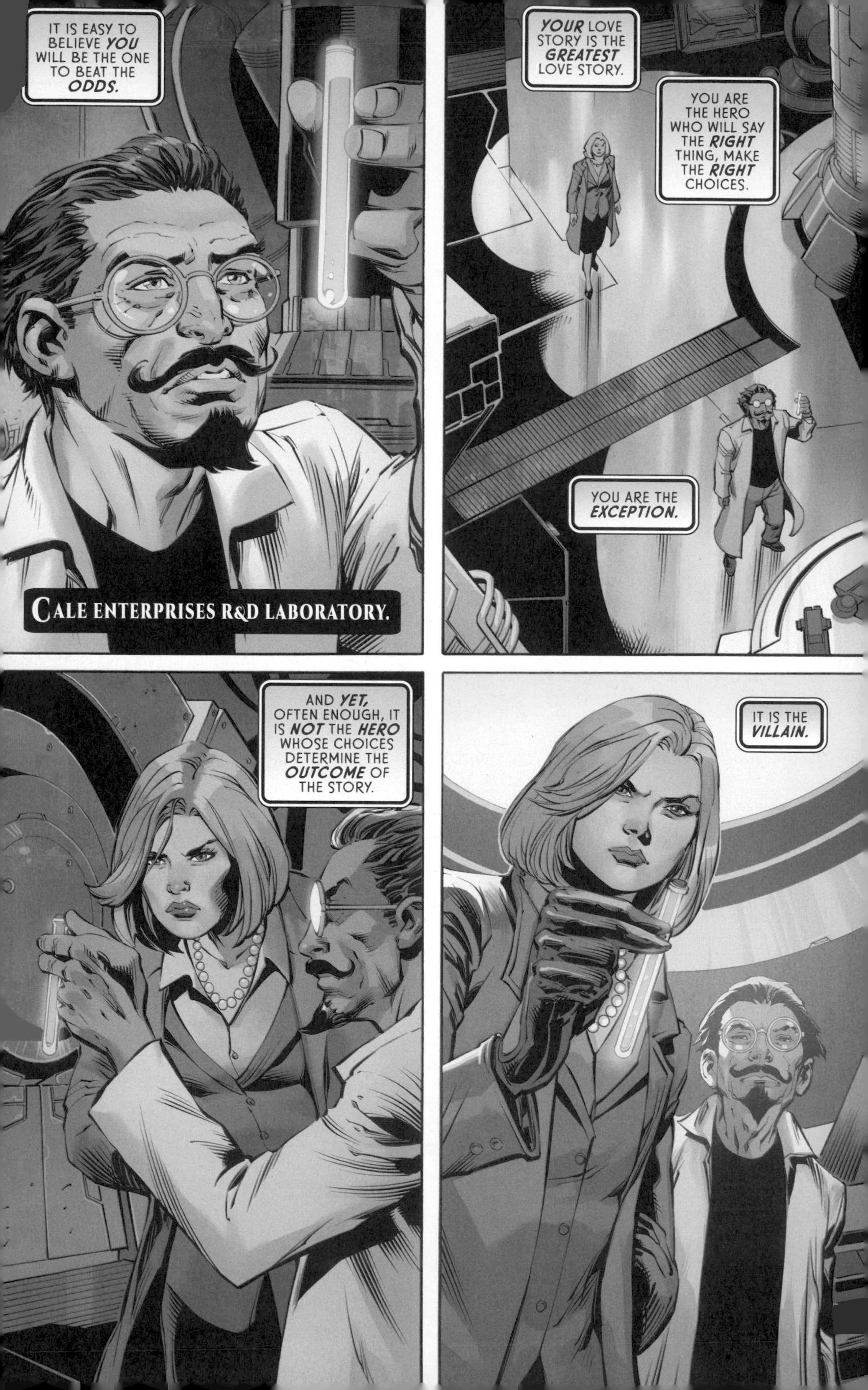
IT IS EASY TO BELIEVE YOU WILL BE THE ONE TO BEAT THE ODDS.
CALE ENTERPRISES R&D LABORATORY.
YOUR LOVE STORY IS THE GREATEST LOVE STORY.
YOU ARE THE HERO WHO WILL SAY THE RIGHT THING, MAKE THE RIGHT CHOICES.
YOU ARE THE EXCEPTION.
AND YET, OFTEN ENOUGH, IT IS NOT THE HERO WHOSE CHOICES DETERMINE THE OUTCOME OF THE STORY.
IT IS THE VILLAIN.

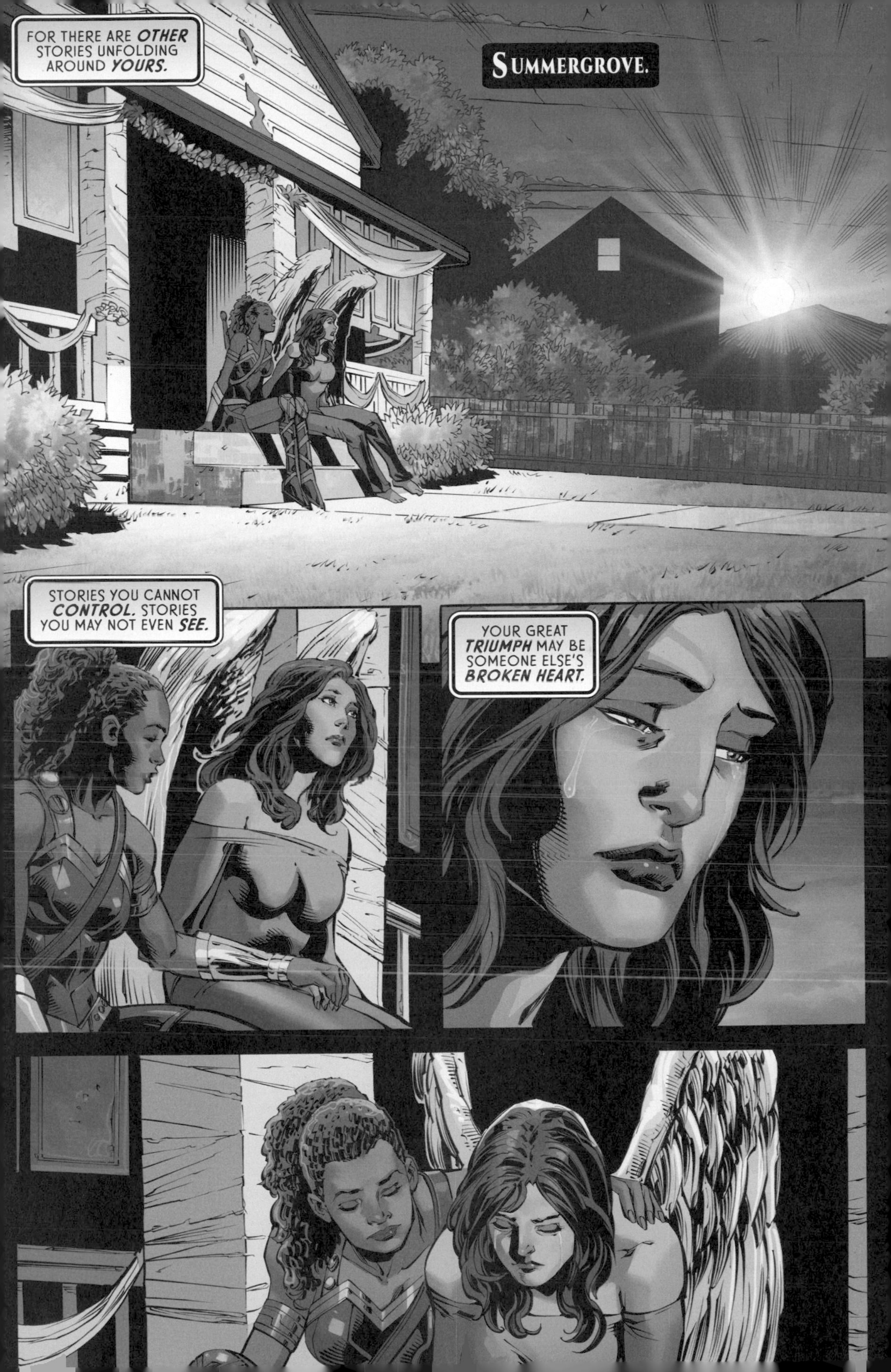
FOR THERE ARE OTHER STORIES UNFOLDING AROUND YOURS.
SUMMERGROVE.
STORIES YOU CANNOT CONTROL. STORIES YOU MAY NOT EVEN SEE.
YOUR GREAT TRIUMPH MAY BE SOMEONE ELSE'S BROKEN HEART.

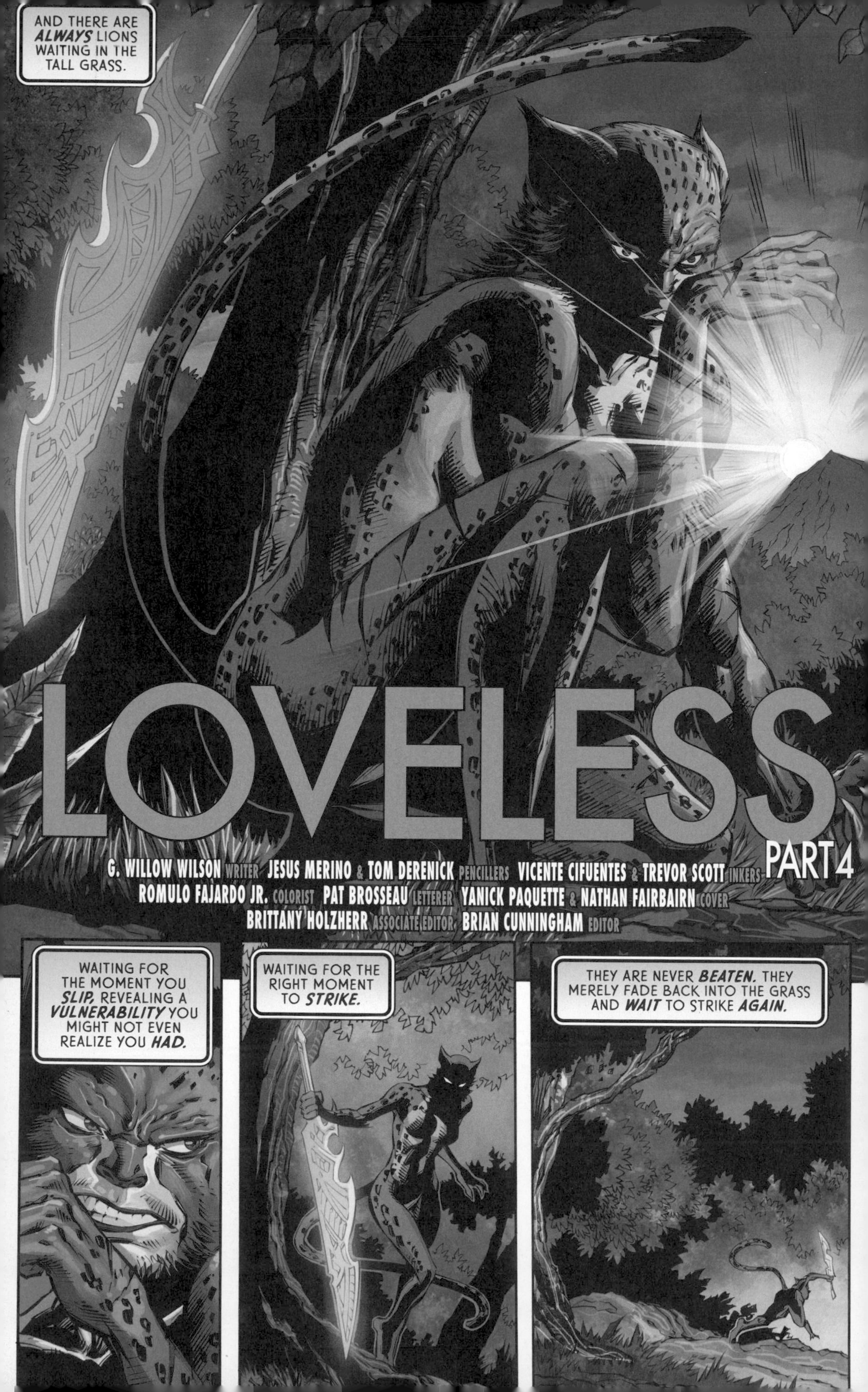
AND THERE ARE ALWAYS LIONS WAITING IN THE TALL GRASS.
LOVELESS
PART 4
G. WILLOW WILSON WRITER JESUS MERINO & TOM DERENICK PENCILLERS VICENTE CIFUENTES & TREVOR SCOTT INKERS
ROMULO FAJARDO JR. COLORIST PAT BROSSEAU LETTERER YANICK PAQUETTE & NATHAN FAIRBAIRN COVER
BRITTANY HOLZHERR ASSOCIATE EDITOR BRIAN CUNNINGHAM EDITOR
WAITING FOR THE MOMENT YOU SLIP, REVEALING A VULNERABILITY YOU MIGHT NOT EVEN REALIZE YOU HAD.
WAITING FOR THE RIGHT MOMENT TO STRIKE.
THEY ARE NEVER BEATEN. THEY MERELY FADE BACK INTO THE GRASS AND WAIT TO STRIKE AGAIN.

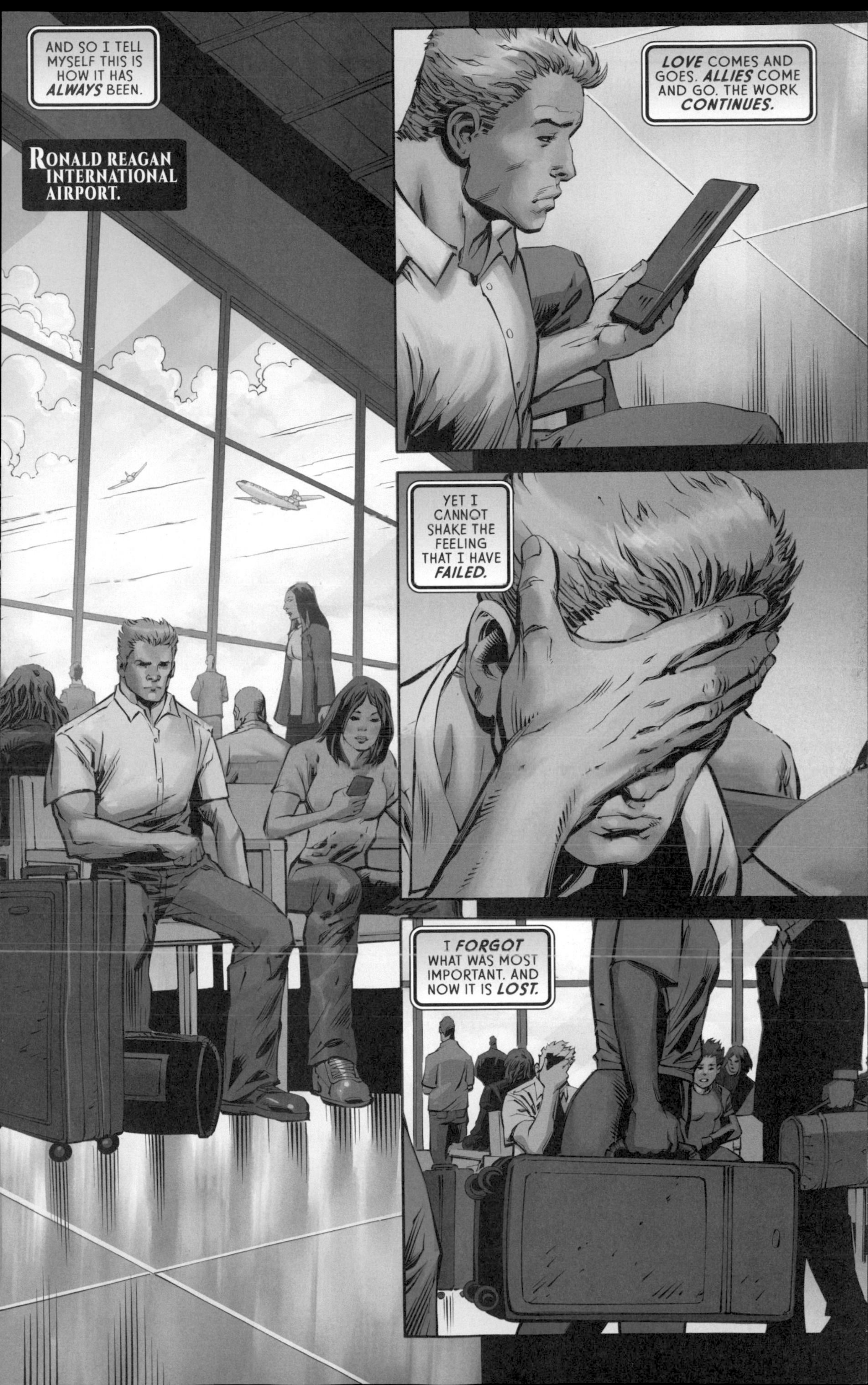
AND SO I TELL MYSELF THIS IS HOW IT HAS ALWAYS BEEN.
RONALD REAGAN INTERNATIONAL AIRPORT.
LOVE COMES AND GOES. ALLIES COME AND GO. THE WORK CONTINUES.
YET I CANNOT SHAKE THE FEELING THAT I HAVE FAILED.
I FORGOT WHAT WAS MOST IMPORTANT. AND NOW IT IS LOST.

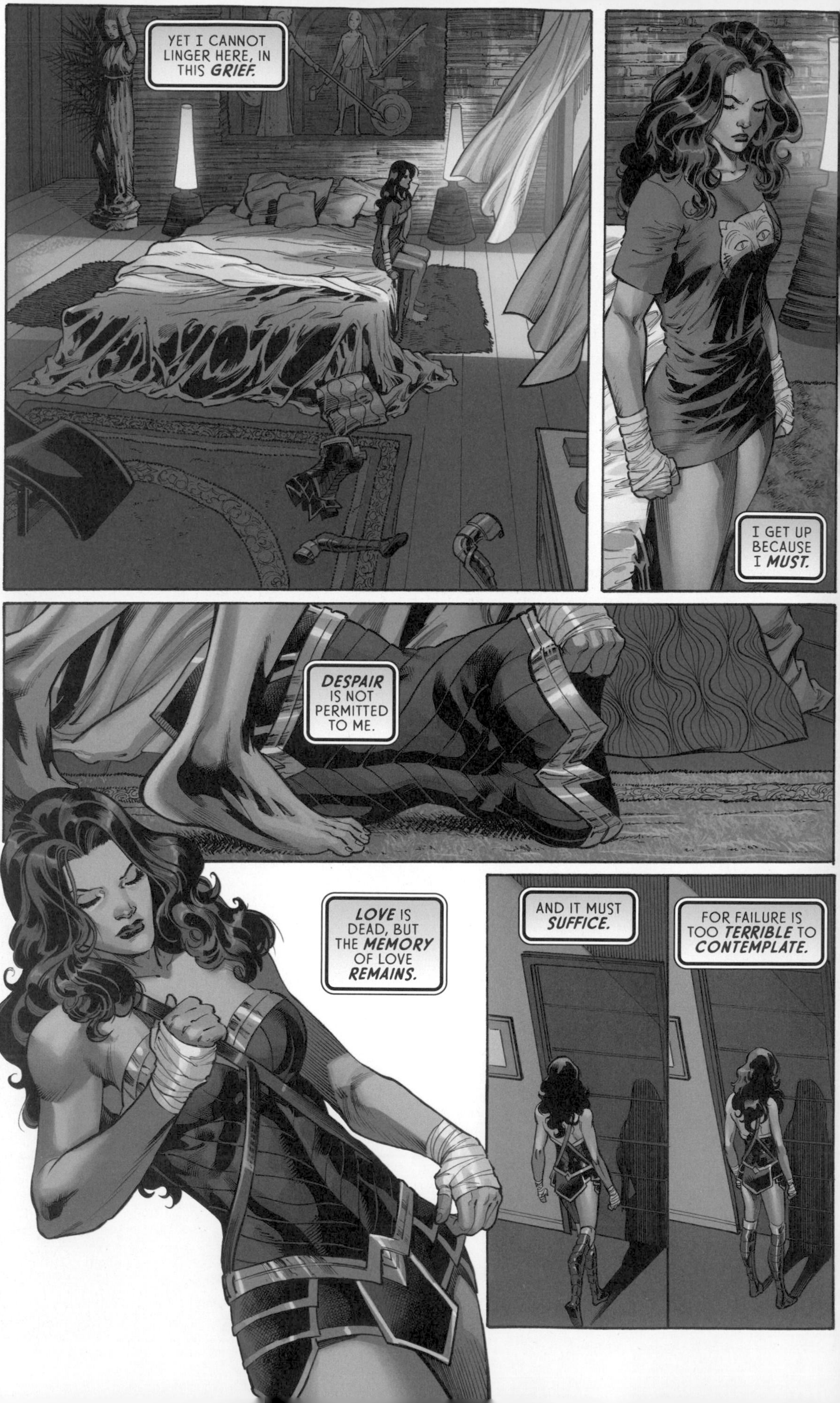
YET I CANNOT LINGER HERE, IN THIS GRIEF.
I GET UP BECAUSE I MUST.
DESPAIR IS NOT PERMITTED TO ME.
LOVE IS DEAD, BUT THE MEMORY OF LOVE REMAINS.
AND IT MUST SUFFICE.
FOR FAILURE IS TOO TERRIBLE TO CONTEMPLATE.

K-CHK

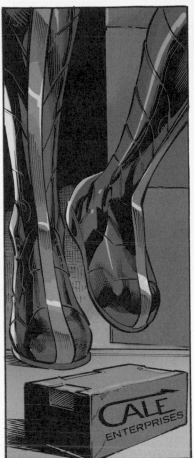

CALE
ENTERPRISES

CALE
ENTERPRISES

VERONICA...

CALE
ENTERPRISES

SO, YOU HAVE
KEPT YOUR
PROMISE...

OUR
BUSINESS
IS NOW
CONCLUDED.
V.C.

CALE
ENTERPRISES

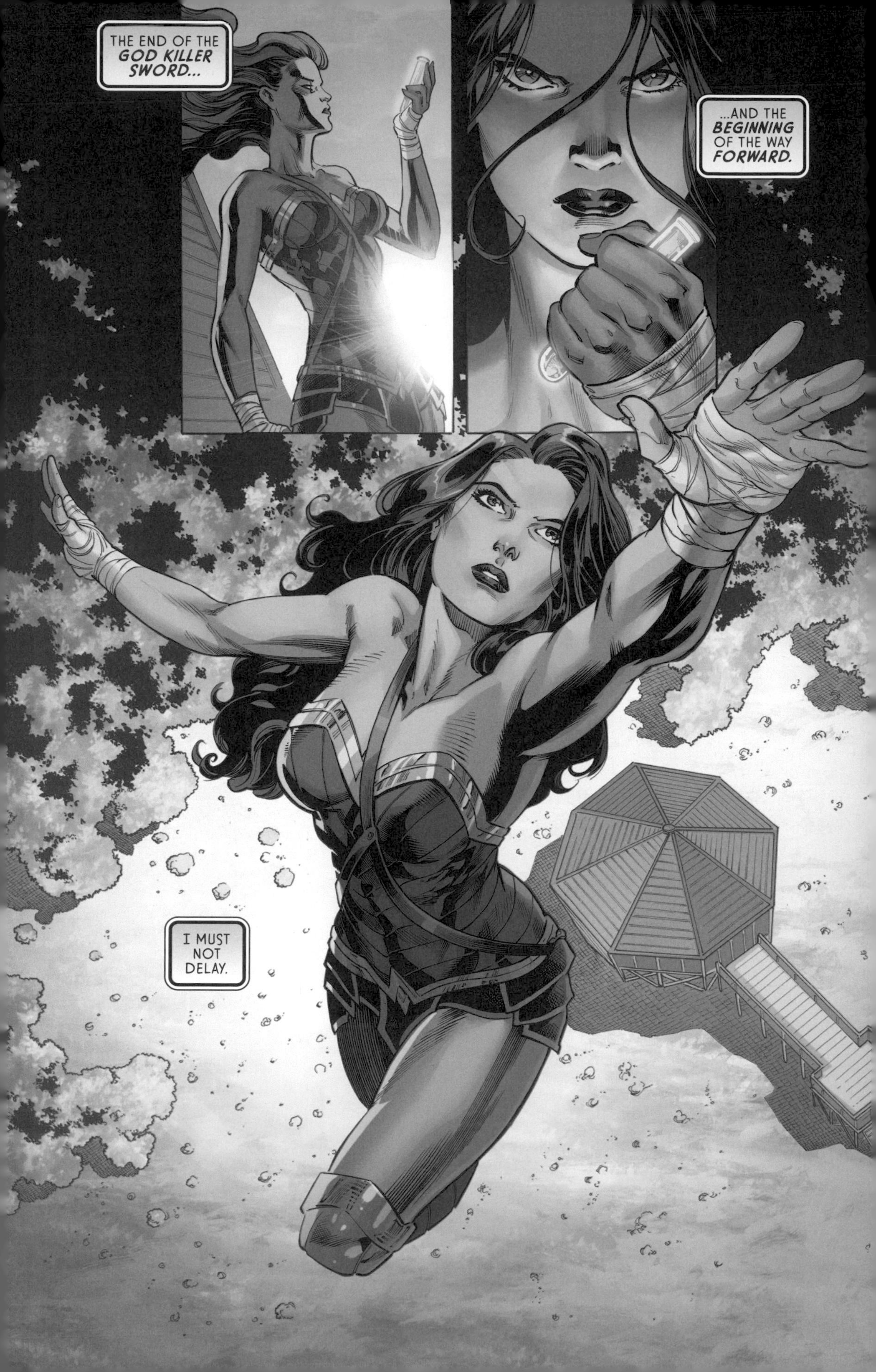
THE END OF THE GOD KILLER SWORD...
...AND THE BEGINNING OF THE WAY FORWARD.
I MUST NOT DELAY.

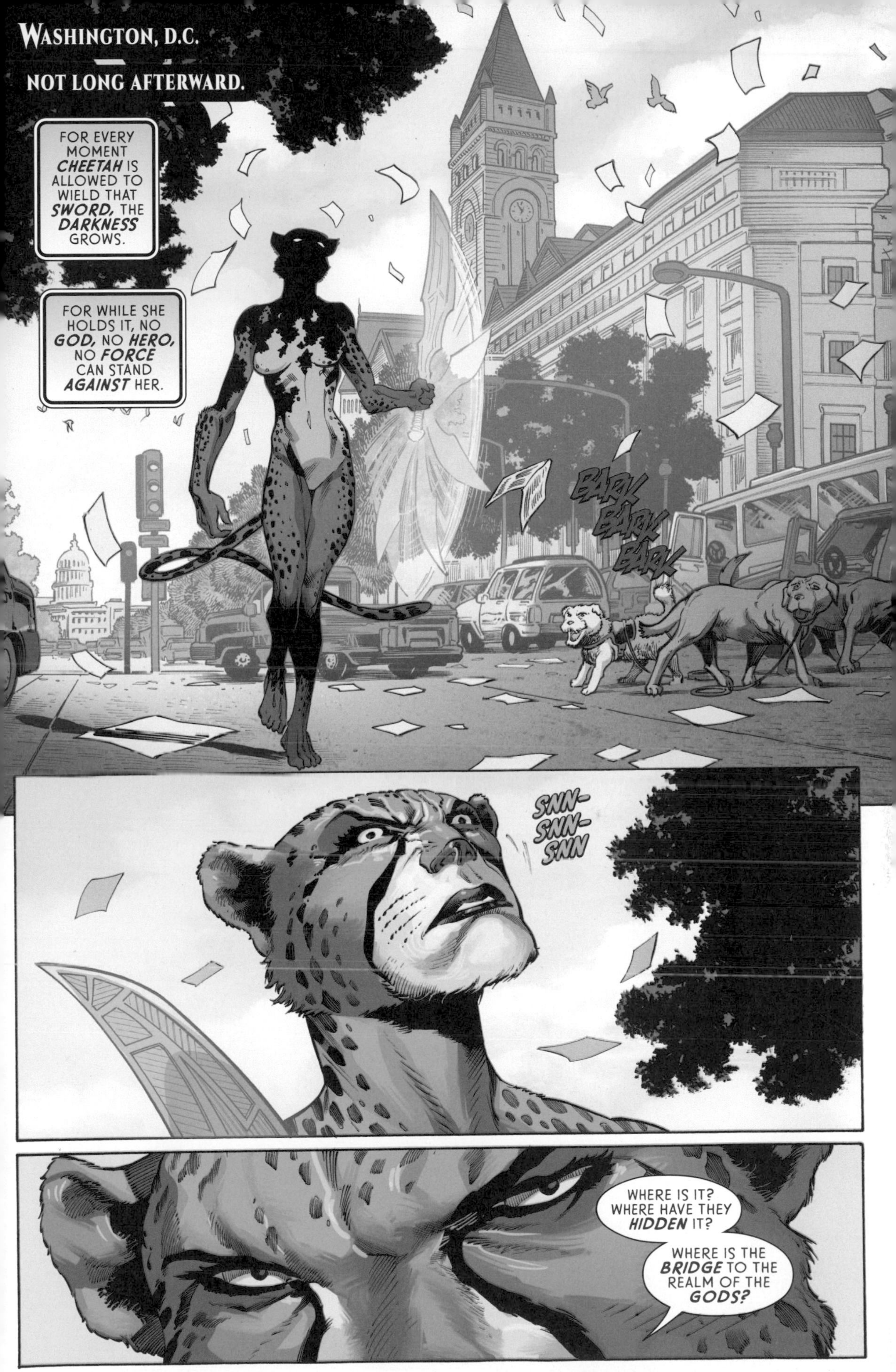
WASHINGTON, D.C.
NOT LONG AFTERWARD.
FOR EVERY MOMENT CHEETAH IS ALLOWED TO WIELD THAT SWORD, THE DARKNESS GROWS.
FOR WHILE SHE HOLDS IT, NO GOD, NO HERO, NO FORCE CAN STAND AGAINST HER.
BARK BARK BARK
SNN- SNN- SNN
WHERE IS IT? WHERE HAVE THEY HIDDEN IT?
WHERE IS THE BRIDGE TO THE REALM OF THE GODS?

I CAN FEEL IT... THE VEIL BETWEEN WORLDS IS THINNER THAN IT HAS EVER BEEN...

THE BLOOD OF THE GODDESS APHRODITE SHARPENS MY SENSES...

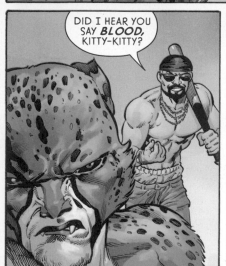

DID I HEAR YOU SAY BLOOD, KITTY-KITTY?

OOH, SHE'S GOT CLAWS.

HERE, KITTY KITTY--

THNK

NNGH!

D-DON'T HURT ME! LEAVE ME ALONE!

HERE, KITTY KITTY. HURRHH HURRH HURRH...

HNNH?

WHUMP

WHAM

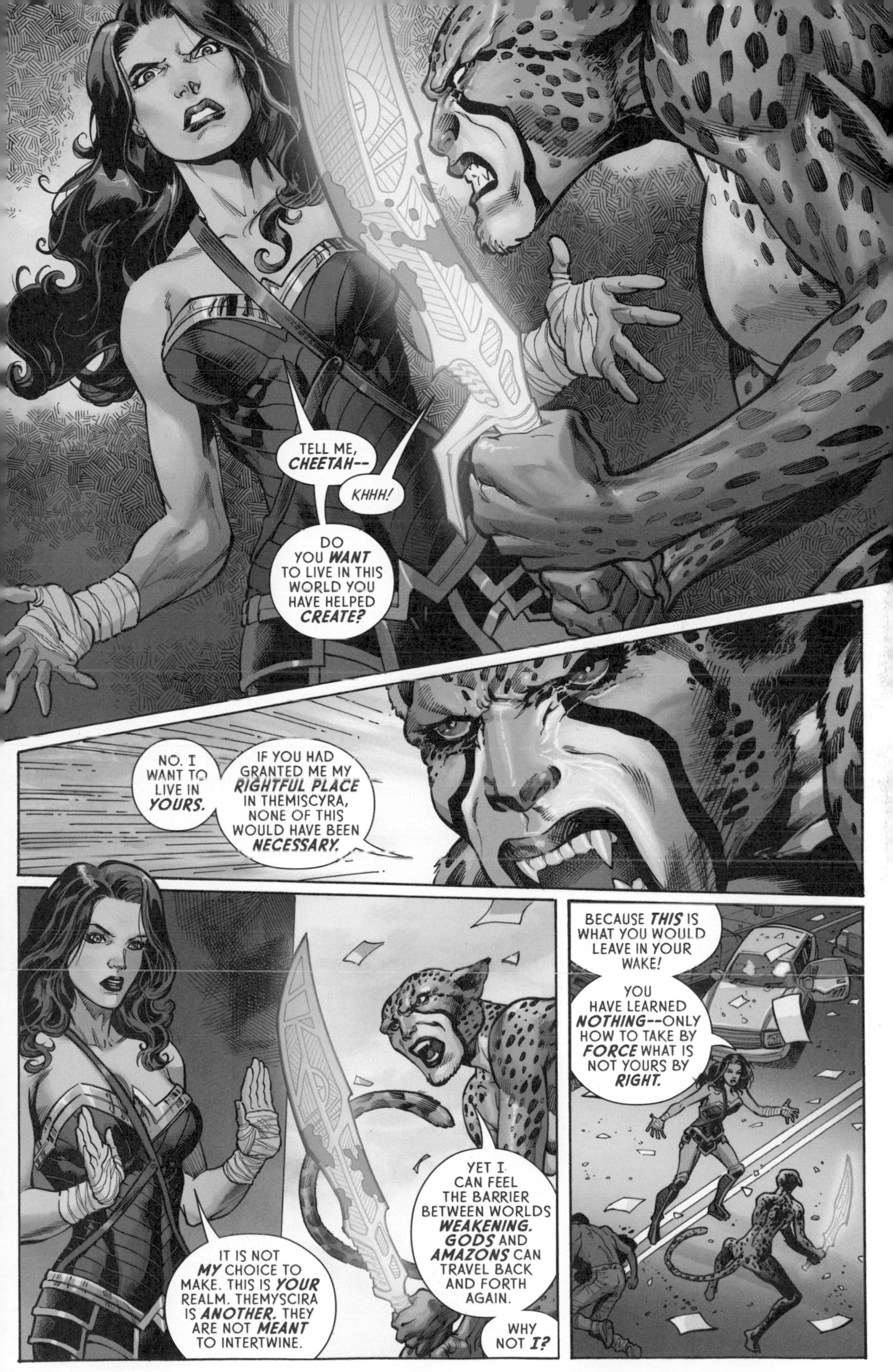
TELL ME, CHEETAH--
KHHH!
DO YOU WANT TO LIVE IN THIS WORLD YOU HAVE HELPED CREATE?
NO. I WANT TO LIVE IN YOURS.
IF YOU HAD GRANTED ME MY RIGHTFUL PLACE IN THEMISCYRA, NONE OF THIS WOULD HAVE BEEN NECESSARY.
IT IS NOT MY CHOICE TO MAKE. THIS IS YOUR REALM. THEMYSCIRA IS ANOTHER. THEY ARE NOT MEANT TO INTERTWINE.
YET I CAN FEEL THE BARRIER BETWEEN WORLDS WEAKENING. GODS AND AMAZONS CAN TRAVEL BACK AND FORTH AGAIN.
WHY NOT I?
BECAUSE THIS IS WHAT YOU WOULD LEAVE IN YOUR WAKE!
YOU HAVE LEARNED NOTHING--ONLY HOW TO TAKE BY FORCE WHAT IS NOT YOURS BY RIGHT.

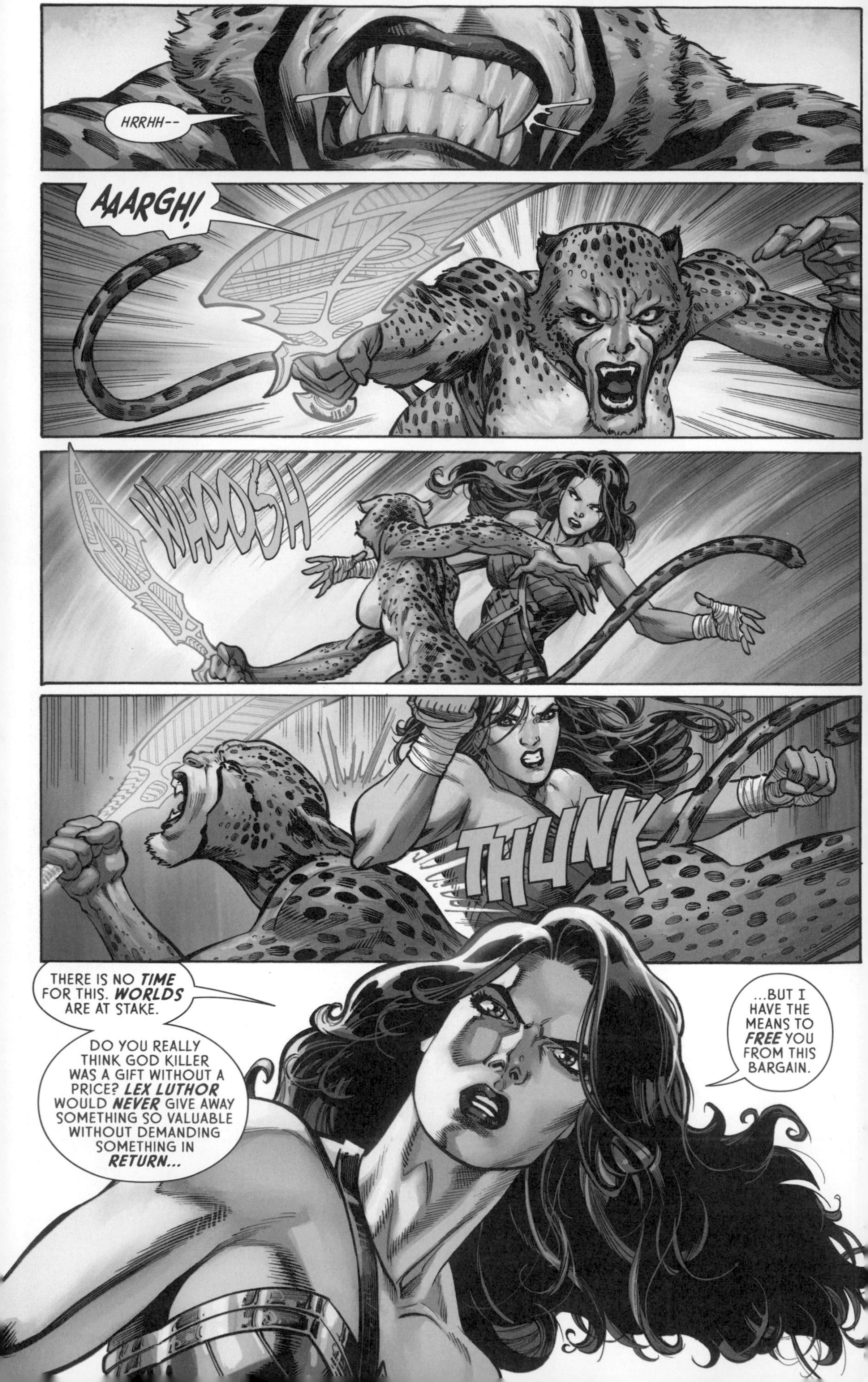
HRRHH--
AAARGH!
WHOOSH
THUNK
THERE IS NO TIME FOR THIS. WORLDS ARE AT STAKE.
DO YOU REALLY THINK GOD KILLER WAS A GIFT WITHOUT A PRICE? LEX LUTHOR WOULD NEVER GIVE AWAY SOMETHING SO VALUABLE WITHOUT DEMANDING SOMETHING IN RETURN...
...BUT I HAVE THE MEANS TO FREE YOU FROM THIS BARGAIN.

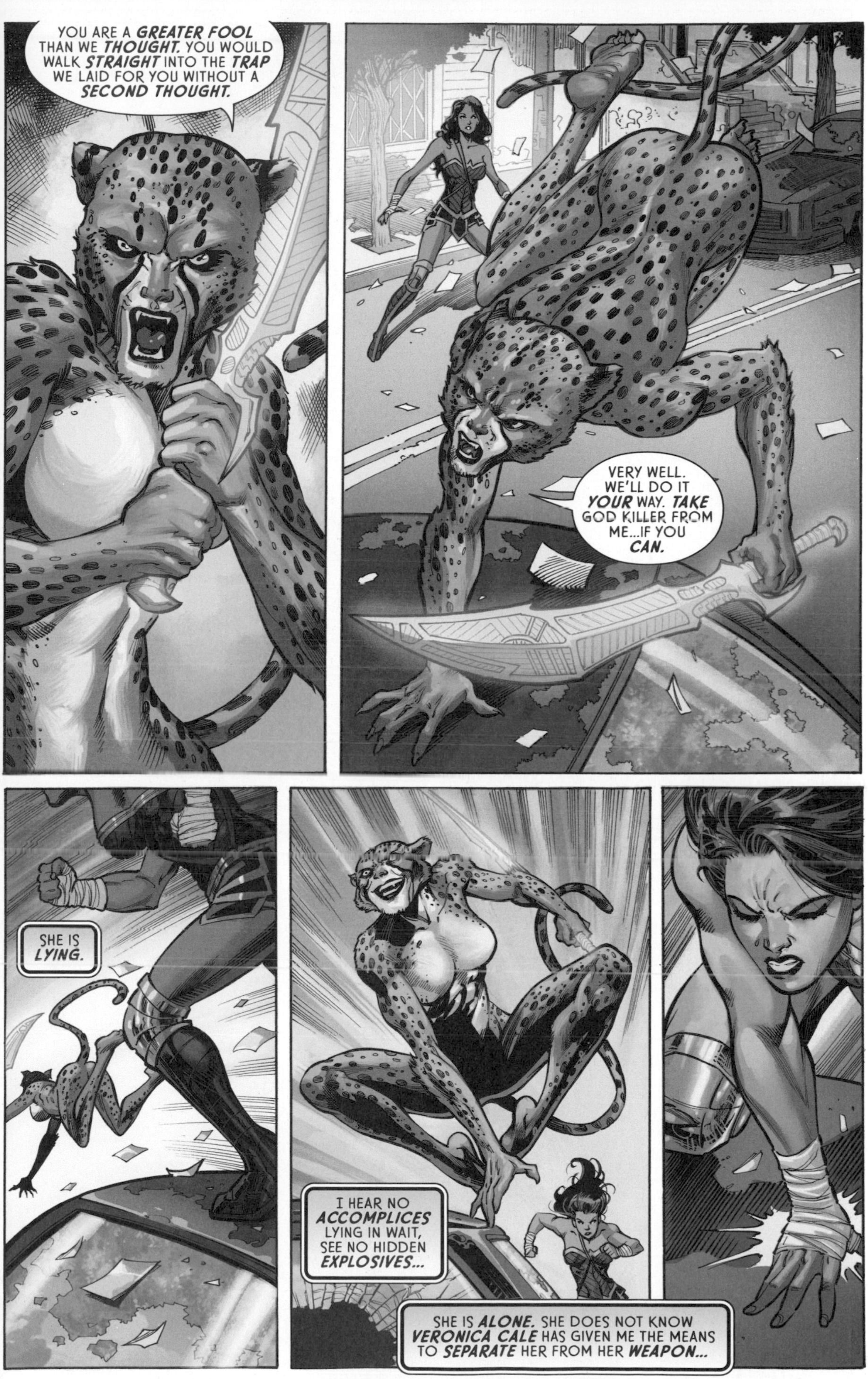
YOU ARE A GREATER FOOL THAN WE THOUGHT. YOU WOULD WALK STRAIGHT INTO THE TRAP WE LAID FOR YOU WITHOUT A SECOND THOUGHT.
VERY WELL. WE'LL DO IT YOUR WAY. TAKE GOD KILLER FROM ME...IF YOU CAN.
SHE IS LYING.
I HEAR NO ACCOMPLICES LYING IN WAIT, SEE NO HIDDEN EXPLOSIVES...
SHE IS ALONE. SHE DOES NOT KNOW VERONICA CALE HAS GIVEN ME THE MEANS TO SEPARATE HER FROM HER WEAPON...

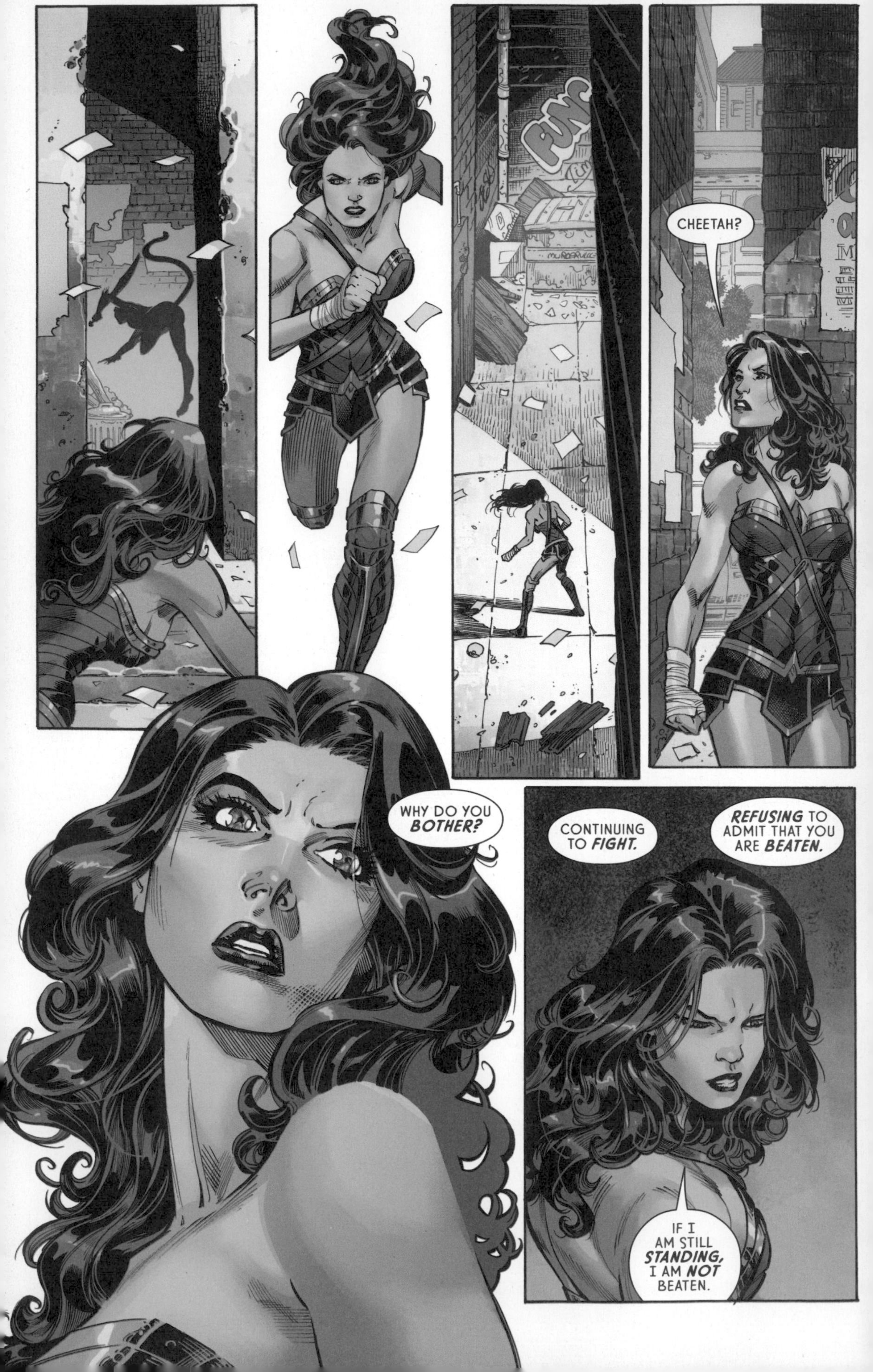

CHEETAH?
WHY DO YOU BOTHER?
CONTINUING TO FIGHT.
REFUSING TO ADMIT THAT YOU ARE BEATEN.
IF I AM STILL STANDING, I AM NOT BEATEN.

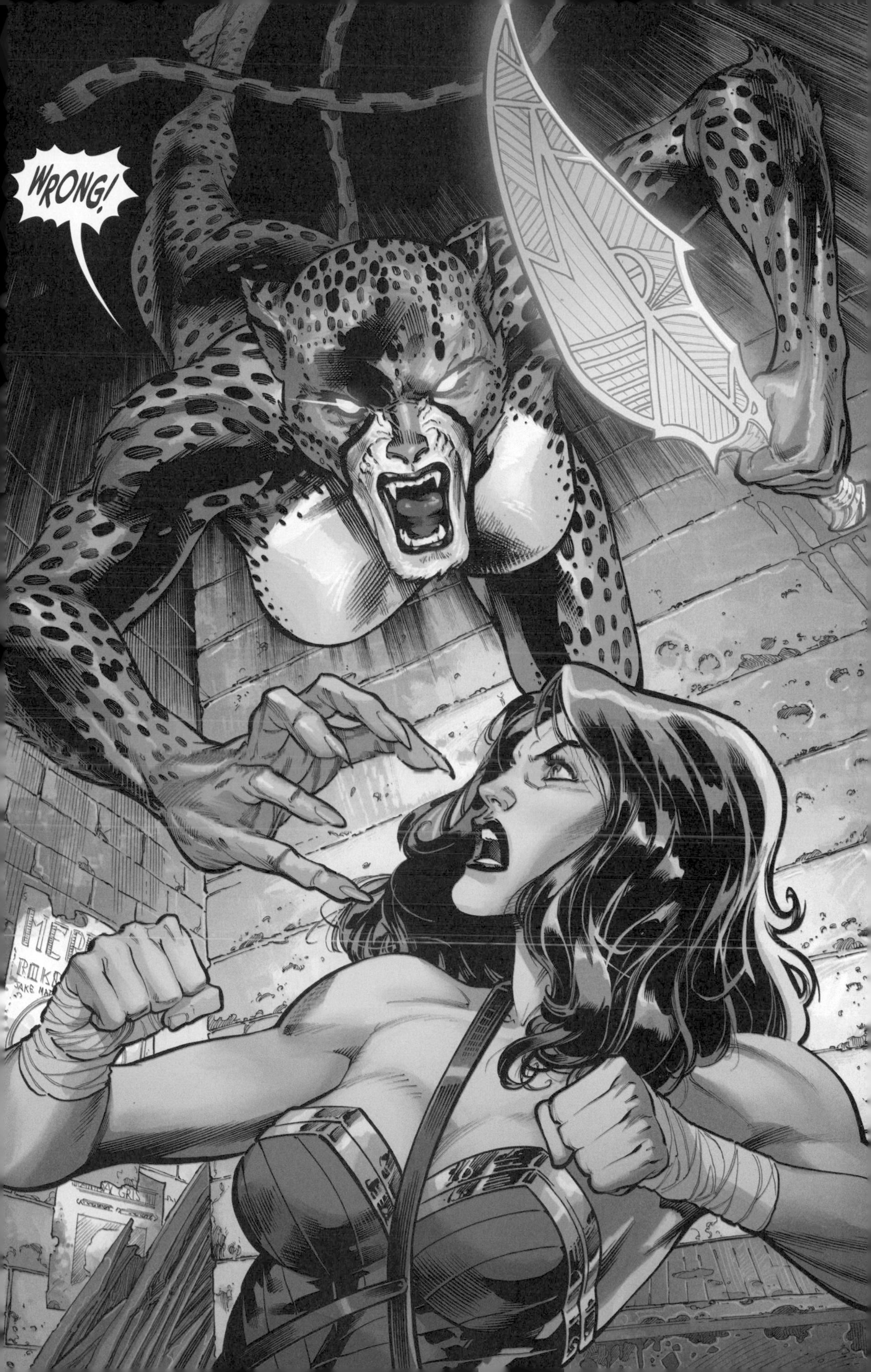
WRONG!

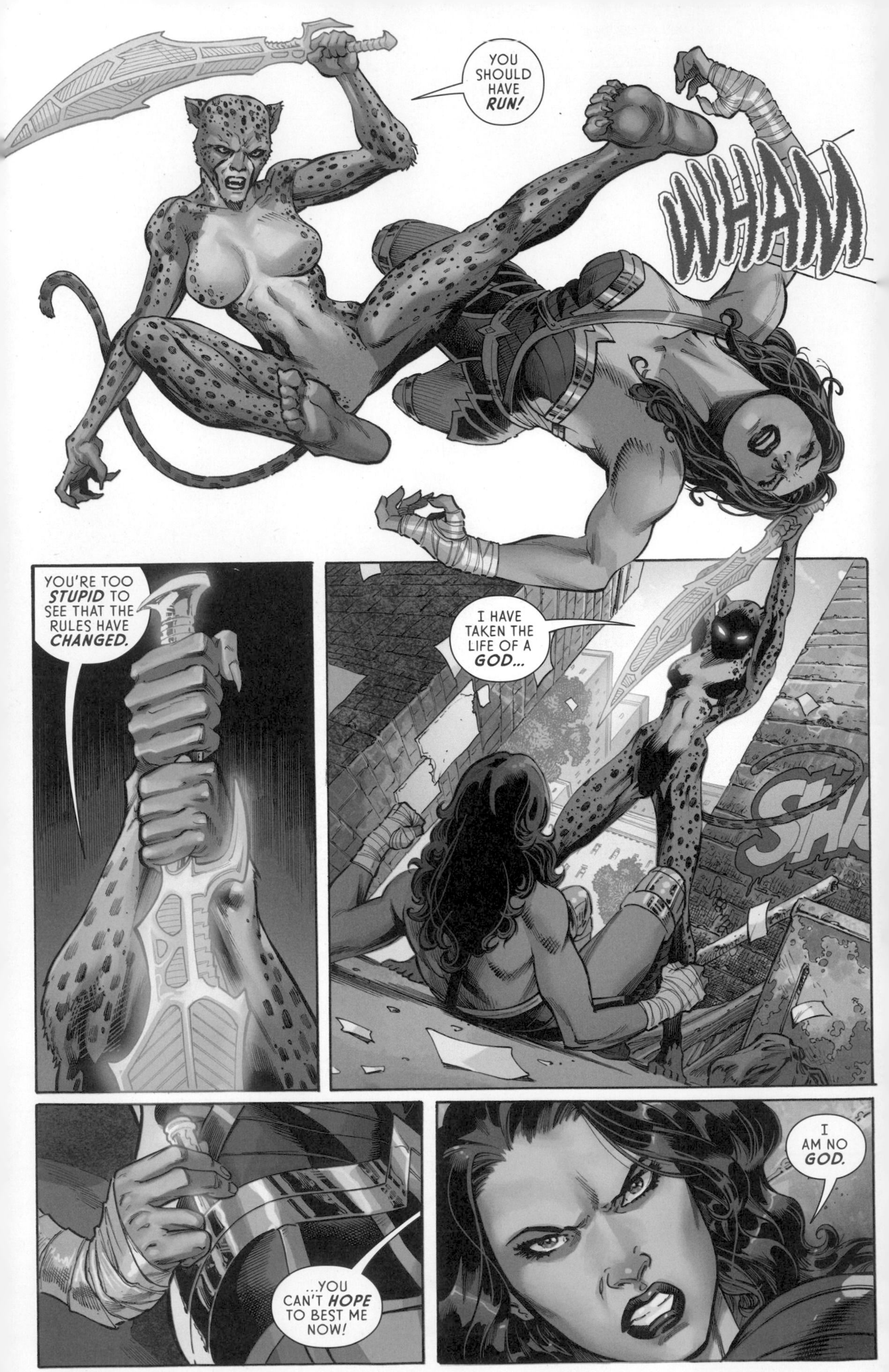
YOU SHOULD HAVE RUN!
WHAM
YOU'RE TOO STUPID TO SEE THAT THE RULES HAVE CHANGED.
I HAVE TAKEN THE LIFE OF A GOD...
...YOU CAN'T HOPE TO BEST ME NOW!
I AM NO GOD.

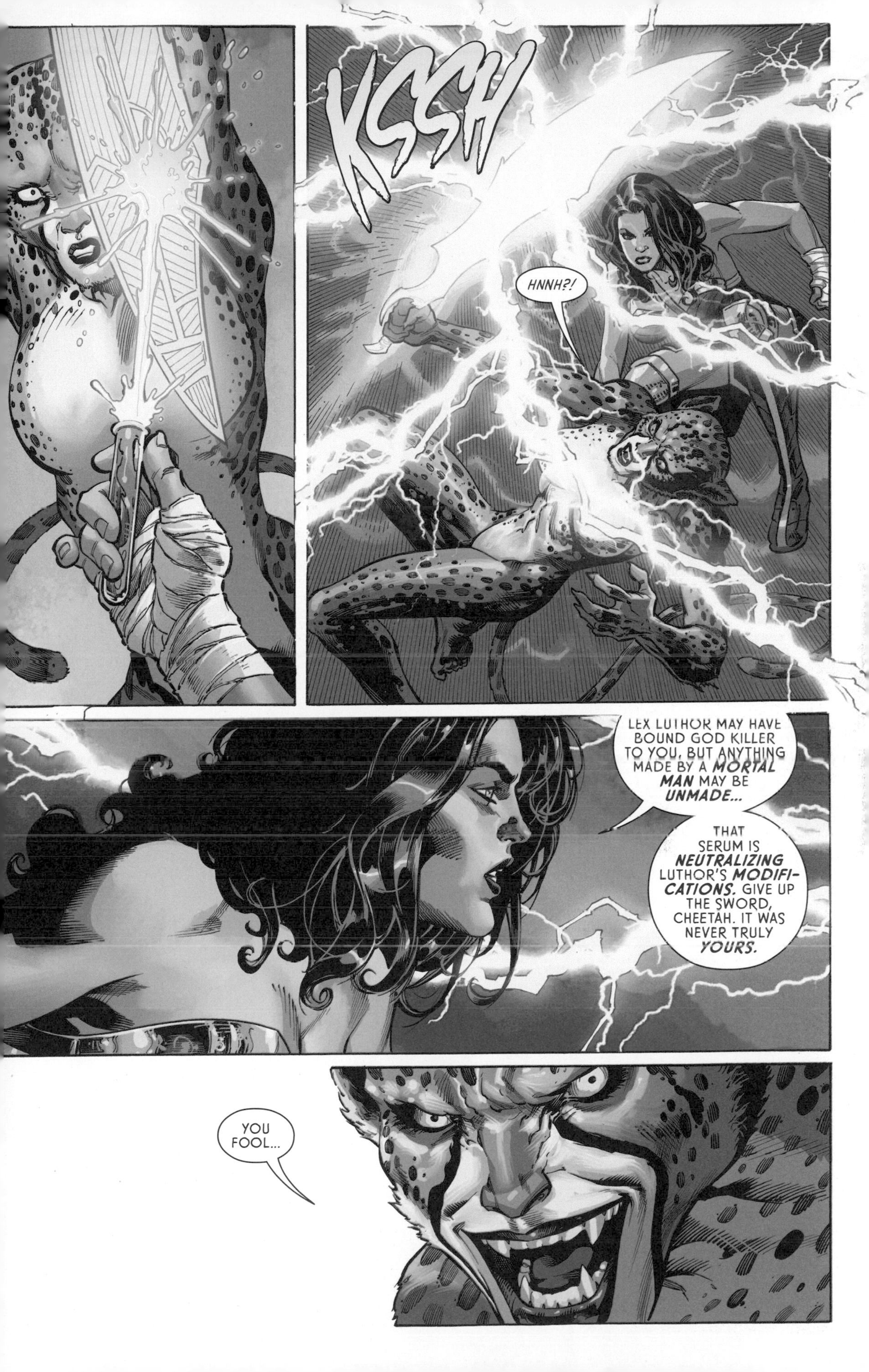
KSSH
HNNH?!
LEX LUTHOR MAY HAVE BOUND GOD KILLER TO YOU, BUT ANYTHING MADE BY A MORTAL MAN MAY BE UNMADE...
THAT SERUM IS NEUTRALIZING LUTHOR'S MODIFICATIONS. GIVE UP THE SWORD, CHEETAH. IT WAS NEVER TRULY YOURS.
YOU FOOL...

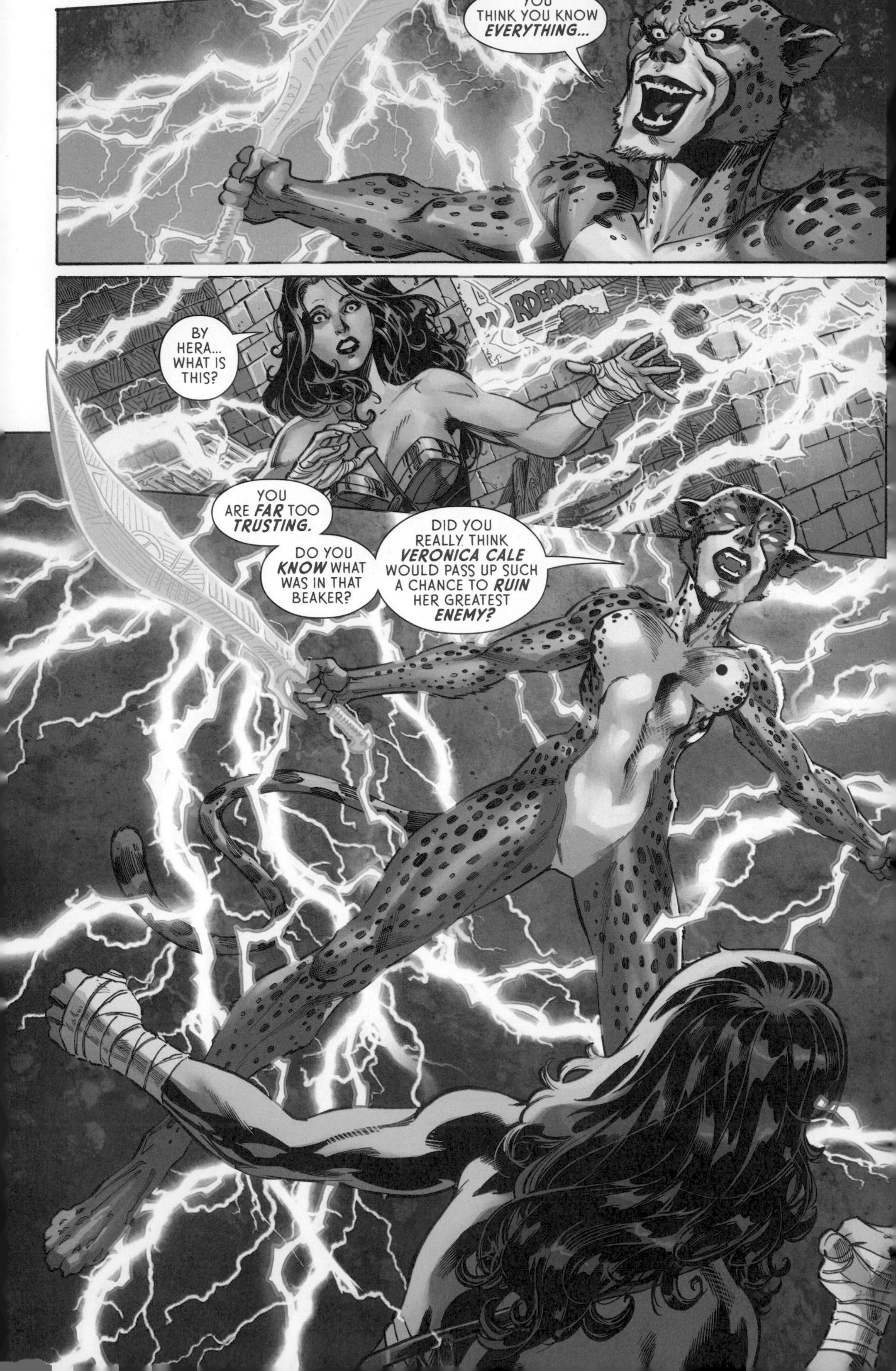

YOU THINK YOU KNOW EVERYTHING...
BY HERA... WHAT IS THIS?
YOU ARE FAR TOO TRUSTING.
DO YOU KNOW WHAT WAS IN THAT BEAKER?
DID YOU REALLY THINK VERONICA CALE WOULD PASS UP SUCH A CHANCE TO RUIN HER GREATEST ENEMY?

"BUT SHE...BUT VERONICA GAVE ME HER *WORD*...SHE OWES ME A *DEBT*..."

"SHE *LIED*."

"THAT DAY...ON THE *ROOF*, WHEN SHE *SHOT* YOU..."

"*STAGED*, OF COURSE.

"I'M HURT YOU THINK IT TAKES SO *LITTLE* TO BRING ME *DOWN*, WONDER WOMAN.

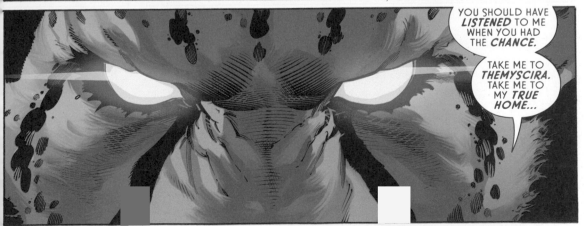

YOU SHOULD HAVE *LISTENED* TO ME WHEN YOU HAD THE *CHANCE*.

TAKE ME TO *THEMYSCIRA*. TAKE ME TO MY *TRUE* HOME...

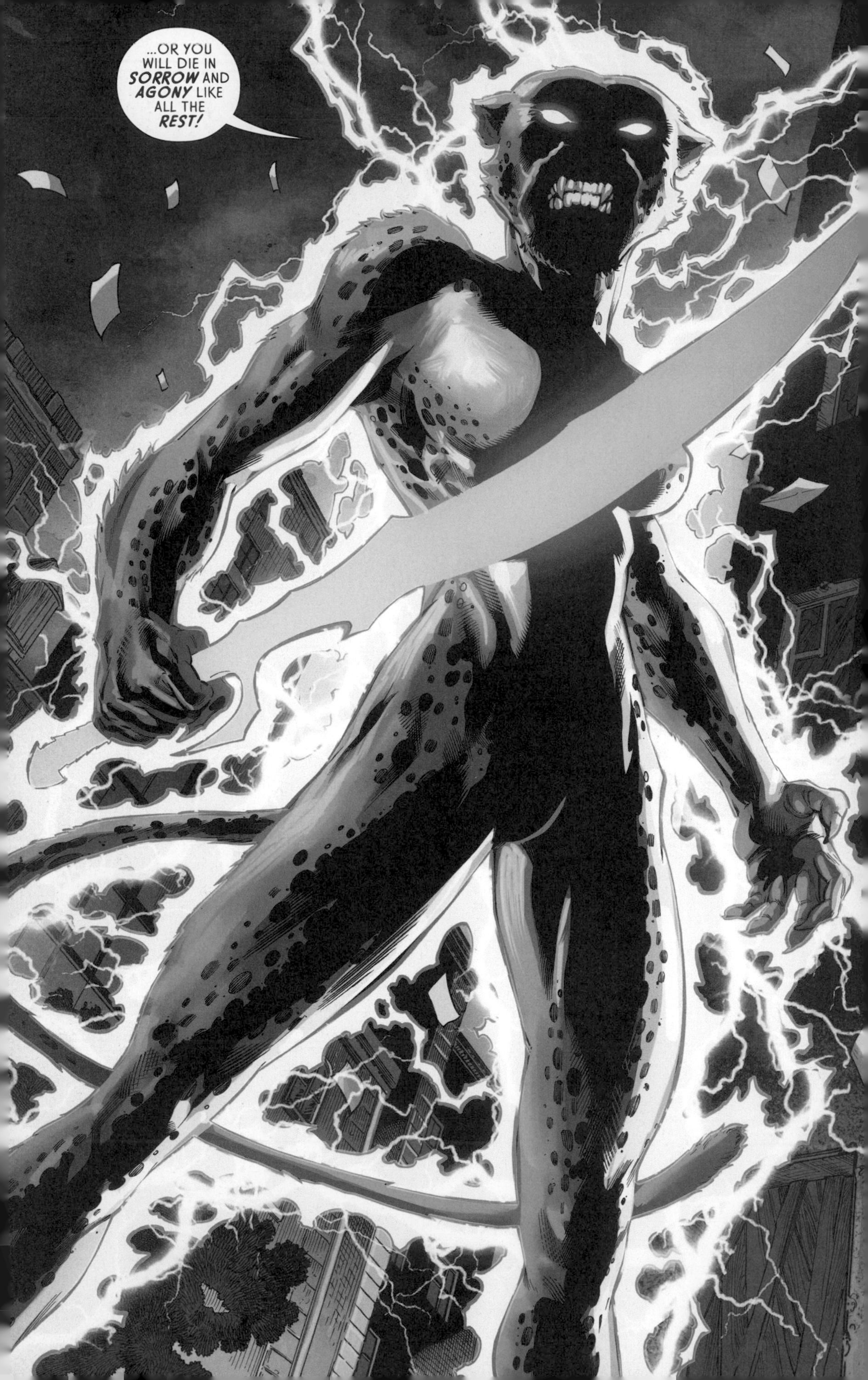
...OR YOU WILL DIE IN SORROW AND AGONY LIKE ALL THE REST!

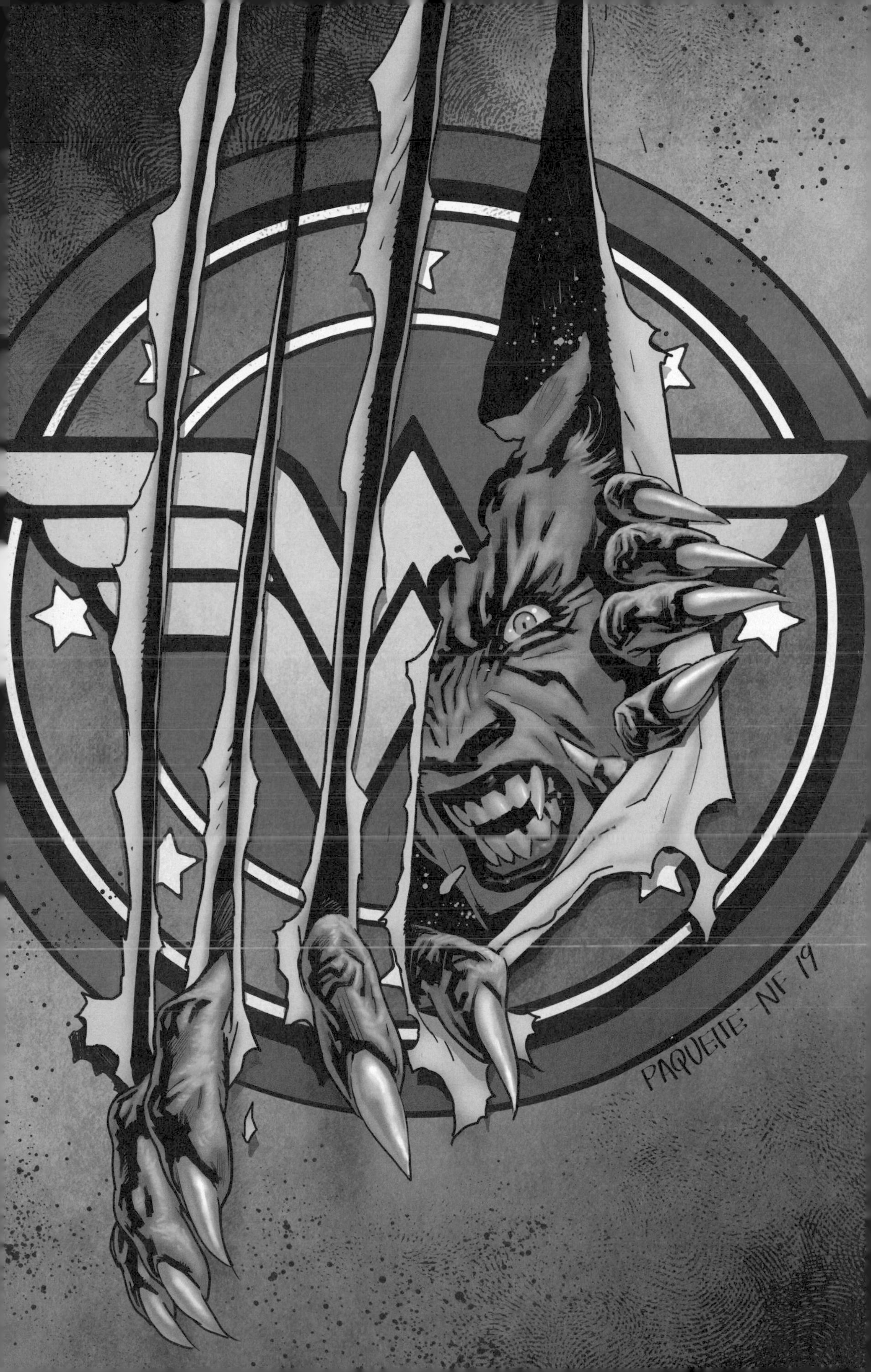
PAQUETTE-NF 19

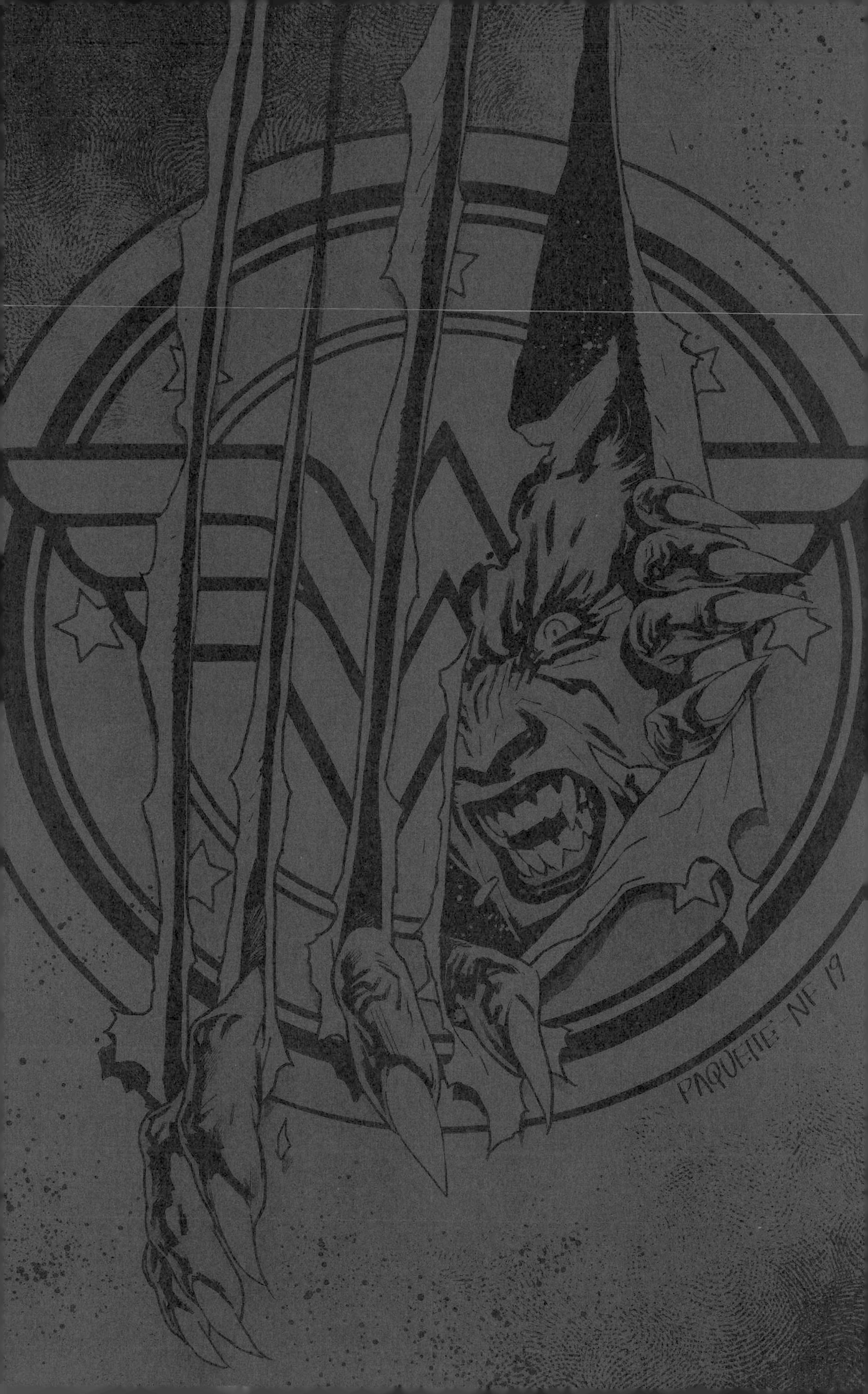
PAQUETTE-NF 19

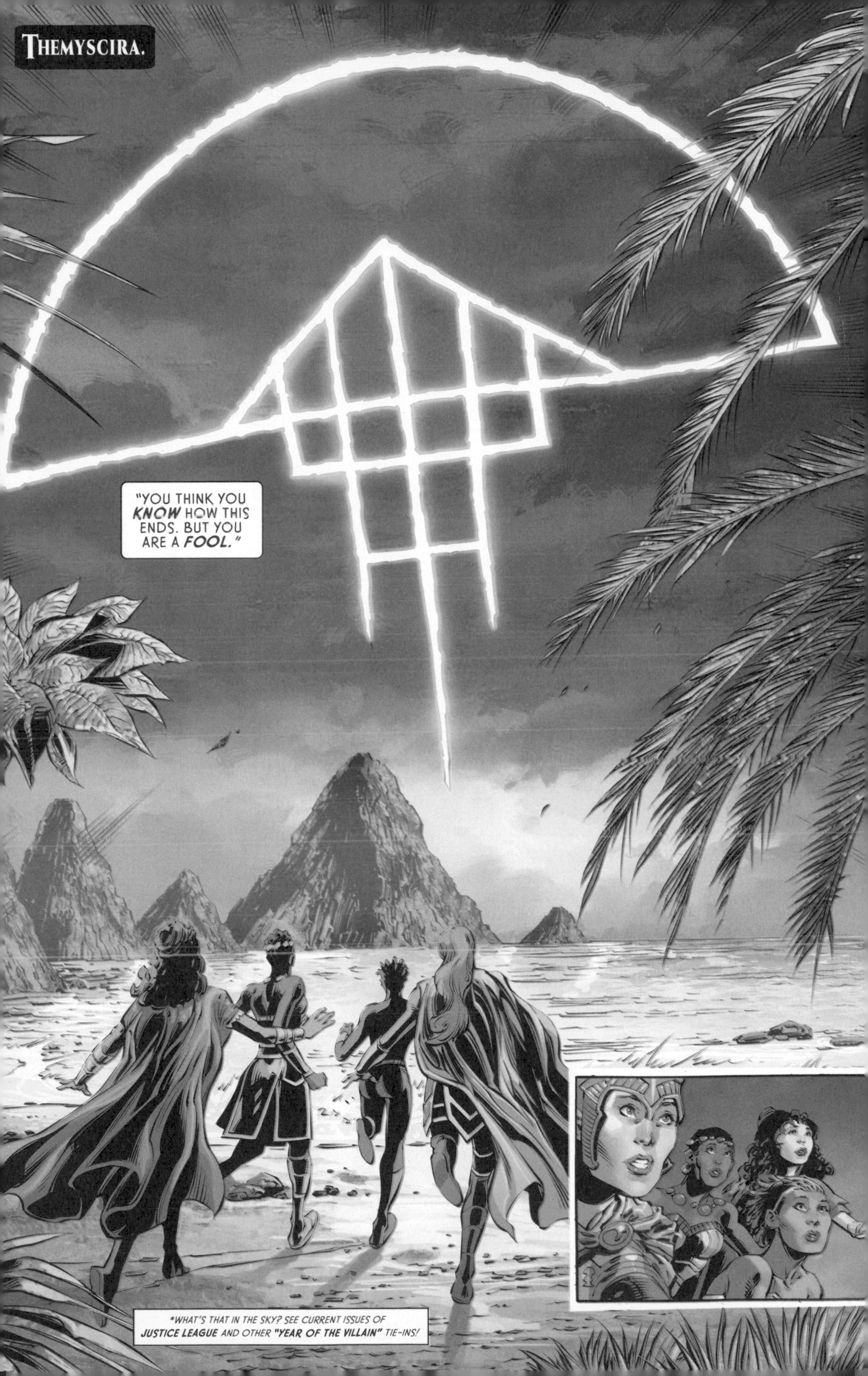
THEMYSCIRA.
"YOU THINK YOU KNOW HOW THIS ENDS. BUT YOU ARE A FOOL."
*WHAT'S THAT IN THE SKY? SEE CURRENT ISSUES OF JUSTICE LEAGUE AND OTHER "YEAR OF THE VILLAIN" TIE-INS!

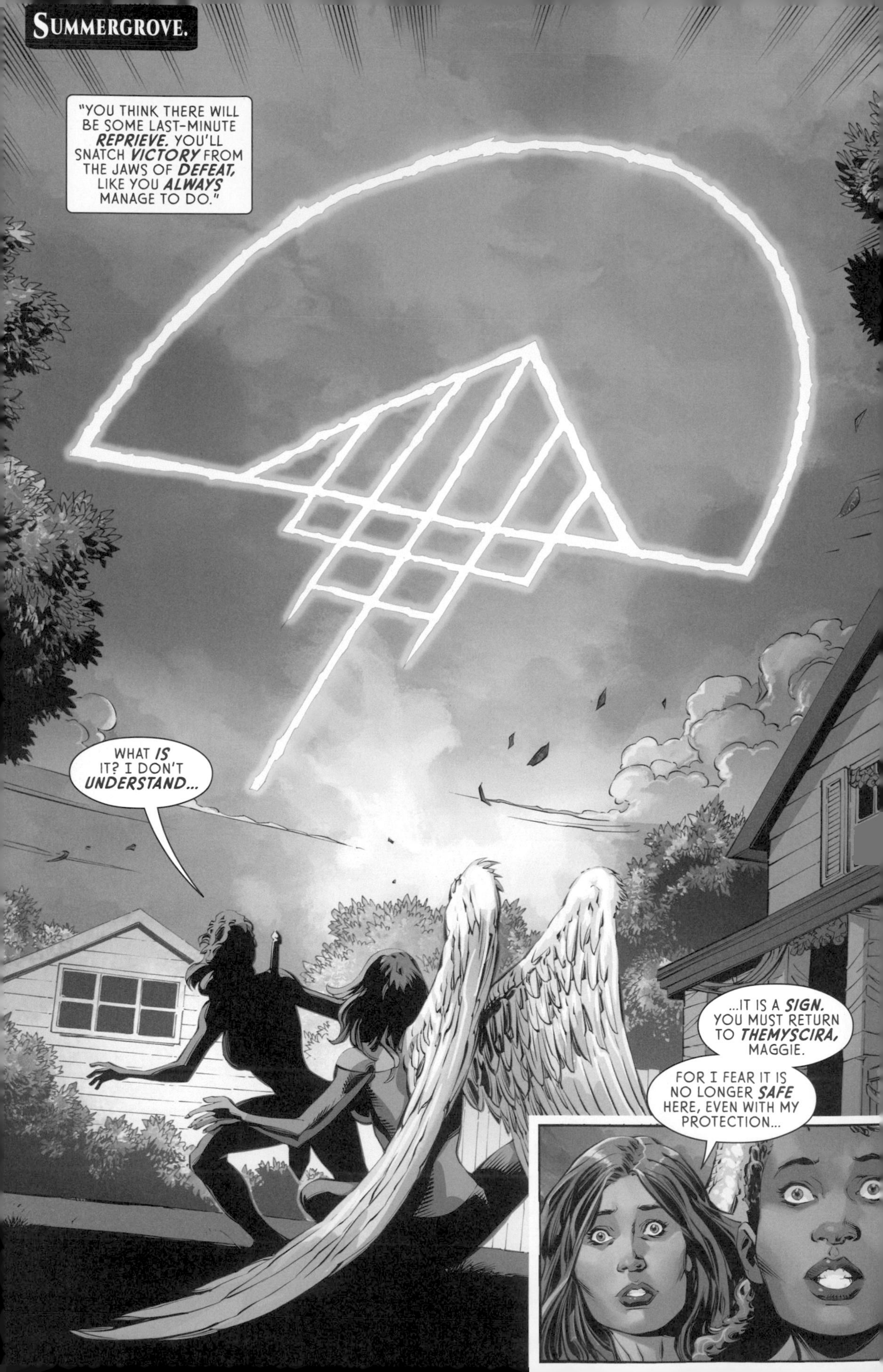
SUMMERGROVE.
"YOU THINK THERE WILL BE SOME LAST-MINUTE *REPRIEVE.* YOU'LL SNATCH *VICTORY* FROM THE JAWS OF *DEFEAT,* LIKE YOU *ALWAYS* MANAGE TO DO."
WHAT *IS* IT? I DON'T *UNDERSTAND...*
...IT IS A *SIGN.* YOU MUST RETURN TO *THEMYSCIRA,* MAGGIE.
FOR I FEAR IT IS NO LONGER *SAFE* HERE, EVEN WITH MY PROTECTION...

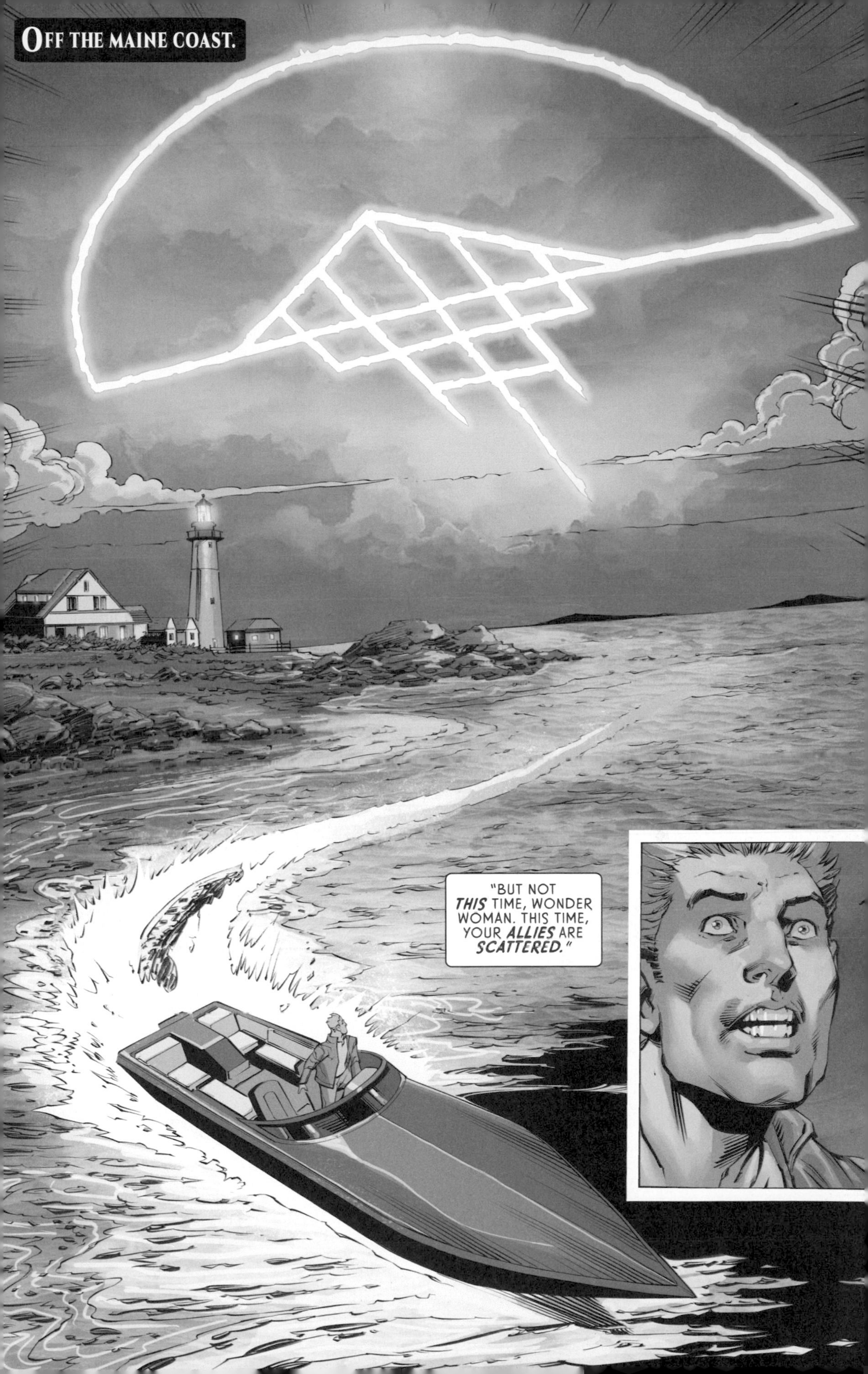
OFF THE MAINE COAST.
"BUT NOT THIS TIME, WONDER WOMAN. THIS TIME, YOUR ALLIES ARE SCATTERED."

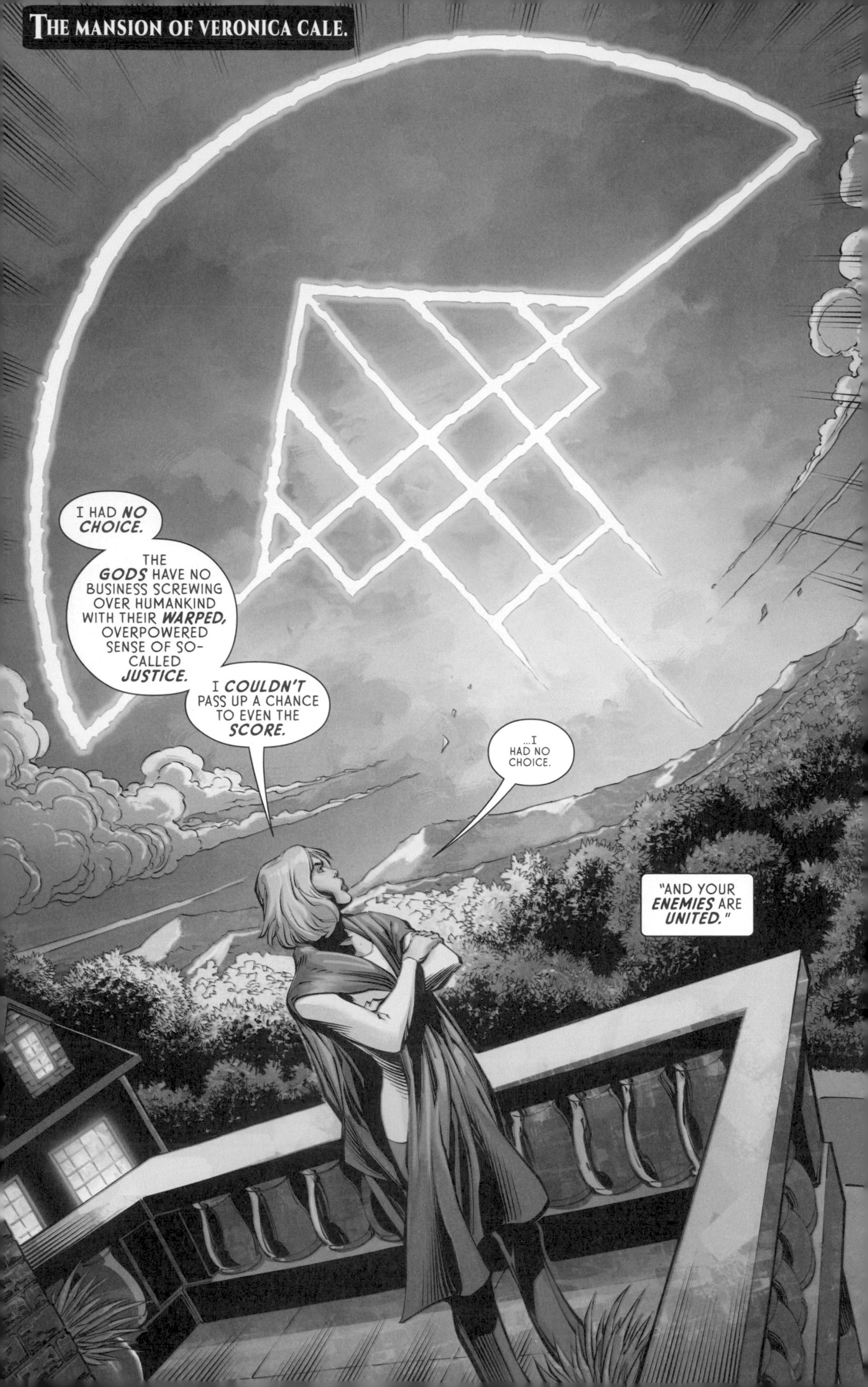
THE MANSION OF VERONICA CALE.
I HAD NO CHOICE.
THE GODS HAVE NO BUSINESS SCREWING OVER HUMANKIND WITH THEIR WARPED, OVERPOWERED SENSE OF SO-CALLED JUSTICE.
I COULDN'T PASS UP A CHANCE TO EVEN THE SCORE.
...I HAD NO CHOICE.
"AND YOUR ENEMIES ARE UNITED."

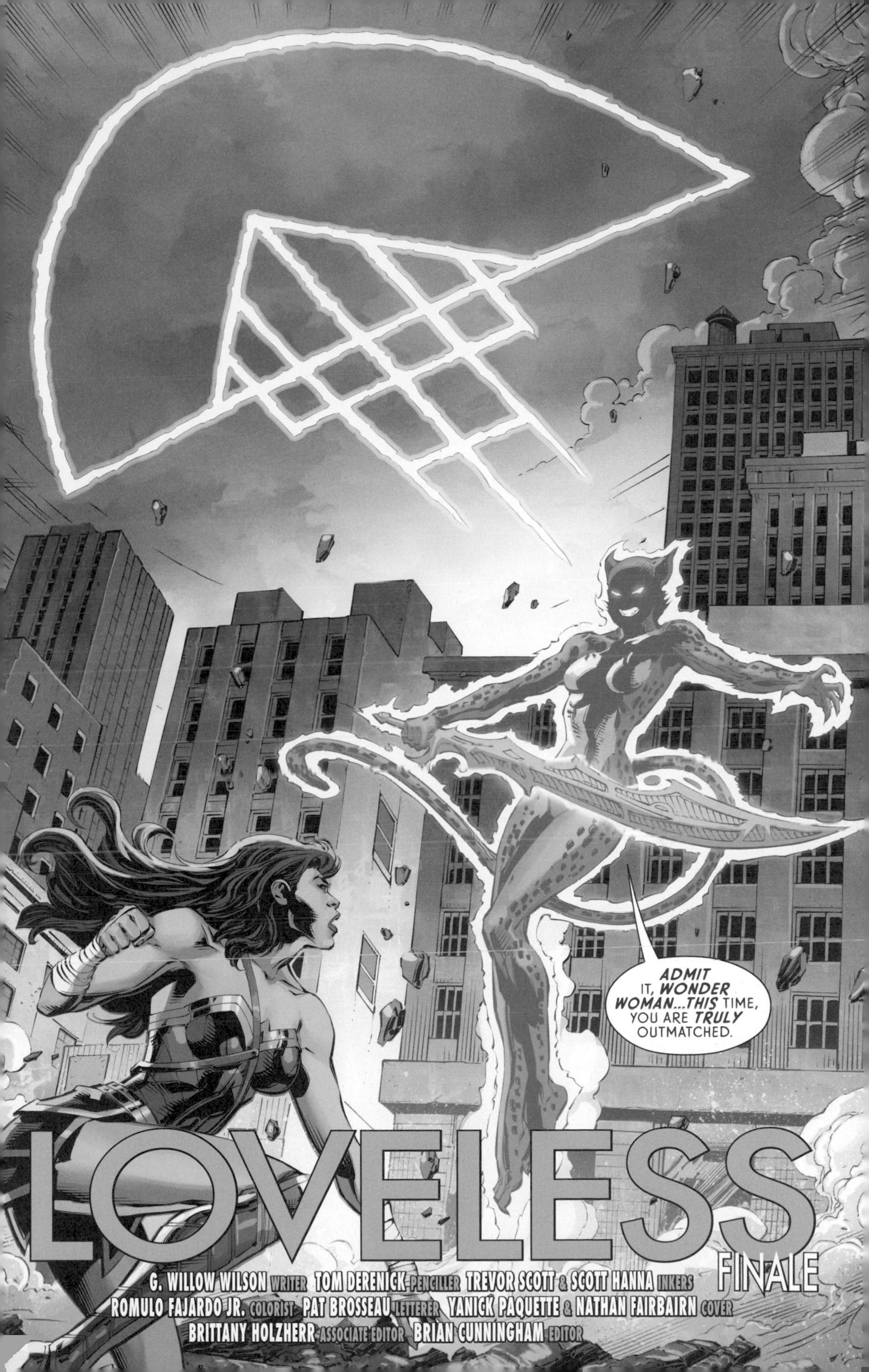
ADMIT IT, WONDER WOMAN...THIS TIME, YOU ARE TRULY OUTMATCHED.
LOVELESS
FINALE
G. WILLOW WILSON WRITER TOM DERENICK PENCILLER TREVOR SCOTT & SCOTT HANNA INKERS
ROMULO FAJARDO JR. COLORIST PAT BROSSEAU LETTERER YANICK PAQUETTE & NATHAN FAIRBAIRN COVER
BRITTANY HOLZHERR ASSOCIATE EDITOR BRIAN CUNNINGHAM EDITOR

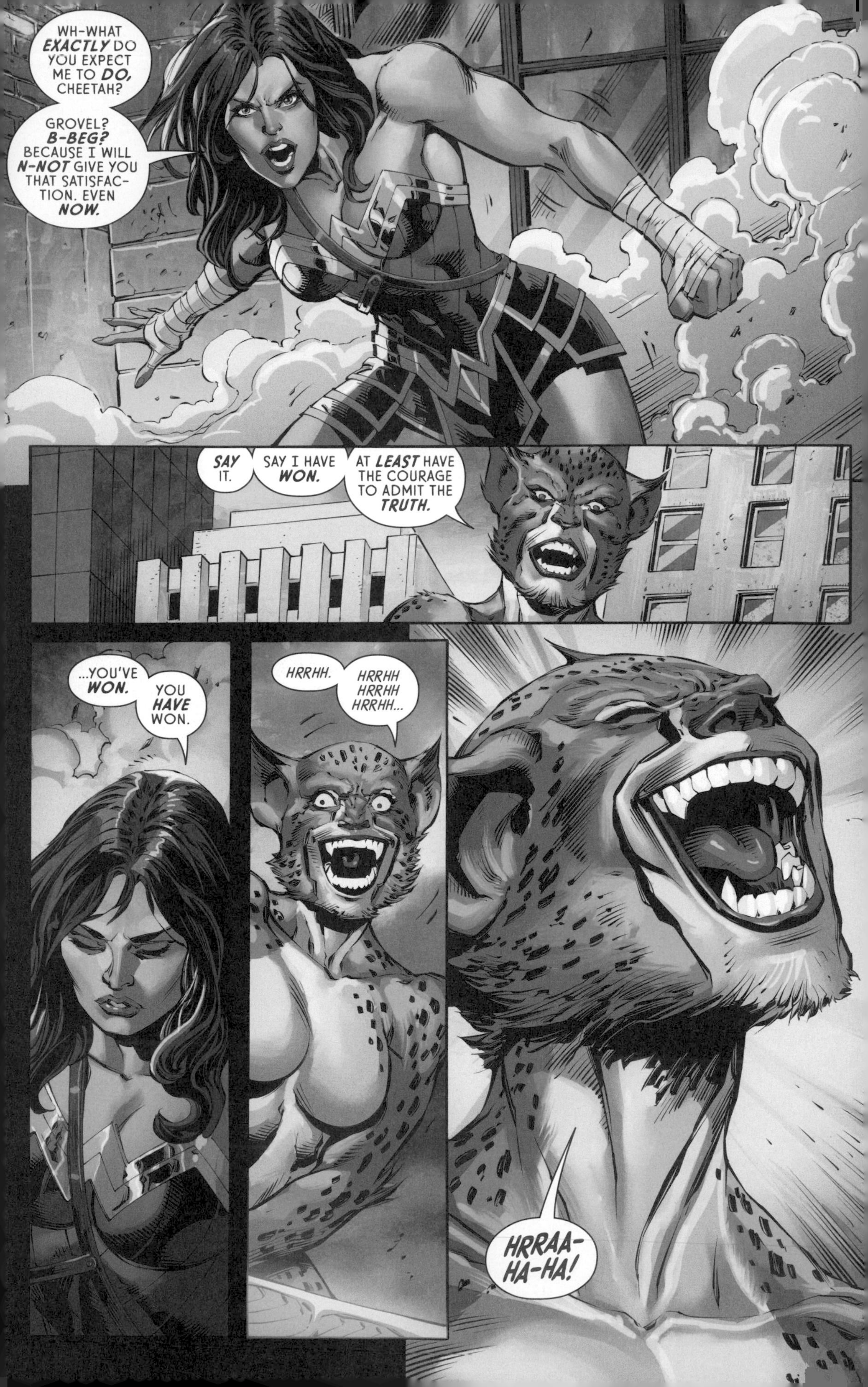
WH-WHAT EXACTLY DO YOU EXPECT ME TO DO, CHEETAH?
GROVEL? B-BEG? BECAUSE I WILL N-NOT GIVE YOU THAT SATISFAC-TION. EVEN NOW.
SAY IT.
SAY I HAVE WON.
AT LEAST HAVE THE COURAGE TO ADMIT THE TRUTH.
...YOU'VE WON.
YOU HAVE WON.
HRRHH.
HRRHH HRRHH HRRHH...
HRRAA-HA-HA!

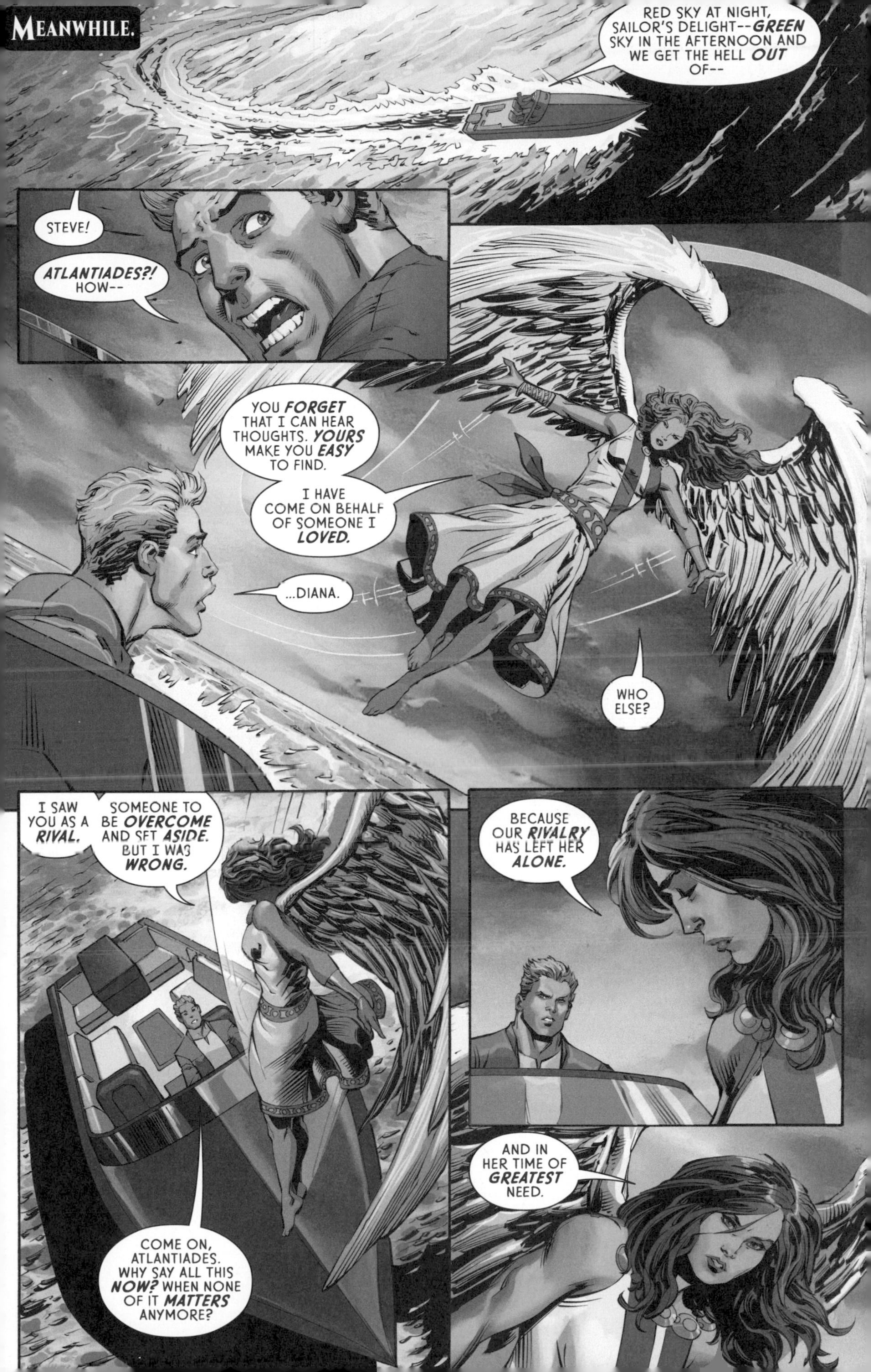
MEANWHILE.
RED SKY AT NIGHT, SAILOR'S DELIGHT--GREEN SKY IN THE AFTERNOON AND WE GET THE HELL OUT OF--
STEVE!
ATLANTIADES?! HOW--
YOU FORGET THAT I CAN HEAR THOUGHTS. YOURS MAKE YOU EASY TO FIND.
I HAVE COME ON BEHALF OF SOMEONE I LOVED.
...DIANA.
WHO ELSE?
I SAW YOU AS A RIVAL.
SOMEONE TO BE OVERCOME AND SET ASIDE. BUT I WAS WRONG.
COME ON, ATLANTIADES. WHY SAY ALL THIS NOW? WHEN NONE OF IT MATTERS ANYMORE?
BECAUSE OUR RIVALRY HAS LEFT HER ALONE.
AND IN HER TIME OF GREATEST NEED.

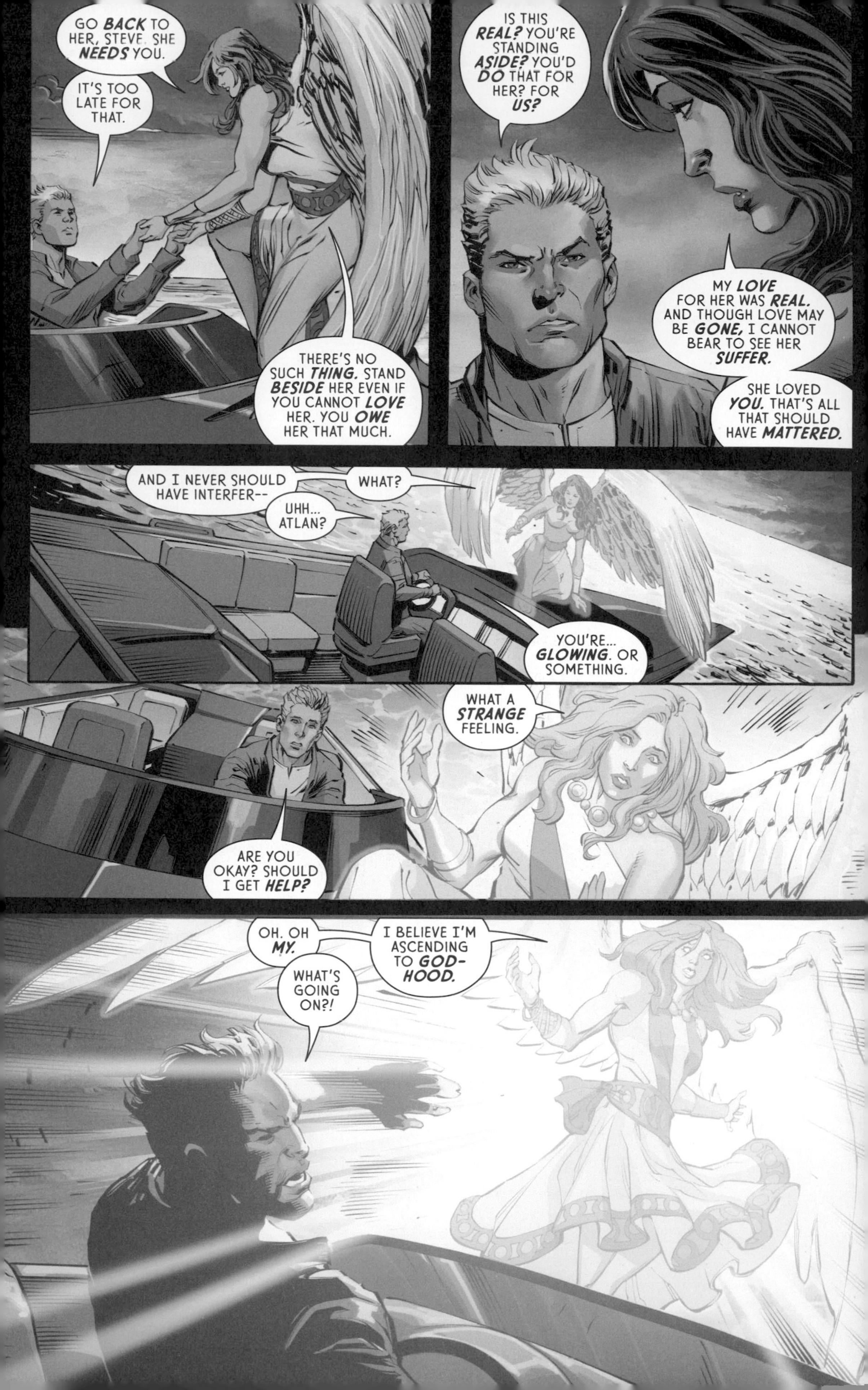
GO BACK TO HER, STEVE. SHE NEEDS YOU.
IT'S TOO LATE FOR THAT.
THERE'S NO SUCH THING. STAND BESIDE HER EVEN IF YOU CANNOT LOVE HER. YOU OWE HER THAT MUCH.
IS THIS REAL? YOU'RE STANDING ASIDE? YOU'D DO THAT FOR HER? FOR US?
MY LOVE FOR HER WAS REAL. AND THOUGH LOVE MAY BE GONE, I CANNOT BEAR TO SEE HER SUFFER.
SHE LOVED YOU. THAT'S ALL THAT SHOULD HAVE MATTERED.
AND I NEVER SHOULD HAVE INTERFER--
WHAT?
UHH... ATLAN?
YOU'RE... GLOWING. OR SOMETHING.
WHAT A STRANGE FEELING.
ARE YOU OKAY? SHOULD I GET HELP?
OH. OH MY.
I BELIEVE I'M ASCENDING TO GOD-HOOD.
WHAT'S GOING ON?!

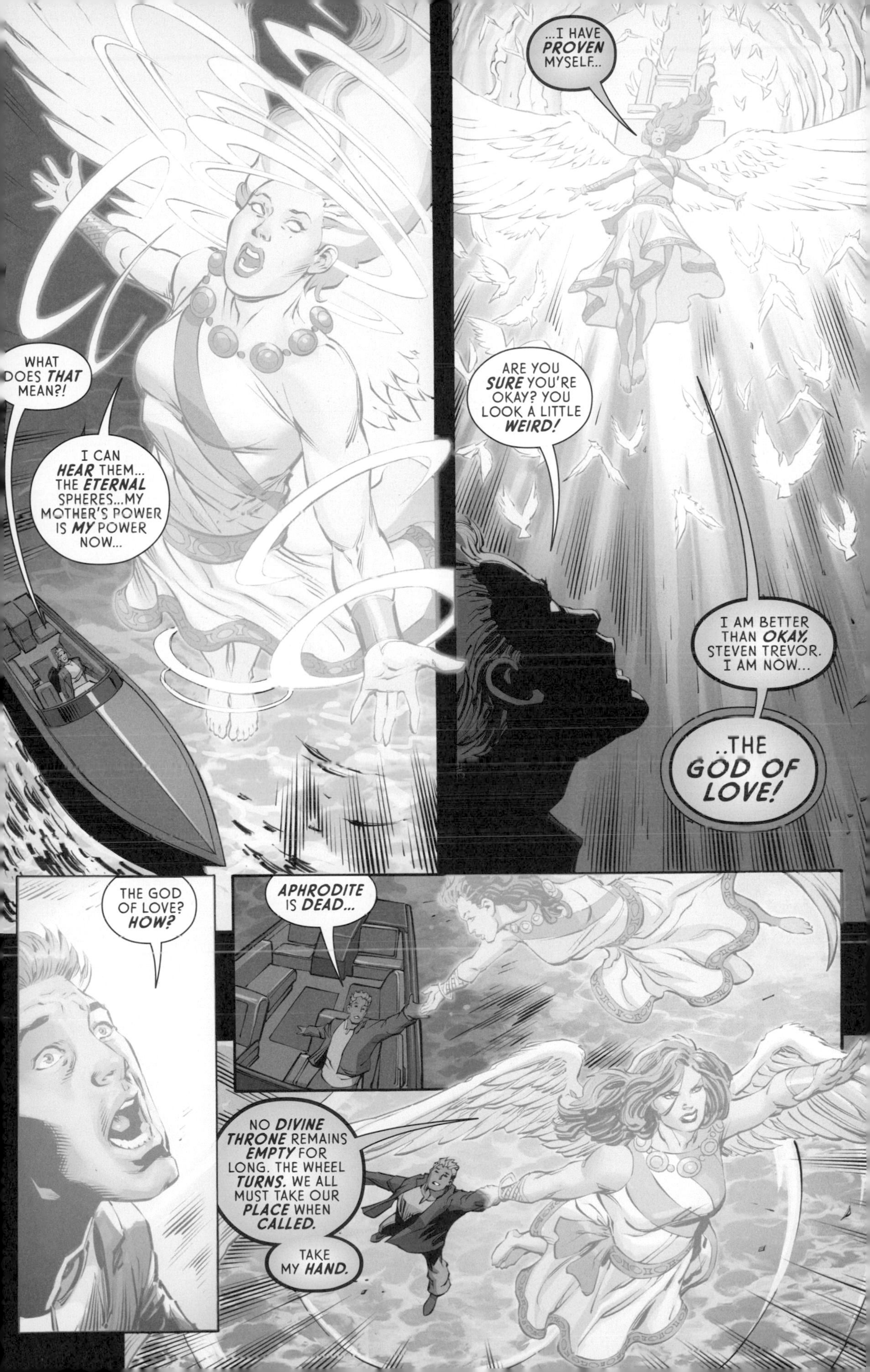
WHAT DOES THAT MEAN?!
I CAN HEAR THEM... THE ETERNAL SPHERES...MY MOTHER'S POWER IS MY POWER NOW...
...I HAVE PROVEN MYSELF...
ARE YOU SURE YOU'RE OKAY? YOU LOOK A LITTLE WEIRD!
I AM BETTER THAN OKAY, STEVEN TREVOR. I AM NOW...
..THE GOD OF LOVE!
THE GOD OF LOVE? HOW?
APHRODITE IS DEAD...
NO DIVINE THRONE REMAINS EMPTY FOR LONG. THE WHEEL TURNS. WE ALL MUST TAKE OUR PLACE WHEN CALLED.
TAKE MY HAND.

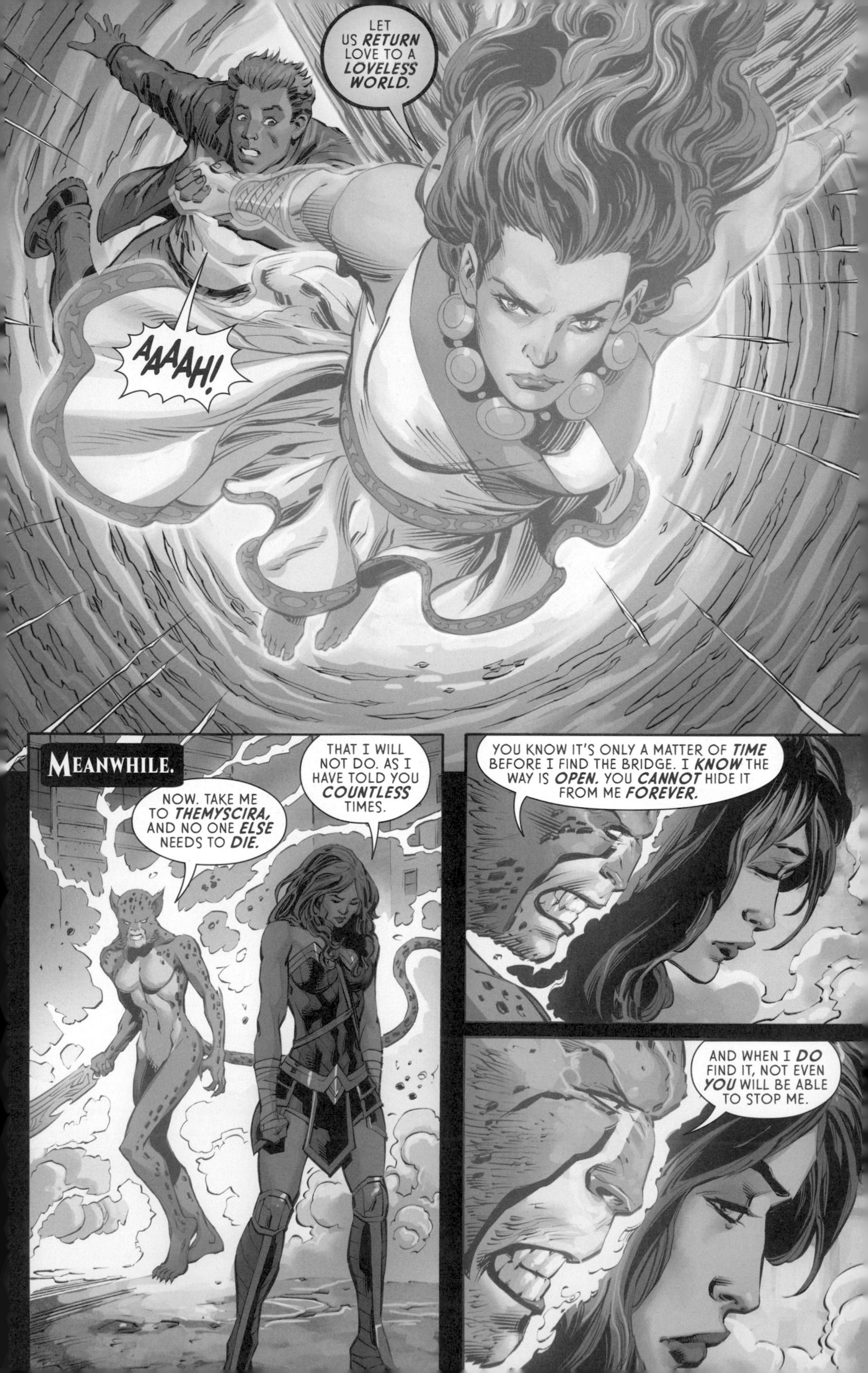
LET US RETURN LOVE TO A LOVELESS WORLD.
AAAAH!
MEANWHILE.
NOW. TAKE ME TO THEMYSCIRA, AND NO ONE ELSE NEEDS TO DIE.
THAT I WILL NOT DO. AS I HAVE TOLD YOU COUNTLESS TIMES.
YOU KNOW IT'S ONLY A MATTER OF TIME BEFORE I FIND THE BRIDGE. I KNOW THE WAY IS OPEN. YOU CANNOT HIDE IT FROM ME FOREVER.
AND WHEN I DO FIND IT, NOT EVEN YOU WILL BE ABLE TO STOP ME.

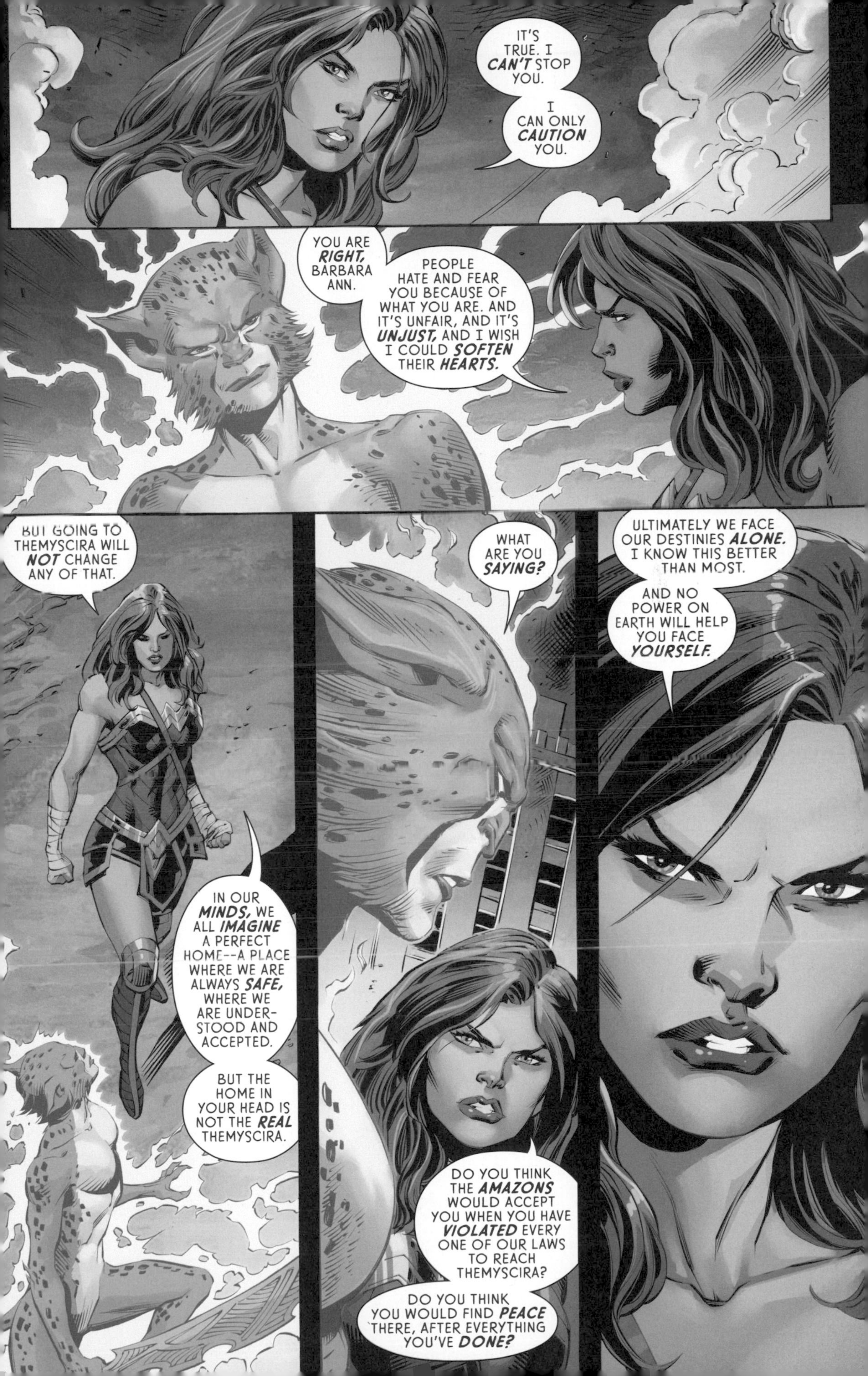
IT'S TRUE. I CAN'T STOP YOU.
I CAN ONLY CAUTION YOU.
YOU ARE RIGHT, BARBARA ANN.
PEOPLE HATE AND FEAR YOU BECAUSE OF WHAT YOU ARE. AND IT'S UNFAIR, AND IT'S UNJUST, AND I WISH I COULD SOFTEN THEIR HEARTS.
BUT GOING TO THEMYSCIRA WILL NOT CHANGE ANY OF THAT.
IN OUR MINDS, WE ALL IMAGINE A PERFECT HOME--A PLACE WHERE WE ARE ALWAYS SAFE, WHERE WE ARE UNDER-STOOD AND ACCEPTED.
BUT THE HOME IN YOUR HEAD IS NOT THE REAL THEMYSCIRA.
WHAT ARE YOU SAYING?
DO YOU THINK THE AMAZONS WOULD ACCEPT YOU WHEN YOU HAVE VIOLATED EVERY ONE OF OUR LAWS TO REACH THEMYSCIRA?
DO YOU THINK YOU WOULD FIND PEACE THERE, AFTER EVERYTHING YOU'VE DONE?
ULTIMATELY WE FACE OUR DESTINIES ALONE. I KNOW THIS BETTER THAN MOST.
AND NO POWER ON EARTH WILL HELP YOU FACE YOURSELF.

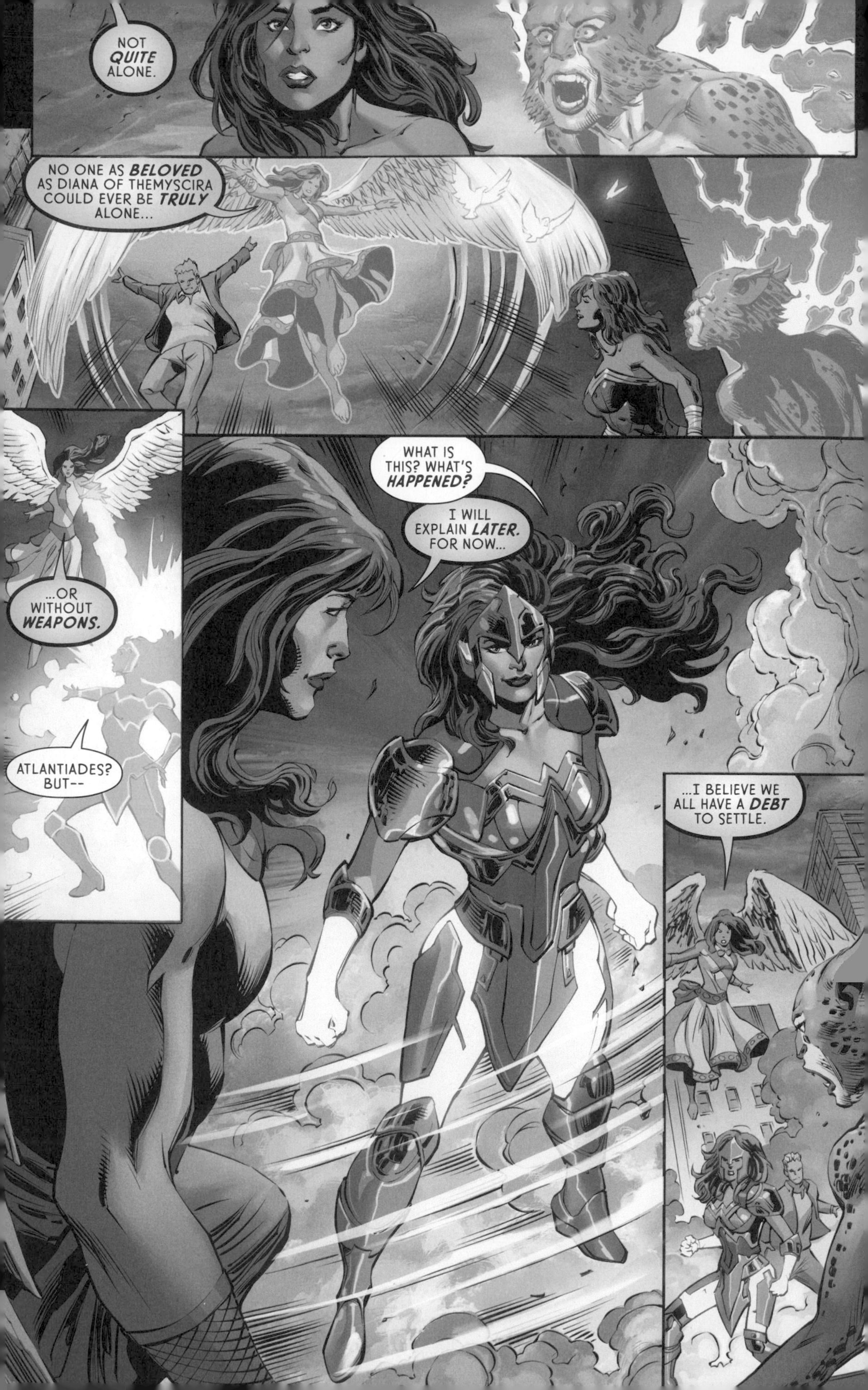

NOT QUITE ALONE.
NO ONE AS BELOVED AS DIANA OF THEMYSCIRA COULD EVER BE TRULY ALONE...
...OR WITHOUT WEAPONS.
ATLANTIADES? BUT--
WHAT IS THIS? WHAT'S HAPPENED?
I WILL EXPLAIN LATER. FOR NOW...
...I BELIEVE WE ALL HAVE A DEBT TO SETTLE.

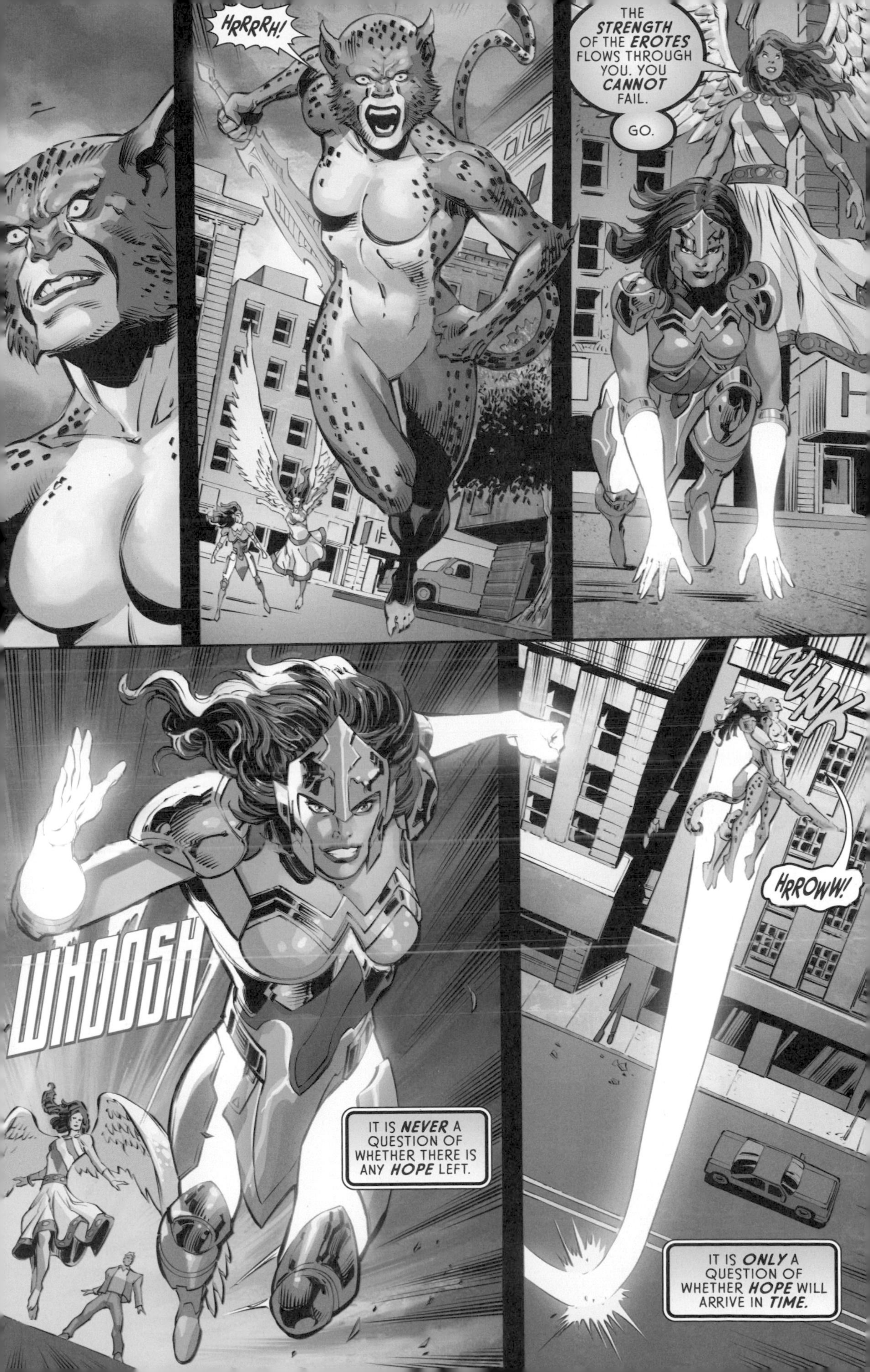
HRRRRH!
THE STRENGTH OF THE EROTES FLOWS THROUGH YOU. YOU CANNOT FAIL.
GO.
WHOOSH
IT IS NEVER A QUESTION OF WHETHER THERE IS ANY HOPE LEFT.
THUNK
HRROWW!
IT IS ONLY A QUESTION OF WHETHER HOPE WILL ARRIVE IN TIME.

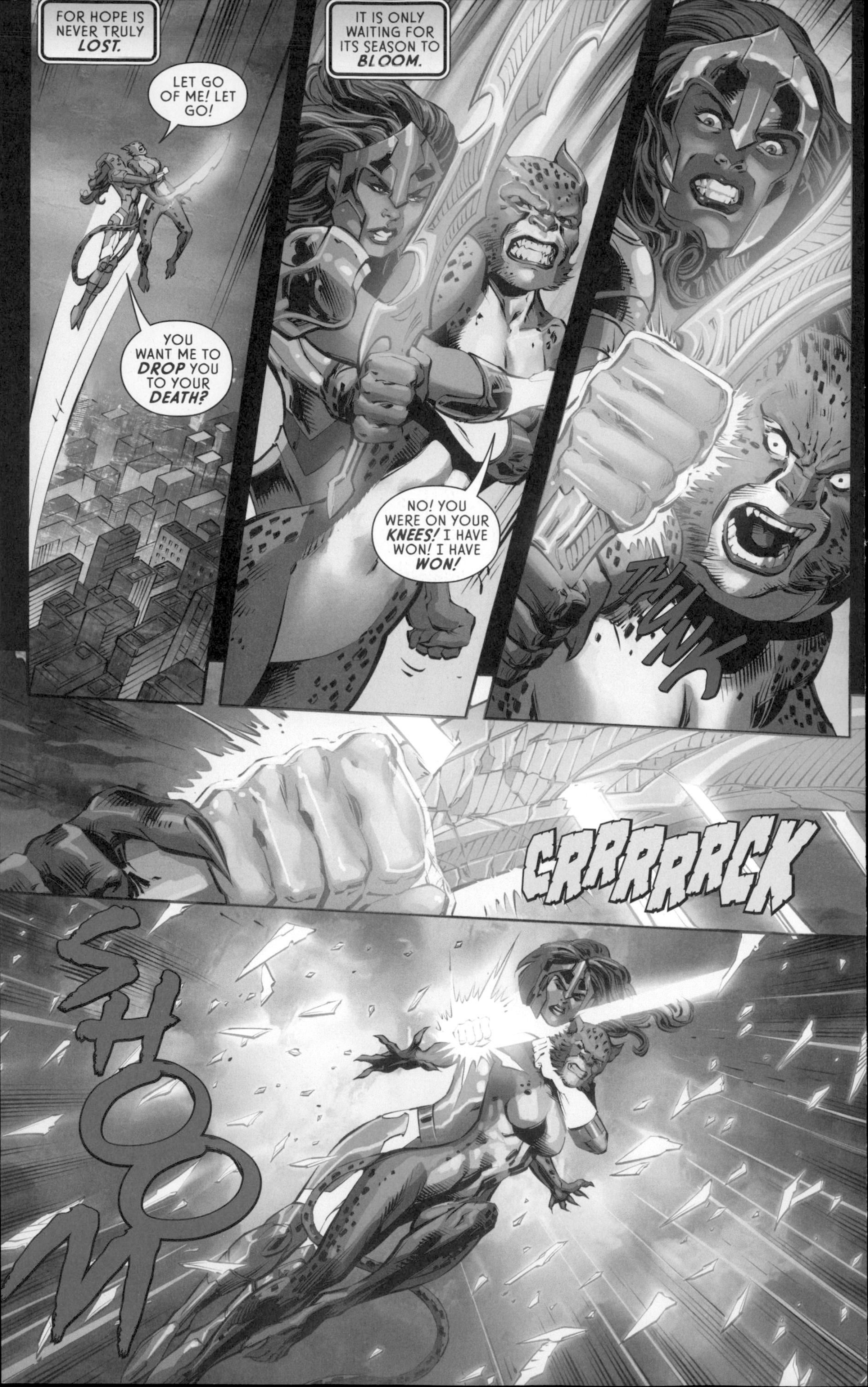
FOR HOPE IS NEVER TRULY LOST.
LET GO OF ME! LET GO!
YOU WANT ME TO DROP YOU TO YOUR DEATH?
IT IS ONLY WAITING FOR ITS SEASON TO BLOOM.
NO! YOU WERE ON YOUR KNEES! I HAVE WON! I HAVE WON!
THUNK
CRRRRRCK
SHOOM

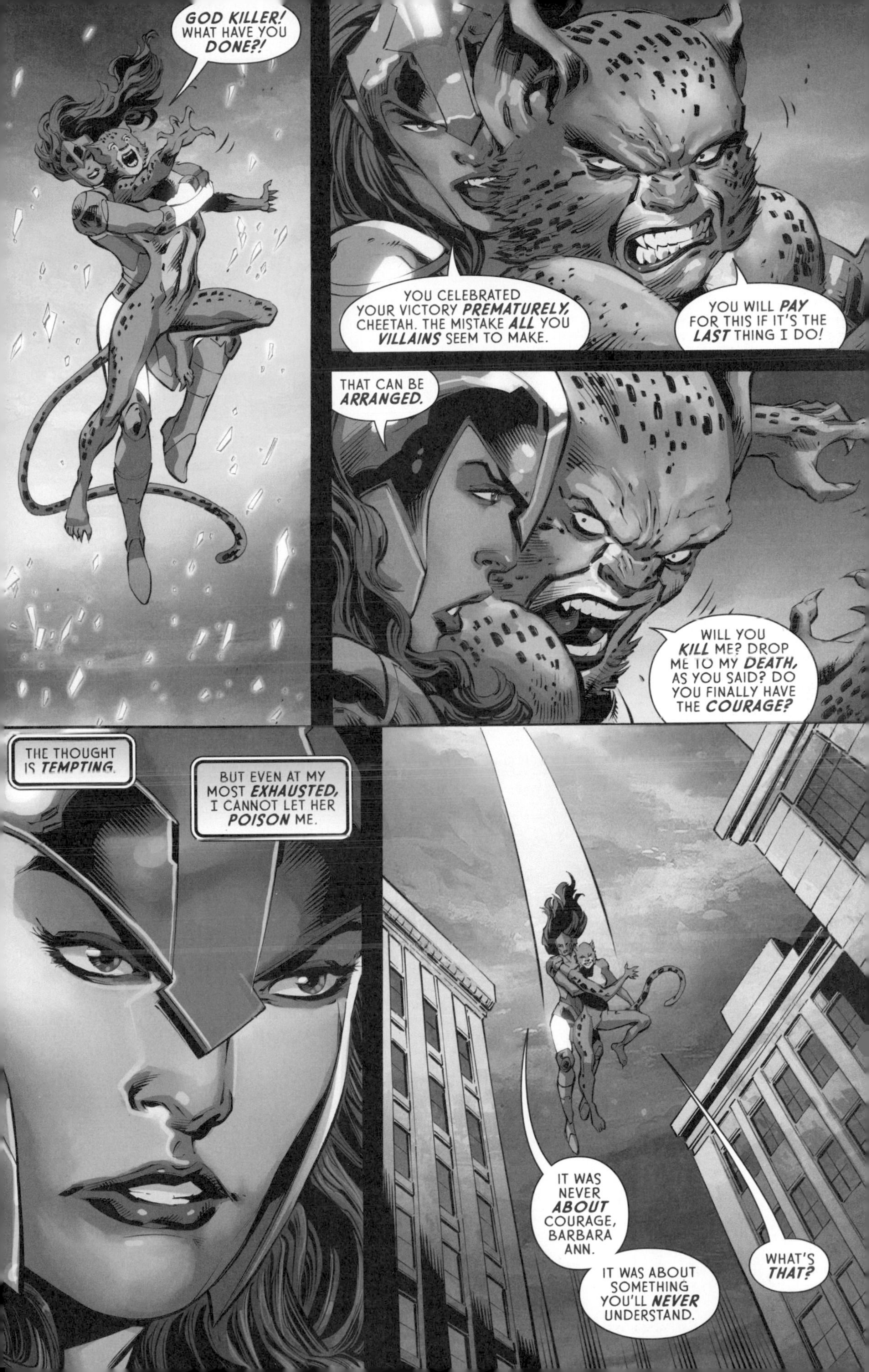
GOD KILLER! WHAT HAVE YOU DONE?!
YOU CELEBRATED YOUR VICTORY PREMATURELY, CHEETAH. THE MISTAKE ALL YOU VILLAINS SEEM TO MAKE.
YOU WILL PAY FOR THIS IF IT'S THE LAST THING I DO!
THAT CAN BE ARRANGED.
WILL YOU KILL ME? DROP ME TO MY DEATH, AS YOU SAID? DO YOU FINALLY HAVE THE COURAGE?
THE THOUGHT IS TEMPTING.
BUT EVEN AT MY MOST EXHAUSTED, I CANNOT LET HER POISON ME.
IT WAS NEVER ABOUT COURAGE, BARBARA ANN.
IT WAS ABOUT SOMETHING YOU'LL NEVER UNDERSTAND.
WHAT'S THAT?

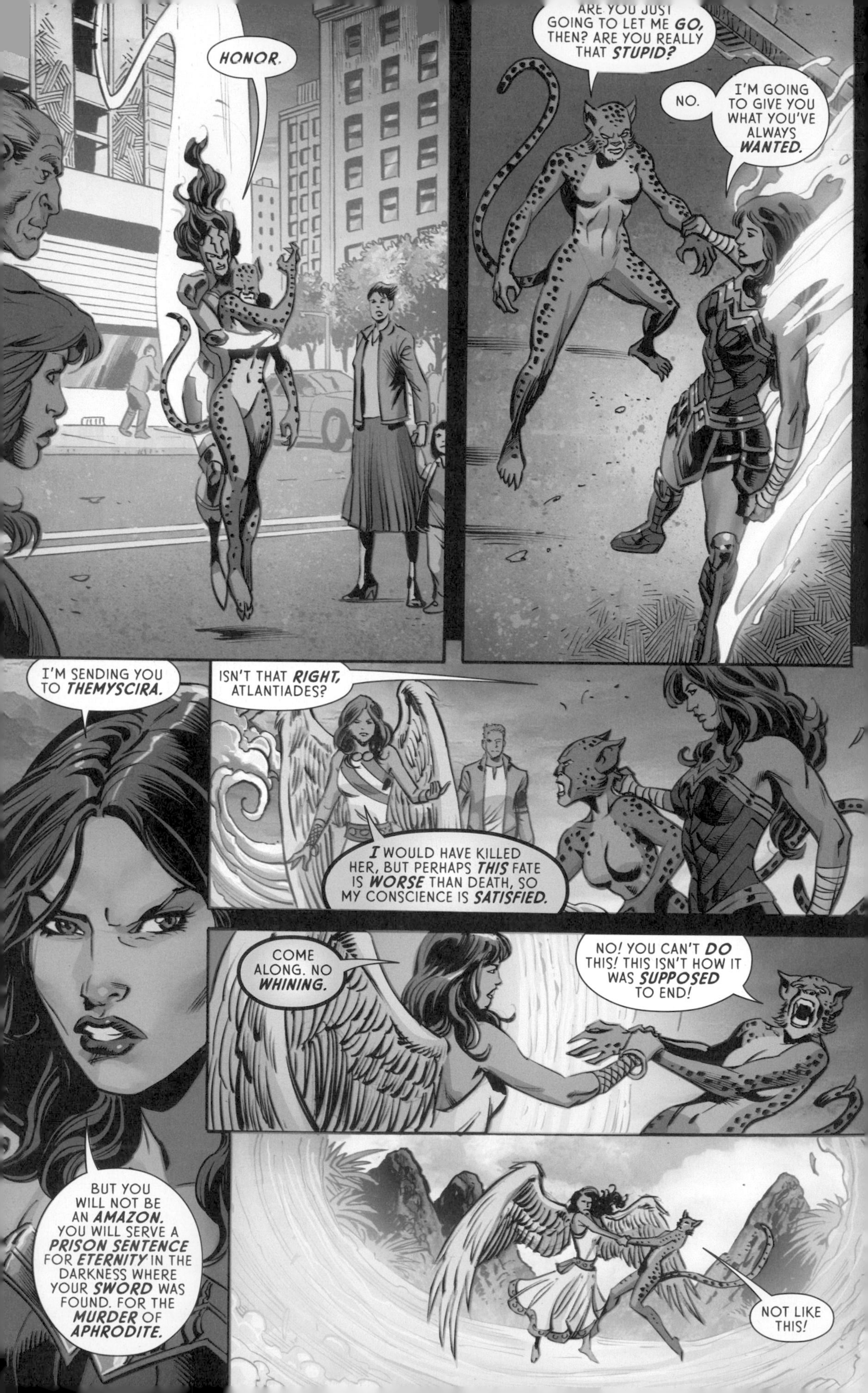
HONOR.
ARE YOU JUST GOING TO LET ME GO, THEN? ARE YOU REALLY THAT STUPID?
NO.
I'M GOING TO GIVE YOU WHAT YOU'VE ALWAYS WANTED.
I'M SENDING YOU TO THEMYSCIRA.
ISN'T THAT RIGHT, ATLANTIADES?
I WOULD HAVE KILLED HER, BUT PERHAPS THIS FATE IS WORSE THAN DEATH, SO MY CONSCIENCE IS SATISFIED.
COME ALONG. NO WHINING.
NO! YOU CAN'T DO THIS! THIS ISN'T HOW IT WAS SUPPOSED TO END!
BUT YOU WILL NOT BE AN AMAZON. YOU WILL SERVE A PRISON SENTENCE FOR ETERNITY IN THE DARKNESS WHERE YOUR SWORD WAS FOUND. FOR THE MURDER OF APHRODITE.
NOT LIKE THIS!

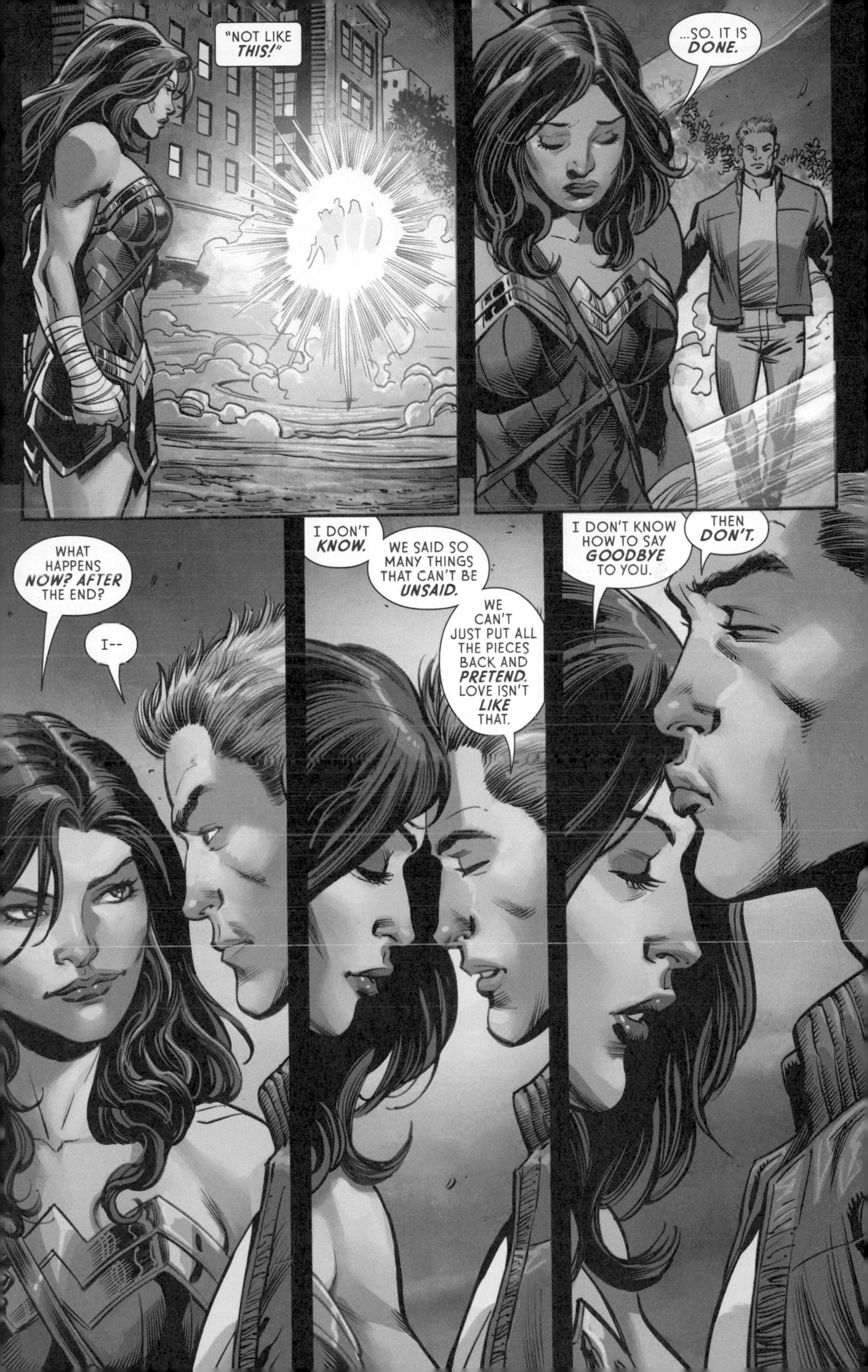
"NOT LIKE THIS!"
...SO. IT IS DONE.
WHAT HAPPENS NOW? AFTER THE END?
I--
I DON'T KNOW.
WE SAID SO MANY THINGS THAT CAN'T BE UNSAID.
WE CAN'T JUST PUT ALL THE PIECES BACK AND PRETEND. LOVE ISN'T LIKE THAT.
I DON'T KNOW HOW TO SAY GOODBYE TO YOU.
THEN DON'T.

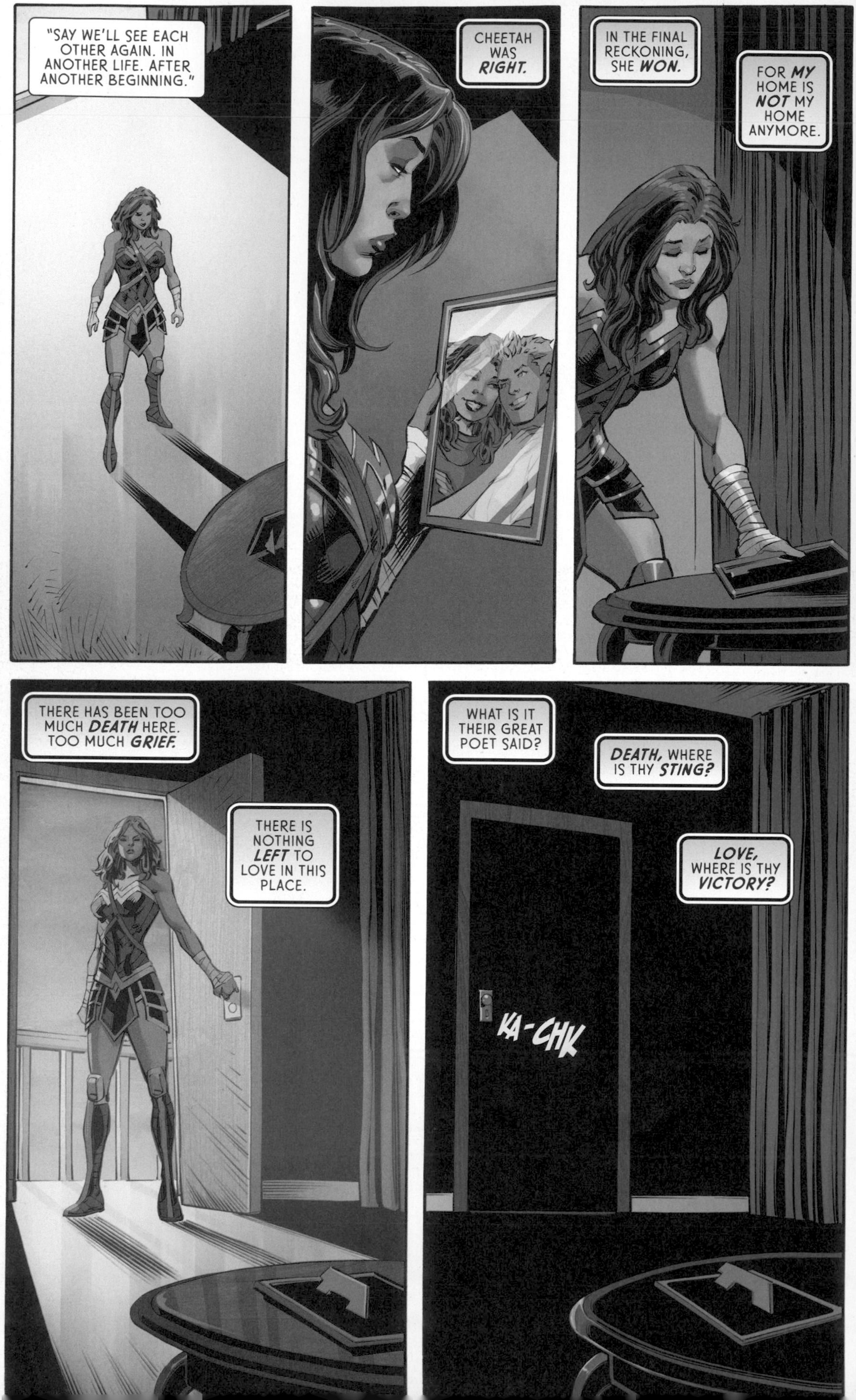
"SAY WE'LL SEE EACH OTHER AGAIN. IN ANOTHER LIFE. AFTER ANOTHER BEGINNING."
CHEETAH WAS RIGHT.
IN THE FINAL RECKONING, SHE WON.
FOR MY HOME IS NOT MY HOME ANYMORE.
THERE HAS BEEN TOO MUCH DEATH HERE. TOO MUCH GRIEF.
THERE IS NOTHING LEFT TO LOVE IN THIS PLACE.
WHAT IS IT THEIR GREAT POET SAID?
DEATH, WHERE IS THY STING?
LOVE, WHERE IS THY VICTORY?
KA-CHK

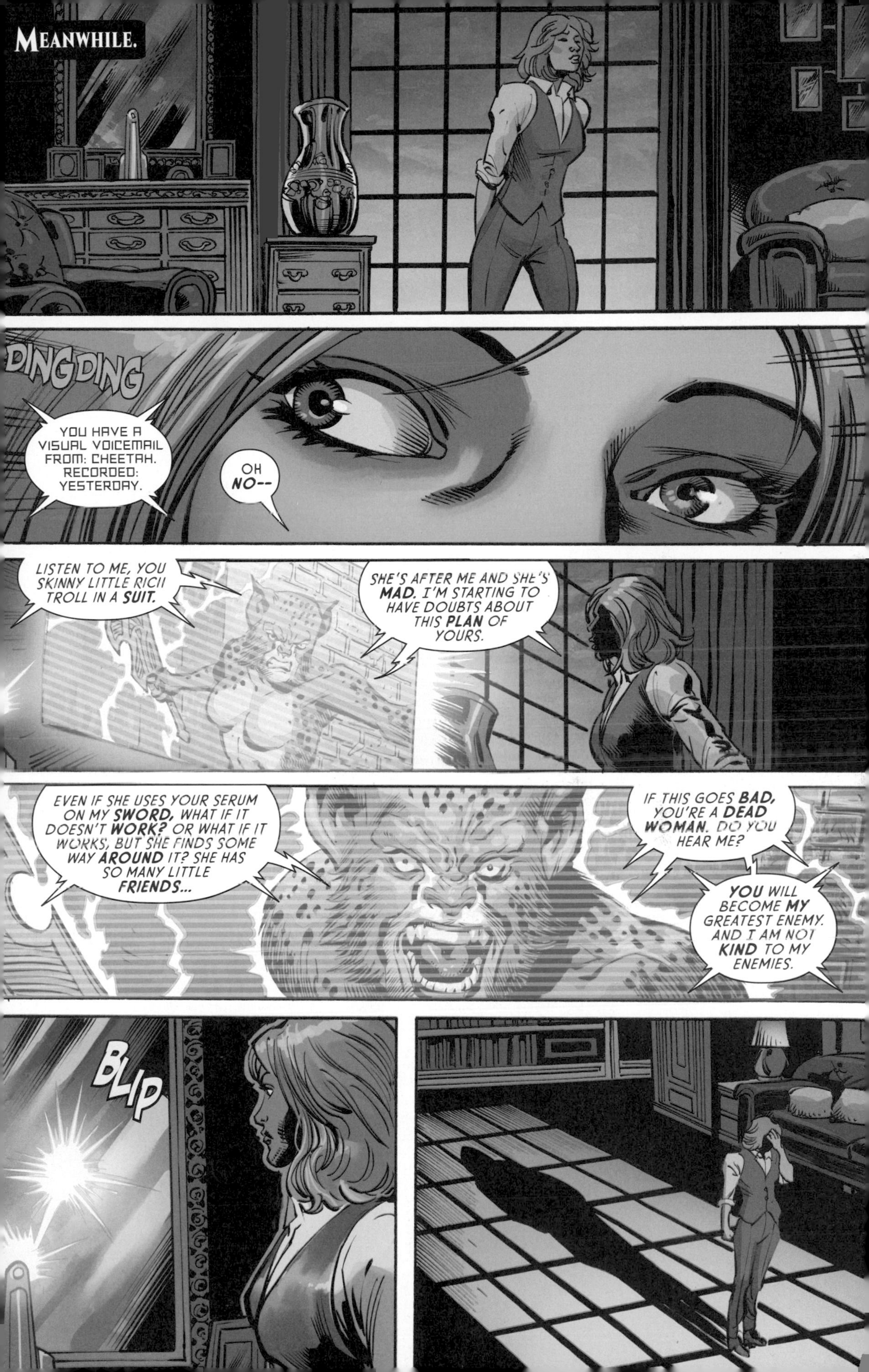
MEANWHILE.
DING DING
YOU HAVE A VISUAL VOICEMAIL FROM: CHEETAH. RECORDED: YESTERDAY.
OH NO--
LISTEN TO ME, YOU SKINNY LITTLE RICH TROLL IN A SUIT.
SHE'S AFTER ME AND SHE'S MAD. I'M STARTING TO HAVE DOUBTS ABOUT THIS PLAN OF YOURS.
EVEN IF SHE USES YOUR SERUM ON MY SWORD, WHAT IF IT DOESN'T WORK? OR WHAT IF IT WORKS, BUT SHE FINDS SOME WAY AROUND IT? SHE HAS SO MANY LITTLE FRIENDS...
IF THIS GOES BAD, YOU'RE A DEAD WOMAN. DO YOU HEAR ME?
YOU WILL BECOME MY GREATEST ENEMY. AND I AM NOT KIND TO MY ENEMIES.
BLIP

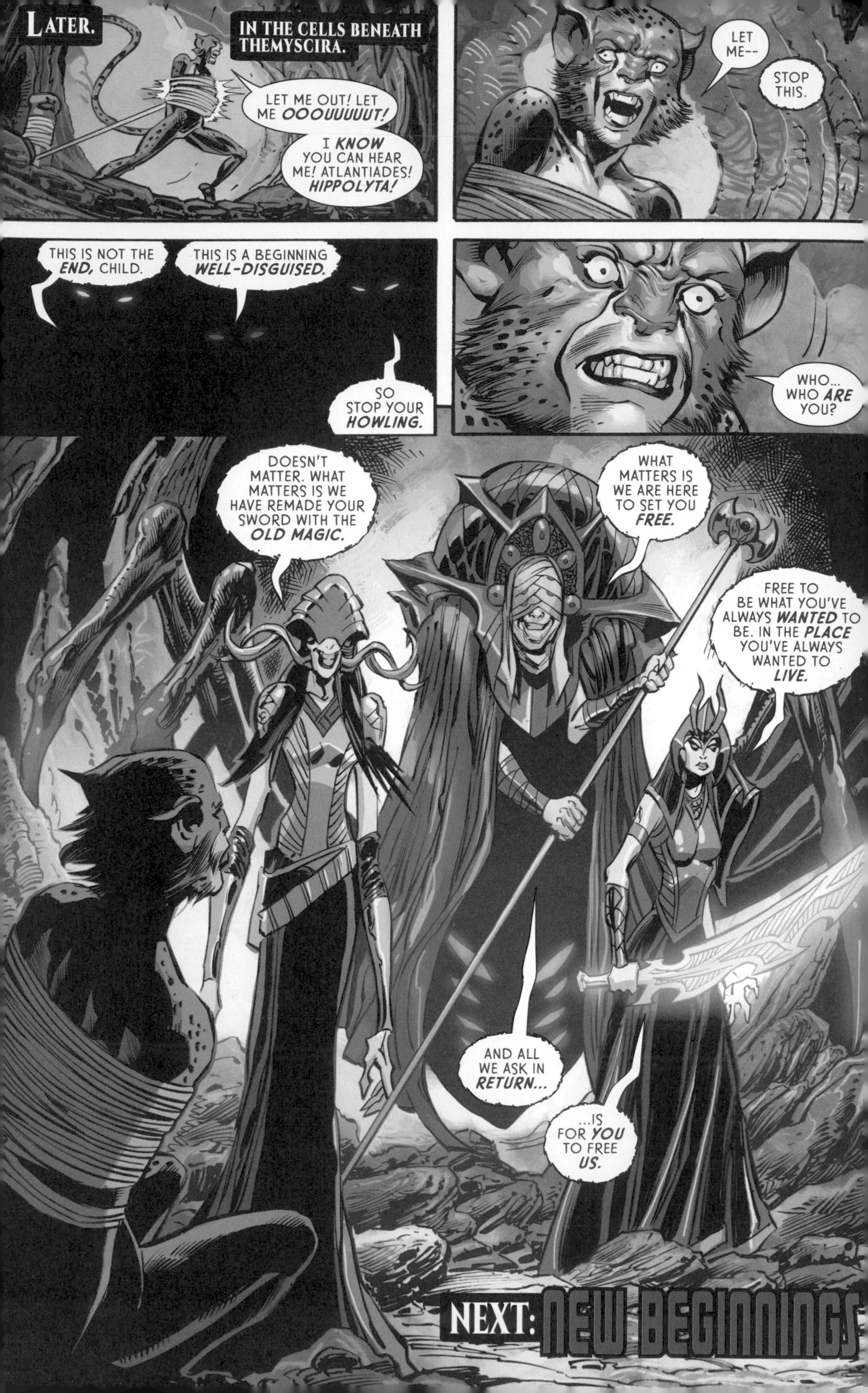
LATER.
IN THE CELLS BENEATH THEMYSCIRA.
LET ME OUT! LET ME OOOUUUUUT!
I KNOW YOU CAN HEAR ME! ATLANTIADES! HIPPOLYTA!
LET ME--
STOP THIS.
THIS IS NOT THE END, CHILD.
THIS IS A BEGINNING WELL-DISGUISED.
SO STOP YOUR HOWLING.
WHO... WHO ARE YOU?
DOESN'T MATTER. WHAT MATTERS IS WE HAVE REMADE YOUR SWORD WITH THE OLD MAGIC.
WHAT MATTERS IS WE ARE HERE TO SET YOU FREE.
FREE TO BE WHAT YOU'VE ALWAYS WANTED TO BE. IN THE PLACE YOU'VE ALWAYS WANTED TO LIVE.
AND ALL WE ASK IN RETURN...
...IS FOR YOU TO FREE US.
NEXT: NEW BEGINNINGS

VARIANT COVER GALLERY

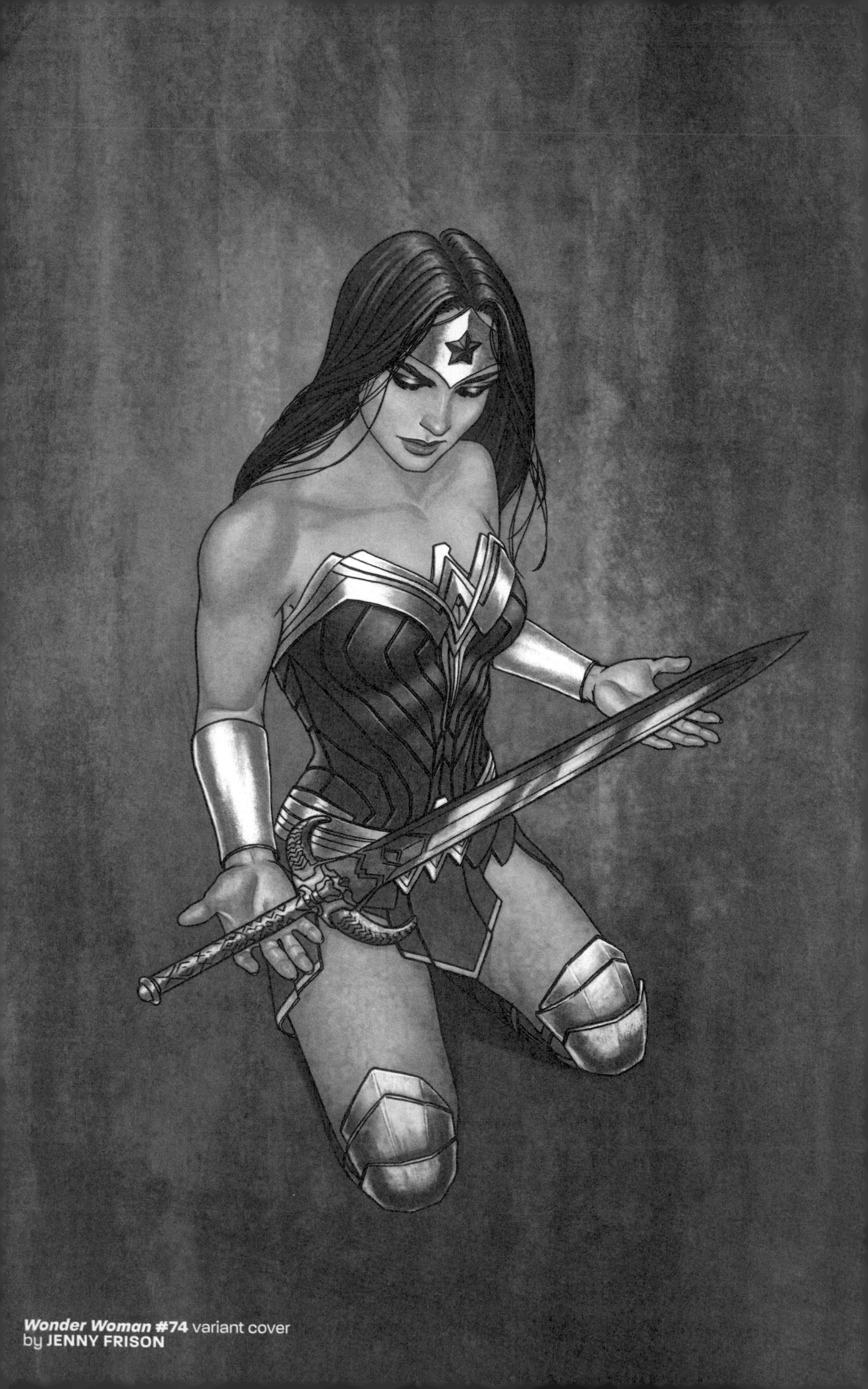

***Wonder Woman* #74** variant cover
by **JENNY FRISON**

***Wonder Woman* #75** variant cover
by **JENNY FRISON**

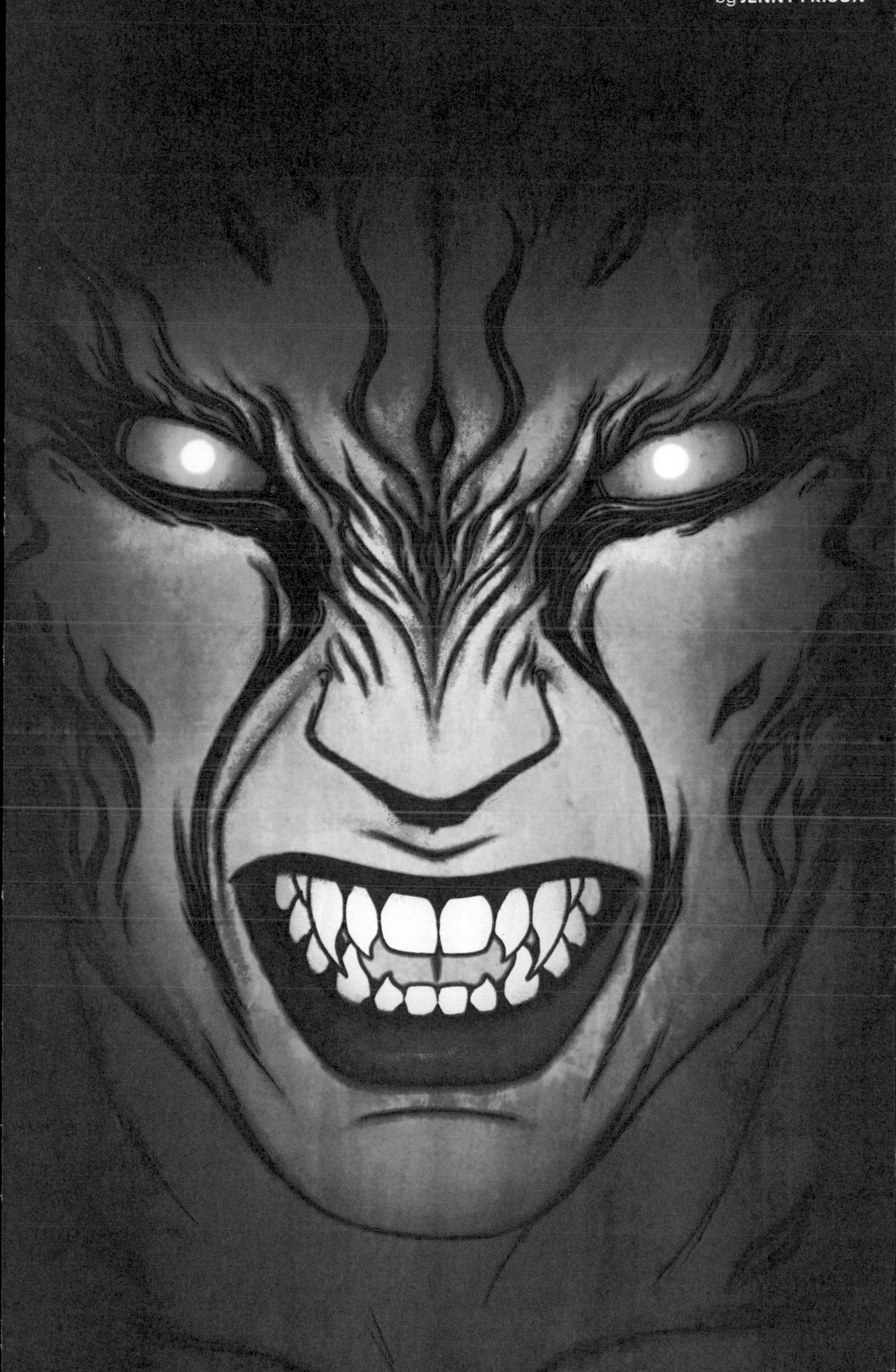

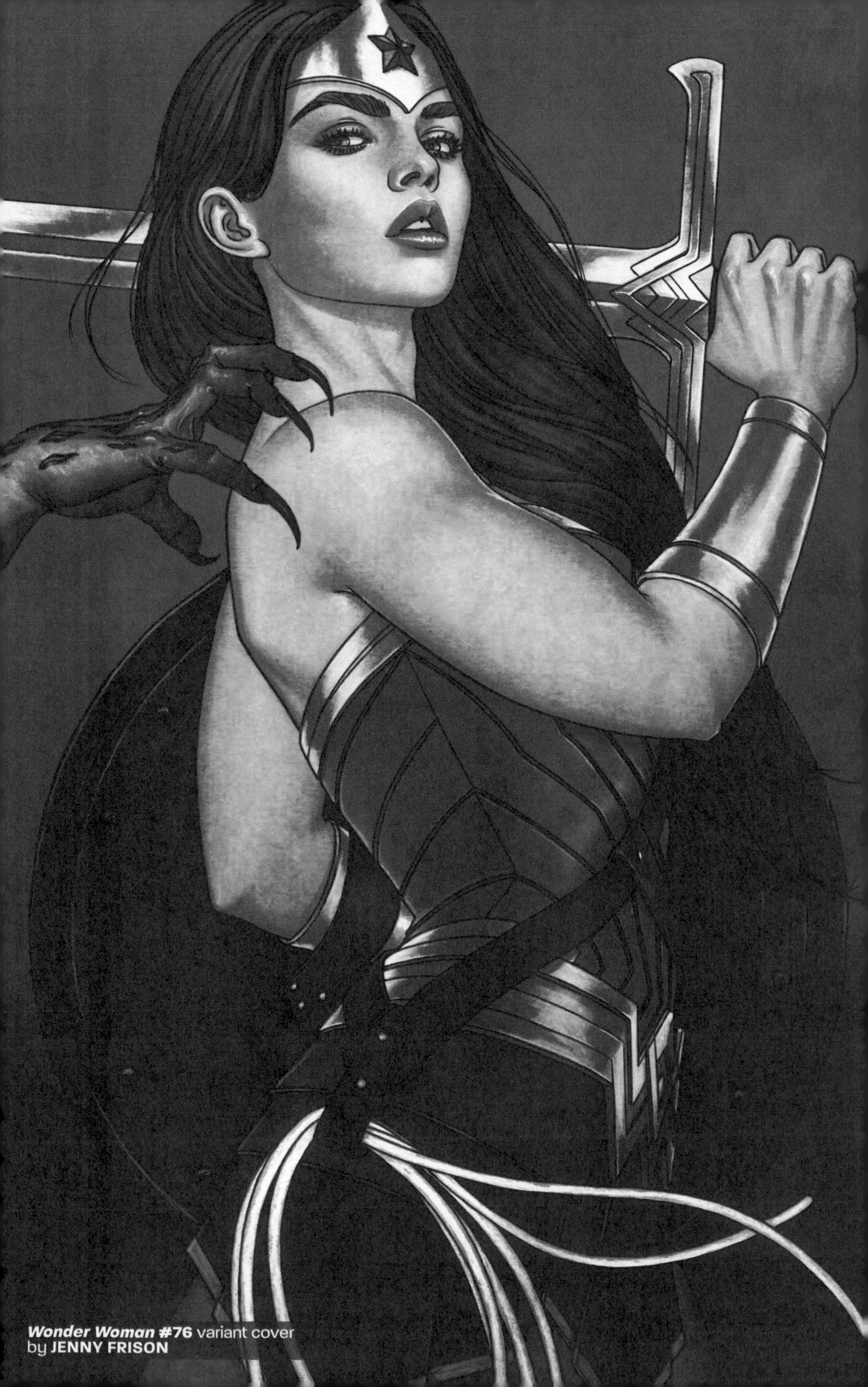

Wonder Woman **#76** variant cover
by **JENNY FRISON**

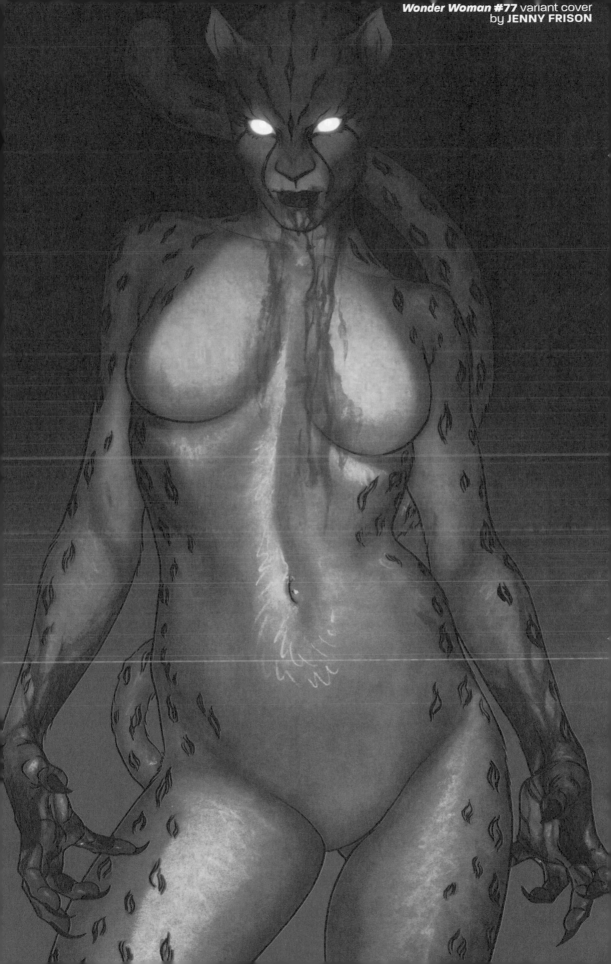

Wonder Woman #77 variant cover
by JENNY FRISON

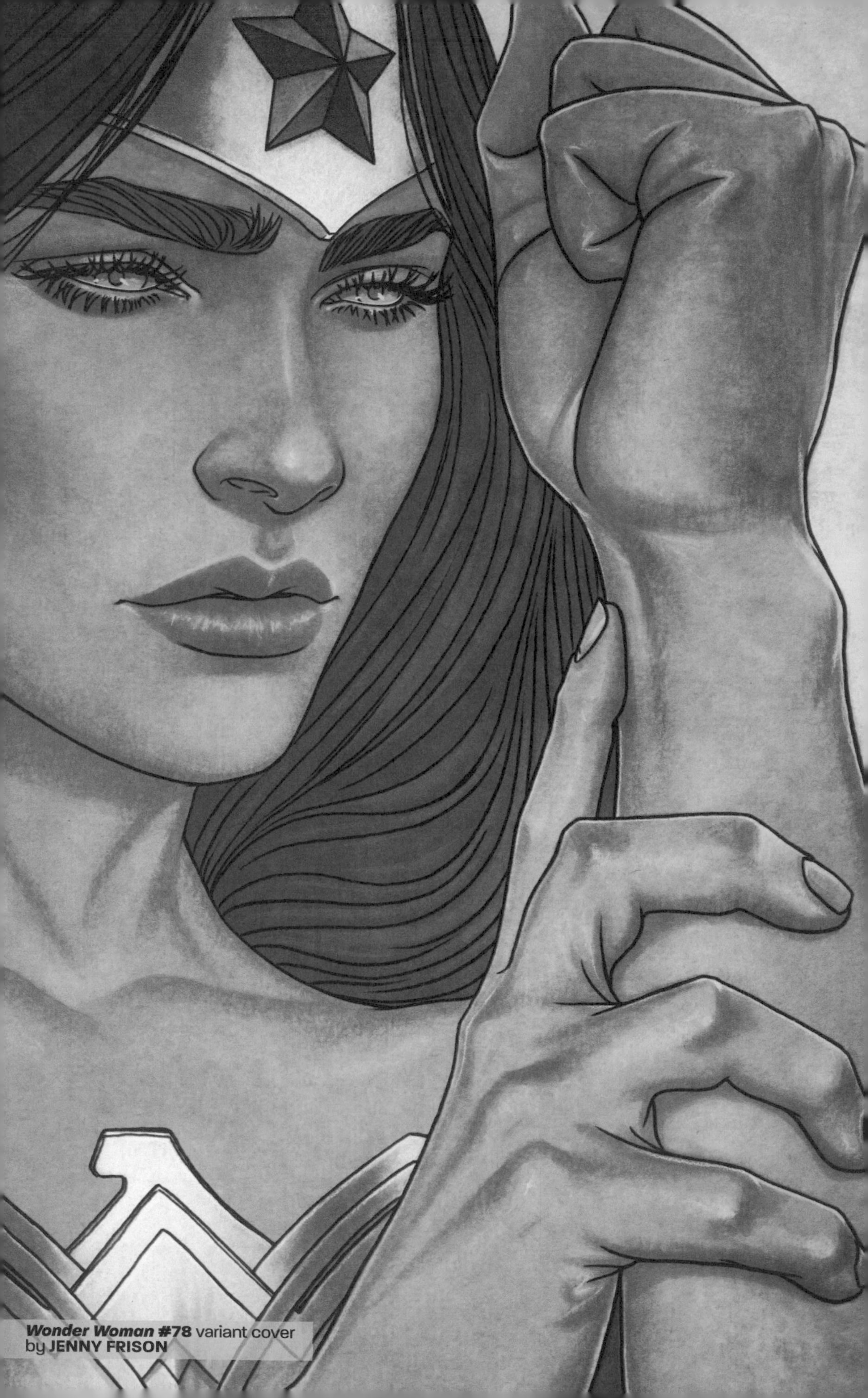

***Wonder Woman* #78** variant cover
by **JENNY FRISON**

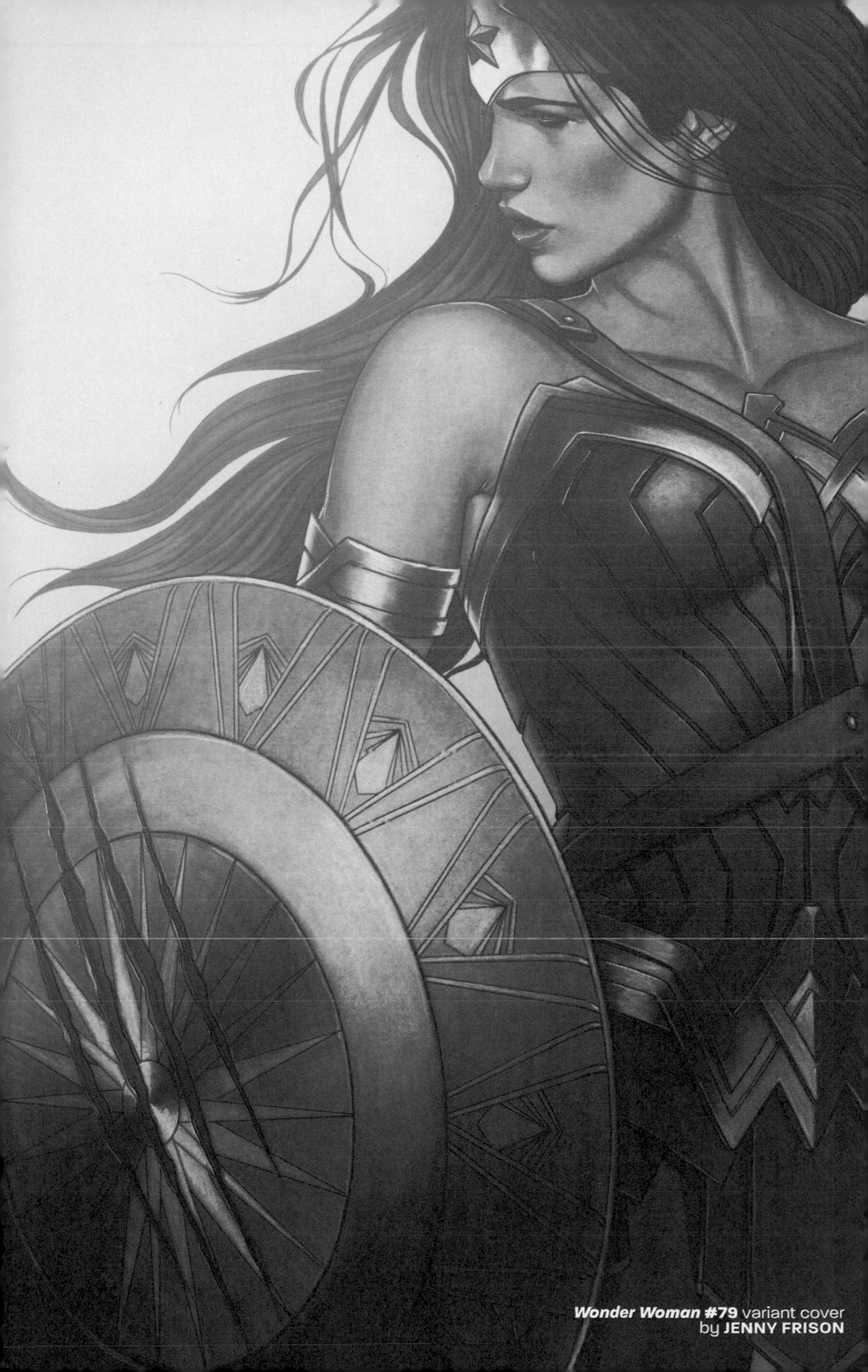

***Wonder Woman* #79** variant cover
by **JENNY FRISON**

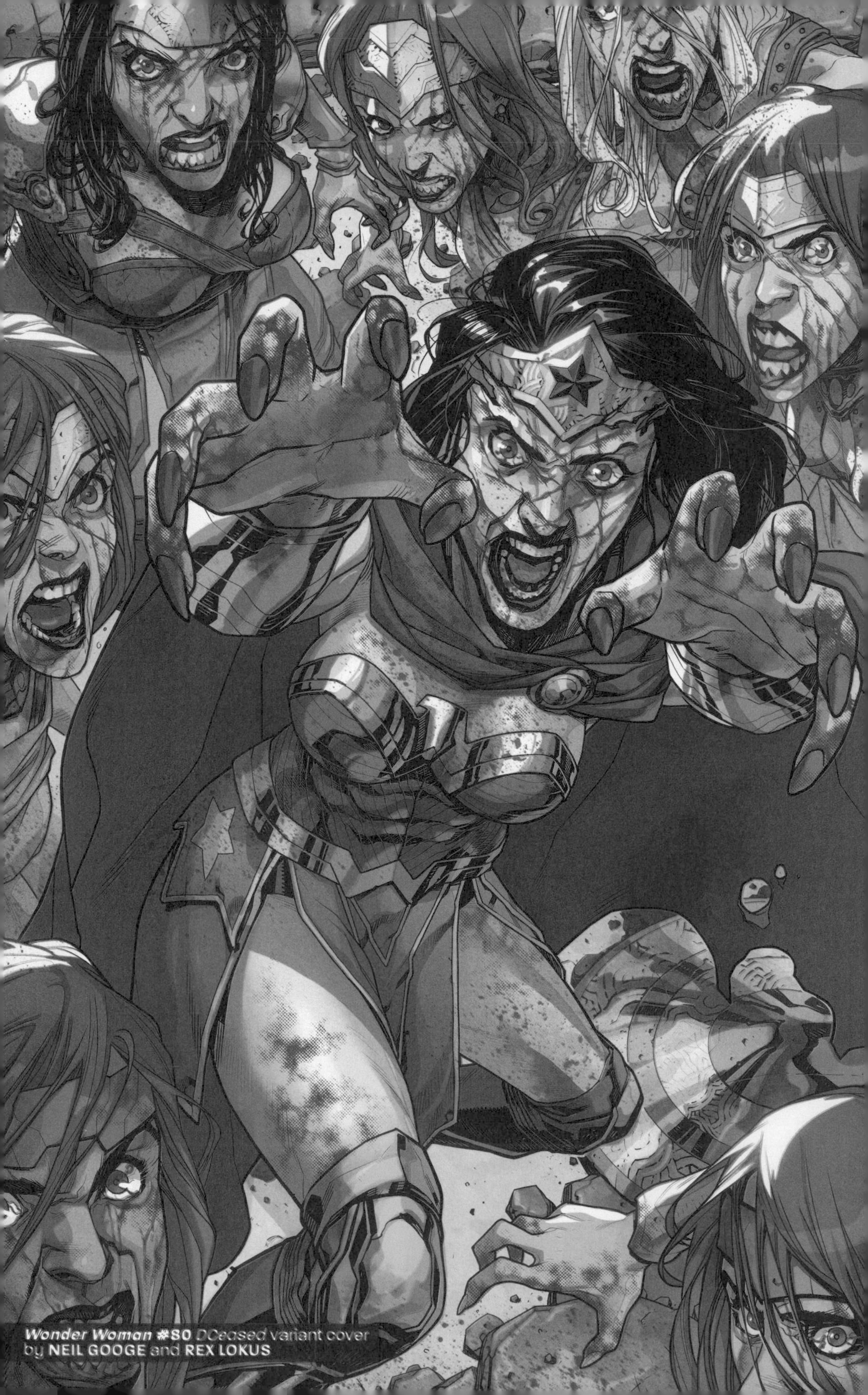

Wonder Woman **#80** *DCeased* variant cover
by **NEIL GOOGE** and **REX LOKUS**

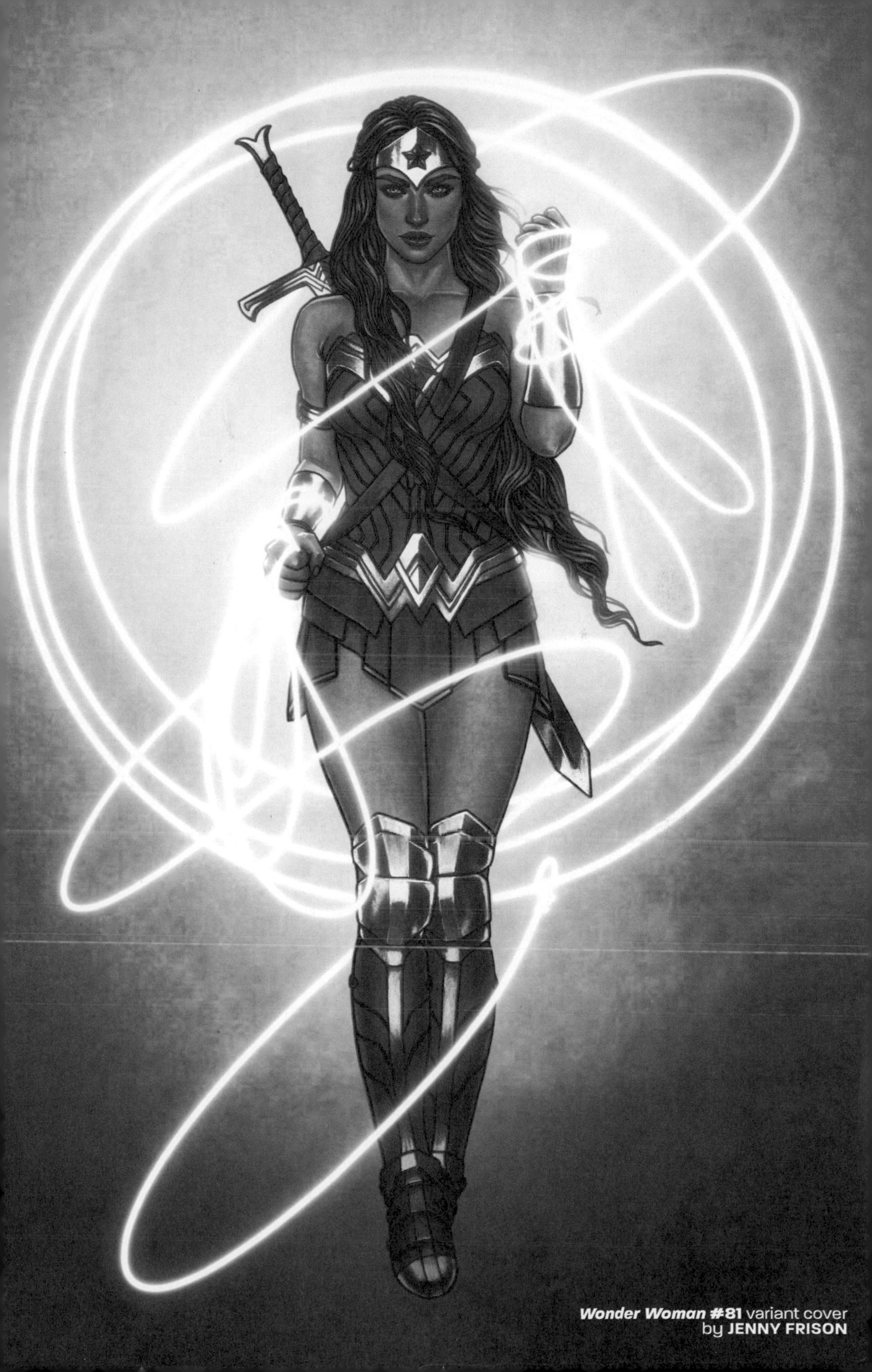

***Wonder Woman* #81** variant cover
by **JENNY FRISON**

> "Clear storytelling at its best. It's an intriguing concept and easy to grasp."
> **– THE NEW YORK TIMES**

> "Azzarello is rebuilding the mythology of Wonder Woman."
> **– CRAVE ONLINE**

WONDER WOMAN
VOL. 1: BLOOD
BRIAN AZZARELLO
with CLIFF CHIANG

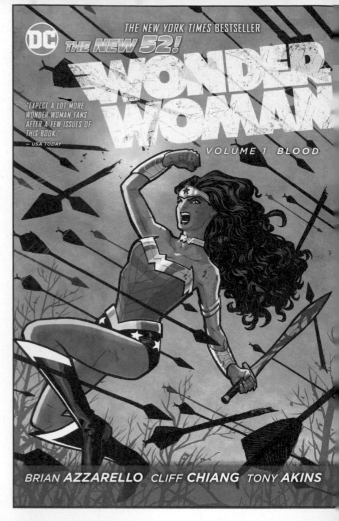

**WONDER WOMAN
VOL. 2: GUTS**

**WONDER WOMAN
VOL. 3: IRON**

READ THE ENTIRE EPIC!

WONDER WOMAN VOL. 4
WAR

WONDER WOMAN VOL. 5
FLESH

WONDER WOMAN VOL. 6
BONES

WONDER WOMAN VOL. 7
WAR-TORN

WONDER WOMAN VOL. 8
A TWIST OF FATE

WONDER WOMAN VOL. 9
RESURRECTION

Get more DC graphic novels wherever comics and books are sold!

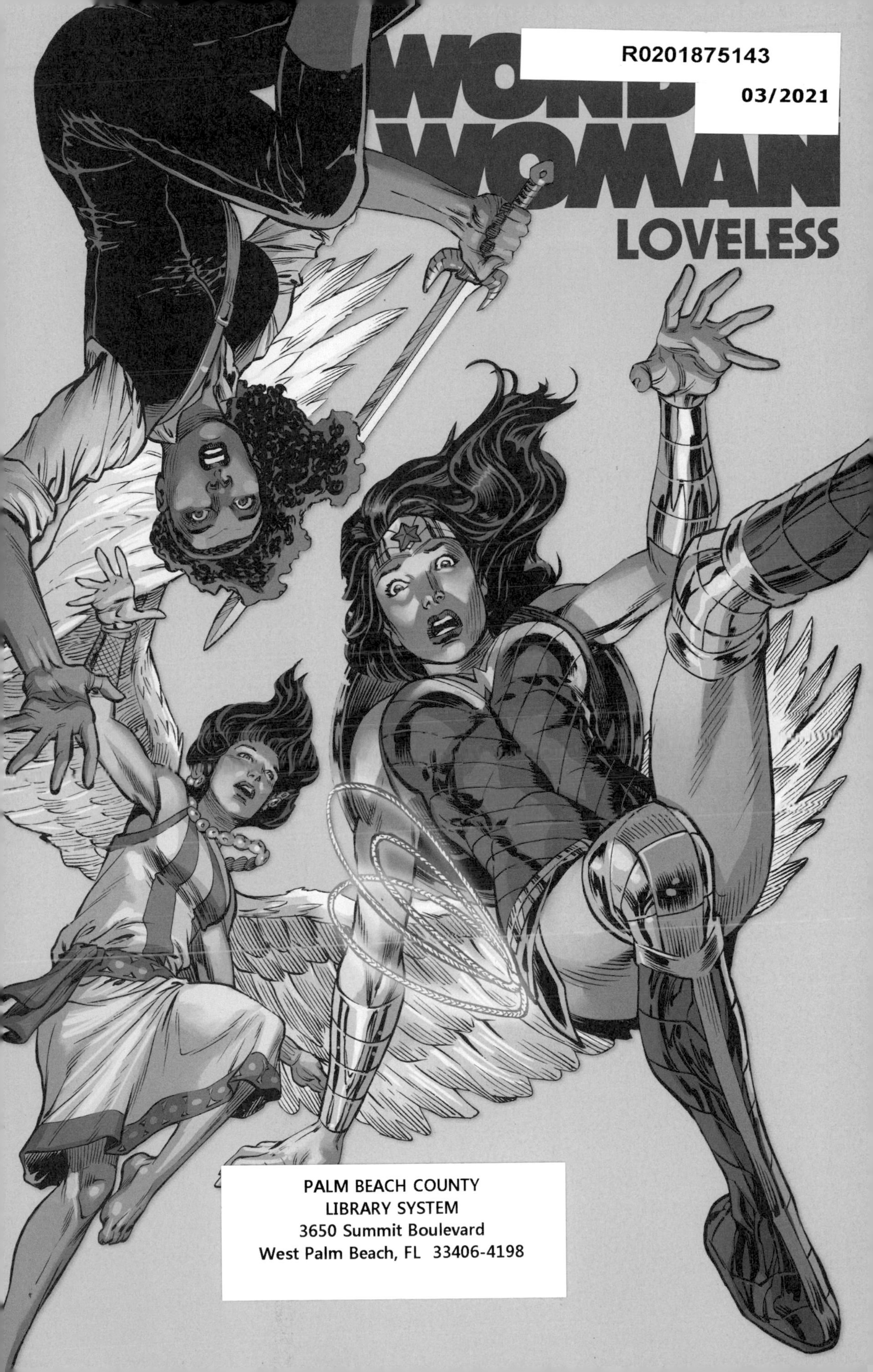
WOMAN
LOVELESS

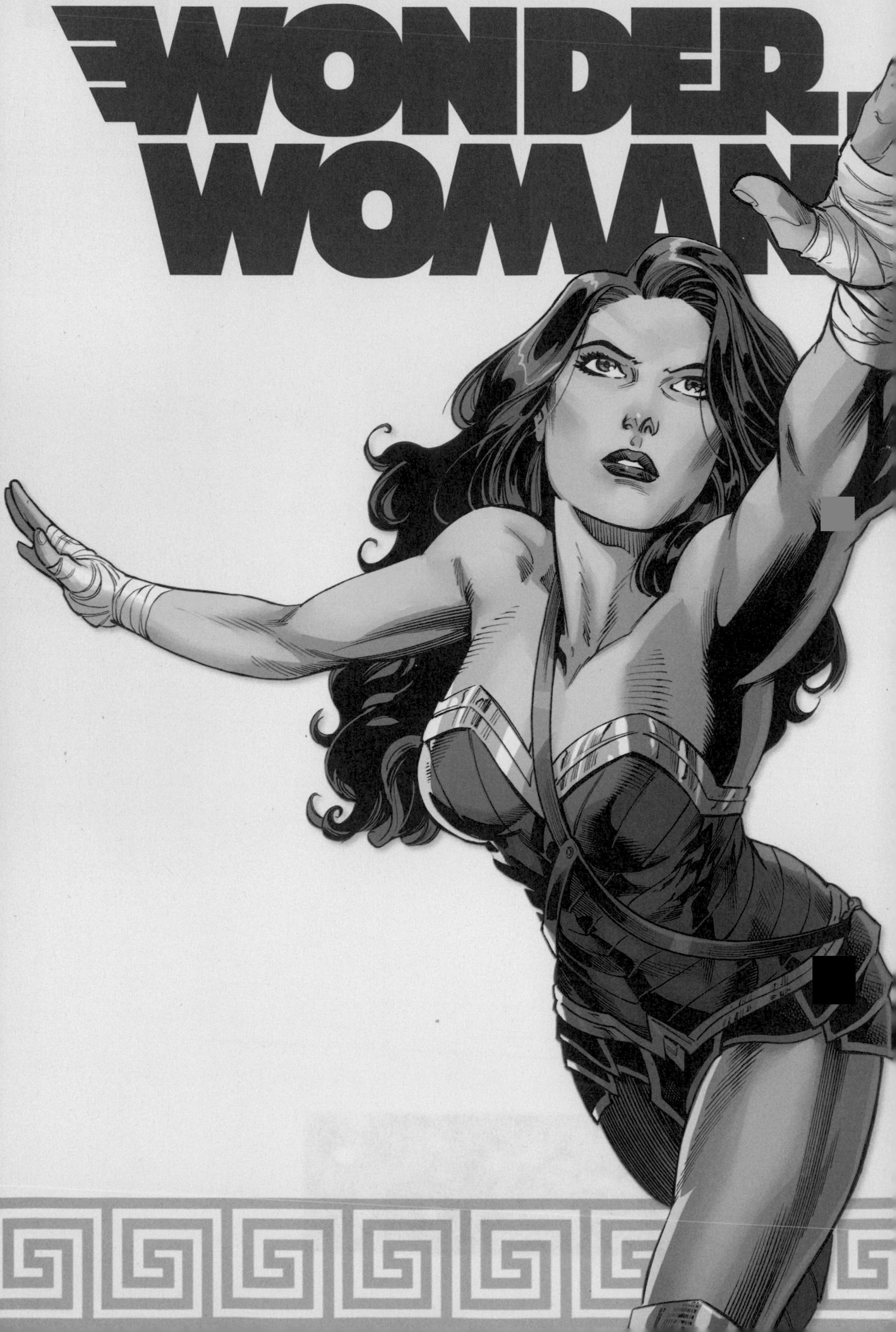
WONDER WOMAN